AUGUST JAEGER: PORTRAIT OF NIMROD

Frontispiece Visiting the sick. Lady Olga Wood and Professor Sanford take their leave of Jaeger and the children outside 37 Curzon Road, Muswell Hill, *c.* 1905.

August Jaeger: Portrait of Nimrod

A Life in Letters and Other Writings

KEVIN ALLEN

Ashgate

Aldershot • Burlington USA • Singapore • Sydney

Published by
Ashgate Publishing Limited
Gower House
Croft Road
Aldershot
Hants GU11 3HR
England

Ashgate Publishing Company
131 Main Street
Burlington
Vermont 05401–5600
USA

Ashgate website: http://www.ashgate.com

British Library Cataloguing in Publication Data

Allen, Kevin, 1945–
August Jaeger: Portrait of Nimrod: A Life in Letters
and Other Writings.
1. Jaeger, August—Correspondence. 2. Elgar, Edward,
1857–1934—Correspondence. 3. Composers—Great Britain—
Biography.
I. Title.
780.9'2

Library of Congress Cataloging-in-Publication Data

Allen, Kevin, 1945–
August Jaeger: portrait of Nimrod: a life in letters and other writings/
Kevin Allen.
p. cm.
Includes index.
ISBN 1–85928–366–7 (alk. paper)
1. Jaeger, August Johannes, 1860–1909. 2. Musicians—Germany—
Biography. 3. Jaeger, August Johannes, 1860–1909—Correspondence.
4. Musicians—Germany—Correspondence. I. Title.
ML423.J12A78 2000
780'.92—dc21 00–23684
[B] CIP

ISBN 1 85928 366 7

This book is printed on acid free paper

Typeset in Garamond by The Midlands Book Typesetting Company, Loughborough, Leics.
and printed in Great Britain by MPG Books Ltd., Bodmin, Cornwall.

Contents

List of Plates

Between pages 206 and 207

Foreword

The most significant event in English musical history during the twilight days of the nineteenth century was the arrival in London in 1878 of the Jaeger family from Düsseldorf. They came as refugees from Bismarckian misrule of Germany. The second son of the family, the eighteen-year-old August, was keenly musical. Otherwise knowledgeable and with good English, apparently without difficulty he found work with the firm of George Washington Bacon & Co., Map and Chart Sellers and Publishers. Apart from work he devoted himself to learning about English music through earnest membership of two choirs: the Novello Oratorio Choir conducted by Sir Alexander Mackenzie; and an amateur choir, with many German members, partial to Brahms, conducted by the Austro-Hungarian Hans Richter. In 1890 Jaeger successfully applied for the senior post in the Publishing Department of Novello, which was responsible for much of the music then being used by choral societies.

In consequence of his appointment, a new future for English music was determined. Jaeger not only supervised the publication of music accepted by the firm (normally requiring the composer to undertake the cost of publication!) but submitted it also to critical examination.

A problem for Jaeger was that there were virtually no professional composers; a livelihood otherwise depending either on the post of organist in a cathedral or, more infrequently, on the post of Professor of Music at Oxford or Cambridge. Of that order, the most senior representatives were Stanford at Cambridge, and Parry at Oxford – the latter, however, being independently wealthy. Walford Davies, at the time, was Organist of the Temple Church in London and Professor in a new post in the University of Wales.

Edward Elgar in 1890 was, on the other hand, solely a composer. His eventual brief tenure in the first Chair of Music in the new University of Birmingham in 1906, however, remains to this day eponymously honoured in the title of the senior Chair of Music.

Such serious examination of new music as there was, was taken from public performance. Jaeger, however, established his credentials as critic by writing copiously on new music in the *Musical Times* (published by Novello). During his time the editors at Novello were E.F. Jacques (until 1897) and F.G. Edwards. The first mention of Edward Elgar in the *Musical Times*, in 1893, commented on the poor audience in Worcester Cathedral, during the Three Choirs Festival, for the first performance of his choral work, *The Light of Life*. Mr Elgar, observed the critic, was still a young man, his sympathies with orchestra rather than voices, and in need of counselling. But 'he is no wayside musician whom we can afford to pass and forget'. Still in the *Musical Times*, three years later, in an account of the Cheltenham Festival, progress in reputation for the provincial composer was slow in coming: 'A musician from Malvern, Edward Elgar, appeared at this Festival as conductor of an orchestral work of his own, a *Sevillana*.'

Gradually Elgar moved forward with a number of choral works and part-songs accepted and published by Novello. In 1896 there was *King Olaf* and, a year later, the *Imperial March* and *The Banner of St George*. In the provinces Elgar was now establishing a place of his own.

At this point, at which serious exchange of correspondence began, a graded course for the composer was enshrined under Jaeger's protection and encouragement. Then the mutual passage of letters began – those of Elgar often marked with characteristic and evocative drawings. When it was advertised in *The Sunday Times* of 5 March 1899, that Mr Elgar intended to follow sad patriotism into a symphony to be dedicated to the late and heroic General Gordon, for performance at the next Worcester Festival, Jaegar called a halt. Elgar was not yet ready, he determined, to compose a symphony. What he did compose in the last year of the century was the *Enigma* Variations, with its own now immortalized tribute to Jaeger as Nimrod.

Elgar's letters to Jaeger vividly show the extent to which he took Jaeger's advice on details of scoring. This remains the case in respect of virtually every major work composed during Jaeger's tragically short lifetime. On 2 June 1899 a characteristic exchange of thoughts found Jaeger suggesting that Elgar should go to a musical festival in Bonn, which Elgar considered an attractive possibility. Otherwise he had this to say to Jaeger: 'I want you to get a further opinion about your nasal business: I have asked a doctor friend in town who recommends Greville Macdonald. I will remind you of this when I am up again next week & we'll talk it over.' Ominously for Jaeger, this was the beginning of an end.

Whatever else Jaeger achieved passes into insignificance beside his involvement with *The Dream of Gerontius*. As is well known, the time allowed for the production of such a major – and controversial – work for an important Festival set a virtually impossible task for the composer to complete, for the publisher to provide the parts, and for the performers to achieve a successful first performance. In their preparations, Elgar and Jaeger – probably for the only time in their relationship – found themselves in disagreement. Elgar knew Newman's mind and thought; Jaeger was less than indifferent about the text. The first performance of *Gerontius* was only just short of a disaster; but the friends of Elgar and the members of the Oratory to which Cardinal Newman had belonged recognized that this was an extraordinary work with a special spiritual intent.

Jaeger was exasperated with the English, to the extent of playing on the most absurd practices (in his view) in English life. Writing to Dora Penny ('Dorabella' of the Variations) he exploded:

> If it were a new oratorio by Mascagni or Perosi, the papers would have rave columns of gossip and gush – Though it is only an English musician (not an actor, or a jockey, or a Batsman) & he is treated like a very ordinary nobody.

In these circumstances Elgar was obliged to point out that he – being treated like a very ordinary nobody – was dissatisfied with Novello's reluctance to pay either promptly or regularly. Once he was angered to the point of desertion in favour of a contract with Boosey and Hawkes. Novello was obliged to heed the signal. Even so, Elgar only ever appeared prosperous.

Jaeger, for the greater part of his commitment to Novello, was a sick man: as his health inexorably deteriorated, he was increasingly forced to spend more time away from work. But even at this time he still pursued the interests of those musicians and friends closest to him. What Jaeger says here is partly true as the relationships within his limited orbit appear. His life was entirely within music. His – often immensely long – letters to his friends thereby expand into a remarkable confession of faith. If his composers forsook their calling, he summoned them back into his confessional. As regards Elgar, Jaeger opined that he spent too much time with the rich.

Jaeger lived through the days which brought *The Apostles* and *The Kingdom* into being. He extolled the beauty of some sixty of Elgar's part-songs (which now remain grievously and undeservedly neglected and unperformed). Jaeger's tuberculosis cruelly advanced, despite being treated – sometimes apparently experimentally – by doctors in expensive 'hotels' (private hospitals) in Switzerland. Jaeger spent much time there during the last winters of his life. His friends did all they could for him in encouragement and generosity. Those who were close to him at the end of his life – he died on 18 May 1909 – were Parry, Dorabella, Walford Davies, and Elgar. For his burial at the Golders Green Crematorium music was provided by the choristers of the Temple Church, directed by Walford Davies. A general thanksgiving for his life in music took place in Queen's Hall on 24 January 1910.

Kevin Allen's approach to an unfamilar period of history is broadly displayed as a colourful background to a remarkable treatment of difficult years in English musical history. This was a time without radio, recording, or brash advertisement. If, as could easily have happened, *Gerontius* had collapsed, so would its composer.

Percy M. Young

Acknowledgements

What August Jaeger attempted and achieved in the Elgar cause was considerable, if very well known. Less familiar, but equally remarkable, are his equally committed efforts on behalf of a variety of other composers and his work as a music critic, which Jaeger regarded as his main vocation. In this book I have concentrated on presenting fresh documentary material relating to these aspects, without attempting an exhaustive study of the Elgar–Jaeger relationship.

My first thanks are due therefore to those who so kindly afforded access to the largely unpublished Jaeger letters which form the basis of this book: Laura Ponsonby and Kate and Ian Russell for the letters to Sir Hubert Parry, Richard Westwood-Brookes for the letters to Sydney Loeb, and the Library of the Royal College of Music for those to Walford Davies. These letters form part of the Walford Davies archive at the Royal College of Music and are reprinted herein by kind permission of the trustees of the late Sir Henry Walford Davies. I would also like to thank Kendall L. Crilly, Music Librarian at Yale University Music Library, for providing copies of Jaeger's letters to Horatio Parker, and for kind permission to include transcriptions of them in this book; the Brotherton Collection at Leeds for permission to include the letter from Jaeger to Herbert Thompson in its possession, and the Taylor Institute Library, Oxford, for providing a copy of Jaeger's letter to Emily Harding. Sylvia Loeb has most kindly loaned her father's diaries and photographs and has been most generous with a rich store of reminiscences. I wish also to record my most grateful thanks to Arthur Reynolds for the loan of photographic and documentary items from his collection, especially a unique volume of mounted press cuttings concerning the Jaeger Memorial Concert. It has been a special pleasure to make contact with Jaeger's grandchildren, Neville Fraser, Gillian Scully, Susan Smith, Jacky Smith, Richard Hunter and Patricia Pamment, and I have benefited greatly from their enthusiasm, interest and support. All have provided family information and anecdote, and I am particularly grateful to Neville Fraser for many detailed letters and for the kind provision of various press cuttings and unpublished photographs.

Of the various institutions with whom I have been in touch during the course of research I would particularly like to thank the Stadtarchiv Düsseldorf, the Russell-Cotes Gallery, Bournemouth, the Bournemouth Orchestras, the Dorset County Library, the Devon County Library, the Local Studies Department of Croydon Public Library, the Royal Society of Musicians of Great Britain, the Public Record

Office, the British Library Music Library, the Library of the Wellcome Institute for the History of Medicine, The Goethe Institute, the German Historical Institute, and the staffs of the Music Reading Room at the Bodleian Library, Oxford, the Great Malvern Public Library and the Worcester Record Office at St Helen's, Fish Street. Marguerite Siegrist of the Dokumentationsbibliothek, Davos, has been most helpful in dealing with my various requests over such a long distance, and I am anxious to record my sincere thanks to Celia Clarke, Oliver Davies and Peter Horton of the Royal College of Music Library, and Elizabeth Wells, Curator of the Museum of Instruments, who have given much of their time in providing material and information. I am grateful to Harry Frost, Curator of the Dyson Perrins Museum at Worcester, for his help with James Hadley, and to Melanie Weatherley, Cathy Sloan and Chris Bennett of the Elgar Birthplace Museum at Broadheath, for their continued patience and helpfulness over my many calls on their time and expertise. For permission to reproduce various photographs from the Birthplace archive I am grateful to the Elgar Birthplace Trust. I am particularly grateful to Chris Bennett for drawing Jaeger's annotated proof copy of Elgar's First Symphony to my attention.

For financial assistance towards the costs of research I most gratefully acknowledge two separate grant awards from the Oppenheim–John Downes Memorial Trust.

I record my grateful thanks to Farrar, Straus & Giroux for permission to use the quotation from *An Arundel Tomb* by Philip Larkin, published by Faber & Faber, and wish also to acknowledge the courtesy of Nicholas Williams, Editor of the *Musical Times.* Oxford University Press have kindly given permission for the use of extracts from letters published in *Elgar and his Publishers. Letters of a Creative Life* and *Edward Elgar. Letters of a Lifetime*, both edited by Dr J.N. Moore. For permission to quote from Mrs Richard Powell's book, *Edward Elgar: Memories of a Variation* (4th edn, 1994) I am grateful to Ashgate Publishing. For permission to reproduce extracts from the letters and diaries of Edward and Alice Elgar, I am indebted to the Elgar Will Trust.

I am indebted to Professor Sir John Crofton for his opinion on the causes and extent of Jaeger's tuberculosis. Extensive help and advice over medical matters has also been provided by Dr John Harcup and Dr E.F. Laidlaw, and I am most grateful for the trouble they have taken on my behalf; ultimate responsibility for the judgements I have arrived at must nevertheless be mine alone.

It is a pleasure to list the names of many other individuals who have contributed towards this book, including Felix Aprahamian, Wulstan Atkins, Pat and Alan Bennett, whose cataloguing of the Elgar letters at St Helen's and Broadheath is a boon to all researchers, Keith Baldock, Charles Beare, Jacob O'Callaghan, Faith Crook, Christopher Fifield, Bernard Hill, Ron Taylor and Geoffrey Hodgkins – past and present Editors of the Elgar Society Journal – Michael Hurd, John and Ann Kelly, Joyce Kemp, Dr Christopher Kent, Catherine Moody, Dr J.N. Moore, Peter and Katrina Norbury, Professor Ian Parrott, Michael Pope, Claud Powell, Ken Russell, Henry Sandon, Geoffrey Scargill, Geoffrey Self, Professor Jack Sislian, Michael Trott, Professor Brian Trowell, Mr C.M.W. Wilson and Dr Percy Young.

Finally I would like to make special mention of Raymond Monk, who has most kindly and generously helped the author in ways innumerable.

I have generally edited Jaeger's letters with as light a touch as possible, preserving his eccentricities of orthography, capitalization and highly expressive punctuation; I have however altered his paragraphing when this seemed appropriate. Frequent underlinings were a feature of Jaeger's style; single underlining is shown in italics, double underlining in capitals, and treble underlining as bold capitals.

A Note on the Elgar–Jaeger Correspondence

The fullest existing published collection of letters between August Jaeger and Elgar is to be found in *Elgar and His Publishers* (Clarendon Press, Oxford, 1987), edited by Jerrold Northrop Moore, who states in the Preface that 'this central correspondence is here presented virtually complete for the first time'. It may, however, be important to remind ourselves of the letters which did not survive to achieve publication.

Jaeger, as we might expect, was fully aware of the importance of many of the letters that Elgar had written to him, and took care to keep them, even proudly offering to show them to friends such as Sydney Loeb and Walford Davies, characteristically describing them as '*deeply* interesting real human documents laying bare an artist's soul'. The subsequent history of these letters is not entirely clear but it is possible to outline one or two developments. After his death, Jaeger's widow Isabella Hunter presumably retained possession of the Elgar letters, although losing many possessions in a serious house fire towards the end of the First World War. Some ten years later, in September 1927, she appears to have given documentary material to the singer Derek Oldham (1892–1968) through a mutual friend, Marguerite Swale. In a letter to Mrs Hunter dated 21 September 1927, Oldham wrote, 'Miss Swale has passed on to me the many precious letters and the Elgar manuscript which you have so generously given to me. I am so very proud to have them in my possession and I promise you they shall be greatly treasured. I thank you most sincerely for giving them to me.'[1] There is no evidence of which letters were involved, or what subsequently happened to them. If the 'Elgar manuscript' referred to was the transcription of the Angel's Song from *The Dream of Gerontius* which the composer made at Isabella Hunter's request in March 1900, the fact that this is now part of the Elgar Birthplace archive may perhaps indicate that the accompanying letters given to Oldham are also safely part of that archive.

Isabella Hunter evidently had Elgar letters in her possession four years later, in November 1931, when she loaned them to Basil Maine to help with research for his biography of Elgar.[2] When he became aware of this, the composer was careful to ask for an opportunity to see the letters, and seemed to want to point Maine in other directions. 'Before you begin to select anything for use from the letters,' he wrote, 'I shall be glad to see them ... I always avoid writing letters when possible and I imagine anything existing might give some very misleading notions. I think I have some from other writers which might be interesting.'[3] So, whatever other depredations the correspondence might have suffered by this time, Elgar had the chance to censor it if he so wished. In addition, he may have chosen to discard letters during Jaeger's lifetime, and accidents happen. For the rest, the Elgar–Jaeger material held at the Elgar Birthplace and the Worcester Record Office represents letters donated by Mrs Hunter in response to the later appeal for letters which Carice Elgar-Blake made to all her father's friends and correspondents.

For whatever reasons, it is clear that the bulk of Jaeger's correspondence with Elgar has not in fact been preserved. From the internal evidence of Elgar's letters as published in *Elgar and His Publishers* I estimate the number of such missing items to amount to at least 240, while the published Jaeger letters number some 167. The overall correspondence should therefore be seen against this background, and certain gaps in it are always going to be suggestive. On a year-by-year basis I estimate the number of missing items as follows; 1897, 3; 1898, 22; 1899, 24; 1900, 18; 1901, 17; 1902, 11; 1903,11; 1904, 9; 1905, 10; 1906, 13; 1907, 6; 1908, 5; 1909, 1.

Notes

1. Letter in possession of Neville Fraser.
2. *Elgar, His Life and Works*, New Portway Edition, 1973, p. xi.
3. Basil Maine, *Twang with our Music*, Epworth Press, 1957, p. 100.

For Laura, Kate, Ian, Harriet and Joanna at Shulbrede Priory

Shulbrede Priory

Part One

1860–1904: 'And your young men shall see visions'

'You see I am conceited enough to think that I too can appreciate a good thing & see genius in musicians that are *not* yet dead, or even not yet well known, or Cathedral Organists or directors of Schools of music in Colleges for Boys!'

1 1860–95: Düsseldorf to London

August Jaeger is widely familiar – if not taken for granted – as the devoted supporter of Elgar and the subject of one of his most inspired movements, the *Nimrod* Variation from the work known as the *Enigma* Variations. It is a piece of music that has taken on a life of its own, entering the national consciousness as an elegy, an adjunct to ceremonial, and latterly as an accompaniment to films, television commercials and even party political broadcasts. The music has found its place – or places – but the life of the remarkable man who inspired it has remained largely unknown, and what is known is in danger of turning into mythology. He is always closely associated with Elgar, but this relationship, more problematic than is usually realized, serves to obscure his efforts and achievements on behalf of many other composers, some of whom are unfairly neglected to this day. The fuller story of Jaeger's impact on the English Musical Renaissance remains to be told.

That impact was the product of a man gifted with a powerful critical intelligence and sensibility, totally devoted to the art he loved. His responses were highly emotional and often directly physical. Like a Romantic poet, he yearned to be possessed by Beauty. He sought music that would satisfy his need to be moved to tears, that would tingle the spine and bring him out in beads of sweat. But music was not just a matter of pleasurable sensation; it was an expression of wider moral and ethical values. Beauty was indeed Truth for him. The search for those values dominated his life, causing him to leave the harsh realities of his native Germany for the 'land without music', where he found his rôle. Jaeger's ethical-artistic outlook may be an unusual combination of German romanticism and Victorian values, but his inbuilt optimism was a corollary of both and provided the basis for all that he achieved.

It was not the least of Jaeger's qualities that he was able for so long to combine his role of visionary and seer with the daily drudgery of office routine, business correspondence and proof-reading. His position within a music-publishing firm, after all, was what gave him the power and influence he exercised to such effect, although art sometimes sat unhappily along with business, and English reserve continued to mistrust continental enthusiasm. An obsessive temperament led to continual overwork, and there were further disappointments when committed efforts were not always appreciated even by those for whose sake he strove his hardest. Perhaps illness was inevitable in one so single-minded and highly strung, and it may be sadly fitting that he died early, ravaged by a disease that was once associated with those with creative talent of a high order. It was a personal and family tragedy, as well as a great loss to the musical life of his adopted country. But we can be grateful that, like Marie Duplessis, August Jaeger perhaps knew that while he may not live as long as others, he promised himself to live more quickly.

Between August Johannes Jaeger's birth in 1860 and the beginning of his preserved correspondence in the 1890s there exists a huge documentary gap. Detailed biographical information concerning the larger part of his life is scanty and the vast majority of extant letters cover only slightly more than his last ten years. Virtually all that is known of Jaeger's earlier life is contained in two articles that appeared after his death, one a brief and anonymous obituary in the *Musical Times*,[1] the other a longer article in the *Spectator* by a longstanding friend, the musical enthusiast and writer, Charles Larcom Graves.[2] In the circumstances it seems possible to do no more than attempt to sketch in various kinds of background to Jaeger's lost years

He was born on 18 March 1860, the third son of the ten children of Gottfried and Caroline Jaeger of Düsseldorf, in what was then Western Prussia. The family name is based on the German word for hunter, and may have associations with towns named Jaegerndorf in Bavaria or Silesia; although it is a documented Jewish surname, there is no evidence that the family was of Jewish descent. There were to be altogether three boys and seven girls, although only three of August's sisters survived to undertake the journey to England in the late 1870s; one of them, Joanna, later remembered the large family living in a house on the Reichstrasse, in the Neustadt area of the city, near the corner with the adjacent Elizabethstrasse. The house was opposite a park with a lake, the Schwanenspiegel, where the children skated in winter. It was a fairly central, prosperous part of town, close to the famous Königsallee on the one hand and the Rhine on the other, offering cherished associations with musical figures such as the Schumanns, Brahms and Joachim. One of August's early musical experiences consisted of following the processions of military bands, and a special memory was of childish pride in being allowed to hold the music of one of the players; Basil Maine found in this a symbol of his whole life.[3] But there was a less pleasant military accompaniment to Jaeger's childhood after the appointment of the ruthless and opportunist Otto von Bismarck as Chief Minister in 1862. Over the next eight years he fought three wars to enlarge Prussian territories and create a unified German state under Prussian control. Earlier the Rhineland had been a French possession, governed under French law, and the majority of its population wished to maintain that tradition and belong to France permanently. The new adjustment was hard to make, especially as in 1871 Bismarck became Imperial Chancellor, dominating Germany for nearly two decades with an increasingly harsh and corrupt regime. It was a process not without significance for the cultural and scientific life of England and America.

The young August attended a Protestant school on the Bilkerstrasse, where the Schumanns had lived, and remained enough of a Protestant to have a portrait of Martin Luther in his house in Kensington, although he would claim to be 'rather an Agnostic than anything else'. This would have been an elementary school, or Volks-chule, where he would have received an efficient training in literacy – at which German schools of that period were notably more successful than those of England or France – together with instruction in religion, arithmetic and singing. The majority of children spent all of their eight years of education at the Volkschulen, and were not expected to progress to any kind of higher education, although Jaeger passed into the Gymnasium,[4] a measure of his abilities. Such establishments featured an emphasis on language teaching, and his later mastery of English must have its foundations here. Possibly he was educated specifically for a business career, for English was the language of commerce; but Jaeger's command of the language went far beyond the merely functional, and he may have studied classics, for he liked to sprinkle his reviews with favourite Latin phrases. But a university education would have been too expensive and socially elitist for the sons of the lower middle classes, and the Jaegers may have felt that in this area as no doubt in others, Germany under Bismarck was a land of limited opportunity. But certainly the zeal with which the basic skills were taught to this able youngster meant that he would become sufficiently well equipped to find initial employment in England as a clerk, to say nothing of the eloquence he would later be able to summon in pursuit of his encouragement of others.

It must have been music above all that became the focus of his efforts and enthu-siasm, and Jaeger evidently made the most of instrumental tuition, becoming 'an able pianist and a brilliant violinist'[5] but his father made him promise that he would not perform in public. Whether this suggests a philistine and authoritarian parent, or just time-honoured concerns about the security of music as a career, it may have been partly the making of the son, by leading him to sublimate the performer into the broader musician and ultimately, the critic. Jaeger would later claim that his piano-playing had been entirely self-taught, and often emphasized the amateur nature of his musical attainments and the inadequate extent of his education generally.

Düsseldorf itself could boast a long and proud musical history. In 1614 the Count Palatine had taken up residence in the city and many Italian musicians, including Giacomo Carissimi, were attracted to his Court. Under the Elector Johann Wilhelm (1692–1716), to whom Corelli dedicated his last Concerti Grossi, the city gained an international status as a musical centre. The celebrated composer and diplomat Agostino Steffani directed the Opera, and in 1711 Handel himself visited, to engage the services of the singer Baldassari for the London stage.

Early in the nineteenth century local music lovers keen to perform large-scale works founded a musical society which made its contribution to the inauguration of the Lower Rhine Festival. This became a triennial three-day Festival held alternately at Düsseldorf, Aix-la-Chapelle and Cologne, a pattern resembling that of the English Three Choirs Festivals with which Jaeger would be associated. Felix Mendelssohn was invited to conduct the fifteenth Festival, that of 1833 at Düsseldorf, and such was his success that the city offered him a three-year appointment to supervise its musical life, sacred and secular. The composer was unhappy as Intendant of the Opera, and the appointment did not run its full course, but before his removal to the Leipzig Gewandhaus, Mendelssohn had made sure to produce as many performances as he could of works by Palestrina, Bach, Handel, Mozart, Cherubini and Beethoven, and he continued to conduct at the Festivals, introducing his *St Paul* at Düsseldorf in 1836.

Mendelssohn's successors, Julius Rietz and Ferdinand Hiller, continued to maintain the city's choral and orchestral forces until Robert Schumann took over the post of Kapellmeister in 1850. After initial success, the appointment ended sadly when his weakness as a conductor became apparent, and with the onset of the mental illness which led to an attempted suicide. Yet Schumann's Düsseldorf years saw the composition and first performance of the *Rhenish* Symphony, together with much evidence of his determination to help young unknown composers, most notably Johannes Brahms, who arrived in the autumn of 1853 with a letter of introduction from Joachim. Schumann's reply included the phrase, 'This is he who was to come', and went on to praise the young composer in a highly eulogistic newspaper article. The model of the musician-writer Schumann may not have been lost on August Jaeger, nor such a precedent of the discovery of new genius.

Musical life continued to flourish during the 1860s, a decade which saw the foundation of a municipal orchestra, led for part of the period by Leopold Auer, and the inauguration of the Tonhalle, the city's concert hall. The Lower Rhine Festivals continued to attract leading figures such as Jenny Lind, Joachim, Anton Rubenstein, Brahms, Hans Richter and Richard Strauss. Julius Buths, who had studied widely in Cologne and Berlin, Italy and Paris, was appointed musical director of Düsseldorf in 1890. His interest in promoting the contemporary as well as the established repertoire may have been the basis for his friendship with August Jaeger, a friendship which would have significant results for at least one composer.

Jaeger retained a life-long affection for the city of his birth, which in addition to its musical eminence, was the home of a distinguished school of painters[6] and the birthplace of Heinrich Heine, the Jewish poet and writer whose lyrics were set by Schubert, Schumann, Brahms and Wolf, among many others, and whose stories provided the bases for Wagner's *The Flying Dutchman* and *Tannhäuser.* Jaeger would have known of Heine's failure to settle happily into the business career planned for him, his dislike of German chauvinistic nationalism and of his lengthy sojourn in a more liberal environment abroad. Jaeger's later references to the poet, even if very occasional, lead one to suspect that Heine might have provided a model in other ways, artistic and political. Like Heine, Jaeger would show himself to be something of an escapist Romantic with a craving for beauty and a need to express strong and immediate feelings. Even in his largely workaday world, Jaeger would be able to share something of Heine's unrestricted, hedonistic enjoyment of life, and at the end, both men suffered from a similar, cruel illness and longed to be done with life. Both men were enemies of tradition in their respective arts, and one or two passing references in Jaeger's letters might demonstrate that he, like Heine, was somewhat antagonistic to the clergy and the aristocracy.

Bismarck was a believer in giving way over unimportant matters. Prussian laws granted much municipal autonomy, and developing civic pride ensured that Düsseldorf itself became a place of genuine beauty. In common with other German cities, it became noted for a carefully planned layout, boasting tidy parks, gardens and tree-lined boulevards, with transport systems, housing projects and public health measures to match. A centrally located Hofgarten, the relic of Residenzstadt days, earned Düsseldorf its 'Garden City' nickname. Jaeger often revisited it and encouraged his friends to do likewise. Writing to the *Musical Times* the year before his death, he mingled schoolboy memories of the city with musical associations.

> Being a Düsseldorfer, I was much interested in the Foreign Note in your September issue which stated that a tablet is to be affixed to the house in the Eilkerstrasse, in which the Schumanns lived for three years. Only I could not remember any Eilker Street in the fair garden city on the Rhine. Then it struck me that no doubt the Bilkerstrasse, named after the suburb Bilk, was meant. That street I know well, for as a little boy I went to school there. I connect it in my mind chiefly with sundry canings – no doubt well deserved – that I received, and with a fascinating baker's shop where we children used to spend our Pfennigs on capfuls of broken pieces of confectionery. Perchance it was the identical shop that supplied bread and cakes to the Schumanns some years before I patronized it to the tune of an occasional farthing. Rather a dull street my memory recalls, but it leads at right angles to the Haroldstrasse, facing the ornamental water, the Schwanenspiegel, where Joseph Joachim lived for a time in 1855 in rooms procured for him by his young friend Johannes Brahms. The latter was then living in Düsseldorf, so as to be near Frau Clara Schumann in her great trouble and anxiety due to her husband's tragic illness. Joachim's rooms would be within two or three minutes' walk from the Schumanns' house. I can well believe Herr Kalbeck's statement in Vol 1 of his Brahms biography, that many Düsseldorfers would foregather on the promenade along the Schwanenspiegel, outside Joachim's rooms, to listen to the performances of quartets and other chamber music given by the young master-fiddler, his pupil K. L. Bargeer, a Danish friend, Waldemar Tofte, and a cultured amateur, Herr Assessor von Diest, who lived in the same house as Joachim, and was a violoncellist of sufficient excellence to play at the Lower Rhenish Festivals at the first desk.[7]

Von Diest seems to have been a friend of Jaeger and only too pleased to tap into a rich memory of Düsseldorf's musical lore, especially when it involved anecdotes of the great.

> We may be sure that young Brahms – 'der blonde Johannes' as his friends called him – profited greatly by these performances under so gifted a leader, for he had not previously enjoyed many chances of hearing classical chamber music. He would sit in the corner of the sofa, cover his eyes with his hand and utter never a word. Once, says Herr von Diest, during the playing of a Mozart Adagio he suddenly jumped up, walked with heavy steps to the door, and closed it behind him with a bang. He had felt like one seasick, he afterwards explained to Joachim, who remonstrated with him for his 'rudeness'; he could not possibly listen to another note, he was too full of music! When a pianoforte was required for the performances, the party met at Frau Schumann's house. Brahms generally played the pianoforte part on these occasions, the hostess explaining her reluctance to take a share in the performances by remarking to Herr von Diest: 'I do not like to play when

> Brahms is present. He is too severe a critic; and, alas, he is always right'. While they are about it, why do not the Düsseldorfers affix a tablet to the house in the Schadowplatz where young Brahms lived at what was a turning point in his career? Are they perhaps ashamed of the notorious fact that when a new Musikdirector had to be chosen in succession to Robert Schumann, they preferred a nonentity like Julius Tausch to the younger genius then living in their midst who had been hailed as a 'strong fighter' and *the* coming man in the clarion-tones of Schumann's famous 'Neue Bahnen' article?[8]

It must have been a difficult step to leave the richness of Düsseldorf's musical life for a country that was later to be dubbed the 'Land without Music', yet August Jaeger was so keen to leave Germany for England that he was granted a passport in 1875, when he was only fifteen. Political conditions were starting to create a regular exodus to Great Britain and the United States, as Bismarck's authoritarianism made itself felt. Perhaps England's lack of advanced development in musical art was compensated for by its greater tolerance, freedom under the law, and parliamentary democracy. Bismarck's domestic policy, by contrast, centred on the subjugation of the people through the creation of what might now be called a police state, with every emphasis on the suppression of political opposition. It is evident that the Jaeger family quitted Germany late in 1878, just three months after the passing of harsh anti-Socialist laws and in a year which saw a flood of emigration. The aggressive nationalism which had supported Bismarck's earlier territorial aggrandisement turned inwards, towards various minorities, religious and racial as well as political. During the 1870s, he initi tated an ideological war, the Kulturkampf, against the Roman Catholic Church, because of its prior claim over purely secular authority on the obedience of the citizen. The Jesuits were expelled, and priests throughout the Reich were forbidden to refer to politics in their sermons; legislation led to the subjection of Church to State, and many priests were imprisoned. And if Bismarck's antisemitism was less extreme in effect than Hitler's, it was no less so in underlying philosophy. Organized German antisemitism seems to have emerged suddenly in the 1870s, fuelled by fluctuations in the economy, and became a focal point for discontented elements seeking scapegoats. Some five hundred publications on the 'Jewish Question' appeared between 1873 and 1890, and antisemitic associations and parties mushroomed. Bismarck used such feelings for his own purposes, and a third of the 30,000 Poles expelled from eastern Prussia in 1885 were Jews. His son Herbert, Secretary of State at the German Foreign Office, was openly and virulently anti-Jewish, and through such endorsement antisemitism became socially acceptable and respectable at Court. It percolated through society, including the army and the educational world, even the universities.

However, admiration for the achievements of German imperialism ran deep and wide, even in the musical world. Brahms would say that the two most important events in his life were the Bachgesellschaft Edition and Bismarck's creation of the German Empire. Bismarck was eventually forced to resign by Kaiser Wilhelm in 1890. Hans von Bulow, after conducting a performance of the *Eroica* symphony in Berlin, dedicated it to the ex-Chancellor and made a speech referring to him as 'the Beethoven of German politics'.

England, meanwhile, prided itself on many freedoms and boasted a reputation for unconditional hospitality to all: between 1823 and 1906 no person who came to her shores was denied entry; partly through economic self-interest, partly through liberal principle, Britain became the most reliable refuge in the world. The arrival in Britain of Prince Albert seemed to set a particular establishment imprimatur on German life and culture. Many of his fellow-countrymen, often Jewish, musical and otherwise, followed in his footsteps to escape the Bismarckian evils. Their contributions to English life were in many cases outstanding and many remain household names. Sigmund Freud enjoyed a family visit in the 1870s and envied his half-brother's freedoms. Longer sojourns were enjoyed by Karl Marx, who made industrious use of his freedom in the British Library Reading Room, and his associate Frederick Engels, who was glad to escape arrest on account of his political activities in Germany. Other noted scholars included the Shakespearians Israel Gollancz and Frederick Boas, and scientists such as Arthur Schuster of Manchester University. Reuter arrived in 1851 and went on to establish his stake in the press. Michael Marks opened his first shop in Manchester, subsequently forming a partnership with Tom Spencer, and Montague Burton began to manufacture clothes for sale in his shops. The worlds of science and industry were represented by Hugo Hirst, who founded GEC, Ludwig Mond who laid the foundations of ICI, and Gustav Wolff who together with Edward Harland created the Belfast shipyard. In merchant banking the Rothschilds were powerful figures of long standing, and Sir Ernest Cassel, who had started as an immigrant clerk in Liverpool at the age of sixteen, went on to become wealthy enough to sustain the monarchy by his assistance to Edward VII, as well as helping to establish the London School of Economics. Edgar Speyer, the banker, subsidised Henry Wood's Promenade Concerts for fourteen years, and was responsible for the Queen's Hall Orchestra Endowment Fund. The presence at varying times in England of such figures as Felix Mendelssohn, Charles Hallé, Edward Dannreuther, Otto Goldschmidt, Joseph Joachim, George Henschel, August Manns and Hans Richter greatly enriched musical life, and when Edward Elgar achieved his first emergence as a composer he received immediate and continuing support from cultured businessmen of German extraction such as Edgar Speyer, Frank Schuster and Alfred Rodewald.

So there would seem to have been every reason for the Jaeger family to be anxious to escape the Second Reich and move to a country which offered everyday freedoms together with scope for economic betterment. They arrived in December 1878, the year in which otherwise August would presumably have left school and started his compulsory year's military service. He never forgot the military arrogance of the country he had left behind, and was prescient of where it would lead. His nephew wrote later, 'Jaeger ... used to impress my father by passionately denouncing the refusal of British politicians to recognise that "Der Tag" was inevitable.'[9] Germans formed the largest immigrant group in England, and there were established areas of settlement in Manchester and Bradford, where Julius Delius had founded his wool business. But London was the major centre and is almost certain to have been the Jaegers' immediate destination; August Jaeger, somehow by nature it might seem a suburban creature, breathed its polluted air for the rest of his life. It was where so much music was to be heard, after all.

The family's security would not have been helped by the death of Gottfried Jaeger in March 1880, some fifteen months after his arrival. His death certificate shows the family living in the Caledonian Road, Islington, and gives his profession as cattle dealer; the census of the following year gives the family at another address, Stock Orchard Crescent, in the same borough. Islington was an area of some degree of settlement by Germans, with a community of immigrant tradesmen, craftsmen, teachers and academics; it contained also the Metropolitan Cattle Market, where the Post Office London Directory for 1888 lists the firm of Jager, Sheep Salesmen, at Bank Buildings. This may be a connection, for the 1881 Census showed the professions of both of August's brothers as being involved in the meat trade, following in their father's footsteps. The eldest, Carl, head of the family now at 23, was described as an 'assistant foreign cattle salesman', while William, 19, was an 'apprentice butcher'. Carl would predecease August, succumbing to a similar tubercular disease, with the possibility of an initial bovine infection affecting both. But the resilience of youth helped the brothers, together with the 21-year-old August, recorded by the census as a clerk, to support their mother and three sisters. To further assist the family economy, the household contained a boarder, one David Davis. Presumably the girls – Emma, 26, Joanna, 17, and Marie, 12, – were supported as long as necessary. Marie would have needed to finish her education, perhaps at the German school at Islington; she later became a successful language teacher working from her home at Orme Court, Bayswater. Joanna seems to have adopted no profession, spending her life helping to look after a variety of relatives and in-laws, a family treasure. The census form gave Caroline Jaeger's age as 54 but she would outlive August, who shouldered his share of family responsibility by taking her under his own roof. His frequent complaints of lack of money begin to ring true when the extent of his responsibilities is realized.

August stands apart from his tradesmen father and brothers somewhat in having joined the ranks of the German clerks, evidence perhaps of greater natural abilities and wider ambitions. Possibly too, other members of the family did not share his passion for music; the resulting emotional isolation may have drawn him further into his chosen path, a mission to explain.

Jaeger's clerkship was with the firm of George Washington Bacon & Co., 'Map and Chart Sellers and Publishers, Map Mounters and Map Engravers', of 127 The Strand, an address shared with three other publishers and a cigar merchant. Although Graves thought that Jaeger was not happy there, the atmosphere seems to have been pleasingly unconventional if not somewhat eccentric. Other interests were pursued as well as maps, with Bacon introducing his 'Patent Domestic Gymnasium', guaranteed to 'cultivate strength, develop muscles, and ensure perfect health'. He followed this up by writing and publishing a series of health booklets, such as 'Our Colds: How Caught, Prevented and Cured', and 'Keeping Young and Well'; Bacon appears to have vindicated his theories by reaching the age of 92. There were also teaching aids for use in schools – the Education Act of 1870 making attendance compulsory up to the age of 13 had opened up new markets – and many maps. Bacon's eye for an opportunity led him to cater for a variety of requirements, including those of the railway traveller ('Bacon's New Railway Map of London & Suburbs Showing each Company's line in a Separate Character'), the cyclist ('Bacon's Cycle Road Map of 150 Miles round London'), and even the temperance movement ('Bacon's New Map of London: The Modern Plague of London, Showing the Public Houses as specified in the London Directory'); but the firm's most notable map publication during Jaeger's time was the 1888 'New Large Scale Ordnance Atlas of London & Suburbs', which became a classic of its kind, unequalled in the extent of the area covered and the amount of information and data provided, from the number of London's gas lamps to the number of passengers carried on the underground per year. Whatever Jaeger's precise rôle in the firm, such an exercise might have interested him, for he had an obsessive eye for detail; but it is difficult to see such a line of employment satisfying him on a deeper level.[10]

But in London there was always music. If violin and piano playing were confined to the domestic circle, there were plenty of opportunities for choral singing. Jaeger joined the Novello Oratorio Choir, conducted by Sir Alexander Mackenzie, in 1885, the year of its formation. There he began a long-lived friendship with his fellow tenor, Charles Graves, partly on the basis of a shared enthusiasm for Brahms. 'Jaeger had no pretensions to be regarded as a singer, and used to compare his voice to a tenor trombone at full blast', wrote Graves later. Both men also belonged to another amateur choir, named after and conducted by Hans Richter, and consisting largely of German expatriates. Again Graves recalls,

> Meanwhile, I had joined one of the worst and the most interesting choirs in London – the old Richter choir, which was periodically mobilized to assist in the performances of the Choral Symphony, Bach's 'Magnificat', Brahms's 'Alt-Rhapsodie', and the few other choral works which were included in Richter's repertory. I have called it the *old* Richter choir for various reasons – partly because it was got together many years ago, partly because of the venerable aspect of the cosmopolitan enthusiasts who composed it. Their voices were like Beethoven's – excruciating – but they were many of them good musicians, and made up in fervour what they lacked in freshness … the great attraction of the choir to me was the privilege which it conferred upon the members of attending the orchestral rehearsals and watching Richter at work with his band – a most illuminating experience. That was something like a revelation, and though in the main a serious business, the proceedings were frequently enlivened by ludicrous 'obiter dicta' from Richter, of which the famous comment on a very tame reading of the 'Venusberg' music is perhaps the best known: 'Gentlemen, you play it as if you were teetotallers – *which you are not!*'[11]

No doubt Jaeger also enjoyed the opportunity of working under such a celebrated conductor as Richter, his status further enhanced by his close association with Richard Wagner. Later Jaeger would write in the *Musical Times*, 'we have ourselves on many occasions been under the spell of that genial eye of Dr. Richter's, and know that he can effect more with a look than some conductors can with hands, and feet, and baton.'[12]

Jaeger also recalled singing in the Novello Oratorio Choir with Graves in the first London performance of Parry's *Judith* at St James's Hall on 6 December 1888. It was an early encounter with the music of a man who was to play a significant role in his life. And if he attended the first performance of Parry's Fourth Symphony at a Richter Concert on Monday, 1 July 1889, Jaeger would have shared the experience with Edward Elgar. No doubt their paths crossed on various occasions during Elgar's year of concert-going in London after his marriage. No one, least of all August Jaeger himself, could have foreseen the role that an obscure music-loving German clerk would have in the lives of these two composers and in the music of one of them in particular.

In pursuit of musical self-education Jaeger attended as many of London's concerts during this period as his pocket would allow, and sometimes more, economizing as much as he could. He was remembered as one of a group of young and enthusiastic music-lovers regularly to be found in a particular corner of the gallery in the old St James's Hall, Regent Street, with its statues of the Muses, many small chandeliers and composers' names inscribed in letters of gold on red panels round the walls. There he would have been able to follow the Richter Concerts, with their revelatory programmes of German music classical, romantic and modern (up to Strauss and Bruckner in the later days), Berlioz, Dvořák and Tchaikovsky, together with works by contemporary English composers such as Parry, Stanford, Cowen and Mackenzie. The formidable Richter set new standards for English audiences, conducting from memory in an undemonstrative style lacking all ostentation. At St James's Hall, too, were held the Monday and Saturday Popular Concerts of chamber music, where Joachim and Clara Schumann were only the most distinguished of the many first-rate artists to be heard from the gallery for a shilling. The musical repertore was wide – again including new works by English composers – and the analytical programme notes provided excellent value for those of enquiring mind. And it was at this hall, just over ten years to the day after the Parry Fourth Symphony première, that Jaeger would hear the first performance of Elgar's *Enigma* Variations. Further afield were the Crystal Palace Saturday concerts under August Manns, and the programmes of the Philharmonic Society, the Royal Albert Hall Concert Society, the Bach Society and the various opera companies.

An outstanding musical experience in these largely undocumented years was provided by the Wagner season which took place in London during 1882. Angelo Neumann presented three complete cycles of *The Ring of the Nibelungs* at His Majesty's Theatre during May, the first to be presented in London. The production, conducted by Anton Seidl, used scenery from Bayreuth and included several singers who had taken part in the original performances of 1876, including Lilli Lehmann. Before the month was out, Hans Richter himself embarked on a season at Drury Lane, again with German singers, and including performances of *Lohengrin*, *The Flying Dutchman*, and *Tannhäuser* together with the English premières of *Mastersingers* and *Tristan.* Between them Seidl and Richter conducted some forty performances and opened up new horizons in English appreciation of Wagner singing and performance. Jaeger followed the performances keenly, for they provided his first opportunity to hear Wagner's music-dramas. His tendency to hero-worship led to a deep admiration of Wagner, although he was evidently broad-minded enough in his approach not to allow this to put Brahms and his music out of court. But in many of his later musical judgements, Wagner was the supreme yardstick.

No doubt Jaeger particularly enjoyed such performances of *Mastersingers* as he was able to attend; the work meant a great deal to him and its music would sustain him during his final illness. But his determination to enjoy the unprecedented opportunities for hearing Wagner that year cost Jaeger dear, for he sacrificed food in order to pay for tickets, and he later traced the beginnings of his poor health to this period, an unscientific explanation that a romantic like Jaeger may have found satisfying. It would be only typical of the man to make such a sacrifice, but his commitment to Wagner's art was not shared universally among his new countrymen. The reviewer of the *Musical Times*, a journal which Jaeger no doubt perused when he could, while by no means withholding from Wagner a due meed of praise, reflected a Victorian response to the story of the *Ring*.

> The character and incidents of the story are naturally much debated – by some from the standpoint of public morality; by others from that of realistic truth. Among the former – if the egoism of the remark be permissible – I number myself. At the same time, I do not forget that Wagner wrote 'Der Ring des Nibelungen' for Germans, and as an embodiment of a new German art. It is possible that even the peculiar Scandinavian-Icelandic-Germanic mixture presented in the great Festival Play commends itself to the patriotic Teuton for whom it was intended. On that point I have small right to speak, and absolutely none to assume the attitude of critic. But when the trilogy, coming out of Germany, appeals to cosmopolitan taste, I am entitled to regard it from an extra-German point of view, and, that state of things being in presence, I contend that the story is not edifying – barely, indeed, permissible ... Its characters have to us no more substance than those of a showy pantomime. They are far removed indeed; and belong to a time and to mental and moral conditions which preclude the idea of sympathy and even of human interest ... It is further unfortunate that the moral atmosphere of the drama is offensive.[13]

Such comments may have proved Jaeger's introduction to the tone of a journal with which he would later be closely associated, and to an approach to the newest music with which he would strongly disagree. It was probably that kind of attitude which led him to describe his adopted land to Elgar on one occasion as 'this tight little island'.

According to Graves, 'Jaeger was not in his element in the map-publishing business ... and he gladly availed himself of the offer of employment in the firm of Novello's, to whom he had been recommended by a musical acquaintance'. Graves seems somewhat diffident about his own role in this, for it was he himself who provided the introduction to the firm,[14] a kindness that was in the fullness of time to have its consequences for English music. Jaeger's appointment to the firm in 1890 was as Chief of the publishing department.[15]

At this time Novello's had been publishing music for nearly eighty years, and had become one of the largest publishers in the world, with some twenty thousand items on its lists.[16] The founder, the organist and scholar Vincent Novello, had originally sought an outlet for his own collections of sacred music, published for the first time with a fully realised accompaniment instead of figured bass. During the 1820s he went on to publish Mozart and Haydn Masses, together with the sacred music of Purcell. The House of Novello formally came into existence in 1830, when it was taken over by Vincent's son Joseph Alfred, who continued to run it for over thirty years.

The Victorian period was one of tremendous expansion of the demand for choral music, in which the spread of literacy, the development of 'sol-fa' singing methods, the resurgence of choral services in churches, and the approval of singing as an activity of high moral and social value, all played their part. Alfred Novello saw the business potential here, and satisfied a growing need for sheet music and vocal scores at unprecedentedly low prices. Under his reign, Novello's began to bring out the works of Rossini, Beethoven, Haydn and Handel, sometimes in monthly parts, and an early coup was the outright purchase in 1836 of the English copyright of Mendelssohn's *St Paul*, a work which successfully established the Novello catalogue. By the late 1850s that catalogue had grown to nearly two hundred pages and included vocal works of every variety, with much of the sacred music that had become the firm's stock-in-trade – oratorios, festival hymns and anthems – together with secular vocal music and a lesser amount of instrumental pieces. Novello began to buy out other firms, and in the 1840s took over the monthly *Musical Times* magazine and set up the firm's own printing works, where the newer method of printing from movable type was adopted alongside the older practice of using engraved plates. Progress continued during the 1850s with the introduction of a highly successful series of part-songs, glees and madrigals and the opening up of an American market. The firm branched out into the publication of books on musical form, orchestration, harmony, counterpoint and fugue – volumes which were to be found on the shelves of Elgar Brothers of High Street, Worcester, 'Pianoforte and Music Sellers, Tuners, Regulators, Repairers, &c', whence they found their way into the critical hands of the young Edward Elgar. Through the huge numbers of its publications, and its policy of selling cheaply, Novello's influence percolated through all levels of society and began to change the musical, cultural and educational face of England. If the example of Elgar is that of the Victorian principle of self-help par excellence, it was Novello's which provided a great deal of study material for him and countless others.

The business rewards were colossal. Alfred Novello retired in 1861 to the family villa at Genoa. He owned railway stock, shares in the Crystal Palace Company, rights in the Bessemer Iron Process, and the income from various properties in and around London. At his death in 1896 his estate was valued at over £63,000, the equivalent of many millions at today's values. However, the larger part of this sum derived from the astute if unusual method he adopted when selling the firm to Henry Littleton, another self-made man who had started as an office-boy at the age of fourteen and who seems to have been invested by the unmarried Alfred Novello with the rôle of son and heir. On the understanding that the family name would continue, Alfred agreed to sell the business over ten years, during which time he would draw £ 2500 from it every six months. After ten years he would have drawn £ 50,000 and the sale would be complete. Such was Littleton's success that the money was paid off in five years, and in September 1866 he became the sole proprietor of Novello and Company. Expansion continued as another rival, Ewer & Co., was taken over, together with its Mendelssohn copyrights. A circulating Music Library was inaugurated, and new premises, where August Jaeger would spend most of his working life, were acquired at Berners Street in Soho. It was an address which, as George Washington Bacon's London map shows, was within walking distance of the Queen's Hall at the end of Regent Street, and Pagani's celebrated restaurant in Great Portland Street – telegrams, 'Soufflé, London'. Jaeger would spend happy hours in both.

Littleton further developed his business by becoming something of an impresario, arranging a series of over two hundred concerts during 1873, to be followed the next year by a further series of daily concerts, 'Prom' style, at the Albert Hall. Full of drive and energy, he travelled far and wide in the firm's interests, attending the opening of the Bayreuth Festspielhaus in 1876 and hiring some expert German engravers in Leipzig. 1877 saw him in America, building up Novello's established links there and opening new premises on Broadway. No musician himself, Littleton felt the need of advice, and he appointed Joseph Barnby as music advisor; he was succeeded in 1877 by the Dutch organist, composer and arranger Berthold Tours.

Littleton retired in 1886, four years before Jaeger joined the firm. He handed the business over to his two sons, Alfred Henry and Augustus James, and the husbands of his two daughters, George Gill and Henry Brooke. Alfred Henry was in overall charge, becoming the first Chairman of the Board of Directors when the firm was formed into a limited company in 1898. The four men were directors for life, able to come and go as they pleased rather than work standard office hours. Three years later Henry Clayton bought his way on to the Board as Company Secretary. In the main, the members of the Board, like Henry Littleton, were more businessmen than musicians, although Alfred had some musical training and became a man of some culture who gathered collections of early printed music and fine composer portraits. But he gave little specifically musical input to the firm, and neither did his brother Augustus, who was more concerned with the practical binding and printing aspects of the business. Henry Clayton had read law at Cambridge and was something of a hard-headed expert on matters of copyright. Only with the next generation would the firm gain a musician as a Director. Harold Brooke, Henry Brooke's son and a good linguist and pianist, joined the editorial department in 1902 after three years at the Leipzig Conservatoire. Later he transferred to the publishing office where he worked with and eventually superseded Jaeger. But in the days when Jaeger joined the firm, the Board of Directors operated in a kind of artistic vacuum, filled only by their musical advisors and editors Berthold Tours and John E. West.

West was an organist and choir trainer who had joined the firm in 1884 and whose contributions included the editing of many services, anthems and madrigals and the arranging of the vocal scores of choral works. Although Tours had had some experience of the orchestral world as a violinist, both men tended to the musically conservative, and their own activities as composers tended to be confined to the many church anthems they contributed to the pages of the *Musical Times*. Likewise, the editor of that 'house journal' from 1897 to 1909, Frederick George Edwards, was an organist and scholar with a particular interest in the history and musical associations of English cathedrals, which formed the subject of many lengthy articles. Edwards was devoted too, to a somewhat heavy-handed style of punning which formed the basis of many shorter contributions, not the kind of humour that appealed to Jaeger, who seems to have felt a complete lack of affinity with Edwards bordering on actual dislike. This was no doubt exacerbated by the older man's devotion to Mendelssohn – the composer with whom Edwards seems to have considered modern music to finish.

If Jaeger with his interest in Wagner was something of a musical left-winger, these men added up to a formidable 'establishment', steeped in the English church music tradition. Their tastes were reflected in the hundreds of hymnals, anthems, services, masses, oratorios and cantatas good and bad to be found in the pages of the Novello Catalogue. In the festival oratorio and cantata market in particular, as well as in churches and concert halls up and down the country, Novello's reigned supreme. In response to the demands of the Victorian singing public, they published dozens of works by English composers, covering apparently every familiar and unfamiliar aspect of the Bible. The vast majority of such works are now forgotten, a fate which has also extended to a great deal of the religious music by the foreign composers Novello's were anxious to publish – Spohr, Félicien David, Niels Gade, Liszt, Dvořák. The important foreign composer had a special status in the English system, and when Charles Gounod agreed to compose his oratorio *The Redemption* for the Birmingham Festival of 1882, it was in return for a then unheard of fee of £4000; Henry Littleton subsequently bought the copyright for £3250 and went on to make a profit out of a work that was thought of at the time as the greatest religious masterpiece of the century. Three years later he was happy to pay the same figure for another now rarely played Gounod work, *Mors et Vita*.

With its unique position, Novello's was a firm that Jaeger felt proud and excited to work for, but it was not destined to be a consistently smooth and happy relationship. As was his nature, Jaeger would give the firm the total commitment of his time, energy and enthusiasm, and his rôle of Publishing Office Manager, with responsibility for overseeing the publication of a wide range of music – including, most importantly, accurate orchestral and vocal scores and instrumental parts against festival and rehearsal deadlines – was only the most narrow definition of his position. His judgement and initiative gradually enabled him to become another, unofficial music advisor to the firm, with different perspectives from West and Tours. He came to feel, however, that he was regarded as little more than a clerk and that he deserved better from the firm in terms of recognition, salary and status. He was understandably frustrated too, when his contributions to the *Musical Times*, over which he took great trouble, were ignored, cut or altered to suit opinions which he did not share.

There can be no doubt that in August Jaeger, Novello's gained an employee with a range of qualities which were assets to them. He had publishing experience, musical knowledge, and spoke German. This would be most helpful in dealing with German engravers on the staff and abroad, and in dealing with the leading musicians of his native land. Jaeger was therefore able to act confidently as the firm's musical ambassador at the great German Festivals, showing charm, tact and diplomacy when dealing with those of 'artistic temperament', to say nothing of the Novello's management. But with his musical tastes firmly rooted in the world of the modern German masters, he could not have felt entirely satisfied with Novello's musical horizons and this inevitably led to friction. It is a reasonable assumption to make that Jaeger gradually defined for himself a role within the firm that would improve matters musically and make use of his more cosmopolitan background; he would seek out and encourage new composers, and in particular he would make it his particular mission to discover and nurture the figure that England lacked above all – a truly great composer.

At that time, a climate of opinion seemed to be developing in the minds of various writers and musicians that such a composer must come. In his notebook for 1890, George Grove made this entry:

> 'While not an English mountain we behold
> By the celestial Muses glorified'.
> So said Wordsworth ... and so we might say of English music, too. The giants Bach and Beethoven and Schubert have taken away all our praise from us, but Wordsworth himself altered the fact as to the mountains, and some one is sure to come and alter it as to music.[17]

Much earlier, the pre-eminence of the foreign composer had been noted by William Henry, father of Edward and senior partner of Elgar Brothers, in an edition of the hand-written 'Worcester Papers' which were circulated among the family for information, amusement and thoughtful consideration during the 1850s.

> ... I consider that the English stand rather in the background as far as regards Musical affairs ... Comparatively speaking how very few English composers are there when we look at the superior number of foreign ... before I conclude allow me to say that I hope the time is not very far distant when England in all her glory will stand pre-eminent, at least in Musical Affairs.[18]

Writing some 40 years later, in an opera review written for 'The World', Bernard Shaw could find nothing in English music since Purcell:

> I wonder how soon strong men in England will begin to take to musical composition. It cannot be said that the national genius is for the genteel, the sentimental, the elegant, the superficial. When I am asked to name a composer who is to England what Wagner is to Germany, I do not cite our elderly imitators of Spohr and Mendelssohn, or our youthful imitators of Gounod: I have to go back to Henry Purcell, whose Yorkshire

Feast suggests that if he were alive today he might give us an English equivalent to Die Meistersinger.

There is a general notion that painting tastes better before dinner, and music after it; but neither is supposed to be in the least nutritious. Too great a regard for them is held to be the mark of a weak character ... Under these circumstances we are kept well supplied with pretty things; but if we want really national music-dramas we shall have to take art seriously, or else wait for the advent of a genius big enough and strong enough to set himself against us all and cram his ideas down our throats ...[19]

Composers themselves felt the need for a leader. Granville Bantock selflessly mounted a concert of works by younger British composers at the Queen's Hall in December 1896. His programme note for the occasion was couched in terms with an almost Old Testament prophetic ring about them:

For the moment any spirit of commercialism is set aside, and the predominant desire has been to advance the cause of British music ... there is no reason why the concert-rooms of this country should be empty when native music is performed; and when that British composer whose coming we await, does arrive, it will be well for his fellow-countrymen to be ready with the bread instead of waiting to place the traditional stone over his grave. Those whose privilege it is to go before, to form as it were the stepping-stones for the god who is to follow, have their little share in their life-time, even though they may be forgotten hereafter; they will continue to work in hope as long as earnest-ness brings no disgrace, and enthusiasm casts no slur.[20]

And in his 'Music and Morals', the writer and essayist the Reverend H.R. Haweis, while remarking on the enormous variety of taste shown by the English music-loving public, considered that:

It may be that we are on the eve of a creative period in the history of English music. This confusion of idea may be nothing but the coming together of what will by-and-by develop into our national school. This eclectic taste, which at times looks much like chaos, may also be the ferment out of which a new and beautiful life is ready to be born.

As an original artist will be caught and absorbed by one influence after another, being possessed by his art long before he learns to possess himself, – as he will at times appear to be swayed to and fro by various distinct impulses, without being able to bring them into harmonious relationship, – as we may watch him year by year melting down one style after another in the crucible of his genius, until he has gained fine gold, and stamped it with his own image, even so we seem to see England now calling in the musical currencies of the world, whch she may before long re-issue with the hall-mark of her own originality and genius.[21]

It was written in fine Victorian-clergyman terms, but it amounted to a not inappropriate explanation of the gradual and eclectic nature of Elgar's development as a composer. Novello's began to have dealings with him in 1890 through Berthold Tours, and it was to be some time before Jaeger was asked to continue the relationship. In the early 1890s a younger figure, still a student at the Royal College of Music, seemed to Jaeger to be the most likely candidate for the rôle of Bantock's 'British composer whose coming we await': his name was Samuel Coleridge-Taylor.

Ironically, Samuel Coleridge-Taylor was described in *Grove's Dictionary of Music and Musicians*[22] as 'a composer whose marked individuality seemed to be peculiarly the product of his mixed race'. His father was a West African who qualified in medicine at King's College London and who subsequently left England for Sierra Leone, having suffered poor treatment on account of his colour. Mother and child took up residence in Croydon, where one day – so the story goes – a leading local music teacher and conductor, Samuel Beckwith, found the small boy playing marbles on the pavement while clutching a newly-acquired violin. Beckwith improved the lad's playing, and another local benefactor welcomed him to a church choir and trained his voice. The family were not well off, and there was some question of the youngster being apprenticed to a piano-tuner, but George Grove admitted the gifted pupil to the Royal College of Music when he left school at the age of fifteen in 1890, and he was to remain there for seven years, sustained by various prizes and scholarships in addition to continued support from various Croydon friends. As well as the privations of limited means, the curly-haired, dark-skinned Coleridge-Taylor suffered taunts and insults on account of his colour, at the College itself as well as on the streets of Croydon.

He began as a violin student at the College but his true bent was for composition, and towards the end of 1892 Grove permitted him to make it his principal study under Charles Stanford, who became the idol of the shy and mild-mannered student. With Coleridge-Taylor, Stanford may have somewhat modified the stimulating harshness whch was his stock-in-trade as a teacher; on one occasion after overhearing a racial comment by another student, the Irishman put his arm round the victim, took him to his room, and gave kindly reassurance and understanding.

By that time, Coleridge-Taylor had already had five Anthems published by Novello, perhaps the earliest sign of Jaeger's interest in his music. The 1890s saw many famous names of the future as students at the Royal College, including Thomas Dunhill, Ralph Vaughan Williams, Gustav Holst and William Hurlstone, but in the short term Samuel Coleridge-Taylor's star outshone them all. Year by year as a student he produced compositions of impressive quality and assurance – songs, chamber works, music for violin and orchestra, and a symphony. Jaeger seems to have become a staff writer for the *Musical Times* two or three years after joining Novello's,[23] probably beginning with the compilation of the 'Foreign Notes', brief listings of musical events abroad culled from the foreign press; he remained particularly well informed of music and criticism on the continent. While it is not always possible to identify his often anonymous writings for that journal, it is possible with hindsight to be reasonably confident in ascribing authorship to him when a young composer's works are praised in enthusiastic terms. Inevitably he focused on the London concerts and would have made sure he kept himself well informed about emerging student composers at the major colleges of music. There was a special encouragement, too, for Jaeger to follow events at the Royal College of Music, in the form of a growing friendship with Isabella Donkersley, a talented violin student. Jaeger's keen patronage of Coleridge-Taylor seems to have mounted with each succeeding work, and his *Musical Times* reviews of the College Concerts were full of praise. Of the Nonet for piano, strings and wind, first performed in July 1894, he wrote:

> It is quite unnecessary to find fault with Mr. Taylor's ambition, both because experience will soon correct that failing and because there is such striking merit in his work as furnishes an excellent excuse. The whole Nonet is most interesting, its themes are fresh and vigorous, and their treatment proves that the writer has learned to compose with freedom and to treat with skill. The *Scherzo* is unquestionably the most striking movement, and few would guess it to be the work of one still a student. We shall look for further work from Mr. Taylor with great interest.[24]

It was perfectly characteristic of Jaeger that he should praise first of all the quality of the thematic invention, and Coleridge-Taylor's was often compared to Dvořák's. A review from the following year of a setting of words by Lockhart for soprano and orchestra showed that Coleridge-Taylor was also able to succeed in another of Jaeger's priorities, orchestration.

> This was the work of Mr. S. Coleridge-Taylor – a scholar of the College, who is already known by a number of compositions published during the last few years. The Ballad in question displays decided talent, the orchestration especially being full of felicitous touches. It was sung by Miss Clementine M. Pierpoint, whose clear, high soprano told well in Mr. Taylor's music. The orchestra was not in its best form; slips were not infrequent, and we have often heard Professor Stanford's young people play with greater finish and refinement.[25]

Professor Stanford would not have liked that. But 1895 proved an excellent year for his pupil, with much more music performed and well received. March saw his five *Fantasiestücke* for String Quartet played at the College, and this work measured up to another of Jaeger's yardsticks, individuality: 'Mr. Coleridge-Taylor is a *rara avis* among students, for he has something to say that is worth saying, and he does so in his own individual way. Considering the lamentable dearth of good string quartet music by native composers, his *Fantasiestücke* should be in request …'[26] The première took place in July of one of the masterpieces among Coleridge-Taylor's early works, his Clarinet Quintet. Jaeger's notice in the *Musical Times* – dignified by another classical quotation – reflected delight and admiration, and placed the work in the context of English music.

> The Chamber Concert of the 10th ult. proved of quite exceptional interest by the production of a Quintet for clarinet and strings by Mr. S. Coleridge-Taylor. To do justice to this work we deliberately apply a different standard from that which pupils' compositions are generally judged. There is little or nothing in Mr. Taylor's Quintet to betray the fact that he is still *in statu pupillaris.* His is, indeed, an achievement, not merely a 'promise'. Mr. Taylor's themes are his own, and very interesting and unconventional the majority are, while the ease with which he handles the difficult form, the freedom and artistic balance of his part-writing, and, even more, the variety and originality of his rhythms, are quite remarkable in one so young. Nor are the higher qualities of imagination and emotion wanting, without which mere cleverness counts for but little. They are most conspicuous in the fine, terse opening *Allegro energico*, and in the Romance (*Larghetto affetuoso*), which is as poetic and suggestive a movement as is to be found in English music. In the *Scherzo* a most complicated rhythm is handled with masterly ease, and in the *Finale (Allegro con Fuoco)* the two-bar rhythm of a theme *à la Dvořák*, kept up with strenuous persistence, produces a most spirited effect. Towards the close the

> expressive theme of the slow movement creeps in unexpectedly and helps to bring the work to a worthy close.[27]

The Quintet was acclaimed by Stanford and taken up by Joachim in Berlin, although it had to wait until 1974 for publication and until 1990 for a recording. Finally in 1895, Novello's brought out Coleridge-Taylor's *Ballade* in D minor, for Violin and Orchestra. Isabella Donkersley gave its first performance, with piano accompaniment, at Kensington Town Hall that year, and Jaeger told her, 'I have long been looking for an English composer of real genius and believe I have found him'.[28] Novello's published the work in an arrangement for violin and piano, an almost unheard-of success for a 20-year-old composer still a student, no doubt the result of persuasive advocacy on Jaeger's part. The following year saw the performance of three movements of the symphony (in a performance which featured Holst playing the trombone and Vaughan Williams the triangle), a string quartet, and, an indication of future inspirations, *Hiawathan Sketches* for violin and piano and *Five Southern Love Songs*, settings of Longfellow.

Isabella Donkersley was a talented Yorkshire girl, from a long-established family of wool-traders of Honley, near Huddersfield. She was born and brought up together with her musical elder sister Lucy, at Ivy Cottage, a delightful family home built into the hillside, with impressive views of Magdale below. She was a student at the Royal College of Music between 1884 and 1890, studying violin under Henry Holmes, Professor of Violin since the College's foundation. Isabella, or 'Bell' as she was more familiarly known, became an outstanding student who took a major rôle in College concerts, on one occasion leading a performance of the Beethoven Septet and on another playing his Violin Concerto under Holmes's direction. But such inconclusive documentary evidence as survives of her studentship tells us less of her violin playing than of the moral régime thought appropriate for musical education at the Royal College of Music in Victorian days. Holmes had spent considerable periods abroad in more relaxed societies, and his relationship with Isabella was considered too informal. Further, he had, according to Sir George Grove, Director of the College, 'radical unbelieving views'.[29] The problem was mentioned in a letter of October 1890, from Grove to his ex-student confidante Edith Oldham.

> Did I tell you about Holmes and Bell Donkersley? Early in the holidays I got an anonymous letter saying that I ought to notice Holmes's conduct with her; that they usually went across the park together; and hinting though very darkly at improprieties I ought to ask the Police men &c &c. Holmes is *very* foolish, but wicked or dishonourable I don't think he is. He was in France, and then I sent him the letter begging him to stop at once any open intimacy that could lead to remark &c. I got a note from him very thankful, and promising all that could be desired. Two weeks ago Watson [the Registrar] spoke to me about the intimacy that existed, & that Mrs. Thompson [Lady Superintendent, housekeeper and matron] had been quite frightened on going in to Holmes Room, on several occasions, to find him alone there with B.D. – that he gave her extra lessons, when no one else was present; that she brought up his lunch & did various

> other personal services to him &c &c. I shd say that Watson knew nothing of the previous letter. On this I wrote another note to him pointing out the inconvenience of such reports, and the danger to B.D. herself of being wounded if such things came to her ears – Then came note No 2 from Holmes; how much he appreciated my good feelings, and everything should cease &c. By Jove! yesterday, I go up between 1 & 2 to consult H. as to having a junior orchestra, and if I don't find him & B.D. alone in the room together! Isn't it foolish & absurd? and also very unfair towards poor D. herself. Holmes has an extravagant opinion of her abilities – I admit she is most praiseworthy and that she plays very well – but she will never be a *great* player. However she is now studying the Beethoven Concerto, to play it at his Concert later in this term![30]

Grove's concern was repeated in a letter of December 1893, three years after Isabella left the College. He had heard that Holmes lectured his girl pupils 'not only on Atheism & Socialism – but on other matters which no man ought to talk to any woman about ...'. A crisis came just a week later, when Holmes was sacked for 'committing the grossest immorality' with several pupils. He went to live permanently in San Francisco, where he died in 1905; it was said that his memorial at the Royal College of Music was the installation of glass panels in the doors of the teaching rooms.[31]

Isabella herself seems to have remained in Kensington on leaving the College, adopting a modest performing career, often as a chamber player, presumably together with teaching. Her name appears several times in the pages of the *Musical Times* during the 1890s and the reviews were consistently good. Her first professional appearance was at Kensington Town Hall, leading a group of ex-College students in chamber works by Brahms, Bruch, Mendeslssohn and Schumann. 'The young lady has a remarkably fine tone and an excellent command of expression', thought the reviewer, and the whole ensemble was thought of sufficient proficiency to play for the Queen on one occasion. There was further praise for later performances, particularly of trios and quartets by Brahms. At a performance of the Brahms C Minor Quartet, in November 1892, 'Miss Donkersley was once more an excellent leader', according to the reviewer, possibly by this time her admiring suitor, August Jaeger. But naturally enough, perhaps, the warmest review was of a performance given in her native Yorkshire in April 1896:

> A high-class Chamber Concert was given on the 15th ult., at the Assembly Rooms, Thirsk, by Miss I.L. Jopling, a talented local pianist and late pupil of the Royal College of Music. The *pièce de résistance* of an interesting programme was Mr. Edward German's delightful 'Gipsy Suite' played, in its entirety, by Miss Isabella Donkersley (violin) and the Concert-giver, with great refinement and brilliancy ... The two artists were also heard in an Adagio and Allegro by Corelli, the *Andante* and *Presto* from Beethoven's 'Kreutzer' Sonata, and two Hungarian Dances (Brahms-Joachim), which served admirably to display the fine tone which Miss Donkersley draws from her beautiful Guadagnini. For an encore, the clever violinist delighted the audience by playing the captivating 'Shepherd's Dance' from Mr. German's popular 'Henry VIII' music.[32]

The Guadanigni violin was another tribute from Yorkshire, for it had been lent to Isabella for life by John Rutson, owner of two estates in the North Riding. A wealthy patron of the arts, a Director of the Royal Academy of Music and a Member of the Council of the Royal College of Music, he was able to acquire many classic violins which he would lend to suitably deserving students to help them start their careers.[33] The Guadanigni family made violins for several generations, and the earlier members claimed to be pupils of Stradivarius, on whose instruments they modelled their own. The most noted was Giovanni Battista Guadanigni (*c.* 1745–90), whose violins were noted for a distinctively highly coloured varnish.[34] Whatever his aberrations, Holmes would seem to have been an effective teacher of an instrument with little place in the English tradition; on one occasion Isabella received complimentary mention from *Corno di Bassetto* himself, George Bernard Shaw.[35]

Another gifted student composer who caught Jaeger's ear during the 1890s was Henry Walford Davies, born on the Wales–Shropshire border in 1869. At the age of 13 he gained a choristership at St George's, Windsor under Elvey and then Parratt, becoming assistant to the latter, and Organist of the Chapel Royal, Windsor Park. In 1890, a shy and serious youth, he was awarded a composition scholarship to the Royal College of Music, studying with Parry and Stanford. Despite the disruption of a serious illness and convalescence, he successfully took a Cambridge Bachelor of Music degree two years later. He began to teach counterpoint at the College, while continuing in a succession of posts as organist and choirmaster. Like Coleridge-Taylor, he produced a flow of compositions during the nineties – a symphony, chamber music, church music, a cantata and most notably of all perhaps *Prospice*, a setting of Browning for baritone and string quartet. If outwardly Walford Davies might have seemed wedded to the conventional musical paths dictated by the organ-loft, his experience of near-fatal illness drew him creatively to Browning's account of the strong man facing death, and resulted in a powerful and dramatic, if neglected, work. The *Musical Times* gave a warm welcome to one of Davies's chamber works, in a review which might seem to reflect many of Jaeger's preoccupations:

> Mr. Charles Jacoby, a former violin pupil of the Royal College of Music, gave two Recitals at the Queen's (Small) Hall, on October 27 and the 5th ult., before large and highly appreciative audiences. His programme ranged from Bach, Beethoven, and Schubert to Wienawski, Sarasate, and Stanford; and both by his selections from these composers and his interpretation of their various works, he proved himself a genuine artist who takes his art very seriously and as an executant of no mean power. He deserves the thanks of music-lovers, and especially of those having the future of English music at heart, for the production of a new Violin and Pianoforte Sonata in D minor by Mr. H. Walford Davies, another erstwhile pupil of the Royal College, and one of the most earnest and talented of our young composers. The new work is not merely the best which Mr. Davies has so far brought to a hearing, but a notable achievement which deserves recognition wherever *res severa verum gaudium* is still the motto of musicians. There is nobility, pathos, and elevation in the opening *Allegro*; the grand first subject sweeps along with rare breadth and dignity, and the composer has succeeded in maintaining almost throughout the whole work the high level thus reached at the very outset. Mr. Davies's workmanship has always been of a high order, and the new Sonata excels in that respect. But what we prize much more is the great advance he has made as a melodist. This, more than anything else, should justify our looking on him as one who will ere long 'arrive' and produce enduring work. At present he is still under the influence of Brahms, though, in spite of his youth, he has not fallen into the error of emulating that master's over-elaboration and consequent occasional diffuseness as

> sometimes displayed in his early works. The movements are, in fact, concise and easy to follow, if we except the *Andantino*, which is so original in design and so sombre, not to say pessimistic in expression, that it is difficult to grasp at a first hearing. In the *Allegretto semplice* he has dared to be unaffectedly tuneful, and a delightful piece of music is the result. The *Finale* is a vigorous, melodious, and exultant movement, which worthily crowns a work in whch noble endeavour is shown in every bar and the 'lion's claw' of something very like genius in its finest moments.[36]

Alongside his cultivation of youthful talent, Jaeger also made contact with more senior members of London's musical world. He dealt with Sir Hubert Parry, whose music Novello's had been publishing since 1880, and who continued to produce a stream of major choral works during the 1890s. A genuine friendship resulted, of much importance to Jaeger in later years. A relationship with another distinguished figure was not without its awkward moments. The ailing George Grove retired from the Royal College during 1895, and went on to devote himself to *Beethoven And His Nine Symphonies*, published by Novello's early in 1896. A second edition was soon called for and Jaeger's help was sought in various revisions and corrections; the first edition had contained no index and no opus numbers for the symphonies.[37] The new edition, however, contained no acknowledgement of services rendered, an omission that Graves considered uncharacteristic, especially as he thought Grove to possess a 'cordial admiration' for Jaeger. Perhaps Jaeger attended a meeting of the Musical Association on 12 February 1895, when Grove read an admirable scholarly paper on the alterations made in the score of Beethoven's Ninth since the composer's death. He provided a meticulous listing of various alterations to the score, concluding with a plea for a return to a strict observance of Beethoven's original scores based on an edition 'of these great works *as Beethoven left them*.' Grove's veneration for the composer as expressed that evening is almost embarrassing to present-day ears. 'Our feeling towards him is one of such utter veneration, such an unqualified desire to do anything he asked – if he could fortunately be here to ask us! – that it is hard to suppose that he could ever have made any request without its being at once obeyed!'.[38] But while emphasizing the authority of purely documentary evidence in support of his argument, Grove had introduced his talk with a modest disclaimer: 'My remarks this evening are not to be taken as those of a musician, to which character I cannot pretend.' It was this elevation of the letter of the law above the spirit which was at the root of the differences that would emerge with Jaeger, who was a musician before everything.

2 1896–97: Composers Old and New

Jaeger had two characteristic contributions published in the *Musical Times* of July 1896. One, a letter appearing over his name, and dealing with a posthumous vocal duet of Tchaikovsky, is easy enough to identify. The other, a report on that year's Lower Rhine Festival at Düsseldorf 'By Our Special Correspondent', is unsigned but contains every evidence of his authorship. Jaeger began by recalling his first such festival in 1878, the year he quitted Germany, and a performance conducted by Joachim of Brahms's Second Symphony, still in manuscript. He compared its enthusiastic reception to that given to Richard Strauss, who conducted three of his works at the 1896 gathering, and concluded pointedly that 'in Düsseldorf, at any rate, unknown works by living composers did not frighten music-lovers away, as is, alas! so often the case at our best concerts at home'. But before dealing with the musical aspects of the Festival, Jaeger could not resist a little scene-painting, evidence of a certain proprietorial pride in the city of his birth.

> No one who has ever been present at one of these Festivals can doubt that the charming 'Garten-Stadt' on the Rhine is an almost ideal place for such meetings; and as the success and enjoyment of the latter depend largely on the surroundings and the 'atmosphere', more or less congenial, in which the visitor finds himself, it will be imagined that Düsseldorf, with its lovely leafy parks, fine, broad and well-built streets, excellent hotels and 'gemüthliche' restaurants ('Kneipen' they call them); with its general look of comfort and cleanliness, its utter absence of noise and stir and bustle; and last, but not least, with its fine 'Tonhalle' can hardly be surpassed as a place for a great musical festival. In the said 'Tonhalle' this fair town possesses a building which is the envy of its neighbours. And well it may be, for, in addition to the 'Kaisersaal', in which the Festivals are now held, a large (but poorly and tastelessly decorated) room of remarkably fine acoustic properties, it includes two smaller rooms, one of which, the 'Rittersaal', is the identical place where Mendelssohn's 'St. Paul' was produced exactly sixty years ago. The cloak-rooms and foyers are on a scale of amplitude altogether undreamt of in the philosophy of the architects of London concert-halls, and, best of all, one of the boasted advantages of the Bayreuth Festival Theatre can here be enjoyed, as the building is surrounded on three sides by a beautiful garden, where, during the long pauses between the parts, refreshments are served *al fresco*, and amid a gay and animated scene mind and body can recuperate till a trumpet signal (another reminiscence of Bayreuth) summons the audience to the second part.[1]

Jaeger devoted nearly a full column of the article to a performance of Beethoven's Ninth Symphony conducted by Julius Buths. With an orchestral body of 130 players available, Buths had decided to use Wagner's changes to the instrumentation of a passage in the *Scherzo*, where the second subject is played by woodwinds only just holding their own against a four-octave ostinato in the strings played fortissimo.

> To remedy this miscalculated orchestral effect of Beethoven's, Wagner suggested that the horns, which are only employed to mark the already very pronounced rhythm, should strengthen the wood-wind, and this is what Herr Buths did. He made his eight horns play the theme *ff*, and his eighty-eight strings hammered out their 'figure' with all their might without being able to cover the melody. The effect was one of tremendous, elemental force. Here was Beethoven indeed in an 'unbuttoned' mood, to quote Sir George Grove's favourite phrase. Some of my readers may hold up their hands and mutter the word 'sacrilege'. But I am happy that in this glorious passage in Beethoven's masterpiece I have at last heard something like the effect which he, the poor deaf master, must have wished to produce.[2]

Jaeger was later to repeat his views in reviews of English performances which adopted Wagner's alterations to this passage, and it was Sir George Grove himself who would hold up his hands and mutter 'sacrilege'. The new edition of his book had included a footnote mentioning Wagner's suggestions over the instrumentation of the *Scherzo* and dismissing them. 'The wonder is that so great a composer should not have felt that *any* alteration of a completed work, by any but the author himself, is impossible ... Make the same proposition in regard to a picture or a poem and its inadmissibility is at once obvious to everyone.'[3]

Grove also held up his hands in horror at the music of the youngest composer appearing at the 1896 Lower Rhine Festival, Richard Strauss. His *Till Eulenspiegel* had received its first English performances at the Crystal Palace in March of that year under Manns, who thought the work so novel and complex that he had it played twice. Of *Also Sprach Zarathustra*, performed at the same venue, Grove wrote, 'What can have happened to drag down music from the high level of beauty, interest, sense, force, grace, coherence and any other good quality, which it rises to in Beethoven and also (not so high) in Mendelssohn, down to the low level of ugliness and want of interest that we had in Strauss's absurd farrago ...?'[4] At Düsseldorf Strauss appeared as very much the coming man to the alert Jaeger. Of *Don Juan* he thought, 'Here we had a work which was calculated to set the enemies of musical progress by the ears!' Of the music itself he wrote that it 'simply glows with unfettered passion and tremendous, restless energy; his orchestration is unprecedented for richness, variety, and novel effects; and conception and execution alike are daring, strong, and masterly.' Jaeger was evidently thrilled by the style, and thought that the 'striking and even beautiful' melodies in the work were an improvement on the 'little scraps of *Motive*' to be found in *Till Eulenspiegel*,

> ... though Strauss, who is still a young man, is not likely to have reached his final development as a melodist. That will come with years, for melodists are not born ready made. The melodic gift, though it must, of course, be innate, is indeed the last to develop, even

in composers of genius, a fact which is too often forgotten by critics judging the works of so young, but so fully, so phenomenally equipped a musician as Richard Strauss![5]

Melody was the supreme test of a composer's ability for Jaeger, and he found qualities in it both mystical and ethical. He did much for the early cause of Richard Strauss in England, although he would be characteristically honest in stating his disillusion with the composer at a later stage. Characteristically honest, too, and perhaps revealing, was Jaeger's admission of emotional exhaustion by the end of the Festival. He concluded the article by admitting that he was too fatigued to stay to the end of the last concert to hear Busoni play in the Beethoven *Choral Fantasia*; 'but as this had not begun when half-past ten o'clock struck, and the Concert began at six, I fled with a jaded feeling that I had had too much of a good thing …'.[6]

Jaeger's love of melody and his emotional response to music would be almost bound to make him an admirer of Tchaikovsky, although in the long term another 'jaded feeling' would set in here as well. His letter to the July *Musical Times* concerning Taneyev's completion and orchestration of an unfinished duet from a projected *Romeo and Juliet* opera by Tchaikovsky, published by Novello's, reflected admiration for the music, together with a degree of irritation with a response which seemed to ignore its emotional nature especially as far as love music was concerned. Jaeger had noticed that the analytical notes for a Richter performance of the *Romeo and Juliet* Overture at the Queen's Hall stated that its composer had given no indication of which aspects of the drama the music described, and he went on to cite the posthumous duet between Romeo and Juliet, which used the love music from the Overture as its material, as evidence of Tchaikovsky's intentions. Jaeger could not believe that the music would not speak for itself, and he concluded the letter with an attack, tinged with sarcasm, on the prudish attitude of the writer of the Queen's Hall notes.

I fancy, with the aid of this clue, it is not difficult to draw conclusions as to the poetical contents of the Overture. But even without it, it appears not a little strange that the clever analyst does not interpret *any* portion of the work as referring to the love element in Shakespeare's drama. He only speaks of *Juliet's* obsequies, the feud and combats between the two rival houses of Montagues and Capulets, the *Prince's* attempt to reconcile them, and the reconciliation on the death of the lovers. Did he not look for such love-music, or has Tchaikovsky so signally failed in his attempt to portray 'la grande passion' that it *required* a clue before intentions could be rightly interpreted?[7]

Jaeger's open criticism of his fellow professional was evidence of his lack of affinity with the English approach to music, and evidence too of an often barely concealed contempt for his fellow critics. It was not the last time he had recourse to a letter in the correspondence columns of the *Musical Times*, and not the last time that he courted controversy and risked odium as a critic.

Since Jaeger's appointment to the the firm in 1890, Novello's had published some eight choral works by Parry, including his setting of Tennyson's *Lotus Eaters*, the Oratorios *Job* and *Saul*, and the *Invocation to Music*, as well as two sets of *English Lyrics* and some violin and piano pieces. Writing to him in the autumn of 1896, Jaeger was on sufficiently good terms with the older man to be able to discuss his setting of words that had evidently been set also by Kate Boundy, an Exeter lady who had several publications to her credit in Novello's catalogue, mainly childrens' songs.[8] Jaeger's letter contained also some gentle cajoling over new works, proposals for finding a Parry score that had gone adrift, and a persuasive recommendation of Elgar's *King Olaf*, one of the earliest of his works to interest Jaeger, although he had also been impressed by the *Black Knight* of 1893.[9] Frank, self-deprecating, tactful, persuasive, businesslike, generous in its advocacy of a new composer, Jaeger's letter gives us a snapshot of the whole man, and contains everything that we have come to recognize about him as characteristic.

1, Berners Street, W.
London.

Sept 25 1896

Dear Dr. Parry,

I am *ashamed* of myself for delaying my thanks for your most Kind letter of the 14th. But I have only recently returned from my holiday (spent in Germany) & have been fearfully busy ever since, one of my assistants having fallen ill while I was abroad. He is still away & hence I am *fully* occupied! Your offer anent Miss Boundy's setting is what an English 'young lady' would call *awfully* Kind, & I thoroughly appreciate your goodness. But I would not dream of availing myself of it! To begin with my judgement may be & very likely is absurdly wrong. I am sure yours is the finer, nobler interpretation of the spirit of the Poem & the more I play & 'hum' it (I cannot aspire to singing) the more I 'see in it'. Its a 'song' i.e. a flowing, songlike melody coming straight & unaffectedly from the heart & appealing to that Organ as well as charming the ear, I like Miss B's better. Hers is a song to sing, yours, to hear *being* sung by an intellectual artist, a fine 'interpreter'. That's how the difference strikes me. Then I may be prejudiced in favour of little Miss B's because my girl (I.D.) is fond of singing it & sings it *very nicely*! Whether it would be a success when published is doubtful. It is at once too good & too 'bad' to be a *financial* success. Therefore once more many grateful thanks, though I don't dare to be in the first place responsible for the publication of the trifle! Your account of the conception of your own version interested me very much, also the news that it had been your intention to set the 'Pied Piper'. Will you ever carry out that design? It would be *extremely* interesting to hear you in a humorous mood!![10]

We have not yet heard anything of the full score of your 'Invocation', *though* we put a paragraph about it in the Sept. Musical Times. I will ask Mr. Alfred to let me put an Advertisement in the 'Musical News', 'Musical Standard' & perhaps one or two daily papers. You are too good natured abut your M. S. S! You lent me the score of your String Quintet once, *though* I did *not* 'bother' you to do so. But I returned *that* by registered Post *long ago* ! When shall we see those *Organ* pieces? Now THEY *would* be in demand!! I'm sure of it.

Look out for Elgar's 'King Olaf'. Though unequal & in places open to criticism I think there is some *fine* stuff in this. The young man has imagination, beauty, strength, 'go'. He is exceptionally gifted & will 'take the shine out of' some of the gentlemen at the top of the profession (Excuse the slang!) I believe in him: and, oh! he has **MELODY**!! melody that touches one. He is not yet very *deep*, but he will grow, I feel sure. 'The Light of Life' I do *not* care for, *nor does he*! He spoke of it as a 'written to order' effort. 'Olaf' is very different stuff. Whether he will ever do anything *great*, the future will prove.

But I am wandering! Forgive this lengthy epistle. It is an *impertinence* I Know, but your super-Human Kindness brings this sort of 'punishment' upon itself. Too Bad!!

Ever yours admiringly & obliged,

A.J. Jaeger [11]

The first performance of *King Olaf* took place at Hanley on 30 October that year, just over a month after Jaeger's letter, although there is no evidence that he attended it. There was however a London performance at the Crystal Palace conducted by August Manns in the following spring, which Jaeger made sure to attend. The review that subsequently appeared in the *Musical Times* for May 1897, while not shirking criticism, concentrated on the work's melody, use of leitmotif and orchestration, all very much Jaeger's priorities.

> After the very successful production of Mr. Edward Elgar's cantata 'King Olaf', on the 3rd ult., it appears more certain than ever that this highly-gifted musician is destined to play an important part in shaping the future of English music. Amongst the qualities which go towards making a composer who shall leave his mark on the history of his art, the inestimable gift of melody must ever be placed first and foremost. This Mr. Elgar possesses in quite an unusual degree, as a perusal of the score of 'King Olaf' proves ... Mr. Elgar has also learned – and without any other teachers than the great masters – the valuable secret of presenting his ideas in the most effective manner. In fact, we know very few contemporary cantatas in which harmony, counterpoint, and orchestration are used with such freedom and force towards the one important end of making the music effective in the best sense of the term. Mr. Elgar employs *Leitmotiven* freely and with admirable judgement. He thinks nothing of using three or four together without being in the least hampered by such an *embarras de richesses.* They are frequently pregnant and expressive phrases which readily lend themselves to the process of metamorphosing, without which the use of the *Leitmotive* is apt to become but the veriest 'dodge' ... Throughout the cantata the work given to the orchestra is of the most important description, so much so that in this respect 'King Olaf' has very few equals in British music. Mr. Elgar does not hesitate to avail himself of almost every known orchestral device, and some splendidly sonorous as well as many highly picturesque or sensuously charming passages are the result. He employs a very full orchestra, and revels in the opportunities for writing accompaniments of symphonic importance which it offers. Thus there are movements ... in which the vocal parts are distinctly subordinate to the orchestra ... That the work is open to some criticism cannot be gainsaid. The composer has still something to learn in regard to the declamation of the text, for which purpose he could not do better than study the works of Dr. Hubert Parry or Purcell. Then he does not exercise sufficient self-criticism when he selects from the wealth of the melodic material supplied by his facile imagination, some few phrases, especially for the solo voices, nearly approaching the trite. It may also be questioned whether a little more reticence in the orchestra here and there would not have added to the general effect by giving relief from the continual chatter of the wood-wind, the never-ending 'effective little bits' for this or that instrument, when the ear and brain, surfeited with so much sonority, colour, and charm, almost demand a rest. But these are but trifles compared with the fine qualities to be found in what is in many respects a masterly work, which deserves and will doubtless obtain frequent hearings.[12]

Even at this stage, Jaeger had completely absorbed the music and the style and his judgements were penetrating as well as prophetic; various points of praise or blame could apply to Elgar's choral works at almost any point in his career. Jaeger pinpointed Elgar's occasional weakness in word-setting and his essentially instrumental thinking. But he mentioned his autodidactism in the most flattering way, and gave credit where it was due over Elgar's manipulation of the leitmotif system. The same issue of the *Musical Times* contained another flattering review of an Elgar work, *The Banner of St George*, composed to Novello's commission for Queen Victoria's Golden Jubilee.[13]

Jaeger's pen was further in evidence in a letter concerning a performance of Beethoven's Ninth Symphony at the Queen's Hall conducted by the celebrated German conductor Felix Mottl.[14] Mottl had used certain of Wagner's re-scorings, but without announcing that he was doing so. Jaeger's point was that none of the critics had mentioned the alterations, presumably because they failed to hear them, and his letter seized upon the lapse of his fellow-critics with glee. 'The London critics have surely been caught napping at last !' he began, and concluded,'Personally, I hope that in future all conductors will follow Herr Mottl's courageous example, whether the critics profess to be 'shocked' or not. The strange thing to me is, Why were they not shocked *this* time?' Again, Jaeger must have failed to endear himself to his colleagues, some of whom he viewed with contempt.[15] Grove, the greatest living English authority on Beethoven's symphonies, presented, as he was bound to, the case for 'authentic' performance in the next issue of *Musical Times*.[16] He allowed himself a passing sarcasm in referring to 'Mr. Jaeger's genial letter' and although he was gracious enough to concede that he was 'no doubt right on his own ground', the problem was 'his ground is wrong'. To Grove it was simply axiomatic that 'the words, notes or colours of a poet, composer, or painter ... must be left as he left them when he quitted the world and his control was taken off them'. Beethoven had scored the *Scherzo* of the Ninth as he wanted to, and that was that.

No doubt Jaeger marked the date of that Crystal Palace *Olaf* performance, 3 April 1897, for the further reason that it was the day on which Johannes Brahms died in Vienna.[17] He must have previously seen the work in proof at Novello's, although strictly speaking a work of its nature came within the province of Berthold Tours. Jaeger's enthusiasm for it may have led to a clear difference of opinion between the two, especially as Tours demanded substantial alterations to Elgar's conception of the work. Originally, the cantata's form was that of a continuous narrative drama with orchestral passages linking the choral and solo items. Tours insisted on the excision of these interludes, and of various other passages, to the extent of about 30 pages of short score.[18] The purpose of these alterations would presumably have been to ensure that it conformed to the standard Novello pattern of a work consisting of a series of numbers with the commercial potential for separate sales. Elgar's idea for a work on the Wagnerian model was something that Jaeger would have understood and supported, but the composer seems to have bowed to the inevitable, including Novello's insistence that the publication and first performance of *Olaf* be made dependent on financial guarantees. When the Hanley première was a success, Novello's decided to take Elgar's music away from Tours, who had not long to live, and put it into Jaeger's hands. So the historic partnership was born; it flourished immediately.

Jaeger's ready sympathy for Elgar and his music was evident from the beginning, and after his previous treatment by the firm, the more personal approach would go straight to Elgar's heart. In the months after the Crystal Palace *Olaf*, Elgar composed a *Te Deum and Benedictus* at the request of his friend G.R. Sinclair, the organist of Hereford Cathedral. Novello's accepted the work and the score was completed and posted to them at the beginning of August. The Elgar–Jaeger correspondence began on the third of that month, when Jaeger wrote an appreciative letter of acknowledgement. Alice Elgar noted its contents with pleasure in her diary, and Elgar was touched by its understanding. He immediately penned a grateful reply, concluding with an early statement of a soon to be repeated theme – 'I told you that I wd. never put pen to paper when I had finished this work; but shall I?' Jaeger could not resist the quasi-sardonic, teasing appeal for sympathy and wrote immediately with further encouragement, and commiserations over the firm's payment for the *Te Deum*, an outright purchase of the copyright for fifteen guineas. So unsure was he of his position at Novello's that Jaeger asked for the outspoken letter to be destroyed. In his reply Elgar thanked Jaeger for putting fresh heart into him, and went on, '... my music, such as it is, is alive, you say it has heart – I always say to my wife (over any piece or passage of my work that pleases me): "if you cut that it would bleed!" *You* seem to see that – but who else does?'[19] The entire exchange of four letters took place over as many days and it was enough to establish the pattern of a friendship based on that quality above all that Jaeger sought in music, and found so completely in Elgar's – 'heart'. So impressed was he by the *Te Deum* that Jaeger broke his return journey after visiting the Donkersleys at Huddersfield to hear the work's first performance at the Festival Opening Service on the afternoon of Sunday, 12 September. He failed to see Elgar there as he had hoped, for the composer installed himself out of sight in the organ loft with Sinclair during the performance. Later, Jaeger was too diffident to call on Elgar at his lodgings, although Sinclair's maid provided the address. But once returned to London he wrote a long letter, commenting on the performance and the subsequent newspaper reviews. He knew the leading critics, and noted those who were present in the Cathedral. He lost no opportunity of pressing Elgar's case with one whose outlook he trusted, Herbert Thompson of the Yorkshire Post. 'I spoke to the latter after the Service & gave him a "piece of my mind" in re your work, and he seemed to be largely agreed with me. Don't laugh when I add that I consider him one of the best, most wideawake & *competent* critics in England'.[20] This was praise indeed, for Jaeger went on to explain how he tended to lump many of the critics together with the senior figures at Novello's.

> ... the critics don't lay half enough stress on the *feeling* in the music, the emotional qualities which *alone* make music live. Our Editor & other good folk keep on saying '*Very* clever, *very* clever' &c &c I say: *hang* your cleverness, *that* won't make *any* music great and 'alive'! *Emotional* qualities never seem to concern our Editor.[21]

Jaeger went on to relate how he had volunteered to write in his own time an analysis of the *Te Deum* for the *Musical Times*, but since Littleton had insisted on other festival works being covered as well, he felt he had to drop the idea. Further dissatisfaction with Novello's and their preference for the 'English Church style' emerged when he lauded Samuel Coleridge-Taylor's music and asked Elgar to encourage the young man, while wishing he could afford to publish his latest music, a Morning and Evening Service. It was not the last time that Jaeger would have been willing to support a struggling composer with financial backing; later, in the case of Cyril Scott, he would be able to carry through the intention. A wealthy Jaeger would have been one of the great patrons of music; as it was, he was often prepared to lend out small sums that he could hardly afford. And Jaeger's appeal to Elgar for encouragement to Coleridge-Taylor gradually bore fruit. The month after the *Te Deum* letter, Elgar asked Jaeger if the young composer might have a work for the newly formed Worcestershire Philharmonic Society, whose programmes he planned and whose concerts he conducted. One of Elgar's aims for the Society was to provide a vehicle for new English composers, and although in the event no Coleridge-Taylor performance resulted, Elgar accepted Jaeger's judgement about the composer's abilities – at any rate for the time being – and kept his eye open for future opportunities. The episode was typical of the personal network of contacts and influence that Jaeger was gradually setting up.

Another glimpse of Jaeger's working methods, this time in dealing with the Novello's management, is to found in his first surviving letter to Walford Davies, written early that December. As well as a not entirely flattering portrait of Littleton, it contained careful criticism of an oratorio, presumably *The Temple*, eventually performed at the Worcester Festival of 1902, together with some business routine over the smaller *Hymn Before Action*. In dealing with an ambitious work by an inexperienced and sensitive young composer, Jaeger used a revealing account of his own evolving responses to new music to lead gently into a discussion of weak points and to encourage the composer to understand the business point of view. He was able to mix such frankness with teasing intimacy at the end of the letter.

1, Berners Street, W.
London.

Dec 4th 1897

My dear Davies,

I have not yet caught Mr Littleton in the proper mood to approach him re your fine Oratorio. I have not forgotten it, I need not say: I am only waiting the best opportunity, when Mr L is in a *very* amiable mood. I think you had better send me the Vocal Score so that I may have something to shew him *at once*, supposing I can get him interested in the subject. I shall take the greatest care of it, I need hardly assure you. If you wish to play it him, a time might be arranged afterwards.

My impression of the music has deepened the longer I look back upon it. It is often so with me. The first imperfect hearing may not leave a *very* decided impression behind, but after I have been separated from it by a short space of time, recollections of particularly striking parts & passages come to me & give me an idea of there being much more in the music than appeared at first. And it is not second rate music which thus 'comes back' to me! Your final chorus especially 'lives' now in my recollection as a piece of splendid strength & elevation. I still can't get used to the 'slow' second Bass Solo. It seemed to me too slow in tempo *for too long a time* & I think with fear of the feelings of the average audience lest they should think it dull. I daresay you won' t care a jot about 'average audiences', but *we* I mean N. & Co. shall. I know that the words required a very reverential setting, but is there not too much slow tempo in *this* setting ? So little movement in the orchestra too, if I remember rightly. It did not succeed in fixing my attention throughout as *everything else* did & I should say: Reconsider it, *though* I Know you are the last composer who would *not* have 'reconsidered' such a movement over & over again before putting it on the paper. You see I give my impressions candidly for I would not insult you by offering hypocritical views & expressing sentiments I didn't feel. A further hearing of the air might of course cause me to alter my opinion, though at present *I don't think so*!

Another thing. I am told you have not yet returned the assignment form for your songs yet. Please do so. As regards the 4 part arrangement of the 'Hymn before Acton', I mean 'Action': Novellos will *not* make any charge for the copies specially printed & sent (for you) to the College. They want you to Kindly add a footnote [to] the Assignment to this Effect:

Note: 'The ad libitum accompaniment for men's voices in four parts is intended to be included in this assignment freed from all Royalty or other payment whatsoever. (Signed) H Walford Davies'.

This will obviate the necessity of a separate assignment for this small thing. Please also send me prestissimo possibile the wording for the *note* at part of the *Poem* relative to the 4 part accpt. You never Kept your promise to send this freshly worded note. Notsy Boy! (*Kick* me!!). Miss D. & her 'boy' (!) enjoyed their evening at Mrs Matheson's *Exceedingly*. Kindest regards to all your Kind friends & yourself,

Ever yours,

A.J. Jaeger[22]

The Mathesons were a cultivated Hampstead family who had earlier befriended Davies as a young and sometimes rather gauche student far from home; their hospitality was evidently extended to Jaeger and Isabella. Mrs Matheson, an excellent pianist, guided his development, organized concerts of his music, and nursed him through illness. Walford was invited to lodge with them and became one of the family, sharing their holidays at home and abroad, particularly in Mrs Matheson's native Switzerland. Some years later, he was briefly engaged to one of the Matheson daughters, but in the event he was not to marry until 1924.

Jaeger's advocacy of the music of Richard Strauss had continued during 1897, with mentions in the *Musical Times* of performances of his F Minor Symphony at the Crystal Palace, and *Don Juan* by Richter. In both cases the audience reception had been lukewarm, but a personal appearance by Strauss at the Queen's Hall on 7 December achieved a better response, although Jaeger was aware of the dangers of such an occasion.

'*Veni, vidi, vici!*' Julius Caesar's laconic despatch might have been quoted by Herr Richard Strauss after his first appearance before an English audience at … the Queen's Hall …

> His 'victory' was to all appearances complete, for he was the recipient of enthusiastic applause and many recalls, and the huge and brilliant audience could not have given him a warmer welcome or bid him a heartier farewell and 'Auf Wiedersehen' if he had been an old favourite whose music they had long known and prized as 'a thing of beauty and a joy forever.' We beg leave to doubt whether all those who so generously showered applause upon the young master really derived any genuine pleasure from his music; but that the occasion was a great one for Germany's foremost living composer cannot be gainsaid.[23]

Jaeger continued by explaining to an English readership something of Strauss's controversial reputation, and the nature of his music as an inevitable new force:

> Richard Strauss is only thirty-three, but already he enjoys the distinction in his native country of being at once the most wildly eulogized and the most bitterly abused musician of the day. The man who can set musicians and critics by the ears as Strauss has done and will continue to do is no ordinary mortal; and ... the writer would fain be 'on the side of the angels' and hail him a genius who will probably force his music upon the world, whether the world likes it or not. Richard Strauss is a great power that cannot be any longer ignored, much less annihilated by adverse criticism and heated warfare of words. We may abominate his music ... but we cannot but grow enthusiastic over the grandeur and masterfulness alike of the conception and execution of his tone-poems, and we shall have to endure that which now seems almost unendurable.[24]

Part of Strauss's greatness lay in the way in which he had raised the limits of orchestral technique, building further on the achievements of the great masters, and Jaeger saw him as part of the old German philosophical tradition, although in reviewing the works which he had conducted at the concert – *Tod und Verklärung* and *Till Eulenspiegel* – Jaeger had to confront his dislike of programme music. Of the poem on which *Tod und Verklärung* was based, he thought it was

> Hardly a new subject to 'yearn for musical expression', but one that would appeal strongly to a typically German composer like Strauss, who is a thinker and an idealist, as well as a realist at the same time – an idealist in his choice of subjects as admit, as this one does, of the widest application to human kind generally, instead of an individual only, and a realist in his means of expression, in which he carries his poetic idea to its logical conclusion with a consistency that is often cruel in its disregard of the laws of beauty. We are no lovers of programme music, but since Strauss will give us none other, we accept the position and do our best to make ourselves familiar with his 'stories', without which much of his music might appear incoherent, extravagant, and unlovely, though even then no one could deny the consummate musicianship and brilliant imagination it displays.[25]

Jaeger provided a poetic and dramatic résumé of the music and programme of *Tod und Verklärung*, and went on to enthuse about *Till Eulenspiegel* as 'this strikingly original and most amusing *jeu d'esprit*, the most remarkable orchestral Humoreske ever penned'. Of both works he thought, 'something like genius scintillates in these scores, or we are greatly mistaken', and to sum up, there could be no doubt where Jaeger's sympathies lay. '... Strauss has written the word 'Progress' on his banner. To him there is no standing still, much less going back to the sweet simplicity of pre-Beethovenism. There is no standing still in art but stagnation and degeneration.'[26]

As Christmas approached, Elgar wrote to Jaeger with news of the commission he had been offered for the 1898 Leeds Festival. Jaeger's letter of reply contained advice over the new work, *Caractacus*, in particular a not entirely heeded warning against excessive length. He mentioned too an earlier, privately published, setting by a certain John Read. Parry came in for some merciless treatment, as he sometimes did between the progressives Elgar and Jaeger, probably on account of his approach to orchestration. 'The "Caractacus" of Read's is a great masterpiece such as *I* might write if I tried *hard*! He (R.) is a gentleman on the Stock Exchange, rather ancient (like his music) & what a certain UNsuccessful musician I wot of called Dr *Parry* – viz: "a bl— amateur"!'[27]

Jaeger had been attempting to increase his income by contributing to a new but sadly short-lived weekly, *The Musician*, which had come and gone during 1897. Its approach must have come as a breath of fresh air after that of the *Musical Times*, for it had concerned itself with the wider world of contemporary orchestral music and published signed articles by such writers as Bernard Shaw, Ernest Newman, Rosa Newmarch, Granville Bantock and Ralph Vaughan Williams. There were also translations of articles from the French and German, and Jaeger's contributions, spread over three issues, were translations of letters written by Wagner during his period in London in 1855.[28] But the journal's formula was too ambitious and novel for economic viability. 'D— "the Musician". They owe me £5! Too bad! Lack of appreciation is the cause of its death … It is a great pity, for it was with all its fault [*sic*] … the only readable musical paper in England. *I* consider the "M. Times" *deadly* dull!'[29]

Christmas that year was a difficult one for Jaeger and Isabella, to whom he was now engaged; an illness of her mother's suddenly became worse, and she died on Christmas Day, as had Isabella's father some eight years previously. But on the last day of the year Jaeger was able to 'ring in the new' with a remarkable and eloquent letter to Elgar which mixed encouragement, exhortation, reprimand and inspiration together with a canny appeal to Elgar's patriotism.

> … let me wish you on this last evening of the old year, a very happy & artistically successful New Year. May you be free from ill health – I agree with Emerson that 'the first wealth is Health' [–] & always in the right mood to compose your best. Let no outside influences affect you adversely too much; steer clear of the 'Howling pelican' days, confound the d— critics & all those that dare to pretend they see spots on the suns of your best works … England expects every man to do his duty & no musician in your great & glorious country has a greater duty to fulfil than you. So don't dare to talk about your new work being squashed. Nonsense! A day's attack of the Blues, due to a touch of indigestion or a blast of eastwind will not drive away your desire, your necessity[,] which is to exercise those creative faculties which a kind providence has given you. Your time of universal recognition will come.[30]

Happy the composer who could receive such a letter from his publisher.

3 1898: The Russian Campaign

At the end of January 1898 Jaeger wrote to Elgar enthusing over choral works by the American composer Horatio Parker. Parker had studied composition in Munich during the 1880s, subsequently returning to the States to work as teacher, organist and choirmaster. His reputation as a composer was established with a series of major choral works, including the oratorios *Hora Novissima*, first performed by the Church Choral Society of New York in April 1893 (and reviewed by the *Musical Times*) and *The Legend of St Christopher* of 1897. A four-column analysis of *Hora Novissima* appeared in the October 1893 *Musical Times*. With an eye to sales of the vocal score, the article concluded with a warm recommendation of the work to choral societies in search of a novelty, but the technique of the music was subjected to rigorous criticism, with references to Dvořák, Brahms and Wagner, and gives every appearance of being one of the earliest major contributions to the journal by Jaeger himself.[1] Parker's works would include incidental music, operas and an organ concerto, and he achieved a high reputation as a craftsman working broadly in terms of his European training. American composers were soon to seek a distinctive voice of their own – one of Parker's pupils was Charles Ives – but Parker's traditional stylistic roots were no doubt something of a recommendation to Jaeger. His music was published by Novello's through their American office, and various works achieved festival performances in this country; Ivor Atkins in particular was a staunch advocate and friend, and Parker's reputation became such that he was awarded an honorary Cambridge degree in 1902. Elgar's response to Jaeger's advocacy of the composer was to emphasize how busy he was with *Caractacus*, but he praised *Hora Novissima* at the expense of the older generation of English composers.[2]

It was one of Parry's works, first produced at the 1897 Hereford Three Choirs Festival, that opened up another gap between Jaeger and the editor of the *Musical Times*. Jaeger wrote bitterly to Elgar at the end of February that he had been told to alter a critical review of Parry's *Magnificat;* 'Such is musical criticism!!! Disgusting! One has to write one's views "to order" when they concern a man who is a "somebody".' Jaeger's respect for Parry the man was high, and he continued, 'Parry of all men in England is the one who would *not* take offence at one's opinion if sincerely stated …'. Such censorship cut Jaeger deep and was an important factor in his periodic frustration with his employers.

In his review Jaeger had taken deliberate opportunity to compare Parry's music with the 'incoherent, noisy and nerve-destroying' programme music included in the concert, and he went on to give vent to strong feelings about the offending item, Mussorgsky's *Night on a Bare Mountain.*

> The programme contained a Russian novelty, a Fantaisie, 'Une nuit sur le Mont Chauve', by Moussorgsky (1839–1881). It is a posthumous work, completed and scored by Rimsky-Korsakow, and as hideous a thing as we have ever heard. The 'story' is of that gruesome, childish description so fascinating to Slavonic composers. There are 'sounds of mysterious voices underground, spirits of darkness, the black god Tchernoborg, evil crews, revels' and, as an artistic climax, a 'church bell'! The music cannot be described. It is very clever, certainly, especially Rimsky-Korsakow's orchestration; but, excepting the *Coda*, 'Break of day', an orgie of ugliness and an abomination. May we never hear it again.[3]

Earlier in the review, Jaeger had dealt hardly more kindly with Borodin's B minor Symphony, and went on to point up the way that the time given to Russian music was squeezing out works by English composers.

> At the concert of January 22 a programme containing Mr. Cowen's "Scandinavian" Symphony attracted but a scanty audience, although those who were present testified their thorough enjoyment of this excellent piece of English music by most hearty applause. At the following concert, on January 29, when Borodine's Symphony in B minor was the *pièce de résistance*, an audience but very little larger seemed terribly bored by one of the most Russian of Russian compositions. In fact, we have never, in all our long experience, heard any symphonic work received so coldly. This state of affairs was hardly satisfactory, and Mr. Newman forthwith decided to mend matters by withdrawing the only other English symphony announced in the prospectus – viz., Mr. Cliffe's No. 1, in C minor. This seems to us a somewhat illogical proceeding after the Borodine fiasco. Certainly it is a distinct slight upon English composers. We have no desire to hear Borodine's masterpiece again. Twice we have suffered it, and failed to see a trace of greatness in music that not once takes us anywhere near 'the edge of the Infinite', as Carlyle would say, or even faintly suggests an inspiration. Colour, glaring and massive, strong rhythms, much energy, and last, but not least, those precious Oriental scales beloved of Mr. E.F. Jacques[4] it gives us, and therefore it may appeal to a few students of nationalism in music. To an average English audience it is, and is likely to remain, caviare. And meanwhile, English symphonies, – the finest efforts of Parry, Stanford, Cowen, German, Cliffe, as well as those of our coming men, Barclay Jones, Walford Davies, Coleridge-Taylor, &c. – rest securely in their composers' portfolios.[5]

That performance of Mussorgsky's *Night on a Bare Mountain* in Rimsky-Korsakov's orchestration, its first in England, had been conducted by the young Henry Wood. It was one of many works by Russian composers that the Queen's Hall impresario Newman, together with his star conductor, had made a policy of introducing and promoting for their success in creating a box-office 'draw'. The Hall, opened in 1893, was built to satisfy a long-felt need for an adequate orchestral concert venue in central London, but it was being run on tight financial margins and takings fluctuated; Newman was no doubt mindful of his earlier failed venture at Covent Garden. Wood himself had a strong personal affinity with Russian music, and as an amateur painter was fully seized of the attraction of 'colour'. In his *My Life of Music* he quoted Ruskin:

'The most thoughtful minds are those which love colour the most', and wrote, 'I flatter myself we gave all these works with some *colour.* I have not been a painter all my life without realizing the value of colour. What, after all, is music but a picture?' It was an approach entirely alien to Jaeger.

During this period Wood produced some forty-two works by eleven Russian composers, which included twenty works by Tchaikovsky alone.[6] His interest in Russian music was to be strengthened in July when he married Olga Mikhailov, a singer of Russian birth whose antecedents were somewhat embroidered when he announced her as 'Princess Olga'. But the colourful and dramatic nature of much of this music provided an appropriate vehicle for a conductor in the process of establishing his name and reputation.

> Wood was always a striking figure and a great draw. He had an unruly mane of black hair, which frequently fell over his forehead and was pushed back with a characteristic gesture of the left hand. His conducting mannerisms were more pronounced – the baton raised high above the head for the brass; his emphatic double nod to the strings in unison passages; his sensitive withdrawal, as if he had been stabbed, when a pianissimo was not pianissimo enough … There is no doubt that his dramatization of the music in this way excited people and made them come again …[7]

So colourful was Wood's approach and appearance that, after he had conducted a command performance at Windsor Castle later that year, he almost failed to pass muster with Queen Victoria. He described the incident in *My Life of Music.* She looked at me rather closely for a moment. "Tell me, Mr. Wood," she said … "are you *quite* English? Your appearance is – er – rather *un-English!*"[8] There would be times when Jaeger would find Wood's style more than he could bear; having attended Wood's Mussorgsky performance together with Isabella, and wrote to Elgar,

> You ought to have heard Moussorgsky's thing! It made me use *wicked* language & my sweetheart laughed. Whether at M's drunken music or my language I don't know. Parry came to me afterwards & said 'Devilish clever'. Well, the cleverness is in Rimsky Korsakoff's scoring which is worthy of that 'clever' fellow. Confound these *Tartars.* I can stand a civilized Russian like now Tchaikovsky & Glazounoff (in his civilized mood) & enjoy their music enormously, but those Heathens a la Moussorgsky are insufferable.[9]

Jaeger could accept only the more Westernized Russian composers. In a short note Elgar promised a proper reply 'sometime soon', but was preoccupied with the Leeds commission and his mind was not easy about it; 'Caractacus frightens me in places', he wrote. There was some homely psychology and understanding reassurance from Jaeger, who replied, 'That Caractacus 'frightens' you is a *good* sign; for directly you become familiar with the 'visions' that now 'frighten' you, they will inspire you & become your friends!' But he could not resist returning to the attack on the musical establishment, and Henry Wood's penchant for Russian music, which Jaeger thought was squeezing out English music at the Queen's Hall.

> Parry's Variations are very good I think, but as usual badly scored. I heard them again last Saturday under Wood. The latter has 'put his foot in it' with Russian music this season. He has played some dreadfully ugly & stupid stuff. Of course it is all well scored,

> but the subject matter & the 'Faktur' cannot interest us Western fellows at all. Those 'old' Russians, Moussorgsky, Balakirew, Glinka, Borodine &c &c are *awful* Bores. I suppose there will be a chance for English composers *some* day at Queen's Hall.[10]

A short, undated letter to Walford Davies may appropriately find a place here, as it continues the theme and shows Jaeger admitting to a veritable personal vendetta against Wood's espousal of Russian music. He seemed proud of his isolation from other critics.

> 16 Margravine Gardens,
> W. Kensington.
>
> My dear Davies,
>
> Thanks for your Kind letter. I will do what I can for Lott. Glad to hear you are happy (you *ought* to be) & fit for work & mean to do something good. We want *serious* work badly, for what we have had to endure of late in the way of 'novelties' is past endurance. Music seems to be going to Hades fast or Wood will do his best to take it there. I have spoken strongly about his Russian craze & done my best to skotch & Kill it. I fancy I alone almost in the press have insisted on the worthlessness of the majority of the Stuff he has played. As if *colour* were of any great account!
>
> Ever yours
>
> A.J. Jaeger[11]

During the last months Jaeger's unmistakable voice had frequently been heard fighting his audacious campaign in the columns of the *Musical Times,* but there was one Russian work in a more European idiom whose emotional power had earlier captured his imagination and support, the *Symphonie Pathétique.*

> ... what in England is considered the greatest achievement of the Russian school so far – viz., the stupendous first movement of Tchaikowsky's 'Pathetic' Symphony, is also the least essentially Russian of that master's pieces. It is great *not* because it is Russian, nor merely because it displays phenomenal strength, superb workmanship, gorgeous colour, &c., though these qualities go for much, but because it is heart-music in which a master speaks to us in accents of suffering and despair, hope and resignation, which go straight to the heart and move us to tears in spite of ourselves. This *is* beautiful, great music, and of such the Russians have given us all too little. They have, in fact, revealed to us next to nothing of the *heart* of their great people. When they begin to do so, they will produce beautiful music which will appeal with equal force to all music-lovers irrespective of nationality, for the human heart is the same all the world over. At present we are too frequently reminded of Bismarck's 'Scratch a Russian and find a Tartar' when listening to the wild effusions which some Russian composers inflict on us.[12]

Other works by Tchaikovsky were not held in such regard by Jaeger, who in various other reviews pronounced *The Storm* 'somewhat oppressive' and the First Piano Concerto 'bombastic' and 'uninteresting and barren in those 'working out' portions in which the great German masters' mastery always shone resplendent'. The Overture *1812* completely failed to find favour with him, although there was qualified praise for the Third Suite. But at the end of the day Jaeger felt that the emphasis on foreign works of all kinds was unfair to home-grown composers, and of

Newman's Queen's Hall Saturday Afternoon Concerts, conducted by Wood, he concluded,

> There is much to commend in the selections of the above concerts, but the entire absence of works by British composers is to be deprecated. There is something anomolous in an English orchestra, conducted by an Englishman, entirely eschewing the compositions of their countrymen. Mr Newman is an astute man, but in this procedure he is manifestly making a mistake or being led astray by bad advisors. There are many fine works by living Englishmen that only need to be made known to prove attractive. Taste grows by what it is fed on ...[13]

That was precisely the philosophy that underpinned Newman and Wood's historic Promenade Concerts at the Queen's Hall, which in 1898 were seeing their fourth season. And amongst the regular Wagner Nights, Tchaikovsky Nights and Beethoven Nights which were the pattern of Promenade programmes in those days, they would include that year an innovatory British Composers' Night, with music by McCunn, Coward, Mackenzie, Pitt, German, Stanford, Elgar and Sullivan. Wood's career as a champion of English music was launched, and Jaeger could take some of the credit.

At the beginning of 1898, with Jaeger's exhortations fresh in his mind, Elgar settled down to complete *Caractacus*, due for its first performance that autumn. Novello's provided another kind of encouragement by agreeing to pay £100 for the copyright, and the work was announced in the February *Musical Times* with the assurance that it 'will furnish Mr. Elgar with a splendid opportunity to still further demonstrate his remarkable dramatic powers, and we may rest assured that he will fully realise all the expectations that have been formed of him as one of our foremost native composers'.

By early April Elgar had made sufficient progress with *Caractacus* to be able to send a first parcel of vocal score to Novello's. But too much work remained to be done for him to be able to entertain a request for a short orchestral work for the Gloucester Three Choirs that autumn. Jaeger's earlier advocacy of Coleridge-Taylor now bore fruit and Elgar suggested that an approach to the younger man should be made. '... I should *dearly* like to see a clever man get on and – upset the little coterie of "3-Choir hacks",' he told Jaeger. It was the Gloucester organist Herbert Brewer's first Festival, and he was determined to persuade a committee bent on economizing, of the importance of introducing new works. Jaeger wondered whether the Gloucester Committee ought to be sent some of Taylor's compositions, and meanwhile found occasion for a brisk 'cheer up' letter to the introspective Walford Davies, who seemed low in spirits despite his recent appointment as Organist of the Temple Church, a post he would fill with distinction until 1923. Once more Jaeger offered some homespun psychology, his interest in his protégés extending beyond matters of musical technique.

1, Berners Street, W.
London.

May 11th, 1898.

My dear Davies,

M.S.S. received. I will try to get them 'settled' soon.

Whatever *is* the matter with you? Liver or love? (notice the capital L to Liver & the small l to love – quite an accident!) You seem depressed. Is it bad Health! Perhaps the reaction after the excitement over your splendid appointment? Cheer up;! the Sun is shining & warmer days are coming. 'Nun muss sich Alles, Alles wenden', for Spring is here. You want a tonic or a change, *or* – fall desperately & *successfully* in love & heigh presto! You'll feel as sound & jolly as can be & your oratorio will rise from the dust of your shelf & be sent to Novello for 'consideration'; & you will think there *never will* be an End to Sunshine & Happiness! Cheer up & compose something good & make other people happy as a first step to feeling happy yourself!

If you are ill, see a Doctor *at once*. Are you going to the Philharmonic Concert tomorrow? Do!

Ever yours,

A.J. Jaeger[14]

(Haste!)

The next day Jaeger wrote to Brewer to add his voice to Elgar's over the Festival commission for Coleridge-Taylor, adding some thoughts on the English festival system in passing.

London

May 12, 1898

Dear Mr Brewer,

My friend Mr Elgar told me a week ago that he has refused an offer to write an orchestral work for your Festival. I am glad to hear it for *his* sake for he has his hands full with *Caractacus* and the haste with which most of you good men have to compose their Festival works is on the whole the great bane of English music. Everybody seems to write under fearful pressure (especially Parry) and the consequences we all know, alas! Well, it is not my business, but I am awfully sorry it is so.

My object in writing is to draw your attention to a young friend of mine, S. Coleridge-Taylor, who is most wonderfully gifted and might write your Committee a *fine* work in a short time. He has a quite Schubertian facility of invention and his stuff is always original and fresh. He is the coming man, I'm quite sure! He is only 22 or 23 but there is nothing immature or inartistic about his music. It is worth a great deal to me – I mean I value it very highly, because it is so original and often *beautiful*. Here is a real melodist at last.

Why not try him and make the '98 Festival memorable by the introduction of young S. C-T. He scores very well, in fact he conceives everything orchestrally and never touches the P.F. when composing! I suppose you know that his father is a negro. Hence his wonderful *freshness*.

Why not give him a commission? He would rise to the occasion and do something good.

His symphony in A major is a most original work. We are doing a short Cantata of his, *Hiawatha's Wedding Feast*, delightful stuff! Won't that do for your Festival? You want a secular work, don't you? I'll send you the M.S. score (P.F.) if you like (though at present in the printer's hands).

At any rate you keep your eye on the lad, and believe me, he is *the* man of the future in musical England.

Yours Faithfully,

A.J. Jaeger[15]

Although the Gloucester Committee seems to have swung temporarily in the direction of Edward German, the commission was definitely offered to Taylor at the end of May. It proved to be the first of a series of Three Choirs commissions over the next five years, including some four orchestral works and culminating in a sacred cantata, *The Atonement*. The combined efforts of Jaeger and Elgar had paid off, and provided Coleridge-Taylor, one of the youngest composers to have had a Three Choirs Commission, with a unique opportunity. His Festival work was the orchestral *Ballade in A Minor* Opus 33, dedicated to Jaeger. Alongside this, he had been composing the choral work that would make his name a household word and vindicate Jaeger's enthusiasm, the cantata *Hiawatha's Wedding Feast*. It was to receive its première at the Royal College of Music in November, and it proved to be a work which rekindled Jaeger's committment to Novello's, for sometimes the firm's attitudes had discouraged his impatient ardour for progress. In an appreciation of Jaeger's life written for his Memorial Concert in 1910, the critic Alfred Kalisch would write,

> ... I well remember one of the first times I had an intimate conversation with him, when he told me that he seriously contemplated a return to map-making, because he did not see that there was hope for any progress, as he conceived it, in British music. At about this time, I once had an appointment to meet him at lunch. He arrived, contrary to his usual regular habits, nearly an hour late, in a state of such excitement and dishevelment that his other friends and myself, who were waiting for him, immediately thought he had had more than a merely verbal argument with one of the official representatives of the older school of music. But he explained to us that his delay was due to his having been busied with the proof-sheets of a new work which had made him forgetful of all prosaic things. The work was Coleridge-Taylor's 'Hiawatha's Wedding Feast'.[16]

Coleridge-Taylor had been closely in touch with Jaeger during the composition of the music. 'I derived great help and much encouragement from my friend Mr. A. J. Jaeger, whose criticisms and suggestions were of the greatest value to me,' said the composer in a later *Musical Times* interview.[17] Jaeger's influence may perhaps be felt in the use of a motivic, symphonic structure which made the work something quite new in English choral music. Jaeger's Yorkshire nephew, the artist and writer Brian Tunstall, thought also that the composer had made considerable cuts at Jaeger's insistence,[18] The work contained too, possibly on Jaeger's advice, something that would recommend it to the publisher, a detachable 'hit' song for tenor, 'Onaway, Awake, beloved'.[19] Unfortunately Coleridge-Taylor initially failed to impress August and Isabella with the celebrated solo due to his limitations as a performer, as Isabella remembered for the composer's first biographer.

> ... Jaeger held ... at this time Coleridge-Taylor was anything but an efficient accompanist. During the composing of *Hiawatha's Wedding Feast* he brought 'Onaway, Awake' for his hearing, with this remark: 'This is the most beautiful melody I have ever written', and sat down at the piano and played and sang it. The result was to leave the Jaegers in complete mystification. His voice was a very different instrument from the pure, clear treble of the solo boy in Colonel Walter's choir; it was a thin, reedy baritone, with many falsetto notes, and the accompaniment seemed beyond his powers. It was only when Mr. and Mrs. Jaeger came to examine the score quietly after he had gone that they recognized how justly he had appraised the melody.[20]

Jaeger, dealing with the printing of Elgar's work as well as Coleridge-Taylor's, had remonstrated over the text of the latter part of *Caractacus* as shown in the proofs he was seeing. The librettist was a retired Indian civil servant who had created a final scene predicting the supremacy of Britain over all other nations, some of which were described as menial and jealous. Jaeger evidently felt that this may have been taken to reflect poorly on Germany, or perhaps he reacted against the essential chauvinism of the whole idea; Elgar agreed to ask for alterations while making something of a joke of it to Jaeger. Some weeks later he added, 'I knew you would laugh at my librettist's patriotism (& mine)'. Jaeger's mistrust of nationalism informed his musical responses, and he would occasionally worry about the warmth of the reception given to Elgar's music by home audiences. But Jaeger himself, always consistent if not somewhat predictable, continued to be guilty of a degree of musical chauvinism; in the June *Musical Times*, another Russian composer, this time Rimsky-Korsakov, came in for an outspoken attack. Hans Richter had programmed *Scheherezade* with Brahms's First Symphony at St James's Hall, a combination providing much grist to Jaeger's mill.

> Nothing could have excelled the playing of the orchestra in the extremely difficult, 'tricky' Symphonic Suite 'Scheherezade' by Rimsky-Korsakoff (Op. 35), which was given for the first time at these concerts, and proved another addition to the lengthy list of Russian works that seem all masterly technique, bewildering arabesques, put together, or rather side by side, in the most whimsical fashion; strange, wayward rhythms, and brilliant, glaring colour, produced by the most daring orchestral devices, frequently new and beautiful, ever and anon bizarre and childish, but always calculated with uncanny certainty ... Do Slavonic music-lovers admire this kind of music, we wonder, and must we Anglo-Saxons, Celts, and Teutons first become Slavs before we can appreciate these strange effusions at their full and proper value? We suppose our Russian friends do derive some satisfaction from them, something more, we mean, than a mere tickling of the senses. To us, we confess it with sorrow and all due humility, they seem like 'linked boredom long drawn out', to vary a famous quotation. Brahms's C Minor Symphony supplied the longed-for contrast to Rimsky-Korsakoff's piece, and never has the great master's magnificent epic seemed greater or moved us more deeply that on this occasion. Its glories seemed to 'bring all Heav'n before our eyes', as its ravishing beauties and touching accents brought tears into them.[21]

Elgar finished the vocal score of *Caractacus* early in June, and the Leeds Festival Secretary began to push Jaeger for the unrehearsed portions of the music before the choir's summer break. With time now drawing short and much to be done before the October première, Elgar pressed on with the orchestration while dealing with the corrections to the vocal score. It became a complicated and worrying business, and Jaeger would have had other equal priorities on his hands. As well as the Leeds Festival items, there were new works for that year's Three Choirs, including Parry's *A Song of Darkness and Light*, and the printing of *Hiawatha* to oversee for its première. It may not have been coincidence, therefore, that in this stressful period Jaeger's ill-health is mentioned in the correspondence with Elgar for the first time. Tuberculosis was not to be positively diagnosed for some years, and in these early stages Jaeger complained only of undefined problems with his nose. Sometime during July 1898 he underwent electric cautery of the nasal passages, to seal blood vessels and prevent nosebleeds,[22] something of an ordeal. 'I don't understand about "hot wires & noses" – I *trust* nothing serious or very disagreeable', wrote Elgar, and followed this up a few days later with 'I hope you are well & quite recovered from your very disagreeable business?'

Walford Davies also wrote to express his concern over Jaeger's condition, and enclosed a list of his chamber works – including three piano quartets and a piano trio, two string quartets and two violin sonatas – hoping that Jaeger would recommend their publication to Novello's. Jaeger, always able to tell hard truths with kindness and sensitivity, replied in a lengthy, patient letter containing much realistic advice, for the firm had found that chamber music did not sell in the English market. He made, too, some further suggestions as to how best to deal with Augustus Littleton.

16, Margravine Gardens,
West Kensington,
W.

17/7/98

Private *and Confidential.*

My dear Davies,

Many thanks for your very Kind letter. Yes, I lost a *lot* of blood; I didn't Know I had so much in my veins – and I feel still a little weak. I haven't done yet either; the other side wants cutting, but that mustn't be yet. I couldn't stand another 'massacre' *now.*

Now as regards your composition. That list appalls me! An English Composer shouldn't write so much high class music except for consumption abroad and for foreign publishers. I Know of no English publisher who would care to publish such a quantity of Chamber music of one composer *however gifted*! Novellos tried Stanford & Parry and lost a small fortune over their things and since then the very names Sonata & PF (or String) Quartet frightens them. Augeners are starting a Series of Chamber works & might include some of your fine things in that. Boosey's have lately published a P. F. Violin & Clarinet Trio by Walther which looks promising. In fact I look to *any body* but Novellos for the publication of high class music other than Choral works. As I said, they have lost their thousands & 'Burnt children shun the fire'. Really I think you ought to try a *German* publisher as *Ashton* has *successfully* done. Your works are such as would appeal to German musicians & audiences & I daresay Simrock or B & H. might be tempted. Even if you produced the works at your own expense you could get them done abroad for less than ½ of Novello's price.

I am depressed to have to write in this forlorn strain; but you Know I have as high ideals in music as any commonplace fellow *can* have and I have long since given up all hope of seeing Novellos do anything for *art's* sake (except publish the works of Your old fogey Purcell!) I *can't* & *don't* blame them, for music publishing is a *business* and not a luxury & they have lost too many thousands over Messrs X & Y & Z (*You* Know!) to tempt fortune again with publishing for art's sake. It is a disgraceful state of affairs but until the *public* begins to 'see something' in English high class music like yours, I see no chance of things mending. You Know my opinion of such of your works as I Know, but if I were adviser at Novellos I should say: Very fine & eminently *deserving* to be published & performed over & over again, but in the present state of public indifference to English Chamber music not likely to prove remunerative. Now there is one thing you might try: Get an interview with Mr Littleton & get him interested in Your plans. (*Confidential)* He is *very* well disposed toward you & might do something in spite of my pessimistic forecast. Your position at the Temple gives you an importance that might have *very considerable* weight with Mr L.

(A Hint!) When writing to him you might refer to his Kindness previously shown in inserting a notice [( ] with portrait) in the M. T. and *thank him* for same. He is very much taken by such recognition of what no doubt he considered a 'good turn' done to a gifted young fellow like you. Such a word of thanks costs nothing & it's often worth much to the giver. Mr L is really a good man who would *like* to do much for *ENGLISH* Art if it didn't mean losing *so much* money.

He might do your Oratorio at any rate & try one Vn. Sonata or one Quartet to begin with, but I cannot of course promise anything. Come & see me one day & I' ll talk this matter over. My spoken word might not sound so cruel as these written cold water sprays look on the long suffering paper. I wish I could make you believe that your fine efforts are the things publishers yearn for instead of seeming feelingless by trying to prove how difficult it will be to find a publisher for them, or *some* of them. What you want is a Louis of Bavaria or a Liszt to help you bring out your works[.] Why can't some rich Englishman put down a few hundred to pay for the production of your things.

I say, have you found that copy of 'Hiawatha's Wedding Feast' which you lost? Taylor told me that as a joke but it is a *really serious matter*, for it might mean our losing the copyright of the work in *America*! If you have not found it I must take immediate steps to get copies printed & sent to the Library of Congress at Washington. *Do tell me at once*, please. Some fellow might also go & crib Taylor's ideas & publish them as his own before we come out with the work. We didn't intend publishing it for some time, perhaps not till next year, but now we *must* [.]

Yes, I received Mrs Mathesons Kind invitation but I purposely delayed replying because I wanted first to see how this operation would affect me *and* also whether I shall this month again have to be Sub Editor of the M. T.; the real 'Sub' is ill and if I have to do his work again I may be prevented! I shall not Know this till the middle of this week. Will you meanwhile Kindly tell Mrs Matheson this? If I *can* come I shall be delighted to avail myself of her Kind invitation.

With Kindest regards & all good wishes,

Ever yours.

A.J. Jaeger.[23]

Elgar's work on *Caractacus* continued through the rest of July and August. It was his most ambitious work so far, and he began to take what steps he could to secure a favourable reception for it. The Cantata was announced as 'ready shortly' in the

August *Musical Times*, as was Coleridge-Taylor's *Ballade*, and Elgar secured the Queen's permission to dedicate the work to her. He wrote to ask Jaeger if he could write a review of its première for the *Musical Times* – 'don't say I suggested it' – as the celebrated *Daily Telegraph* critic, Bennett, was not going to be able to attend.

Elgar's estimation of Coleridge-Taylor remained high at this time. Writing to Jaeger after a successful *Caractacus* rehearsal in Leeds at the end of August, he somewhat cynically commented on articles in the September *Musical Times* on Brewer and Taylor, 'Brewer is very lucky – or rich – to get into the M. T. before he's done ANYTHING – Samuel Coleridge-Taylor deserves it & I rejoice thereat. (I really must pick up some shares)'. He met Taylor at the London rehearsals for the Three Choirs at the Queen's Hall, and complimented him after hearing the *Ballade* for the first time. But some of the other works drew out his 'Three Choirs' prejudices and he evidently unburdened himself to Jaeger in no uncertain terms. He subsequently wrote to apologize, the first letter to Jaeger in which Elgar dispensed with the formal 'Mr' at the beginning, with the punning comment, 'The M*i*ster-y is soluted', and it might seem that the conversations during the London rehearsals had taken their friendship to a new depth of intimacy. Moore considers that this would have been the occasion when, in response to Elgar's complaints and evident lack of confidence in his future as a composer, 'Jaeger responded with warm encouragement through a long evening during which he compared Elgar's uncertanties with those of Beethoven at a similar point in his career'.[24] Elgar subsequently told Dora Penny that 'He went at it … hammer and tongs, and … preached me a regular sermon and sang Beethoven at me! … he said that Beethoven had a lot of worries, and did *he* give it all up? No. He wrote more, and still more beautiful music – "And-that-is-what-*you*-must-do"'.[25] And on Elgar's return to Malvern Jaeger followed up the attack with a letter: 'He wrote me such a screed, reams and reams of it, all about my ingratitude for my great gifts, as he called them, and he abused me for my wickedness – and I don't know what else.'[26]

Clearly Jaeger had intervened in what he thought a major crisis. He had taken Elgar's threats to give up composing very seriously, and no doubt they had been forcibly and bitterly expressed. Dora Penny tended to be dismissive of Elgar's feelings and of Jaeger's reaction. She had heard similar suggestions, but couched in more flippant terms for her benefit: 'I had had a letter from E. E. myself in which he said he was sick and tired of mouldy music and was going to take to kite-flying! Of course I knew he didn't mean it and that everything would be all right again soon, but one could quite imagine that a foreigner might not understand.'[27] Possibly at this stage Jaeger might not have had time to know Elgar's capacity for extremes of mood but there was a moral earnestness in his approach to music as an art, which led him to make judgements about the 'wickedness' of Elgar's 'ingratitude' for his gifts, and there was enough of the Victorian in Elgar to respond. Jaeger was becoming more and more ready to take responsibility for the insecure Elgar's state of mind, and was creating a rôle second only to that of Alice herself. At times indeed by virtue of his superior musical knowledge Jaeger would be able to take the lead, and Alice would work through him to influence her husband. Jaeger was coming to realize Elgar's needs for reassurance and encouragement, and how his own intuitive, empathetic nature could satisfy those needs and help realize his vision of a great new English composer. Further, Elgar's gradual emergence would vindicate Jaeger's self-appointed rôle as champion of the new at Novello's, and although his dissatisfaction with the firm continued, there were to be no further documented threats of a return to map-making. But Elgar tended to play down the importance of Jaeger's intervention. 'I am certain that he thought he had saved a critical situation …', said Elgar to Dora Penny, concerning the Beethoven conversation, somewhat ambiguously; but it was of course music by that composer that provided the intimate reference towards his portrait of Jaeger in the Enigma Variations.[28]

Jaeger's screed, 'reams and reams of it', seems not to have been preserved, but Elgar wrote on his return to Malvern, 'Very many thanks for your letter which soothed me immensely', and continued in self-exoneration, 'a 3-choir festival always upsets me – the twaddle of it & mutual admiration'. If Elgar at this time felt himself to be something of an outsider, it was another link with Jaeger, who had been long enough with Novello's to thoroughly understand the firm's limitations and to have had various divergences of judgement with those in charge. He must have had few illusions on the question of his position in the firm and his future prospects within it. Head of the publishing department seemed as far as he might rise at Novello's, for the directorships were firmly in the hands of the Littletons and their relations, and he could not afford to buy his way on to the Board as Henry Clayton had done. As far as his earnings were concerned, Jaeger was awarded a pay rise during 1898 of a pound, bringing his salary to five pounds weekly.[29] This was as much as five times the average working man's wage at the time, about the same amount as a general practitioner might earn and considerably more than a teacher.[30] The increase in salary, a hefty one in proportion, was a handsome recognition of Jaeger's contribution to the firm after eight years, but there were to be no further increases for the remaining nine years of his employment. In those virtually inflation-free days a salary of five pounds per week[31] over such a period would have been a comfortable enough income, and presumably there were further payments for his *Musical Times* reviews, but Jaeger was supporting others at this time, and would soon have family responsibilities of his own. His dissatisfaction with the Novello directors may perhaps have turned to resentment when fuelled by awareness of their wealth. The firm had become a limited company in April 1898, and the five directors had been issued with a total of 13,500 ordinary £10 shares, also buying in preference shares to the value of £90,000. The amounts were staggering for those times.

Amid the pressure of further proof-reading and correcting of the *Caractacus* score and parts against rehearsal deadlines, Jaeger, significantly perhaps, complained again of poor health. There was a suggestion that Elgar would go to London himself to help but in the event he remained in Malvern, fretting. 'I am past swearing & am sitting in my shirt with my feet in a bucket of water (it's hot) drivelling …', he wrote. Orchestral rehearsals were held at St James's Hall at the end of September. Elgar was uneasy and stopped the orchestra frequently, but generally the rehearsals went well and on the final day Alice Elgar confided to her diary, 'Finished the rehearsal of Caractacus. Very brilliant & splendid. Much excitement and applause'. There was an opportunity for Jaeger to introduce the Elgars to his fiancée, and just before going to Leeds Elgar wrote, 'I am going to congratulate you on your charming Miss D. & my wife is also charmed with her – you are a lucky fellow & she – well I think she is worthy of one of the best fellows that ever lived'. Perhaps also there was an opportunity for Jaeger to tell Elgar proudly about an article he had written, 'A Wagner Novelty', for that month's *Musical Times*, published over his initials.[32] In it he discussed cuts that Wagner had made in the Prelude to the third act of *Tannhäuser*, and described the differences between the two versions, concluding with a direct appeal for a performance: 'Will not Mr. Henry J. Wood endeavour to trace the full score and orchestral parts and complete arrangements for a speedy production of the "Prelude to Act III., 'Tannhauser' (Tannhauser's Pilgrimage), *First Version*"?' Wood took the hint, and there was in fact a Queen's Hall performance early in 1900; in mentioning it to Elgar, Jaeger described it as 'the Wagner *novelty* which *I* have unearthed'. The hackneyed nature of the frequently repeated standard Wagner orchestral excerpts was another of Jaeger's themes in his writings for the *Musical Times.*

The *Caractacus* première went off well enough, but Elgar was thought by one friend to leave Leeds at the end of the Festival week 'with the air of one who has fought, and is inclined to think he has lost, a heavy engagement'.[33] He had been invited to contribute a work to the 1900 Birmingham Festival, and on his return to Malvern was disappointed to find a letter from Novello's advising him to write something short and easy, ignoring his artistic ideals. Once again there was a bitter complaint to Jaeger, promising 'no more music for me', although, bearing in mind Jaeger's likely reaction, he qualified this with 'at present'.

Once more Jaeger responded imaginatively. Possibly he had sensed that after the composition and first performance of a major work, Elgar would be depressed and in need of a new project to work on; it would prove to be something of a pattern in the future. Jaeger suggested an orchestral work, one which would give Elgar scope for his artistic ideals, a symphony based on the life of General Gordon, and sent a draft programme synopsis.[34] The proposal reflected too his understanding of Elgar's need at this period to focus his music round a hero-figure, but Jaeger was pushing him to compose on a scale for which he was not then ready, and Elgar later admitted as much to Ivor Atkins.[35] But he was sufficiently taken with the idea initially to promise it for the 1899 Worcester Three Choirs, Atkins's first, and the work was noticed as being 'on the stocks' in the *Musical Times* for March of that year, together with *Sea Pictures* and the Variations. The paragraph may well betray Jaeger's authorship or influence in its reference to Beethoven, and in the absence of other documentary evidence must represent our closest approach to the nature of the suggested programme itself.

> Mr. EDWARD ELGAR has several interesting compositions 'on the stocks'. Chief among them is the new symphony for the Worcester Festival, which is to bear the title 'Gordon'. As in the case of Beethoven's No. 3, Mr. Elgar has selected a great hero for

his theme, though one of a very different type from that of the 'Eroica'. The extraordinary career of General Gordon – his military achievements, his unbounded energy, his self-sacrifice, his resolution, his deep religious fervour – offers to a composer of Mr. Elgar's temperament a magnificent subject, and affords full scope for the exercise of his genius; moreover, it is a subject that appeals to the sympathies of all true-hearted Englishmen.

Perhaps Jaeger had learnt the lessons of the *Caractacus* correspondence, and realised the extent to which Elgar's patriotism might stimulate composition; the Nelson reference in the New Year's Eve letter had been another imaginative stroke. What in all probability he could not have known at that point was Elgar's personal connection with Gordon through a poem by Cardinal Newman that had been in the General's possession at Khartoum. Elgar's copy had Gordon's markings copied into it; the poem was *The Dream of Gerontius.* That Elgar took the Gordon idea as seriously as he did was a sign of his fascination with the man, as well as of Jaeger's emerging power to directly influence his music. Over the following years Jaeger would return again and again to the Symphony question, as if he had to test Elgar against the supreme yardstick of the Classical tradition. When the A flat Symphony arrived some ten years later, a heroic model was evident. But even with strong support for the earlier concept from Ivor Atkins, including a proposal that the Worcester Committee should consider a payment, Elgar knew the time was not right and that Novello's staple fare was choral music. He wrote to Jaeger,

'Gordon' Sym. I like this idee but my dear man *why* should I try?? I can't see – I have to earn money somehow & its *no good* trying this sort of thing even for a 'living wage' & your firm wouldn't give £5 for it – I tell you I am sick of it all: why can't I be encouraged to do decent stuff & not hounded into triviality.[36]

But that day he notated at length a magnificent melody for the Symphony, later used as the 'Committal' theme in *Gerontius.*[37] The day following this letter - 21 October 1898 – saw the inception of a work that Elgar quite evidently was ready to write, although the resulting masterpiece vindicated his predictions about Novello's financial attitude towards orchestral works; indeed the quoted figure of £5 was much in excess of what he received for the copyright of the score. Elgar had undertaken a hard day's teaching at The Mount, the Malvern school his daughter attended, and whose headmistress, Rosa Burley, was a strong-minded believer in his genius. In the evening he relaxed over a cigar and indulged a favourite habit of extemporizing at the piano, hardly aware of an emerging theme which Alice noted and approved. 'What is that?' she asked. 'Nothing', answered Elgar, 'but something might be made of it'. He went on to play the theme in a variety of styles in imitation of the personalities and mannerisms of various friends. Alice was immediately able to recognize William Meath Baker of Hasfield Court, in a version of the tune which parodied his behaviour, and told her husband, 'You are doing something which I think has never been done before'. Three days later Elgar wrote to Jaeger about the newly-evolving work, explaining his amusement with the idea of portraying friends. With the Beethoven conversation still fresh in his mind, the *Nimrod* movement had already been conceived; and he concluded, 'it's a quaint idee & the result is amusing to those behind the scenes & won't affect the hearer who "nose nuffin"'.

Although Elgar thus revealed an enjoyment of the idea of a certain amount of secrecy over the identity of each variation, there was at this stage no mention of the 'enigma' idea, which would only emerge after the whole work had been sketched, finished and scored. After the initial rapid inspiration, in fact, work on the Variations appears to have proceeded slowly, although further stimulus came when Elgar spent the last weekend of October at Hereford with George Robertson Sinclair, the Cathedral organist. During a riverside walk, Sinclair's bulldog fell into the Wye, and paddled downstream a little before scrambling up the bank with a 'rejoicing bark'. Sinclair challenged Elgar to set the incident to music, and the result was to be the eleventh Variation. But it was not mentioned in Dora Penny's account of her visit to the Elgars on the following Tuesday, 1 November, when he seems to have played her just six of the movements, including her own.[38]

Elgar wrote to Jaeger some ten days later confessing his slow progress, and confirming the other commissions in the air – for Birmingham, Worcester and Norwich. Again the financial complaint was aired. 'You see, none of this will pay me a cent !' he wrote, and went on to reveal why progress on the Variations was so slow, and how he was boosting his income. '... I am doing hack work – orchestrating a comic opera for another chap! for which I shall be paid. Such is life. (distinctly private – Beware! the knout is at work!!!' A few years later Elgar would be happy to have his work on the orchestration of Brewer's cantata *Emmaus* publicly known, but he enjoined Jaeger to strict secrecy over his orchestration of a less artistic kind of work, and very effectively too, for no suggestion has ever appeared as to the identity of the work in question.

With Jaeger's marriage just over a month away, Elgar renewed his congratulations and his compliments to Isabella.

> Well & so the day is fixed – I am very, very happy thinking of your new life, because I've seen Miss D. & can, thank God, congratulate you & believe you *will* be happy – one can very seldom say this to men who shew you the 'modern young women' they are going into partnership with: Lord pity 'em ! More of this some day: all good to you both for the present.[39]

The day of Elgar's prenuptial letter marked a triumph for Coleridge-Taylor and for Jaeger too, for it was the day of the first performance of the young composer's *Hiawatha* cantata, which was launched on its highly successful career at a concert given by students of the Royal College of Music and conducted by Stanford himself. Jaeger had successfully urged an otherwise indifferent Alfred Littleton (who told Coleridge-Taylor 'we do not expect to sell a copy of it') to publish the work, although it was done, as was usual in those days, on the basis of an outright purchase of the copyright. There was some ineffective bargaining on Taylor's part, but he settled for fifteen guineas, a very modest sum indeed for a work the phenomenal popularity of which would have made him a rich man had Novello's dealt with him on a royalty basis. Instead, he would be forced to adopt a hectic lifestyle of teaching, adjudicating and conducting, alongside composing to Festival commissions, a process of overwork that weakened the quality of his output and clearly contributed to his early death. But in earlier and happier times Coleridge-Taylor visited Jaeger several times a week to accompany his sweetheart Jessie singing his songs and to receive advice and encouragement. Berwick Sayers considered that Jaeger's influence was of unusual formative value and that their relationship was an intimate one. Of Coleridge-Taylor's behaviour at their meetings he wrote, 'When he was not trying over and discussing his compositions he seemed quiet, with little conversation; but he was delightfully unaffected and lovable, and the possessor of an irresistible sense of the comedy of things, which caused him to explode with laughter at the least of Jaeger's witticisms'.[40]

As far as Jaeger's sense of humour was concerned, Jessie remembered helping to check some proofs of a choral work and finding mistakes in a part written in the alto clef, whereas Jaeger

> … in his hurry had thought of the notes in the soprano clef; when the sheets were returned to him, of course, the alterations in the margin caused him some amusement and he sent the following, enclosed to me in one of Coleridge's letters:
>
> There was a young lady called Jessy
> Perused C-T's proofs rather messy,
> Poking fun at old Jaeger,
> Which his knowledge is meagre,
> This sharp-eyed young lady called Jessie.[41]

Jaeger characteristically seems to have done everything he could and more to establish *Hiawatha.* In the *Musical Times* for October he reviewed the work on its publication in vocal score. He noted the influence of Dvořák and, while careful not to overpraise the work, could not resist concluding with a significant Schumann reference.

> There is real grip, real heart and soul about this music. To be sure, it is all very simple and natural and not at all 'profound'. But if 'Hiawatha's Wedding Feast' cannot perhaps be called a great work, these simple and natural outpourings of our young friend are prophetic of great things in the future. Here is a real, Heaven-sent musician, and we feel inclined to quote Schumann *apropos* of Chopin: 'Hats off, gentlemen, a genius!'[42]

And a paragraph appearing in the next month's issue ended with a biting comment that presaged certain ideas of Elgar himself.

> Mr Coleridge-Taylor's 'Hiawatha's Wedding Feast' in spite of the absence of the prestige attached to a work that has been produced at an important Festival, is making remarkable headway. Performances are already announced to be given at the Royal College of Music (London), Plymouth, Torquay, Sunderland, Glasgow, The People's Palace (London), Bridlington and Middlesborough. Mr Coleridge-Taylor's Gloucester Festival work, the Orchestral Ballade in A Minor, is to be performed at several musical centres, London, naturally, not included. In such a respect London is a musical *dis*centre.[43]

Possible reasons for the later decline in Jaeger's relationship with Taylor were touched on in a quotation Berwick Sayers used, taken from Graves's article of December 1909:

> I think Jaeger's secret was his unfailing ear for the emotional signs in music. From that point of view alone he could register how much vitality there was in a new work. His defects in judgement arose from the same cause. He believed in a piece if it made him feel like tears. But he did not only bid for emotion. He demanded noble effort and sanity, and sometimes came to hate that which once moved him but subsequently showed its over-emotion.[44]

This described perhaps the characteristic behaviour of a man with an essentially Romantic outlook and a highly strung temperament, with a tendency to commit himself to emotionally highly charged relationships with similarly highly strung, creative people. Such relationships are notoriously unpredictable and are liable to burn themselves out and there are traces of this in Jaeger's friendship with Elgar as well as with Coleridge-Taylor. The judgement concluded, 'His help to young composers was marvellous. If he gave us over-praise he tempered it with much candid criticism'.[45]

One candid criticism of Coleridge-Taylor that Jaeger made, and that Stanford shared, was of his lack of self-criticism,[46] a lack which became more and more evident as he left behind the spontaneous and convincing instrumental and chamber works of his College years, in favour of commissioned choral works written under pressure. But for the moment the *Hiawatha* première, following on the heels of the success of the *Ballade* at the Three Choirs, made its composer famous overnight. It was played to a full audience which included a delighted Arthur Sullivan, who had made a special effort to attend despite increasing infirmity. Taylor himself shyly listened to the performance from behind the scenes, but appeared afterwards to acknowledge a warm reception and was recalled many times. Even after the acclaim, he was seen dodging into doorways to avoid being spotted as audience and musicians made their way home through the South Kensington streets. Jaeger again emphasized his modesty in his review of the performance.

> That the orchestral colouring improves the cantata immensely we need hardly say, for Mr. Taylor has proved ere this that he handles the colour-machine yclept the full modern orchestra as to the manner born. We have brilliancy, sonority, daintiness, and sensuous charm side by side, and the strongly marked and much-varied rhythms appear yet more marked and yet more varied in the full score, in the beat of drum, the crash of brass, and the elastic stepping of the violins. But, as we are never tired of insisting, orchestral colouring alone will never make great music. There must be melody, melody, and again melody! And that Mr. Taylor has in abundance. Though we do not of course, consider the little cantata a great masterpiece, nor hail the twenty-three-year-old composer as one who has nothing more to learn, we would fain protest against the assumption that the work is a lucky fluke. Mr. Taylor is no novice at composing, and the present work is but the outcome of the legitimate, though very rapid, development of his powers. That he adopted an original and peculiar style for a peculiar and original poem, and that he set that poem so successfully is in itself no mean achievement. It does not follow that he cannot write in another style. He has long learned the art of symphonic development, as other and earlier works of his have shown. But that art would not have availed him much in this particular cantata, and so we have what we consider a wonderfully fresh, buoyant, vigorous, and, especially as regards the latter portion, quite beautiful and poetic little work, which appeals to all and yet repays close examination. And now let us leave the gifted young composer happy with his remarkable success. He will do much better yet, for he has the gifts and strength and the modesty for higher things.[47]

Meanwhile, Walford Davies had not been forgotten and Jaeger again approached Elgar to use influence to secure a Three Choirs commission. His efforts to pull strings on behalf of a young and little-known composer were eventually rewarded when the Worcestershire Philharmonic took up a Davies work some two years later. The hoped-for Festival commission arrived in 1902, and proved to be the first of a series.

Jaeger's wedding was now fast approaching and he had invited Elgar to the ceremony, which was to take place in London on 22 December. Possibly the invitation had been rather shy one, for Elgar replied in one of two letters he wrote to Jaeger five days beforehand. 'This is to wish you every good thing now and always; you are too sensitive about the invitation'. However he was non-committal over his attendance and apologized for what would be the late arrival of a wedding-gift, a faience inkstand from James Hadley's Diglis factory which was incorporated into the nearby Royal Worcester Porcelain Factory on Hadley's death in 1905. The firm was a family concern, producing distinctive high-quality ware of their own design; one of Hadley's sons had been a violin pupil of Elgar. The inkstand stood some five inches high, and was urn-shaped with an embossed lid. Three winged beasts stood around its sides, with their feet on the points of a triangular fluted base. With its suggestion of German-Romantic style it was a compliment to Jaeger's background, and on a practical level it was a recognition of the committed and supportive writer, critic and correspondent.

That support was urgently called for in the second letter Elgar wrote to Jaeger that day, enclosed with the first and marked 'private'. In it he confessed that he had been 'very sick at heart over music' for the last six weeks – roughly the period since the conception of the orchestral variations – and the reasons were financial. He had receieved no answers from Littleton to recent queries about the firm's interest in his new Birmingham Festival commission, and about his debt to them over 'King Olaf'; and what annoyed him still further was a suggestion that he should write some light pastiche-style music such as Edward German's highly successful *Henry VIII* Dances. 'I can't write that sort of thing & my own heartfelt ideas are not wanted', he wrote, and went on to discuss his income in terms showing it to be about the same as Jaeger's own. 'You see I want so little: £300 a year I must make & thats all – last year I subsisted on £200', and claimed that he was asking only for sufficient income in order to be able to continue composing: 'It seems strange that a man who might do good work shd. be absolutely stopped – that's what it means ... I did not intend to write as it may seem disloyal to the firm but apparently this is the end of all things so it doesn't matter'.[48]

In the depths of the winter, with little apparent prospect either of increasing his income or writing the music that he wanted to despite the efforts of the previous few years, Elgar's discouragement was such that work on the Variations had slowed down to a stop. Busy as he must have been with preparations for his wedding and honeymoon, Jaeger recognized that another crisis was at hand. He sent immediate reassurance, and Elgar replied wth a grateful note to arrive on the morning of the wedding, confirming that he would not attend. 'I am just in & find your good letter: I will not say a word now. This is only coming – because I cannot get away alas! – to wish you once again *everything* & may you be as happy together as I & my dear one have been and are'.[49]

August Jaeger married Isabella Donkersley on 22 December 1898, at St Mary Abbott's Church, Kensington. He was 38 years old, and she 34. The Public Record Office has no record of Jaeger becoming naturalized,[50] and by virtue of her marriage, Isabella took on German nationality. Among the family witnesses were the bridegroom's younger sister Joanna, and Isabella's sister and her husband; the world of music was represented by Kate Boundy and Samuel Coleridge-Taylor. As his 'rank or profession' on the certificate, Jaeger entered the role he was presumably proudest of, 'musical critic', preferring to ignore his position at Novello's. The honeymoon was spent at Düsseldorf, although even this visit seems partly to have been a working one and Isabella would have discovered, if indeed she did not know already, the extent to which her husband's work was his whole life. There were just over ten years of that life to be lived and Jaeger became a devoted family man who enjoyed the domestic happiness that came to him relatively late. The marriage was founded on a common love of music, and on intense responses to it, for Isabella could be just as openly emotional as her husband. Jaeger was also intensely proud of his wife's accomplished musicianship and the enjoyable domestic music-making they were able to share.

The couple settled in West Kensington, at 16 Margravine Gardens where August had been living since April 1894 and which would have been large enough to be shared with others of his dependants. It was a substantial four-storey terraced house, with dormer windows above, a basement below and an imposing flight of steps leading up to the front door. A near neighbour, later to be a friend, was the artist and photographer Edgar Thomas Holding. The area was low-lying, just north of the Thames and liable to London's 'pea-soupers', which would not have helped Jaeger's nose and throat problems. But the house was close to Baron's Court Tube station for the daily journeys to Berners Street and various concert venues, and during the following years it would see much music-making at regular 'at-homes' and many musical visitors.

As the year came to a close with his marriage that December, August Jaeger might have taken some further satisfaction and pride in various strongly-argued reviews of his appearing in that month's *Musical Times*. He continued his audacious campaign against aspects of the Wood–Newman programmes at the Queen's Hall, beginning an article with a protest against the continued use of Tchaikovsky's 'Pathétique' as a 'draw':

> ... Mr. Newman's hobby-horse, 'Symphonie Pathetique', was once more ridden to the admiration of a crowded house. Moral for all orchestral conductors everywhere: Play the 'Pathetic' for the remainder of your days and you will please the dear public evermore. We do not know how the work fared on this occasion, for we purposely absented ourselves *pro tem.* We cannot endure this nerve-shattering music any more, and shall give it a well deserved rest till further notice.[51]

It could have been worse; at least Wood had not acceded to the requests of the Queen's Hall management to play the symphony every night during the Proms season.[52] But Jaeger went on to attack Wood with a series of questions after an unimpressive performance of Edward German's Symphonic Poem, *Hamlet*.

> When will Mr. Wood remember that he is an Englishman and should take a pride in doing his utmost for his countrymen whenever he gets the very rare chance of performing one of their compositions? He takes enormous pains over novelties of the Russian school; his performances of these could not be surpassed for finish, brilliancy and insight. When will he do the same for British works?[53]

Finally that month, Jaeger took up the cudgels once more in the controversy over the re-orchestration of certain passages in Beethoven's Ninth. A performance of the work under Wood at the Queen's Hall provided an opportunity to respond to Grove with a convincing statement of the case for alterations to the score, and to offer some further suggestions. After paying warm tribute to the conductor and performers for a 'dignified and impressive' performance, Jaeger continued,

> Mr. Wood adopted Wagner's suggestion as regards the scoring, by letting the horns play with the wood-wind in the famous second subject of the *Scherzo* and giving to the trumpets the whole of the opening fanfare in the *Finale*, instead of merely the A's and D's. The effect was correspondingly much greater, and, accepting the responsibility of a mere personal opinion, we confess to complete approval of Mr. Wood's course. Nothing seems more ridiculous to us, or more in direct contravention of what must have been Beeethoven's intention, than to hear some sixty stringed instruments suddenly drop to a *pp* (after they have given forth a truly magnificent body of tone in all loud passages during the rest of the evening) at the very point where Beethoven particularly wishes them to hammer out his figure of accompaniment with all their weight, *ff* in four octaves! If the strings played *all ff's* throughout the evening as *pp's*, the ludicrous anti-climax would not be apparent; but the ordinary performance of the passage 'as Beethoven wrote it' seems to us an absurd sacrifice of the Beethoven spirit on the altar of the poor printed letter! When will our purists remember that Beethoven never wrote for sixty-four strings and never dreamt of his wood-wind (one each flute, oboe, clarinet, and bassoon) playing that pretty tune against sixty-four strings, and English strings into the bargain? If he could hear Mr. Wood's orchestra, would he not shout with delight at the superb quality of the strings? but would he not proceed forthwith to re-score that passage, especially if he compared the refined tone of our oboes and clarinets with the coarse, penetrating quality of the instruments for which he wrote? But why not let the trumpets join in the theme too, Mr. Wood? You may as well be hanged for a sheep as for a lamb. *Then* only will you be able to let the strings play a *real ff*, and then only shall we have Beethoven in his most 'unbuttoned' mood! Either reduce the strings or let them play *pp throughout the concert,* or adopt Wagner's suggestions as regards this passage *in toto.* Any compromise appears to us ludicrous and a misrepresentation of the great master. We look forward with pleasure to indignant protests from all sorts and conditions of Beethoven lovers, but they will never cause us to change our rebellious mind.[54]

Thus Jaeger the unrepentant.

4 1899: A Quaint Idee

During his Christmas and New Year honeymoon at Düsseldorf Jaeger had taken the opportunity to lobby musical contacts on Coleridge-Taylor's behalf. Early in January, Taylor wrote to the Principal of the Croydon Conservatoire where he taught,

> As I have so many commissions to complete within the next three years, my friends have strongly advised me to give up my teaching after this term, more especially as I am expecting to go to Düsseldorf at Easter for a time. So will you kindy arrange so that I may have no fresh pupils during this term … these arrangements rest with Mr. Jaeger, who is now in Düsseldorf, and I cannot say for certain until I see him again.[1]

The commissions included a continuation of *Hiawatha* for the North Staffordshire Festival, an overture for the Norwich Festival, and another orchestral work for the Three Choirs. No Düsseldorf performances seem to have resulted from Jaeger's efforts and, despite further hopeful references in various later letters and efforts to learn the language, Taylor was never to undertake a visit to Germany.[2] Isabella told Coleridge-Taylor's biographer Berwick Sayers that the German conductors did not find his music favourable because they considered it to lack philosophical qualities.[3] But Jaeger was successsful in persuading Novello's to give the young composer a five-year contract, which guaranteed an annual retainer of £100 in return for first refusal of anything he wrote. Jaeger fully realized a composer's need to be free from the drudgery of teaching and yet have a background of financial security, and in securing the retainer he had won a victory for his hopes for Taylor's future development. He would later ask the firm for similar regular financial support for Elgar, but with less success.

Just at that point, in January 1899, such an income would have been greatly welcome. The new year had begun conspicuously badly for the Elgars, as the composer recounted in a 'strictly private' letter to his Bishop Auckland friend Nicholas Kilburn. Alice was 'worn to a shadow' by the cook having gone down with scarlet fever, the consequent fumigations and sending away of their daughter Carice. His career as a composer was at crisis-point, with the financial return having been so disappointing that a continuation of the hated teaching was the only resort. But the decision had been made to give composing one last try, to avoid 'breaking my dear wife's heart'. And he continued, 'I go to London on Monday to see what can be done: I have completed nearly a set of Variations for orchestra which *I* like – but commercially nothing.'

The Jaegers had invited Edward and Alice Elgar to their first 'at-home' at Margravine Gardens on Saturday, 7 January, but a Worcestershire Philharmonic Concert supervened and it was not until two days later that they were able to travel to London for a week's stay. It was a busy and fruitful visit, with outings to theatres, concerts, art galleries and the London Library. A commission for the Norwich Festival, a song-cycle for Clara Butt, was settled. There was much social contact with various friends including the chamber-music partners Basil Nevinson and Huw Steuart-Powell, and Rosa Burley, and several calls were made on the Jaegers. 'We were glad to get a small peep at your home & the pretty picture dwells with me,' wrote Elgar later. Most importantly of all, Elgar used one of these visits to give Jaeger a hearing of the uncompleted Variations on the piano, no doubt together with a verbal performance reflecting his state of mind at the time. Finance would have been a complaint, and the necessity to teach, and perhaps too the difficulty of securing a performance of the Variations, even if they were completed; Worcester would be unlikely to provide the kind of players capable of doing justice to the complexity of such music.

Jaeger responded immediately in terms of his knowledge of London's musical system; he realized that the prospect of an adequate performance in the metropolis, and one under the imprimatur of the great Hans Richter, would do more than anything else to get Elgar to finish the work. He realized too that among his network of contacts, far and away the best person to make the first approach to the great man would be Hubert Parry, in whose discretion, selflessness and goodwill Jaeger knew he could trust entirely. Accordingly he went to see Parry at his house in Kensington Square. Parry's son-in-law, the singer Harry Plunket Greene, created a somewhat dramatic myth out of the incident in his biography of Stanford. Parry 'was sitting at home after dinner one evening at his house in Kensington Square, when ... A. J. Jaeger of Novello's turned up and asked to see him. He had the score of the "Variations" under his arm and showed it to Parry. It was a terrible night with a howling gale and sheets of rain, and any sensible man would have put off his good deeds till the morrow. But one look at the score was enough for Parry. He jumped into a hansom and drove straight off with them to Richter, and Richter did them at his next concert'.[4] It would have been impossible for Jaeger to have had the score of the Variations, since the orchestration of the work had not then been completed. However, there is evidence that Parry, together with Jaeger, did in fact visit Richter one rainy night, although it was only to find that the great conductor was abroad.[5] Undaunted, they went to the home of Narcisco Vert, his London agent, who promised to forward a completed score, together with a strong recommendation. Jaeger's initiative won the day, and the subsequent completion and London première of the Variations marked a new era in English music and launched their composer on an international career.

Towards the end of the Elgars' stay in London, on 15 January, Alice Elgar recorded a busy day of music and friends in her diary.

'E. badsley cold – Pouring rain – E. & A. & B.G.N. (who came to lunch) to Queen's Hall Concert at 3.30. E. saw Randegger, Mackenzie &c. Miss Burley, Miss Gillis, Mr & Mrs Jaeger to tea at Mandeville. E to Banquet to Cowen Maccabean Club'.[6]

It was the first time that Miss Burley had met Jaeger, and he was as yet unknown among the Elgars' Malvern circle. Apart from his friendships with Edward and Alice, and with Dora Penny, he would tend to remain somewhat isolated socially from the other variants, many of whom were interconnected by ties of family or friendship. On one occasion Winifred Norbury noted in her diary that she met him in the slips at a Covent Garden Wagner performance, but despite their close proximity as Variants, she referred to him formally as 'Mr Jaeger'. Miss Burley subsequently left an account of him at that tea at the Mandeville Hotel, and described her feelings about him and his influence, characteristically mixing headmistressy assertiveness and native shrewdness with occasional touches of jealousy, cultural chauvinism and anti-semitism. But her judgements are often stimulating, even if sometimes by virtue of their eccentricity. She had been a strong supporter and encourager of Elgar all through the nineties, and in recent months she had heard the gradual development of the Variations at close quarters during Elgar's teaching visits to her school. She noted Jaeger's ability to give the composer hard criticism while smoothing his path at Novello's, and she saw his tendency to hero-worship Elgar, something that might carry with it the seeds of future disillusion. Already, too, she could not help but notice another worrying pointer, Jaeger's cough.

> ... I first met Mr Jaeger at a little hotel in Manchester Square, London, where the Elgars happened to be staying. He was a lovable but rather typically commonplace little German with a very large head and a guttural accent and it was apparent from the outset that he was not only deeply impressed with Edward's ability but inclined to worship him as a hero. If this was the man who was to handle Edward's work at Novello's in future, I felt that we could look forward to an easier passage. And indeed his value to Edward became very great. As editor of 'The Musical Times'[7] and reader to Novello's he wielded a great power and, although he often irritated – in fact infuriated – Edward by criticism of points of detail, there is no doubt that he managed to lubricate a relation between composer and publishers which without his patient intervention would have been anything but smooth. His appearance in *Grove's Dictionary* is avowedly due to the help he gave in advancing the reputation of Edward's early work, but, much as I admired him, I have often wondered whether his influence was quite as beneficial as is usually supposed.
>
> At that time, although an English school was arising, musical opinion in this country was largely dictated by German, Jewish and otherwise, and it was these people who, if they did not discover, were most successful in popularising Edward's music. So much was Mr Jaeger's encouragement valued indeed that he once complained to me that Alice was perpetually writing to ask him to stir Edward into fresh activity. This championship by Germans did not, as Mr Nettel points out, help Edward's cause with the English school but there was an even more serious disadvantage. For Edward's genius, much as its development may have owed to the example of Wagner and Brahms, was not really Teutonic in spirit but akin rather, even in some of its faults, to that of Cesar Franck[8] should not have been constantly assessed by exclusively German standards. One may therefore be a little doubtful of the value of a mentor whose principal requirement of a work of genius was that it should move him to tears.
>
> Nevertheless poor little Mr Jaeger was probably the most faithful friend Edward ever had and when he died in 1909, racked by the consumptive cough which I had noticed with concern at our first meeting, he had probably done more for his hero's music than anyone else before or since.[9]

Short in stature and slightly built, 'rather typically commonplace … poor little Mr. Jaeger' may not have been outwardly prepossessing, but Elgar and those who knew him best understood his qualities of mind. Something of Rosa Burley's attitude may have been reflected by Dora Penny when she asked Elgar why he gave Jaeger 'such a grand and noble tune' for his Variation. The reply was, 'Don't you think him grand and noble? His *mind* is!'[10] Later, Dora would come closer in friendship to Jaeger than any of the variants apart from Edward and Alice, and would know the truth of Elgar's comment.

Jaeger had intervened decisively to secure the completion and first performance of a great orchestral work, and it was to Hans Richter, a German, that he had looked for the promotion of a new work by an English composer. That month Jaeger had been allowed two outspoken, anonymous columns in the *Musical Times* to restate his case against Wood and Newman and their neglect of native composers. Under the dramatic headline, 'LOST! BRITISH MUSIC AT THE QUEEN'S HALL', the article took as its starting point the repeat of a concert of German, French and Russian music which had earlier been given for Queen Victoria at Windsor Castle. The lack of British music on the programme predictably roused Jaeger's ire and he deployed the by now familiar arguments, although accepting that a whole programme of British music might prove unprofitable. But Jaeger argued for the inclusion of single works, and went on to develop his case against Newman in typically audacious, even threatening style.

> … we appreciate Mr. Newman's difficulties as thoroughly as we are convinced of his duties to native art. It would be idle to discuss whether a man in Mr. Newman's position has other duties besides that of money making which he owes to himself. But he has so far failed to fulfil them. He seems to be gradually assuming the *rôle* of a monopolist in orchestral concerts in London, and unless he uses his power wisely and well, he will share the fate of most monopolists and, by creating that irritation, distrust, and envy, which ultimately lead to a revolt against a tyranny, he will alienate the very public upon whose support he has to depend. It is time to speak out strongly; time to assure Mr. Newman and Mr. Wood that their present policy of novelties at any price so long as they are not British will not do, and that they may bore and annoy the public once too often with works suggesting an utter absence of critical acumen in those responsible for their selection.
>
> We have faith in the future of British music, for we know sufficient of our young composers to believe that the time will come, and that soon, when Londoners will clamour for those British orchestral works that are now denied them. Then will also come the time when the public will want to know what evil influences have been at work to retard the recognition of our best men, to thwart the urgent and just claims of our budding native art …[11]

Fortified, Elgar returned to the Variations and completed them. Before beginning the orchestration, he travelled to London again to attend the inaugural meeting of the Folk Song Society, returning to Malvern amid snow and cold weather on the morning of another of the Jaegers' 'at-homes'. Coleridge-Taylor was present and wrote his thanks for Elgar's past support in a letter which gives some flavour of the musical evenings at Margravine Gardens.

> I was so sorry to find on my arrival at Mr. Jaeger's 'at home' last evening, that you had already returned to Malvern ... Mrs Jaeger played one of your early & short pieces for violin last evening & charmed her small but highly critical (!) audience. We also scrambled thro' the new part of 'Hiawatha'! Mrs Jaeger was Soprano, Miss Boundy Contralto, Mr Jaeger a kind of Bass & Tenor mixture. I played the Piano, & thanked my stars you were not within hearing distance![12]

The orchestration of the Variations was achieved in a fortnight, 5–19 February, and the March *Musical Times* announced their performance in London in the spring. The previous number had devoted several paragraphs to the programmes of the forthcoming Norwich and Three Choirs Festivals and the Queen's Hall season, Jaeger's fingerprints much in evidence. The Norwich programme found favour through its inclusion of *Hiawatha's Wedding Feast.* 'It speaks well for the Norwich committee that they have selected a work by a British composer purely on its merits – a work that is rapidly making its way without the prestige attached to a Festival novelty.'[13] Elgar's Symphony – the *Gordon* – was predicted for the Worcester Three Choirs Festival, in terms that may have done as much as anything else to convince its putative composer that the time was not right: 'Special interest attaches to Mr. Elgar's symphony, as it will practically constitute his *début* in the highest form of purely instrumental music.'[14] There was also a biographical paragraph on the American Horatio Parker, whose choral work *Hora Novissima* would feature at Worcester. It had been premièred in New York in May 1893, to a warm review 'from our own correspondent' in the *Musical Times,* which included a reference to 'the brilliant young composer from whom we may hope so much'.[15] It was just the kind of phrase to whet Jaeger's appetite, and the October 1893 number carried a two-page analysis of *Hora Novissima* which in its references to Brahms and Wagner, and in its honest refusal to discuss one movement 'until we have heard it ... the effect one cannot judge at all on paper', bears every sign of coming from his pen.[16] Novello's published the work in England and America, perhaps another sign of Jaeger's advocacy, and the analysis concluded with a recommendation to choral societies to take up the work. But the article reflected Jaeger's excitement at a new discovery as much as purely commercial priorities; his notice for a Worcester performance six years later would still advise, 'Professor Parker is a young man of whom great things may be expected'.

Consideration of the Queen's Hall programmes ('we cannot feign any surprise at observing that they do not contain a single note of British music, old or new') gave Jaeger opportunity to follow up his outspoken article of the previous month. As he had no doubt hoped, it had provoked interest and reaction in wide circles, from a speech at the annual conference of the Incorporated Society of Musicians to articles in the national and musical press. Jaeger's points about English composers needing to handle the orchestra as well as their 'foreign rivals' were endorsed, although again he was at pains to point out that orchestration was but a means to an end. He went on to dismiss suggestions from the *Standard* that greater recognition be given to

English music in 'high quarters', so that it might become fashionable to support it, and gave short shrift to remarks by 'an esteemed contemporary' that 'Individuals ... must conquer recognition not by grumbling, but by good work'. It was the kind of Victorian-homily touch that gave Jaeger the cue to press the point home once more.

> ... Mr Edward Elgar, whom he mentions as proof of his assertion that 'if an Englishman writes a good work he has as fair a chance of fame and profit as his foreign rival', is the very composer who has so far been utterly ignored by Messrs. Newman and Wood, except that they performed a few light dances from his pen at their Promenade concerts, which they evidently think quite good enough for native composers. Moreover, nothing but 'good work' has brought Mr. S. Coleridge-Taylor as with one bound to the front. His beautiful and original cantata, 'Hiawatha's Wedding Feast', and his striking Orchestral Ballade are being heard throughout the country, but not at Queen's Hall. Instead, we shall no doubt ere long hear young Perosi's works there. They are being exploited in the Italian press. That suffices. Meanwhile, our composers will spend anxious, despondent months, aye, years, waiting for a performance that never comes. We repeat, is it not time that something was done?[17]

Jaeger knew only too well of the 'anxious, despondent months' that Elgar had lived through recently, and how nearly a great orchestral work had been stifled. But his tactics over that work began to pay off when early in March, Vert wrote of Hans Richter's interest in the Variations. Elgar proceeded with a piano arrangement of the work, pointing out to Novello's that several of the movements would arrange well as separate numbers. But he wrote more personally to Jaeger the same day concerning the *Nimrod* movement, 'Mrs J. will recognise your portrait quicker than you will: I have omitted your outside manner & have only seen the good, lovable honest SOUL in the middle of you!' Elgar, with the achievement of the work behind him, certainly realized how much he was beginning to owe to Jaeger, and what a powerful sensibility lay behind the frail exterior.

The March *Musical Times*, much as Jaeger might have foretold, contained an article on Perosi. As far as the Queen's Hall concerts, and Henry Wood in particular, were concerned, Jaeger evidently felt it was time to redress the balance somewhat, and give credit for performances of high quality, although he was unable to resist a sideswipe at Tchaikovsky's Fourth Symphony.

> ... with the first concert of the new season, given at the Queen's Hall on January 28, came the proof that the splendid orchestra conducted by Mr. Wood is still the finest and most highly trained body of instrumentalists in London. We do not approve of all that Mr. Wood does; we may occasionally find fault with his selection of novelties, or cavil at his reading of recognised masterpieces; but it is impossible not to feel genuine admiration for the magnificent performances he secures of those works which appeal to his temperament. At the concert under notice the band displayed a beauty of tone, a brilliancy of colour, and a finish that were absolutely delightful. Even Mr. Wood has never given us a more gorgeous performance than that of some new Symphonic Dances (Op. 64) by Edvard Grieg. They are, to be sure, scored with consummate mastery and glow with exquisite colour; but their beauty of raiment seemed intensified in the superb playing of the band. The symphony was Tchaikowsky's original but distressingly Slavonic No. 4 (in F minor), one of those works which one completely exhausts at a first hearing, and whose repeated performances leave one less and less impressed.[18]

Far more to Jaeger's taste was the chamber music of Walford Davies, and the next issue of the *Musical Times* contained a notice of a concert which had introduced his Piano Trio.

> The trio for pianoforte, violin, and violoncello ... is one of Dr. Davies's ripest works, in which his sound musicianship goes hand in hand with an unaffected and wholesome directness of expression that is quite refreshing. He dares to be simple, lucid, and concise and his melodious strains have the true ring about them. Simple as they are they come from the heart and go to the heart; of nervous excitement there is nought, nor of ranting loquaciousness. It is an eminently sane work, which is more likely to speak lovingly to a few intimate friends in the chamber, for which it was written, than to the crowd in a large concert-room.[19]

Davies wrote his thanks while Jaeger and Isabella were taking a short break at Ivy Cottage. In reply Jaeger took the opportunity to enlarge further about his feelings about the contrast between Russian and German styles, as well as saying something about the difficulties of criticising the works of friends.

[no address]

5/4/99

My dear Davies,

I received your note while away at my wife's Home in Yorkshire, where I spent a few quiet & happy days. Yes! I wrote that little paragraph about your Trio & am glad to think that I seem to have understood your work. At the same time, you ought not to 'thank' me. Supposing I had *not* liked the work & said so? Would you have 'gone for' me & considered me unkind & unfriendly? It is sometimes *very* difficult to express one's honest opinion on the works composed by friends without running the risk of losing those friends' friendship. I have experienced that ere this.

As for your Trio I am *sure* some of my colleagues judged it too hastily & too severely. They expect to be impressed with such a work as if it were a nerve-exciting orchestral novelty by a Russian. They seem to lack the *patience* to quietly listen to unaffected, sincere & 'innige' strains such as yours. Everything must be in this style at the present day: (I mean as regards expression marks)

N. B. This is *not* supposed to be a 'Theme'.

as loud as ever possible & every note with a dash or dot or sforzando. Our ears are rapidly becoming quite spoiled for all *quiet* music. But I fancy I can still enter into the spirit of it & enjoy it quietly & serenely. I should *much* like to hear the Trio again & hope an opportunity will soon be found. And I am *longing* to hear your splendid Violin Sonata (No 4) again.[20] Is that never again to appear in a Concert programme?

How is the new overture getting on? Mind you give us plenty of *tune* & *rhythm* & *sonority*, as well as 'Brains'.

Goodnight! I am dead-tired & must go to Bed. Much happiness & good Health to you[.]

Ever Yours

A.J. Jaeger[21]

A few days later Jaeger told Elgar that the Variations score had been received at Novello's from Hans Richter in Vienna, and he made some corrections at Elgar's request. Further, Jaeger at this time added the word 'Enigma' on the first page, above bars two and three of the theme itself; he would have to have been acting on Elgar's instructions, or, if the suggestion had been his own, with Elgar's approval. And so the saga began, with almost immediate effect. During that month and the next, Elgar received several letters from the composer and writer Charles Ainslie Barry, who was responsible for the programme notes for the Richter Concerts, asking for help with preparation of the notes for the Variations première. The first letter was dated 10 April, and already Barry had heard something of the 'enigma' idea.

> I shall be very pleased if during your visit to Town you will come here some day to lunch, at which I shall be glad of any hints as to the 'composer's intentions'. It would be best if you could *send* me your score in advance, as in that case I should perhaps be prepared with some questions on moot points. I will send you some Variations of mine of thirty years ago. Don't think me impudent in saying that I think I *discovered* a 'trick', which I will impart to you. You won't guess it, so I am glad to think that there is something enigmatical about *my* Variations, as well as yours.[22]

So a rumour of the 'enigma' was current in London musical circles and could only have come from Jaeger, whose love of gossip might have been deliberately indulged to arouse special interest. It is clear that the whole idea was developed during this period, after the work had been finished, and with a degree of collaboration from Jaeger. No correspondence with Elgar on the matter appears to have survived, which may in itself be suggestive, although it might have been discussed between them during various visits to London that Elgar made during March to rehearse for an Albert Hall performance of *Caractacus*. The possibility exists that Jaeger himself was an influence in the creation of the 'enigma' concept. His own interest may perfectly properly have been in the question of 'marketing', something that appealed to what Elgar referred to as 'the cheap publisher's side' of his mind. The choice of title for a new work might be a crucial factor in sales terms. The March *Musical Times* paragraph had referred to the work as simply as a set of 'symphonic variations', and this was reinforced in a sentence in the next month's number: 'Mr. EDWARD ELGAR's "Symphonic Variations" will be introduced at one of the Richter concerts, under the direction of Hans Richter'. Jaeger's knowledge of contemporary music would have told him that there were at least two notable works with just that title, Dvořák's of 1877, popularized in England by Richter ten years later, and Parry's of 1897. He may have felt that a distinctive identity for a new work by a new composer would help to establish it in the public mind, although he cannot have had doubts about the appeal of the music itself.

Speculation and detective-work over the mystery has continued ever since, but no decisive conclusion has been reached. It seemed to be accepted among Elgar's friends that the 'enigma', whatever it was, was known only to three people: Edward and Alice Elgar, and August Jaeger. It must also be said that little or no attention has been paid to Alice's possible rôle as the originator of the idea. In her undated, unpublished essay, *The Ideal in the Present*,[23] a consideration of contemporary developments in art, literature and music, she wrote, 'Let us now pass on to the works of Watts. Think of the 'Enigma' the embodied striving of the mind of man to pierce the Unseen, the Unknowable ...'. It was of course Alice who had first recognized the potential of the improvised theme. Moore says of the 'enigma', 'It was the inchoate blackness out of which creation comes,'[24] and if indeed the 'enigmatizing' contained something of the element of a 'publicity stunt' it has since proved one of the best, if with hindsight one of the most unnecessary, in the history of music.

The May *Musical Times* carried an advertisement for the piano arrangement of the Variations, now described as 'Variations on an Original Theme for Orchestra', together with reviews of Elgar conducting *Caractacus* at the Albert Hall, the 25-year old Rachmaninov conducting his *Fantasia in E* for Orchestra Op. 7 at Queen's Hall ('... the themes are small and ill nourished. Nearly all creep about in apologetic half-tones. They never grow to anything, and their gorgeous Byzantine apparel accentuates their want of distinction ...'), and a symphonic poem based on Chaucer by the former Royal Academy student William Henry Bell. Bell would become another of Jaeger's protegés, and the review praised his craftsmanship, but *The Pardoner's Tale* itself was pronounced as being based on a 'sordid' subject: 'This want of perception of what is suitable for musical treatment is a common failing amongst composers of to-day'. Jaeger's most characteristic and interesting report that month, however, was a review of a concert by the pioneering Bournemouth Municipal Orchestra under Dan Godfrey at the Winter Gardens which had taken place on 17 April. Possibly at Jaeger's suggestion, Isabella played Coleridge-Taylor's *Ballade in D Minor* of 1895, in its first performance with orchestral accompaniment; Godfrey remained a staunch champion of the composer. Jaeger himself found much else of interest in the programme. He praised the modest size of the orchestra, which he found ideal for the Beethoven symphony that was also on the programme, and went on to argue a case which, while putting a new perspective on his disagreements with Grove, was somewhat in advance of its time.

> Londoners of the present day hear Beethoven's symphonies played by orchestras of from eighty to a hundred players, which mean that the proper balance between strings and wind, such as Beethoven had in his mind when he wrote his immortal works, is completely upset. We have to go beyond the Metropolis to hear them performed with the small 'Beethoven orchestra' of the beginning of the century; and it was new, and, we may add, delightful experience to us to listen to the great master's ever-fresh 'No. 2' as interpreted on the 17th ult., by the Municipal Orchestra, at the Bournemouth Winter Gardens, under the direction of its energetic and enthusiastic conductor, Mr. Dan Godfrey, jun. This capital band consists of thirty-eight performers – viz., twenty strings and eighteen wind and percussion. They play like true artists and seem competent to appear anywhere and do anything in the way of interpreting the utterances of the masters of music. They perform in a concert-room of such excellent acoustic properties that the faintest *pianissimi* of string or wind carry with charming effect to the farthest corner, the *Tutti* reveal a rich and full sonority without calling up even the semblance of an echo, and the *fortissimi* of the brass never degenerate into a noisy blare. Moreover,

> they display the finish and spirit of a highly trained and intelligent body of musicians, so that their performance of the aforesaid symphony came as a rare surprise to one who, from one year's end to the other, is condemned to listen to many ponderous battlings of huge orchestras with small scores of a dozen staves or so. There is nothing in a Beethoven symphony that a first-rate and perfectly balanced 'small' band, such as Mr. Godfrey's, cannot do better, given a suitable room, than a modern 'playing-machine' of a hundred men. That, at any rate, was our impression after the most enjoyable performance under our notice, and it might be worth the consideration of London conductors to give us occasionally a Beethoven or Mozart symphony as nearly as possible under the conditions that obtained in those composers' days.[25]

Jaeger went on to praise Godfrey's promotion of works by native composers, and explained how Coleridge-Taylor had re-orchestrated the *Ballade* especially for the Bournemouth performance, the original score being in possession of 'a well-known conductor who has it still'. Taylor said he was unwilling to 'bother' the conductor concerned, but Jaeger thought that the new version was an improvement. He analysed the work briefly, and concluded by paying gracious but suitably restrained tribute to Isabella in one of her apparently infrequent appearances with orchestra. 'Her beautiful tone and excellent technique were well displayed ... and she left little or nothing to desire on the score of expression.'[26]

Jaeger began to see his hopes for the Variations brought to fruition, as he attended the rehearsals – three altogether, a good number for those days including a special extra rehearsal called and paid for by Vert – that Hans Richter devoted to the work. There was a preliminary rehearsal at the beginning of June, another on the 17th, and one on the morning of the première, giving him several opportunities to gauge the orchestral effect of music previously heard only on the piano. He would thus have had several hearings of his own variation, allowing its impact to sink in. There is no record of his feelings about *Nimrod*, but he must have viewed the music with a certain justifiable pride. On a personal level he must have felt that it vindicated beyond all expectation the paths he had taken since Düsseldorf days. He would have known, too, that his variation grew directly out of German roots, and when Hans Richter wanted to praise the climax of the *Nimrod* Variation, it was in terms of the one to be found in the *Mastersingers* Prelude. But there was another, quicksilver side to Jaeger's personality apart from the serious German one which shines through many of his letters and writings, as well as many of his actions. Elgar summed it up best in a note for the programme of the Jaeger Memorial Concert in January 1910, where he wrote that something 'ardent and mercurial' would have been needful to portray his character and temperament as well as the slow movement of the Variation.

Whatever his personal feelings as he listened to his own music and that of the other friends during the rehearsals, Jaeger did not allow his critical faculties to be blunted. He began to focus ideas about the work's finale which emerged immediately after the first performance. This took place on Monday 19 June 1899, at St James's Hall in Regent Street, where Jaeger used to sing in the Novello Oratorio Choir concerts. Many musicians and 'variants' were present among a large audience, including the figure who had, together with Jaeger, intervened so decisively to ensure the progress of the work, Hubert Parry. The audience's reception of the work was warm and enthusiastic, with Elgar being recalled twice. In the artist's room afterwards Richter was joined by Elgar, Jaeger and Ivor Atkins, who remembered Richter enthusing about the work in his deep toned voice while Elgar remained 'singularly quiet'. Atkins recalled also how Jaeger stated his opinion that the Finale was too short and needed strengthening, and although Richter was of a broadly similar view, Elgar would have none of it; indeed he became quite hurt as Jaeger continued to press the point, and 'argued strongly that the ending was exactly as he wished it to be, and that any alteration would defeat his object'.[27] Richter paid Elgar more enthusiastic compliments at an after-concert supper, but he continued to feel hurt, according to Atkins, for some weeks; Jaeger had extraordinary confidence in his own judgement and had enthusiastically pursued his point without regard for the composer's feelings. Once Elgar returned to Malvern, Jaeger continued the campaign by letter. In the end, Elgar gave way and not only lengthened the finale, but did so in a way that convincingly clinched the argument of the work by uniting the two parts of the 'Enigma' theme. And he admitted to Dora Penny, who remembered how he roared with laughter as he played her the new ending from proofs, 'the old Moss was right'. It was not the last time that Jaeger would seem to know what Elgar wanted better than the composer himself did, nor was it the last time that Jaeger would focus on Elgar's codas and finales, about which he seemed to develop something of an obsessive concern.

Jaeger wrote a review of the Richter season for the July *Musical Times*, necessarily covering various other works before dealing with the concert which included the Variations. Richter's performances of the established classics of the German repertoire were briefly dealt with as 'glorious readings of glorious masterpieces'. Much more space was devoted to works by Russian composers, with the by now predictable criticisms. He then continued:

> Of a very different calibre was the one English novelty of Dr. Richter's season – viz., Mr. Elgar's 'Variations on an original theme' (Op. 36). Our opinion of Mr. Elgar's gifts is by this time known to our readers, but after making ourselves thoroughly acquainted with his latest work, and listening to a splendid performance under the greatest living conductor, we say more emphatically than ever: here is an English musician who has something to say and knows how to say it in his own individual and beautiful way. He does not pose as a 'profound' and learned master of his craft; he writes as he feels, there is no affectation or make-believe. Effortless originality – the only true originality – combined with thorough *savoir faire*, and, most important of all, beauty of theme, warmth, and feeling are his credentials, and they should open to him the hearts of all who have faith in the future of our English art and appreciate beautiful music wherever it is met.[28]

The article discussed the personalities behind the music, the nature of the theme and the ensuing variations, the orchestration, the 'all too short' Coda, and concluded,

> And thus ends an original, masterly and poetic work, which not only grows upon one enormously, but which we are convinced more than justifies our faith in Mr. Elgar's genius and in his future. The performance was almost ideally perfect and Mr. Elgar was repeatedly called to the platform and enthusiastically applauded. Madame Brema gave

an intensely dramatic and moving, we might even say 'inspired' performance of the wonderful final scene of 'Gotterdamerung', and Mozart's delightful 'Prague' Symphony closed a most interesting – may be historic! – concert.[29]

Historic indeed, and evidence too that Jaeger had found his man. He would continue to encourage other composers, but there could now be no doubt in his mind that the hoped-for genius had arrived, and that Elgar's future would be to some extent his own as well.

But that future was immediately threatened by difficulties that had arisen over the business arrangements for the Variations. As Elgar had earlier told Kilburn, the work was 'commercially nothing'. Novello's would offer just one guinea[30] for the copyright of the orchestral score, and royalties would be payable only on separate arrangements. Elgar had been disappointed to learn of the royalty he was to receive from the sale of the piano arrangement, but the hard-headed Henry Clayton would not increase it and insisted that Elgar was being offered the usual percentage. Further fuel was added to the composer's simmering resentment when he heard that Novello's charged Vert the standard 30-shilling hire fee for orchestral parts for the extra Variations rehearsal, for which he had already paid some £40 out of his own pocket as a favour to ensure a smooth launch for the work. Matters went from bad to worse when Elgar heard that the management's view was that the orchestral players should have foregone their fees.

When he came to London in August to rehearse *Sea Pictures* for the October Norwich Festival with Clara Butt, Elgar went to Novello's and had what Alice described as a 'stormy interview' with Clayton. A week later he again went to London and broke with the firm, signing a contract the next day with Boosey & Co. for the publication of the new song-cycle; it gave him £50 for the copyright and a small royalty on any of the songs sold separately. At the beginning of September Elgar, still furious, wrote to Jaeger to express his anger over the wealthy Alfred Littleton's attitude to poorly paid orchestral players and his disgust over the whole business side of publishing, and concluded that he thought himself 'well out of the vortex of jealousy, chicanery, fraud and falsehood' that he considered typical of the 'farcical and depressing' state of music in England. It was a bruising encounter, but the breach was healed through Littleton's diplomacy and Elgar signed the Variations contract without further protest, virtually giving away a masterpiece of English music which would have made him a rich man had he been given a royalty on it. Indeed the 'enigma' word itself had earlier been connected in Elgar's mind with financial matters when he wrote to Jaeger in May 'Another "Enigma" – the Black Knight you say is unsuccessful commercially – and its the only thing I ever recd. any royalty on yet –'[31] Whatever the significance or otherwise of the reference, it was providential that Jaeger was at Berners Street to smooth the path in the future.

Jaeger spent some time in Germany that summer, and returned to oversee revisions to *The Light of Life* and the Variations finale for that year's Worcester Three Choirs, which would also feature another Festival commission by Coleridge-Taylor, a *Solemn Prelude* for orchestra, as well as Parker's *Hora Novissima.* The September *Musical Times* repeated the recent short feature about the American composer with a photograph, together with a similar informative article about Ivor Atkins, whose first Three Choirs Festival it would be. The step from cathedral organist to orchestral conductor was encouraged: 'He has doubtless been equipping himself for the proper discharge of his arduous duties (we fancy that we saw him at a Richter rehearsal one day!)'. As regards Elgar, the Festival programme included *The Light of Life* and the first performance of the Variations with the revised Finale. After the performance of the Coleridge-Taylor work, Elgar wrote to Jaeger that he thought the composer a 'dear chap' and the music '*human* & yearning'. Jaeger's next and last big priority that year was the preparation of the orchestral parts of his first protegé's new cantata *The Death of Minnehaha*, the continuation of *Hiawatha's Wedding Feast*, due for its first performance at the North Staffordshire Festival at the end of October. Early October saw the *Sea Pictures* successfully premièred at Norwich, and such was the attraction of the work and its performers – Elgar himself accompanied Clara Butt at the piano – that Jaeger was unable to get into their performance of four of the songs at St James's Hall two days later. He was further disappointed not to be able to attend a highly successful performance of *King Olaf* at Sheffield on 11 October, but wrote to Elgar with news of a particularly good review by the critic Vernon Blackburn, together with a complaint about John West's likely slowness in correcting proofs of the Variations score, and an invitation to Margravine Gardens. He finished with a plaintive mention of his overdue midday meal, for he was writing from his Berners Street Office on a Saturday: 'I must stop, for it is 2 pm & time to go home to my little wife *&* a little dinner'. Elgar's visit took place just a week later, and he played Jaeger some music intended for the Apostle Judas in a big but otherwise undefined choral work intended for the Birmingham Festival the following year. Shortly afterwards the Jaegers left for two days at Hanley for the North Staffordshire Festival. Jaeger had been permitted to contribute over his own initials a lengthy and thorough analysis of *The Death of Minnehaha*, spread over two issues of the *Musical Times*,[32] and his commitment to the work and its composer was further demonstrated in his review of the Festival for the December number. Jaeger emphasized the emotional impact of the work and made a vehement plea for the primacy of melody over the tendencies of the modern school, even as displayed by Richard Strauss.

> ... such was the spell which Mr. Coleridge-Taylor's music cast over the large audience that not a soul, from her Grace the Duchess of Sutherland to the humblest amateur in the gallery, moved before the echo of the last chord of the beautiful work was drowned in a spontaneous and splendid ovation for the happy young composer. We have written at length about the cantata in another column. We need therefore only say that our highest expectations were most fully realized, and even surpassed. The little work worked a great wonder: we saw grey-bearded critics moved to tears, and there were many in the audience who made no attempt to hide their emotion. Whoever can do this with the force of his simple melodies is no ordinary musician. For we must here insist, as we have insisted elsewhere, that the music is simplicity itself. There is no elaboration,

> no striving after new and sensational effects; of development into lengthy movements there is very little, for the poem does not lend itself to such treatment unless the words be repeated *ad nauseam* and thus all dramatic force be spent. But our composer has the precious gift of inventing melodies which seem the very soul of the words or of the poetic idea, expressed in the greatest of languages: music. Their spontaneity is as striking as their simplicity and their beauty as moving as their directness. We seem to possess in Mr. Taylor that *rara avis*, a new and original melodist. *A new melodist*! Do we fully appreciate the significance of the term and the priceless value of the possession? Music is sick for the want of such an one, for the spring of melody seems in danger of running dry, and to take its place, harmony, polyphony, development *in excelsis*, and orchestration (*alias* colour) are vainly called to the muse's aid to charm and move us. We fully appreciate the value of these qualities in modern works, provided they are displayed with a master's mastery; and we can be roused to genuine enthusiasm over some of the most daring efforts of that *facile princeps* amongst advanced harmonists, polyphonists, and colourists, Richard Strauss. Yet what avails the heavy armour, the veritable 'Giant's robe' of these modern musical Goliaths against the sling and stone of the simple but inspired melodist? It is the latter who will sway the hearts of countless thousands, as the touching melodies of 'The Death of Minnehaha' swayed us and caused our eyes to become dim with a deep and true emotion.[33]

The quality of the work came through despite an indifferent performance, exactly as would happen with Elgar's *The Dream of Gerontius*. Jaeger went on to point up the lack of an orchestral rehearsal: inadequate rehearsing was a notorious feature of the Festival system and of English musical life. On his return he wrote to Elgar from Berners Street, again emphasizing the emotional response the work had received from the 'old stagers' and from Isabella. 'As for my little wife she cried half the time. I was too much concerned about the bad orchestral performance to cry. (I have done that *at Home* over the vocal score & at the Piano!)'.

It had been a busy period and Alfred Littleton had been away from the office, unwell, for a fortnight; significantly Jaeger complained of being unwell himself – 'that *nose* of mine will kill me ... I hope you are well and jolly[.] I am neither'. Elgar sympathized but kept Jaeger busy by asking him to attend a performance of his unpublished *Sursum Corda* for Strings, Brass and Organ of 1894, which was to be given at Marylebone Church one Sunday afternoon in November, with a view to judging its suitability for publication. Elgar claimed that he had been offered good terms for it by a German firm, but was patriotic and waited, and the piece had been forgotten. Jaeger was prepared to disrupt his Sunday in order to hear it: 'I will certainly go & hear the Sursum Corda if I can possibly get away from Home & from my cup of coffee & cigar *&* from the little wife & my easy chair,' he replied. He liked the music and promised to speak to Alfred Littleton about it, but the piece was eventually published by Schott in 1901. The journey from West Kensington to Marylebone by underground for the performance would have done nothing for Jaeger's health.

> I 'did went' to Marylebone Church to hear your Sursum Corda & was nearly poisoned dead on the fearful 'Sewer' line between Baker Street & Portland Road. Well, That's neither here nor there, for your music made me forget about the fumes of poison down below in the bowels of the Yearth. The Sursum was very well played, *considering*.[34]

Elgar was properly grateful. 'You are an angel to have went & I send a very dutiful, especial little bundle of thanks to Mrs. Jaeger for letting you go,' he wrote, and promised to send a 'refreshing' theme 'some day' to compensate for the Underground. Meanwhile he enclosed a four-bar phrase scored for five tubas from the new choral work, relating to Judas. Jaeger replied describing the idea as a 'discovery', and referred memorably to the proposed tone-colour as 'dark copper glow & gloom'. In the same letter he had one more suggestion to make concerning the Variations Finale – the orchestral score being now in proof stage. His idea brilliantly matched a technical point with dramatic effect, and was couched in typically persuasive, tactfully modest terms, with Wagnerian overtones.

> Look here! you wont call me a d– fool & impertinent Hass for making another suggestion re *the* Skore, will you? When I heard the new Finale, *both* at the Worcester Rehearsals & the Richter, I was a little disappointed that the sudden Burst into Eb at 82 did not 'come off' quite as *explosively* & surprisingly as I had anticipated. When I look at the score page 126 I put it down to the fact that the 1st Fiddles have *not* the short quaver rest that many of the other instruments have. They seemed at the performances to glide up to the Bb instead of *sharply plunging, hammering* on it as with stroke of Thor's War Axe! Would it not give you a *stronger* Bb & a stronger Eb chord & a greater *surprise* if **ALL** instruments had the crotchet rest before 82? The Wind could take breath for the fff & not merely use their *last* breath of a *crescendo* for THE effect; & the 1st Fiddles could get a better *grip* of the Bb & give greater *brilliancy* to it? You know I am not such a d– ass as to want to *teach* **YOU!!!** scoring. *I know nothing about it* & make my suggestion with all humility. I may be quite wrong.[35]

The alteration was duly made, clinching the superb effect of the modulation at the climax of the Finale.

That December marked a year since Jaeger had promised in the columns of the *Musical Times* to give the 'nerve-shattering' *Symphonie Pathétique* a 'well deserved rest', although Novello's had been sufficiently impressed by its business potential to issue an arrangement of the last movement for harmonium solo. Now for one of his final notices for 1899 he returned to that work, and another Tchaikovsky piece, with a humour now black and mocking, and a bitter repetition of his case against Wood and Newman.

> At the Tsar's – beg pardon, the Queen's Hall in Langham Place, the sentimental and unhappy hero of the 'Pathetic' Symphony has once more been killed with stroke of tam tam and decently buried with much growling of double-basses. The interesting event took place on the afternoon of October 28, and the occasion was the first of Mr. Newman's Symphony concerts. But weep not, gentle reader, he is not really dead; alas! he will come to life again to be scotched and killed many more times ere we have quite done with him. Not that we really object to the gentleman, for we have taken the liveliest interest in his 'life and death' ever since he made his appearance (and disappearance) at the Queen's Hall in 1894, under the aegis of kind and sympathetic Sir Alexander Mackenzie. But even you, gentle reader, cannot deny that the *toujours perdrix* of tam tam suicides (for it *is* a suicide, of that we are convinced) and weeping double-bass funeral mutes does become monotonous.
>
> Mr. Wood and his merry men played the work quite magnificently. This much is due to them. Equally fine was the performance of a symphonic poem, 'Fatum' (Destiny), a

> posthumous work of unhappy Tchaikovsky, who suffers much from those who, ghoul-like, dig up his musical remains, however bad. This 'poem' is unworthy of Tchaikowsky, and its 'Fatum' should have been what the composer doubtless meant it to be – viz., oblivion. If Mr. Wood spent half as much time in the preparation of some representative British work as he must have devoted to this wretched 'Fatum' how happy some native composer might be made! British art is just good enough for the Promenade concerts, in the estimation of the Queen's Hall authorities; but 'taboo' is their motto for the higher class Symphony concerts. In no other country in the world is such an unjust and unpatriotic insult to native art possible or even conceivable, and nowhere in England except at the Queen's (save the mark!) Hall.[36]

Earlier, in November, Jaeger had shared some more banter about the English and patriotism with Elgar and had referred to the Boer War as 'this glorious campaign for Goldmines' – but in matters musical Jaeger was evidently more English than the English.

5 1900: Mystic, Sublime, Superb

Jaeger seems to have been unwell during the last weeks of 1899, and early in the new year Elgar wrote anxiously to enquire after him. Jaeger replied with a long, now-lost letter which seems to have mentioned various works by the other composers he supported, including Coleridge-Taylor. But Jaeger's estimation of his latest works, the *Hiawatha* Overture and the *Solemn Prelude*, had evidently declined dramatically. Elgar agreed, and could not resist emphasizing his own efforts on behalf of the composer at Jaeger's behest.

> I think you are right about C. Taylor – I was cruelly disillusioned by the Overture to Hiawatha which I think only 'rot' – & the Worcester prelude did not shew *any* signs of cumulative invention or effect: the scoring is altogether uninteresting & *harsh* of both these works: wherever I've been people are sympathetic & kind on acct: of the colour question and he is well advertised & backed but his later work is insincere & cannot do any real good: this is what I feel: I have never worked so hard for any man before – on *your* recommendation – & I took a real pleasure in him.[1]

The charge of insincerity was a serious one to both Elgar and Jaeger, who thought alike in many ways, and Coleridge-Taylor's lack of self-criticism coupled with his work pressures were seeming to retard his development. Elgar had also changed his opinion of *Hora Novissima*: 'I fear I didn't make much of Parker – I think that's the last item in your scrawl.'

That January the arrangements for the Birmingham Festival were at last finalized, largely due to the diplomatic efforts of the Festival chairman, George Johnstone. The biblical subject for which the Judas music had been intended was put aside, and Elgar decided upon a setting of Newman's *Dream of Gerontius* poem. Johnstone went to London and negotiated personally with Alfred Littleton, who agreed to publish the work and who noted after the meeting that the sum of two hundred pounds had been agreed for all rights. But Johnstone's letter to Elgar confirming details of the meeting referred to a royalty as well, 'if there is any profit on the Sale after the Two Hundred pounds has been cleared'. And there for the time being the matter rested.

Jaeger returned to the attack on Wood, Newman and Russian music in the January *Musical Times*, but his main victim on this occasion, Alexander Glazunov, was criticized more in sorrow than anger. Tchaikovsky's Fifth Symphony evidently found favour and gave scope for some pictorial imagery, although Wood's reading was compared unfavourably to that of Nikisch, the German conductor on whom Wood and later Adrian Boult modelled themselves; he had conducted four concerts in London in 1895, at one of which he introduced the Tchaikovsky Symphony.

> Glazounoff's latest novelty, produced with his usual loving solicitude for Russian art by Mr. Henry J. Wood, at Mr. Newman's Symphony Concert of November 25th, was a Suite drawn from a ballet, 'Raymonda' (Op. 57), ten movements of greatly varying character, some of them of such short duration that even much finer music could not possibly have made an effect in such small forms. They include more or less fantastic Dances, Fanfares, Preludes, *Entr'acts*, &c., and, with the exception of the final number ('Triumph of Love and Nuptial Fete'), not one leaves a satisfactory impression, though they are invariably scored with the rarest art of an acknowledged master amongst orchestral colourists. We doubt whether we shall ever hear the Suite again, for its reception was chilling ... The Symphony was Tchaikovsky's gorgeous No. 5 (E minor), with that most voluptuous of symphonic slow movements, and the dashing, exciting *Finale*, which always suggests a battle with triumphant issue to us (a cavalry charge and much flashing of sabres bare, for choice). Mr. Wood and his orchestra were at their best in this Symphony, but why the conductor should completely ignore the composer's distinct direction, *'molto piu tranquillo'*, when attacking the yearning syncopated subject in the first *Allegro*, is a mystery. Those who heard Herr Nikisch's performance in the same hall some years ago will remember the great effect he produced with just this theme by taking it at a slower speed. Mr. Wood scampers over it in feverish haste.[2]

Jaeger had been trying to persuade Wood to mount a performance of the Variations, as he told Elgar:

> I am always bothering Wood about them, but I fear me (*Entre nous*) the Q. Hall management is summat in a 'badish' way. Don't whisper a word to anybody!!! For I MAY be wrong. Won't you come on Saturday & hear the Wagner *novelty* which *I have unearthed?*[3]

Perhaps Jaeger's attacks over Russian music had somewhat prejudiced Wood, although he had always been anxious to pay tribute to the quality of the conductor's performances. But the conductor had certainly taken note of Jaeger's suggestion that he perform the original version of the Prelude to Act III of *Tannhäuser*, which Jaeger had made the subject of a *Musical Times* article some two years previously. He rather pathetically concluded the letter to Elgar by admitting that, in company with Ivor Atkins and others, he was 'saving up' for a copy of the Variations full score, although the composer immediately wrote to suggest Jaeger took one and had it charged to his account. In the same letter, of 5 February, he told Jaeger for the first time of the background to the Birmingham commission, and that he was setting Newman's *Gerontius*; he would have to use the Judas music in it. Preoccupied, he asked Alice to write to Jaeger a week later with press cuttings of performances of the Variations at Birmingham and Manchester under Richter, suggesting that they might be shown to Alfred Littleton or Edwards. The result was to be found in the next month's *Musical Times* in the 'Occasional Notes' column:

> There is no variation in regard to the success which attends Mr. Elgar's 'Variations'. Herein is no 'enigma'. Wherever and whenever these orchestral dainties are performed they naturally charm the ears of those who listen to them. Under the fostering care of Dr. Richter the work has recently conquered the strongholds of hardware and cotton – Birmingham

> and Manchester to wit. In both these centres of musical activity the 'Variations' and their composer have been received during the past month with genuine appreciation and enthusiasm. As with the London critics, the initials at the head of each variation seem to have been the initial difficulty of the provincial gentlemen of the press in enigmatising – if the word be allowed – the conception of the composition. Especially is this the case in regard to that mysterious individual, 'Nimrod' (No. 9), who is thus speculated upon by one of the critical fraternity: 'No. 9, perhaps, refers to a mighty hunter (Nimrod); but we rejoice to record that no tarantivys are heard, though perhaps Dr. Richter, who was once an orchestral horn-player, even as the composer was a violinist, would have taken especial interest in the feature. They key, however, is E flat, which is in itself suspicious. Mr. Elgar's 'Nimrod' appears to be enjoying a peaceful old age, marked by Handelian aspirations. A pearl in a string of pearls.' This is exceedingly imaginative. Supposing, however, that the veteran 'Nimrod' is really flesh and blood, and that he is an out and out Wagnerite, what must be the old gentleman's feelings in regard to these deductions? But the question is: Has anyone yet succeeded in hunting 'Nimrod' down?[4]

The punning indicated F.G. Edwards's hand, but no doubt the paragraph represented a private conspiracy of humour with Jaeger. If so, it was a rare example of public collaboration.

Elgar was pressing on hard with *Gerontius*, but he and Alice took a break in London for a few days at the end of February, attending a Crystal Palace *Sea Pictures* with Rosa Burley and spending a 'nice evening' with the Jaegers at Margravine Gardens. It would have been a first opportunity for them to hear parts of the new work, and they were so taken with the 'Angel's Song' that Elgar was asked to write it out for them to sing and play at home; Isabella was by then some seven months pregnant. Five days later, on 3 March, Jaeger received the vocal score manuscript of the work as far as the beginning of 'Sanctus fortis', and the remainder of Part 1 followed on the 20th. Elgar anxiously asked for confirmation by wire that the manuscript – the only copy – had arrived, and requested two copies of proofs. Jaeger was unwell at this time and may have been away from the office. Elgar received only one proof copy from Berners Street, but on his return Jaeger wrote promising three, and praised the music so far as 'shivery' and 'awe-inspiring'. He went on to tell how he had had lunch with Robert Newman and the Belgian violinist Ysaÿe, and had persuaded Newman to put on the 'Triumphal March' from *Caractacus* at Queen's Hall. Jaeger also seized the opportunity to suggest the Overture *Froissart* when Newman asked for a short English novelty for the forthcoming London Musical Festival.

There had been signs recently that Jaeger's persistent campaign against Russian music at Queen's Hall was paying off. The March *Musical Times* noted gratefully that

> The prospectus of the new series of Symphony Concerts at the Queen's Hall is a document that caused us to rub our eyes. It did not contain a single specimen of the Russian school, but, on the other hand, quite a respectable selection from the works of our native composers! Have our protests against the anti-British policy of the Queen's Hall authorities availed, and are the classics, as well as our own representative composers, to come by their own at last? It is devoutly to be hoped ...[5]

In the same number Jaeger began his review of some of the earlier concerts that year with

> How does the public appreciate the change of policy at Queen's Hall? The answer was given by the very large audiences that flocked to the first two concerts and expressed their satisfaction with the new order of things in enthusiastic applause. So far, so good. Let us hope that Messrs. Newman and Wood will have no occasion to regret their right about face. The public will show them that the announcement of an English work does not frighten them away if only the rest of the programme be made attractive. They have on many previous occasions proved their willingness to give the heartiest welcome to our native composers' best works.[6]

Meanwhile Jaeger had begun to take the measure of the *Gerontius* poem and wrote to offer encouragement over the challenge Elgar faced in setting it. He was still unwell and in concluding the letter he mentioned his cough to Elgar for the first time; 'Good night, I am very tired, have a dreadful cough & feel altogether out of sorts. Want a change, but can't get one.' Elgar was concerned; he wrote to Jaeger three times over the following three days on a variety of matters, and each time invited him to Malvern for the much needed change. 'Why shouldn't you come down this week over Sunday?' was the final appeal. 'You could if you tried & wouldn't sulk in state: do try – it might do you good. I've pills – draughts – lotions – whiskey – tobacco – golf – all waiting for you.' It was a bad time as Isabella, now in the final month of her pregnancy, was unwell also, and there was staff absence at Berners Street. Jaeger declined: 'I have to work hard & I'm poor, 2 good reasons for staying in London, worse luck.' He was so tired and busy that he even admitted to not having looked at the set of *Gerontius* proofs that he had taken home. But he thanked Elgar for the copy of the Angel's Song which had arrived at last, although both Jaegers were so unwell that it would have to wait nearly a fortnight for a run-through. Isabella, a capable singer, was the first to perform the haunting music. She wrote to Elgar to thank him – 'I have gone through the day with the opening bars ringing in my head' – and Jaeger followed up next day with comments of his own, finding the music 'uncanny'.

Jaeger had found time to study the proofs of Part 1 of *Gerontius.* His immediate point of reference was Wagner, and he looked forward to the climax of the work in Part 2.

> There is some gorgeous stuff in it ... Since 'Parsifal' nothing of this mystic, religious kind of music has appeared to my knowledge that displays the same power & beauty as yours. Like Wagner you seem to grow with your greater, more difficult subject & I am now most curious *and* anxious to Know how you will deal with that part of the poem where the Soul goes within the presence of the almighty. *There* is a subject for you! Whatever else you may do, *don't* be *theatrical*![7]

Elgar would reply that none of the action takes place in the presence of God, implying that no theatricalism would be necessary. Jaeger continued by comparing *Gerontius* with Horatio Parker's new work for that year's Hereford Three Choirs, *A Wanderer's Psalm.* The comparison enabled him to point up Parker's weaknesses together with the limitations of Novello's advisors.

> Parker's Stuff is what *pleases West & Button*! It is such good church Style!! I don't at all wish to sneer at it, for it looks powerful enough stuff. But the more nearly a composer

> goes to that precious 'Church Style' the greater he is in the eyes of W, B & Co so it seems to me. They cannot see much beyond the 'what is' & what-used-to-be! Freshness, originality, individuality & the great Beauty that creates *new* wonders for us & goes for more than much solid workmanship leave them untouched & un-excited.[8]

That freshness and individuality Jaeger continued to find in the choral music, at any rate, of Coleridge-Taylor, and he devoted two columns of the April *Musical Times* to what had now become the *Hiawatha* trilogy, for a third and final part had been added with the composition of *Hiawatha's Departure*, given its first performance on 22 March. Any doubts concerning the *Hiawatha* overture for Norwich were cast aside as once more Jaeger sang Coleridge-Taylor's praises in extravagant terms. Twice in the first paragraph he repeated Schumann's phrase welcoming Chopin:

> ... we say once more to all who have ears to hear: 'Hats off, gentlemen, a genius!'... Need we hesitate to say this, or stop to criticise, when in the presence of a work so absolutely beautiful and so absolutely unique? We think not. Here we have at last what England has been waiting for ever since she began to repudiate the taunt that she was unmusical, that the creative gift was denied to her musicians. 'Hiawatha' is a creation if there ever was one in our art. It boldly crosses the line that divides the abnormally clever from the simply beautiful, the obviously inspired. Who can define inspiration in music? Who can analyse the qualities in Mr. Coleridge-Taylor's music that touch singers until they can hardly produce their notes, and audiences so that they cannot read their programmes or scores? ... We have it on the authority of the soloists engaged on these occasions, and we have heard it from many members of the choir, that hardly anything they have ever sung has moved them to attempt, and yet (for the reasons stated above) prevented them from achieving their very best, as has this beautiful music of our young countryman. And the indefinable Something that can produce this greatest of 'Marvels and many wonders' must be, *is* inspiration.[9]

In a piece of writing that once again reflected Jaeger's strong emotional responses, some mention of an especially warm reception for the composer himself on the occasion was inevitable. Any previous criticism of Coleridge-Taylor, and thoughts of the music of *Gerontius* that he had heard so far, were swept away in something of a tide of hyperbole.

> Coming now to the performance of the 22nd ult., let us say at once that the young composer's triumph was complete. Rarely, if ever, has such a spontaneous outburst of genuine enthusiasm been witnessed in London at the production of a new work than that displayed by the large audience after the first part of the concert, which concluded with 'The Death of Minnehaha'. The pent-up feeling of the deeply moved audience relieved itself in such cheers and shouts of approbation as must have warmed and gladdened the heart of the composer and, if we may incidentally say so, also of those who for some years past have hailed the young Anglo-African as *the* coming man in music.[10]

For Jaeger, who had so much personal commitment invested in his protegés, and for Novello's, who had made their own business investment in Coleridge-Taylor at Jaeger's insistence, the vindication was sweet, even if the judgement as a whole has not stood the test of time. Indeed *Hiawatha's Departure* had been achieved under Jaeger's harshest criticism.

> The earliest draft of *The Departure* was a failure in several ways ... Jaeger played over the manuscipt, and came near to tears; he thought the choruses commonplace, the melodies in the setting of the scenes where the Black-Robed Chief appears little better than mediocre hymn tunes. 'This will never do,' he wrote frankly to the composer. 'The public expects you to progress, to do better work than before; this is your worst.' It was not simple advice to offer to one whose name started out [*sic*] from every important newspaper of England as one of the most remarkable men of his day; but the advice was given, and it is to Coleridge-Taylor's credit that he received it modestly and admitted its truth. At once he recast the whole work, consulting Jaeger at frequent intervals; and the final draft was worthy to be a pendant to *The Wedding Feast* and *The Death of Minnehaha*.[11]

And in the book of words for the Royal Choral Society concert, Jaeger perhaps sought to give the completed trilogy greater status in the eyes of those like Hans Richter who tended to dismiss Coleridge-Taylor's music, by comparing it to a symphony. *Hiawatha's Wedding Feast* was the opening allegro, *The Death of Minnehaha* the slow movement, and *Hiawatha's Departure* comprised elements of scherzo and finale.

Two other works by other young composers of interest to Jaeger were given notices in that month's *Musical Times*, Josef Holbrooke's setting of Poe's *The Raven*, and William Henry Bell's *Walt Whitman* Symphony, which had been given without its second movement. Both works had been played at the Crystal Palace. Bell was a former student of composition at the Royal Academy who had also taken lessons in counterpoint from Stanford; since 1893 he had held an organist post in St Alban's. Jaeger appeared to prefer his latest work to the *Pardoner's Tale* Symphonic Poem of the previous year; he thought the work 'made a most favourable impression by reason of its manly sentiment and masterly development ... Mr. Bell is to be heartily congratulated upon his healthiness of mind, and we hope to hear his symphony at an early date in its entirety in central London.'[12] Holbrooke was a younger figure, having left the Royal Academy as recently as 1898, and while making appearances as pianist and conductor in the cause of British music, attempted to devote himself to composition. He was a brilliant composer but a difficult man, as both Jaeger and Elgar were to discover; Jaeger summed up *The Raven* as a work of 'decided promise, for it attests to the possession of lively imagination, invention, considerable knowledge, and resource.' But there were aspects of the work that may have seemed similar to the approach of the Russian Nationalists.

> ... his 'Raven' is deficient in regard to balance of tone in orchestration. There are invariably two ways of creating a desired effect. The one is allied to beauty, the other to ugliness. Of late a preference has, in most instances, been shown for the latter, because the writers had not sufficient strength to seek the former without becoming sentimental and undramatic; but ugliness is bad art. Mr. Holbrooke shows that he can invent expressive melodies, can develop them in a musicianly and interesting manner; but his endeavours to support in his orchestration the supernatural in Edgar Poe's lugubrious poem result, for the most part, in crudities and harsh sounds that seem to blaze forth their inability to combine with anything approaching a harmonious whole.[13]

Jaeger's daughter, christened Mary Eva Lucy and later known in the family as Maimie, was born on 26 April at Margravine Gardens. As he confessed to Elgar, the new parent doted on his daughter; in return she remained devoted to her father and his memory all her life. The exchange of letters with Elgar concerning the happy event marked another intimacy in their friendship. Elgar had apologized for troubling Jaeger over some MS; Jaeger replied with news of his daughter, and a warm response to the apology.

> ... my dear wife gave birth to a little *girl yesterday* morning at 3 a.m. Both she & the little bundle of sweet Humanity are doing well, I'm happy to say, & though Bell 'wanted' a boy, *I wanted a girl*, & she has kindly & sweetly 'obliged' me. I have always been devoted to little girls & love their pretty ways & prattle. The wife is most happy with what Providence has given her, & to watch her fondling the little stranger sends a thrill of Happiness through me. But enough of this ... Go on 'troubling' me, my dear friend, I love to do all I can for one whom one loves as a man & friend, and admires sincerely, greatly, as an artist, a weaver of most wondrous sounds, whose genius, moreover, I had the happiness to appreciate & extol before almost any one of my colleagues! Bless you & 'trouble' away.[14]

Elgar, deep in work on *Gerontius*, responded to the news about the birth with a suitable phrase from the poem, although, like Jaeger, he thought a little male gruffness appropriate.

> I was thinking very much of you & your house during the last few days & as I was making the copy for the printer of this:-
>
> 'Hark to those sounds!
> *They come of tender beings angelical*
> Least and most childlike of the sons of God'
>
> my thoughts somehow, illogically, connected the words with you & I wondered if anything were happening.
>
> Your letter gave us the very welcome news – we do hope, pray & trust that all goes on well with both your dear ones; I *quite* know your joy – great & deserved, dear man – in your little one, for I have been thro' it all & know the strange, new feelings that come into life – however I won't preach.[15]

And he signed himself 'With much love'.

Jaeger at last took up Elgar's invitation to stay at Malvern early in May, after a visit to Ivor Atkins at Worcester to take in a Festival Choral Society performance of the first two parts of the *Hiawatha* trilogy under the composer's direction. He arrived at Craeg Lea, the Elgars' handsome detached house on the eastern side of the Hills at Malvern Wells in time for lunch on Friday 4 May, and stayed until the Sunday afternoon, a little guilty at leaving Isabella and the baby. But it was a musical weekend, for there was to be a rehearsal and concert by the Worcestershire Philharmonic Society. Both occasions were followed, as custom dictated, by a substantial tea for various members and friends at the home of Martina Hyde, with Winifred Norbury joint secretary of the Society. It would have been a first opportunity for Jaeger to meet many of Elgar's local circle, although the day of the concert itself was best remembered by another 'variant' who lived at something of a distance, Dora Penny, the daughter of Alfred Penny, the Rector and Rural Dean of Wolverhampton. A widower, he had married Alice Elgar's close friend Mary Frances Baker of Hasfield Court. 'Dorabella', as she became known, had first met Elgar as a new family friend in 1895. An attractive, musical girl of twenty-one, she had become fascinated by Elgar from that first meeting and became devoted to him and his music. She left an account of her visit to that Worcestershire Philharmonic concert of 5 May which shows that her friendship with August Jaeger began as easily and spontaneously as had that with Elgar. Jaeger was by no means lacking in susceptibility to what he liked to call in Goethe's phrase the 'ewige-Weibliche'; family legend tells how he would happily go past his stop in order to continue studying a pretty face on the bus. His friendship with Dora Penny brought out the racy, sociable pleasure-loving side of his character. She wrote that

> After the concert we had a most hilarious tea at the Hydes, and when tea was over we said our farewells and went to Foregate Street station on our way back to Malvern. Mr. Jaeger and I became fast friends at once. He *was* a most delightful person. His English was fluent, not to say voluble, but with a strong German accent. He asked me if I knew Gilbert and Sullivan well and we sang 'Oh, Captain Shaw!' on Foregate Street platform while waiting for the train. E.E. in the background remarked, 'Now they're off.'
>
> That journey was one of the noisiest I have ever made. Our party filled a compartment, and all the way Mr. Jaeger was telling me with great volubility and much gesture how wonderful *Gerontius* was. E.E. was trying to stop him and was calling him a whole string of comic names, and the rest of the party were in fits of laughter.
>
> On Sunday E.E. and Mr. Jaeger shut themselves into the study all the morning ...[16]

Another 'variant', the Malvern architect and painter Arthur Troyte Griffith, came to lunch, and Dora wrote that Elgar 'was in the best of good spirits', with a good deal of chaff and repartee being exchanged. 'We coruscated like mad', she noted in her diary, together with her estimation of Jaeger – a 'charming person'. Jaeger told her about his work and promised to send a copy of an analysis of *Hiawatha* that he had written. In future he would write her many letters about Elgar's works as they were written, together with proof copies, although she confessed to destroying many of them in a fit of tidying up in 1914.[17] Dora Penny was a genuine student of music, taking regular singing lessons, belonging to the Wolverhampton Choral Society for many years, and forming a string band which she conducted. Together with the element of mutual attraction, there was in the relationship something of the teacher-pupil element as well.

> In the years to come he was very good to me and was a most delightful and interesting friend ... I went with him to a great many orchestral concerts, which was not only extremely enjoyable, but was quite a musical education. What I enjoyed most of all was when he took me to a rehearsal in the morning, followed by luncheon at some restaurant, and the concert in the afternoon. That I usually came armed with miniature full scores seemed to please him very much. He used to say:
>
> 'Ha! very good. That is the way to enjoy the music.'
>
> But there were many times when he wrote and asked me to go up for a concert, and when I had said I was uncertain if I could manage it – much as I should like it – he wrote back:
>
> 'Now, Dorabella, naughty girl, you must not tease small Germans so!'[18]

Dora Penny was also a lifelong seeker of the truth behind the 'Enigma' puzzle, and Jaeger seems to have had little confidence in his ability to keep it from her.

> It was on one of the first occasions when I met Mr Jaeger in London – at a rehearsal of the *Variations,* I think – that I tackled him about the Enigma.
>
> 'Now, Dorabella, you must be a good girl and not ask me about that. I do not suppose that I could keep it from you of you were to plead with me, but the dear E.E. did make me promise not to tell you.'
>
> 'Oh, he did, did he?' I said slowly, 'then I will never ask you.'
>
> He kissed my hand.'Forgive my funny little foreign ways, Dorabella dear?'
>
> I never mentioned the subject to him again.[19]

Jaeger's departure from Craeg Lea was something of a scramble owing to confusion over train times, and Alice wrote to apologize, 'forgive such mistakes, it must be owing to the 'Martha' like duties I have to accomplish while wishing to dwell in the IDEAL'. Jaeger responded with a 'thank you' letter in which he reinforced Alice's 'ideal-ism'.

> ... I enjoyed my stay at your hospitable House *immensely* & thank you & Mr Elgar very much for your kindness. I can quite appreciate how two 'ideal angeleyte' people like yourself & E.E. must suffer occasionally when coming into contact with the common-place in things or men – (e.g. Philistines like 'Nimrod!'). Though I am made of commoner clay, I can sympathize with you twain most throughly, & wish you could be spared all unpleasantnesses. But it has ever been a law, I daresay, that genius must suffer ...[20]

If it was a diplomatic letter in the circumstances – the mistake over train times had been Alice's – nevertheless Jaeger meant every word of it and a friendship with Alice as well as Edward Elgar was being cemented, especially as she asked Jaeger to polish the translations from German literature which she continued to produce. They were all to meet up again in London on 10 May, when Elgar conducted *Sea Pictures* at the Queen's Hall with Clara Butt. It was a busy and sociable day. Both lunch and supper were taken at nearby Pagani's, the Italian restaurant in Great Portland Street which had become a Mecca for artists, writers and musicians, and which was no doubt the scene of many of Jaeger's working lunches with a wide variety of contacts. Established some thirty years before as a *patisserie*, Pagani's had developed into a large and important concern, with several floors, a lift and a Masonic banqueting-room with mirrors and painted trellis-work. But its pride and joy, and a great source of attraction for Jaeger no doubt, was the second floor Artists' Room, the walls of which were covered with autographs, caricatures, photographs and sketches of the great. The autograph collection grew to include those of Paderewski, Chaminade, Tosti, Tchaikovsky, Calvé and Melba, Toscanini, Richard Strauss, Leoncavallo, Mascagni, Lamoureux and Kreisler; after the maladroit cleaning efforts of a well-meaning waiter they were protected by sheets of glass. The room, and Pagani's spaghetti, were renowned far and wide; one wit had contributed 'Abandon all hope, Oh ye who go out!' to the graffiti.

Back at work, Jaeger began an article for the *Musical Times* about *Gerontius.* He had also been discussing with Elgar a new separate piano arrangement of the 'Dorabella'

Intermezzo from the Variations. Jaeger revealed to Dora Penny just how hard he was working on what would become a full analysis of the new work, in a letter that, like many others, was only partially preserved in her book.

> May 25th, 1900 [.] Gerontius grows more and more masterly as it proceeds. It is quite wonderful in parts: mystic, sublime, superb. I have to write a preliminary review of the work in the Musical Times for October, so I am already studying it hard, in Buses, Trains, everywhere. Have it always in my pocket, in fact & go to Bed with it.
>
> We are now discussing the publication of a new pianists arrangement of 'Dorabella' separately and I hope something will come of it. I shall harp on the subject till I have found a good pianist-arranger to make the proper (difficult) P-F arrangement, and till I see the thing in print with a portrait of the original 'Dorabella.' Eh? Fine idea! Send your photo at once!![21]

With just four months to go before the Birmingham Festival, Elgar was working intensively at the second part of *Gerontius*. That month he had sent Jaeger vocal score manuscript up to the beginning of 'Praise to the Holiest,' together with the Angel of the Agony music – originally intended for Judas. When he had had a little time to absorb the music, Jaeger wrote of his reactions in one of his most eloquent letters. Wagner and Tchaikovsky were immediate points of comparison; but there was a prophetic warning as well.

> I have just spent an hour over your last batch of proofs ... and, Oh! I am half undone, & I tremble after the *tremendous* exaltation I have gone through. I don't pretend to know *everything* that has been written since Wagner breathed his last in Venice 17 years ago, but I have not seen or heard *anything* since 'Parsifal' that has stirred me, & spoken to me with the trumpet tongue of genius as has this part of your latest, & *by far* greatest work. I except, *perhaps* [,] the Pathetic Symphony, although *that* is but wordly, pessimistic, depressing, whereas your wonderful music is inexpressibly & most wonderfully elevating, 'aloof', mystic, & heart-moving as by the force of a great *compassion.* I cannot describe it!
>
> But that solo of the 'Angel of the Agony' is overpowering & I feel as if I wanted to kiss the hand that penned these marvellous pages. Those poignant melodies, those heart-piercing, *beautiful* harmonies! I recognise the chief theme as having belonged to 'Judas'. Nobody could dream that it was not originally *inspired* by *these very words* of *Newmans.*
>
> You must not, *cannot* expect this work of yours to be appreciated by the ordinary amateur (*or* Critic!) after once hearing. You will have to rest content, as other great men had to before you, if a few friends & enthusiasts hail it as a work of genius, & become devoted to its creator.[22]

Jaeger concluded by expressing doubts over his ability to tackle the analysis of the work – 'I am such a wretched *amateur*' – and reserving some points of criticism for a later occasion. But the letter had found its mark. Two days later Elgar sent the finished 'Praise to the Holiest' and wrote, 'I can't tell you how much good your letter has done me: I *do* dearly like to be *understood.*' Elgar wrote again the next day, 1 June, to return some proofs. Publication day for the *Musical Times* was the first of the month, and he addded a postscript, 'M. T. just come – good! but no time to read just now'.

Jaeger had several contributions in that month's edition, including reviews of Newman's second London Musical Festival at Queen's Hall, the *Sea Pictures* concert, a new Suite by Coleridge-Taylor, and a National Sunday League concert of English music. But Elgar's interest would have been in Jaeger's article on the Worcestershire Philharmonic Concert he had attended over the recent Malvern weekend. The review began however with mention of the *Hiawatha* and *Minnehaha* concert given by the Worcester Festival Choir conducted by Coleridge-Taylor. The performance of the Choir, trained and prepared by the 'young and enthusiastic' Ivor Atkins, met with warm praise.

> We have heard many performances of the two cantatas, but can honestly affirm that the small, but most excellent Worcester Society was an easy first as regards those qualities which constitute good chorus singing – *e.g.*, a good, round 'musical' tone, crisp attack, and exact release, true intonation, clear enunciation, and an intelligent appreciation of the emotional side of the music in all its varying moods. These points are not brought out without much careful and systematic work by a thoroughly competent choir-trainer, and to Mr. Atkins are due the thanks of those who were at last enabled to hear such beautiful works beautifully and expressively sung.[23]

Unfortunately the instrumental accompaniment seemed no match for the standard set by the Choir:

> Would that the orchestra had been as efficient. But, truth to tell, it was not, the wood-wind and percussion especially leaving not a little to desire. Though drums and cymbals were represented, the frequent and often striking effects of the cymbals struck with drumstick were omitted; the tambourine was conspicuous by its absence, though, surely, any amateur might have struck it; and the triangle had no more music in its soul than a tin spoon.[24]

It was a pity that Coleridge-Taylor's delightful percussion effects should have been spoiled, and Elgar may have especially noted Jaeger's points in this regard. When extra percussion was occasionally required for his Worcestershire Philharmonic Concerts, he would make sure to cover all the requirements, commandeering friends as necessary. On one occasion Winifred Norbury, an excellent pianist and singer, was not only asked to play the triangle, but expected to undergo some personal tuition with Elgar himself. But Jaeger was able to add a word of praise for the orchestra elsewhere, as under Atkins's 'spirited direction' they enterprisingly tackled Tchaikovsky's *Romeo and Juliet* Overture-Fantaisia in tandem with the posthumous duet of the same name which had been the subject of Jaeger's 1896 letter to the *Musical Times*. The combination, perhaps a result of his suggestion at the end of the letter, together with some subsequent verbal hints, must have given Jaeger some satisfaction. He noted, 'These two works were on this occasion performed side by side for the first time in England, and probably anywhere'.

Before moving on to discuss the full programme conducted by Elgar at the Worcestershire Philharmonic concert Jaeger could not resist a teasing comment about the Society's personnel – all the Society's rehearsals and performances took place in the afternoon, which says something about music and the leisured classes at that time; 'It was a smart enough function in all conscience. A dream of fair women! Such gowns! such hats! But the music's the thing we have to discuss.' Jaeger praised the variety of music chosen, including works by Wagner, Brahms, Beethoven, Granville Bantock, Arcadelt, Bellini and Ponchielli; 'There is eclecticism for you, ye London compilers of hackneyed programmes!' He could not care for the Bantock work, but was prepared to follow Elgar's lead over it.

> Mr. Bantock's 'Scene' left us (and the public) utterly unimpressed. Much as we desire and strive to appreciate native music, we confess that this most productive of English composers has not yet succeeded in convincing our dull brain that his 'Kehama', in nineteen (or is it twenty-nine?) movements – most monstrous of wild-fowls amongst many modern developments of the symphony – contains any beautiful music. Yet there must be something 'in it', or why should a brilliant musician and trenchant critic like Mr. Elgar perform it? We cannot solve the riddle, but wait and hope that our eyes may be opened to perceive beauties to which we are still blind, alas![25]

Bantock himself had remembered his prediction of 'that British composer whose coming we await', and proved an immediate champion of the Variations, inviting Elgar to conduct the second performance of the work with his municipal orchestra at New Brighton, just outside Liverpool, at a concert which included various other Elgar works. Elgar was no doubt happy to return the compliment by producing one of Bantock's works on this occasion, and despite the wide differences in their musical natures, the two men always got on well in a jocular kind of way; tobacco and horseracing in particular were shared interests. To Jaeger Bantock's music, with its programmatic nature, highly coloured orchestration and its leanings towards the oriental and exotic, may have resembled the modern Russian school too closely. Although Novello's published some of Bantock's music, he was one progressive, active figure with whom Jaeger's dealings seem to have been minimal.

Jaeger's comments on the comparative merits of the performances put up by the two Worcester bodies showed him anxious to be seen as even-handed; he seems to have thought Elgar's orchestra the better, while Atkins's chorus took the laurels. There was, as well, admiring praise of Elgar the conductor.

> ... Mr Elgar conducted with the thorough *savoir faire* and *sangfroid* resulting from a most intimate acquaintance with the technique of the orchestra, long experience, and an inborn aptitude, allied to an artist's temperament and a genuine enthusiasm for the beautiful or worthy wherever found in our art. We shall hear more of Mr. Elgar as a conductor in the future, or we are much mistaken.[26]

Jaeger was right to point up Elgar's long orchestral apprenticeship, but many of the Worcestershire Philharmonic Society musicians under his baton might not have been quite so complimentary about his conducting. As a final kindness, no doubt at Elgar's request, Jaeger made mention of another Worcester concert that took place the day after he left Malvern, when 'the "Civil–Military Band," conducted by Mr. Frank Elgar (brother of the composer), performed a highly interesting programme of pieces to a crowded and most appreciative audience'. The review concluded with even-handed compliments all round to Worcester's musical societies, and one of the classical quotations that Jaeger still liked to embellish his writings with. 'Altogether, music seems in a most flourishing condition in the old Cathedral town. There seems plenty of room for the various societies. May they grow and prosper side by side in wholesome and stimulating rivalry, and may their watchword ever be: 'Res severa verum gaudium!'[27]

The second of June saw 'E's dearest birfday', part of which he spent playing golf; he was just days away from finishing the vocal score of *Gerontius.* Jaeger continued to enthuse about the work to Dora Penny, and in a preserved fragment of a letter written to her that day, hit for the first time on an idea which has become essential in any description of the composer's work: Elgar the dreamer.

> June 2nd, 1900 Dear Miss Allegretto (♩ = 80) G major = $\frac{3}{4}$
>
> ... In Gerontius we have a great, deep *thinker* & *dreamer* allying wonderful music to wonderful words, a powerful intellect doing its greatest for a great poem ... There is stuff in Gerontius that is perfectly beautiful, original & heart rending![28]

Five days later Elgar sent the last vocal score pages of *Gerontius* to Jaeger, adding 'God bless you, Minrod. Here's the end.' Jaeger telegraphed 'Finis coronat opus' in reply. There now remained almost four months to the day to have the work printed and rehearsed for the Birmingham première. The engravers at Novello's were still working on the vocal score of Part 1; not a note of the demanding music had been rehearsed, and all the orchestration remained to be done.

Elgar went to London for a few days, staying with his Malvern friend Jebb-Scott at the Grand Hotel. It was a well-deserved break and he took in a variety of diversions from 'Rip van Winkle' to *The Twilight of the Gods* to a Richter concert followed by supper with Jaeger, who had invited him to Margravine Gardens to meet the tenor Henry Beaumont and the conductor Allen Gill, soon to become Director of the Alexandra Palace Choral Society. Jaeger was keen to 'enthuse them' over *Gerontius.* He mentioned the meeting to Dora Penny, whose Aunt was a member of the Birmingham Festival Chorus, awaiting her first sight of the music, and repeated his anxieties concerning the reception of the work.

> June 9th, 1900. Dear Friend of E.E. He has arrived ... and is going to the Götterdämmerung tonight & the Richter Concert on Monday. Why cometh No. X of Variations Op 27 [*sic*] not to that? ... E. E. has sent the completion of his blessed Gerontius. The work undoes me utterly if I am in the mood. A few friends are coming to my house tomorrow to hear some of it. Elgar, whom I saw half and hour ago, says that perhaps he will come too. The Chorus parts will not be in the hands of the B' ham Singers for another 3 weeks or more; so your honoured aunt must possess her soul in Patience. I'll send you an advance copy of the Vocal Score for your very private use (mind you: Private!!) as soon as I possibly can. But that will not be for a week or two or three.
>
> ... No, the majority of the B'ham audience will not be able to appreciate Gerontius first time; too subtle & original & too mystic & beautiful, but a few like yourself & others will wax 'Wild' with enthusiasm.[29]

One other aspect of the new work which Jaeger thought might further militate against its acceptance was its Roman Catholic theology. 'There is a lot of *Joseph &*

Mary about the work', he wrote to Elgar on 14 June, and described the adverse reaction of the Secretary of a Glasgow Choir whom he had been trying to interest in performing *Gerontius*. The exchange of letters over the subject provides some of the only documentary sources we have for Jaeger's religious outlook. In suggesting that it would be realistic to modify the Catholic element in Newman's poem he claimed to be 'rather an Agnostic than anything else', and he finished the next letter by saying '"Religion" (Dogma) is a damnable thing at times & responsible for more misery & cruelty & General *Badness* than any other thing the Devil ever invented'.[30] Elgar would not hear of the poem being altered, and Jaeger was to be vindicated on later occasions when the Anglican authorities of the time insisted on changes being made for cathedral performances.

Jaeger continued to write to Elgar praising the musical achievement that *Gerontius* represented. 'I ... *must* write a line to let off steam, lest I explode during the night!' was how he began one letter, but his response was not merely subjective. Jaeger attempted to see the work in the widest possible context. '... with all my appreciation of English music I did not expect such a work to come out of this tight little island', he wrote, and 'This "Gerontius" is the most *beautiful* & *elevating* work since "Parsifal". Your music is in turn as original as Bruneau,[31] as "wild" & strong as Strauss, as impassioned as "Tchai", as ecstatic as Verdi (the latest Verdi) & as sane & noble & dignified as Brahms knew how to be. In fact to *me* who know *some*thing of modern music Your Gerontius is the finest, because the most *beautiful*, & *ennobling* work since Wagner's Sacred Drama'.[32]

However, Jaeger made many criticisms and detailed suggestions for improvement, many of which Elgar adopted.[33] As with the Variations, Jaeger did not allow his overflow of emotion to blunt his acute critical powers; indeed, the two seemed to go together. A point to which he returned several times was the treatment of the reaction of Gerontius to his momentary glimpse of the Almighty, 'Take me away'. In Elgar's original version this followed immediately after the three-part 'Lord thou hast been our refuge' chorus; Jaeger thought it weak and lacking in drama. Elgar set himself adamantly against any alteration to the passage, only to receive a further letter, one of Jaeger's toughest, pointing out that Wagner would have made it the climax of the whole work and accusing him of shirking the challenge. The accusation stung, but Elgar sent a revised version along with some doggerel verses and an extract from the 'Nimrod' Variation in two keys at once. Despite all the teasing Jaeger would not accept the new effort, and suggested that the vision of the Almighty be undertaken by 'the whole force' of the orchestra. Once again he hit hard by claiming that only a Wagner or a Strauss could achieve such a passage, and claimed to believe in Elgar's powers more than the composer himself. Finally Elgar gave way and added the orchestral passage, although claiming that he had thought of such an idea 'at first'. So the work became as it stands today, with a sense of complete inevitability about the sequence of orchestral crescendo leading to the momentary vision, followed by 'Take me Away', 'Lord, Thou hast been our refuge', and the Angel's Farewell. As with the Variations Finale, Jaeger's acumen had unerringly pinpointed a weakness in an otherwise inspired work, a passage where Elgar's judgement seemed to have deserted him and where Jaeger's intuition enabled him to know what Elgar wanted better than the composer himself. Moore has summed it up : 'These relatively small changes had the effect of altering the climax – and thus the emphasis – of the entire work from theology to drama. It made a creative contribution to Elgar's masterpiece without parallel in the history of relations between composer and publisher'.[34]

With the Festival deadline of early October looming ever closer, Elgar had begun to orchestrate *Gerontius*; Alice's first diary reference to the process was on 19 June. Meanwhile he was unable to correct the proofs of the final pages of vocal score because Novello's had not returned the manuscript to him, and further delay would be caused when the firm failed to agree to the provision of a second copy of the full score. Jaeger reported 'As to a *Duplicate* Full score, I spoke to Mr L. about it some days ago. He says, quite rightly I guess, that you must supply *one* Score to the publishers to work with – whether that be the original or the copy he careth not'. It was a typically businesslike if not cynical response and Jaeger was suitably apologetic about it, using a word with intimate resonance between them, again in the context of the firm's tight-fistedness. '... DON'T let the enigmatical, evasive answer annoy & worry You! *It's a way they's got at Novellos.*' But the lack of a second full score played its part in the difficulties and delay experienced by all concerned in the preparation of the work for its première, not least the conductor Hans Richter, whose first sight of the music was not until 23 September, just ten days in advance.

Jaeger had many other matters on his hands that summer as well as the problematical *Gerontius*, his continued reviewing for the *Musical Times* and a new baby in the household. He would have been responsible for seeing through the press the new works by Parry, Coleridge-Taylor and Parker commissioned for that year's Hereford Three Choirs Festival. Parker himself arrived in England from the States early in July, to conduct a performance of his *Hora Novissima* at Chester later that month. Jaeger wrote to welcome him and to deal with various details concerning the Festival work, *A Wanderer's Psalm*, about which he was duly complimentary; but his disclaimers of musicianship, after his recent creative contribution to *Gerontius*, speak overmuch of modesty. Jaeger seems never to have been perfectly at ease in dealing with Parker himself. The letter provided another opportunity to enthuse about *Gerontius*, although Parker seems to have been initially unsympathetic to Elgar's music.

1, Berners Street, W.
London, July 11th 1900

My dear Parker,

Welcome in old England & all good wishes for your success both at Chester & Hereford! Many thanks to you & Mrs Parker for your Kind words àpropos the birth of my little girl. Both Mother & cheeild are doing nicely [&] seem quite adorable to this proud Pa!

You *have* led me a nice dance over those things of yours. Why don't you *register* proofs that come from your benighted, 'star' bespangled (H. W. re)[35] fatherland?

Those last 20 odd pages never reached us! Now tell me please at once: 1stly Is 'A

Wanderer's Psalm' to remain the more or less 'aloud' title? (I have no views myself, I *never have* in writing to a big powerful chap like yourself, I only *quote*!) Sinclair don't like it, and his clergy don't, & nobody don't, only H.W. do!! *Secondly*. Are we to put on the Title: 'Composed for the Hereford Musical Festival 1900'? We don't *want* to, but will do so if you & Sinclair wish it.

You will make a *big* success with the work, I'm sure. Chori & audience will like it muchly & of the critics only the ridikkerlus Reminiscenten-Jäger (not A.J. of that ilk) will be 'narsty'.

Fine, wholesome, big & most effective stuff. No wonder our Readers revelled in it. Not being a musician, I don't Know anything about your masterly workmanship which they rave over.

A Full score of the *Hora* went to Chester yesterday. We pasted the proof-sheets together & made quite a nice job of it, as you will see. Strongly Bound too!

I hope I shall see something of you when you do come to London [.] Will you stay over the B'ham Festival? It will be the most memorable Festival to *English* Art since Festivals began [.] *2* REAL creations, *original, strong & beautiful*: Taylor's 'Hiawatha' & Elgar's extraordinary, *inspired* Gerontius, the biggest thing *any* English Composer has *ever* done. In fact, the most inspired work since Parsifal though of Course E. is *not* a Wagner quite! You don't think much of E.E. I Know, but wait till you hear this Gerontius. He has produced now what I prophesied years ago he *would* eventually produce, a master-piece of creative & original art.

Much love!

Ever yours

A.J. Jaeger[36]

Jaeger was preparing a lengthy *Musical Times* preview[37] of the new Hereford Festival works, which included a *Te Deum* by Parry and a song-cycle, *The Soul's Expression*, by Coleridge-Taylor, as well as the Parker work. The day after his letter to the American, Jaeger wrote to Elgar, 'Parker's stuff will make you laugh', although he was more complimentary about Coleridge-Taylor's song cycle. But he seized upon the orchestration of the Parry work unmercifully. 'Parry! oh. Parry!! very MUCH Parry!!! Toujours Parry!!!! Fiddles sawing all the time!!!!! DEAR old Parry!!!!!! Now if you could compose & Skoughre like that!!'.

With one of his staff on holiday, Jaeger was particularly pressed at this time, and he complained of regular late nights working at his *Musical Times* reviews. He had completed an analysis of *Hiawatha's Departure* for the Birmingham Festival, and became anxious to have confirmation of an earlier proposal for a similar publication about *Gerontius*, so that he could organize his time: '... I ought to know soon, for I do this kind of work in my own time after 6 p.m. So it takes me many days to concoct such an analysis.' Elgar established with the Festival authorities that Jaeger's analysis would be acceptable, although no mention was made of the amount of payment that would be made for it. Jaeger replied gratefully, although he was unwell, complaining of a new degree of malaise: '... Sunday I was really *very ill* – with the fearful Heat, I fear, I could not move, but lay on Sofas & Bed all day more or less, a perfect wreck. I have never felt like that before'. He mentioned a possible fee of ten guineas for the analysis, and although being prepared to accept less, thought that seven guineas, plus the copyright, would be his lowest price; he had spent much time working on it already. In the event, Jaeger seems to have had to settle for five guineas for all rights.

The letter concluded with a reference to Walford Davies, who had been encouraged to play parts of *Gerontius* from proofs; Jaeger continued to rate him very highly, and could not resist prophesying to Elgar that he was another composer whose time would come. Jaeger also acted as propagandist for *Gerontius* with Henry Wood at this time; 'Thanks amany for tackling Wood & Co but I fear they are quaint,' responded Elgar. But Jaeger's main preoccupation was the Analysis, which he worked at during a holiday in the fresh sea air of Cliftonville. From there he wrote on 12 August to ask Elgar for help in providing examples of the themes with their orchestration – the lack of a second copy of the score was felt here too – and in naming the leitmotives; 'You could then correct me & add where you wish.' He seemed almost desperate at the amount of work involved and the lack of time for its completion, and characteristically felt that he must overwork if he was to do it at all, even if it meant returning to the office on Sundays.

> Remember I have to write the thing in my 'spare' (!) hours after 8 hours work at no. 1 Berners Street & on Sundays. I mean to spend the next few Sundays at no. 1 working all day, for that's the only way to do it. I cant work at Home, with the Baby Squeaking perchance! So please think what you can do for me, will you, & I'll not fail to do all I can for you & your works on every available opportunity. You know *that*![38]

Elgar promised all help with the analysis, and Alice sent some background reading from the Newman literature together with encouragement of her own. Nearly a fortnight later, on 26 August, Jaeger sent some draft pages for comment, although repeating his diffidence about taking up the Analysis in the first place – 'I am no musician!!!', he insisted. He subjected everything to Elgar's approval, especially the one-word names that he wished to give to the themes of the Prelude. Next day he had to write to a discontented Horatio Parker, who was travelling in Europe, concerning proofs of his *Wanderer's Psalm* which was due for its Hereford première two weeks later. Jaeger's zeal had made him the object of some crossfire between Parker and Augustus Littleton, and he had been hurt too by a simultaneous 'growl' from Elgar. The letter showed the kind of stress that Jaeger might be subjected to in the office, and the extent to which his hours there could be taken up by the day-to-day minutiae, not only of parts and scores and proofs, but of parcels and post and addresses.

> 16 Margravine Gardens
> West Kensington W.
>
> London, August 27 1900
>
> My dear Parker
>
> Your letter reached me shortly after I had returned from my holiday & as I Knew *nothing* about your Parcel of H. N. & St. Ch. And felt *sure* that you had just cause for grumbling, I spoke to Mr Augustus L. about your growl & read some of your words to him to show him how *annoyed* you were (*rightly* I felt sure!)

By Jove! I put my head in a Hornet's nest, for he was a bit upset by your sarcasm & growling. He saw himself at once to getting a *Second* Parcel of Vocal Score off to you & he wrote to you. Now I'm *awfully* sorry if I have caused any disagreeableness between you & the firm! I daresay it is my fault, but I acted in perfect good faith because I thought the Heads of the firm *ought* to see how seriously annoyed you were (I had a similar growl from Elgar on the *same day*, & the 2 attacks, combined, upset *my* equanimity.) I daresay you will make it allright with Mr. A. for he is a good fellow. Anyhow, believe me, I thought I was doing the right thing. *I* didn't Know the firm had already sent a parcel off.

Now as to the 'Psalm' parts I have everything ready, String Parts already read once with the Full score & revised so that I can send you *second* proofs! The Score is nicely bound & the Wind parts copied, BUT – is it SAFE?? – seeing that a parcel sent to Braunenburg did not reach you – to entrust this precious score and parts to the post to a little place which we can't find in any Gazetteer or on any map in our possession. I think its MOST risky. Are we to send the things *Postlagernd*? And is the damned place called Braunenburg or Brannenburg?

I think you had better come to England & read the things here. There is no time to be lost as the printing of the String Parts will take some days. I confess I am in a fix not Knowing *what* to do! Tell me!!

In great Haste

Yours very sincerely,

A.J. Jaeger[39]

Parker did not remain for the Birmingham Festival and the *Gerontius* première but Jaeger, mindful of future performances in the States, made sure the American had an early copy of the vocal score to study on his return journey; two of Parker's colleagues at Yale University, Samuel Sanford and Stanley Knight, had been impressed by private performances of the tenor solos from the work given by Edward Lloyd during the Three Choirs Festival. The first American performances of *Gerontius* were not to be given until March 1903, in Chicago and New York, and in writing to Berners Street about them, Novello's American agent Herbert Gray referred to his feeling of 'enthusiasm caught from my old friend Jaeger when the work was first published'.

Jaeger had sent Elgar a draft copy of his *Gerontius* analysis as far as it went, and in his acknowledgement Elgar seemed in two minds about the general approach, for Jaeger seems to have used, not unexpectedly, the standard analyses of the Wagner music-dramas (some of which were published by Novello's) as a model. The result was a tendency to produce somewhat simplistic labels for each theme which belied the purely musical processes at work. Elgar gave general encouragement but quibbled about some of Jaeger's ideas, and ended by quoting predictable support from Alice: '... my wife fears you may be inclined to lay too great stress on the *leitmotiven* plan because I really do it without thought – intuitively, I mean.'[40] Jaeger was evidently anxious to show understanding of Elgar's reservations and in the analysis as published he put his labels in brackets next to the musical quotations, and made them more a matter of suggestion than of dogmatism when referring to them in the text.

Sometimes, too, he amplified his explanations by quoting Elgar's own comments, for example in referring to the 'sleep' motive as 'the ghastly troubled sleep of a sick man'; and in a prefatory paragraph he described Elgar in terms that have become common usage as 'a poet, a mystic, a dreamer of dreams'. Elgar summed up the treatment of the motives in a letter to Herbert Thompson of 5 June 1902; 'Yager's analysis is practically authorised by me as far as the choice of themes is concerned, but not always the actual naming of them.'[41]

Elgar visited London for several days at the beginning of September, and enjoyed 'jaw & japes' at Pagani's with Jaeger, who asked him to write an introduction for the *Gerontius* analysis. Elgar could not in the event oblige, but promised to read and amend the proofs, although expecting proofs of the String parts and copies of the Wind parts to correct as well. Matters were complicated when Jaeger became uncertain of Elgar's wherabouts; two days after returning from London, he went to the Hereford Festival for the week, although stopping over at Birmingham for one night to attend a *Gerontius* rehearsal. Jaeger wrote of his confusion over Elgar's movements, and went on to relate an encounter at the London Three Choirs Festival rehearsals with the tenor Edward Lloyd, who was to be the first to sing the role of Gerontius: '... I spoke to Lloyd re Gerontius at the London Rehearsals. He said very fine 'music' but wants 'getting at' & 'understanding'. Just so, I said, I *hope so. Brains* generally want understanding.'

Jaeger himself was not able to go to Hereford and missed hearing the new works that he had seen through the press and previewed in the *Musical Times*. He also nearly missed an opportunity to add to his collection of signed photographs but a short reminder to Horatio Parker brought results.

1, Berners Street, W.
London, 8/9 1900

My dear Parker,

My dear little wife (& the Baby, Evchen) were quite distressed when I told them that you had gone to Hereford without giving me one of your photos with your name on't, as you had promised to do nearly a year ago. My wife particularly requested me to remind you of the promise when I saw you & she sent her Kindest greetings, but like the d– ass that I am I forgot *both* messages!! I blame my wooden head exceedingly & any racy Yankee expression that you could find to describe a doddering Hidjot won't offend me if uttered con amore in your mellowest Baritone.

To appease the Wife (plus the aforesaid Evchen) send me that promised picture! My wife has already found a lovely place for it.

Goodbye once more & good luck attend your Psalm. Wish I were there to enjoy the Festival. Pleasant journey to you & Prof Sanford & Mr Knight. (to Whom Kindest greetings.)

Ever yours

A.J. Jaeger[42]

Jaeger continued to battle with increasing last-minute problems over *Gerontius*, even sending Elgar second proofs unread as he knew that West would not be able to cope with them in the time. Edwards was preparing a leading article about Elgar for the *Musical Times*, and Alice asked Jaeger to pass over to him the Newman material she had sent. With just over a fortnight to go before the première, Jaeger replied with apologies over the analysis which he felt did not match up to the work itself, and gave some idea of the pressure he had been under, although careful to acknowledge that the composer had felt it too. '... I also, (like E. E.), have been driven nearly crazy over this Festival – Working late every night on that analysis, which after all is not worthy of the work ...' And he went on to mention to Alice the initiatives he had made concerning her husband's music with the Director of Music at Düsseldorf, Julius Buths.

> I sent the other day a Score of E's Variations to Professor J. Buths of Düsseldorf, one of the *Ultra moderns* of Germany, great propagandist for Richard Strauss ... The Firm at my suggestion, have invited him to B'ham to hear some English music. He is conductor of the Lower *Rhenish Musical Festivals*! Do you guess something? But mum's the word ... Good night! It is past 9 p.m & I am still here at 1 Berners Street.[43]

Thus Jaeger began to pave the way for the successful performances of Elgar's music in Germany which set a special imprimatur on the composer's reputation. But the wretched nature of the *Gerontius* première at Birmingham was now grimly inevitable. Much proof-correcting still remained to be done, and Jaeger asked Elgar to do the work in London, eliminating postal delays. Initially he refused, but changed his mind when he realized that Jaeger was being reduced to desperation. 'I'm nearly off my head with your & Parry's & Taylor's things. ALL BEHIND! For God's sake return all PROOFS at once or we shall get landed in a fine quandary', wrote Jaeger on 18 September, and two days later Elgar booked into the Langham Hotel to be at hand. He had been suffering from a tell-tale sore throat, and Alice wrote to Jaeger to ask him to 'take all the care you can of him' until she joined her husband in order to attend the first orchestral rehearsal at Queen's Hall on Monday, 24 September under Richter, who had seen the score for the first time only the day before. Her letter also made plain her debt to Jaeger over the analysis: 'May I send a line & say how *beautiful* I think yr. analysis – For once my poet tone painter is absolutely understood & appreciated – which means *much* to me', and on his return to Malvern Elgar himself echoed her appreciation, although repeating the qualifications he had previously expressed. '... I read your stuff in the train & it's clever beyond words I think & thank you for it – save & except your adjectives over some of which I "splutter & growl"'. The praise, even if qualified, must have gone some way to make up for the degree of financial disappointment that Jaeger seems to have experienced over the analysis. He wrote to Dora Penny promising a copy and informing her of his rôle at the Festival.

> September 29th, 1900. In a few days I will give myself the pleasure of sending you a copy of my wretched analysis. I hope your ladyship will deign to consider it not unworthy of His Excellency's magnum bonum, I mean opus. (though it *is* bonum, in fact 'optime'). Mr Johnstone the chairman of the Committee (B' ham) told me yesterday that Richter likes the work as much as I do! If that's so he must indeed think much of it. I am going to the whole of the Festival chaperoning a German musician, Professor Buths, of Düsseldorf, my native town. I hope to see you there after all.[44]

In the event, Jaeger was too fully occupied during the Festival to have opportunity to talk with Dora. He wrote to explain, and gave vent to his reactions to the English cultural scene in its response to *Gerontius.*

> October 14th, 1900. I have been 'pitched into' for being enthusiastic over Gerontius. I don't mind a bit. It was lack of enthusiasm both in the performance & amongst the critics which riled me at B'ham & afterwards, when I read the critiques. Now you Englishers have a composer at last you might be excused if you waxed enthusiastic over him for once in a way. But oh dear no! If this were only a wretched new opera or a dull new oratorio by Mascagni or Perosi, the papers would have had columns of gossip & gush about those 2 frauds. But it is only an English musician (not an actress or a jockey or a Batsman) and he is treated like a very ordinary nobody. Oh you unpatriotic creatures. I won't say a word about the performance, but I suffered purgatory!! this disenchantment after my hours of exaltation & refreshment at the Pianoforte was too cruel. I was of course unfortunately placed in a way, for the music was so very familar to me that I concentrated all my attention on the actual performance, never glancing at the score or analysis, old St- the choir-mess-ter ought to be boiled & served on Toast for having had us in Purgatory for nigh 2 Hours ... You ought to come to Düsseldorf (my native place) & attend a Festival (under Buths) to get an idea of an ideal Hall for such a gathering. Such ample corridors, cloakrooms, Restaurants; and a big lovely garden (with al fresco refreshments) all round the Hall!
>
> All the Germans I spoke to at B'ham (Richter, Dr Otto Lessman,[45] Prof. Buths, etc. etc.) were enthusiastic about Elgar's work. Directly it was over Buths grasped my hands (coram publico) & blurted out: 'Ein wunderbares Werk; eins der schonsten Werke die ich kenne' etc. etc. ... To be with Buths for a whole week continuously (except bedtime) exhausted me, & I longed for a chat with a woman. And it was a fruitless longing. So I say: Where was my co-variation? In Print No. 9 & 10 'were not divided'. Then why in festive Brummagem? I never forgive you that! ...
>
> Dear E.E. sent me quite a depressing letter last week. I told him it was *weak* and *wicked* to write like that. So he replied at once in a better strain. I told him to look at the Introduction & first Allegro of Beethoven's 'Pathetique' (Sonata). That is the mood in which to look adverse circumstances in the face & defy them ...[46]

The notorious première of *The Dream of Gerontius* is now regarded as one of the great disasters of English music. Its late completion, complicated by the massive amount of time-consuming proof-reading required, Swinnerton Heap's untimely death and Novello's refusal to expedite the process by providing a second full score, together with the sheer difficulty of the music itself, led to a performance at Birmingham on 3 October which was under-rehearsed and conspicuously weak in terms of tempi, ensemble and intonation. Richter inevitably took a good deal of the blame at the time, but he had done wonders with a complicated score in a matter of days, and could not be held responsible for the shortcomings of the chorus. He had, as well, many other works to deal with during the Festival, including *Hiawatha* which was given later on the day of the Elgar première. It went well, a source of some annoyance to Richter, who seems to have shared the antipathy to the work which had been shown by other German musicians. He noted in his diary, 'In the evening conducted that rubbish *Hiawatha*. It was well received, Oh!'[47]

In the aftermath of the nightmare performance, boiling over with disappointment and frustration, Elgar had written bitterly to Jaeger, '… I always said God was against Art & I still believe it. Anything obscene or trivial is blessed in this world & has a reward – I ask for no reward – only to live & to hear my work …'.

Jaeger himself was unwell during the Festival, which for him was the climax of months of work and commitment, in and out of office hours; it was inevitable that he should have become physically and nervously exhausted. As a result a great deal of the responsibility of looking after Buths during the Festival was shouldered by Ivor Atkins, who remembered,

> … Elgar was in good form. Novellos … had told him that Julius Buths, the Conductor of the Lower Rhine Festival, was coming to Birmingham, and that he and August Jaeger were to be quartered together at one of the hotels. He asked me to get in touch with both … Unfortunately, Jaeger was not well … throughout the Festival, and Buths was thrown largely on my hands. After the performance of *Gerontius* he and I met and compared notes. Notwithstanding the poor performance there was no mistaking his enthusiasm for the work. I well remember how impressed he was by its daring originality. His words tumbled over each other as he pointed out passage after passage …[48]

The irrepressible Buths returned to Germany keen to promote *Gerontius*, as Jaeger had intended. Elgar, for his part, received a letter shortly after the Festival from Cambridge offering a Doctor of Music degree; his initial reluctance to accept due to the expense of the robes was overcome when Granville Bantock organized a collection among Elgar's friends. Jaeger contributed a cheque for one guinea to the fund and sent it with an undated note to Bantock, adding a pointed postscript. 'Can't *you* get our esteemed & brilliant friend to write more satisfactory & satisfying Codas to his works?'[49] It was to become one of Jaeger's Elgarian hobbyhorses.

There were other financial vexations for Elgar at this time. It was emerging that there had been a complete misunderstanding between Novello's and Johnstone in the negotiations over the terms for *Gerontius*. At his earlier meeting with Alfred Littleton, Johnstone had raised the question of a royalty, and thought that the point had been accepted. Now it emerged that there was no written confirmation of such an agreement, and Littleton jibbed at further payment for a work that he described as a 'commercial failure'. For Johnstone it became a matter of honour, for he had given his word to Elgar, and correspondence continued over several weeks until Littleton finally gave way. Meanwhile at the end of October Elgar wrote complaining to Jaeger that he was at the end of his financial tether, that he was considering taking up a coal or house agency, and even threatening suicide. He had been asked to write something for the Philharmonic Society, although there was no question of payment and the expenses of rehearsal and copying parts would amount to £21: 'I really cannot afford it', he added. Jaeger's reply is missing, like many of his responses to Elgar's most desperate letters, but he was able to write early in November to Alice to say that Buths was intending to mount *Gerontius* in Düsseldorf and he offered to recommend an article by Otto Lessmann for publication in the *Musical Times*:

Yes, I saw Dr Lessmann's fine critique on Gerontius & had been thinking of translating it, or some of it, for the *Ml. Times.* But I feel *sure* you can do that better than I can, & moreover, I have so little time now. I get home at 8.15–8.30 now & am generally too tired for any more work.[50]

Jaeger also apologized to Alice for his delay in writing:

I meant to do so last Sunday, but in the morning there were so many serious & jolly things to discuss with that little Baby of ours, & she is such a time-killing fascination, that the morning went, & nothing in the way of work or correspondence was done; and in the afternoon friends came & *they* argued with that baby & we looked on; and nothing was done, again.[51]

Not surprisingly, Jaeger was continuing unwell and Elgar wrote to commiserate before meeting up with him in London towards the end of the month. The Elgars made the Langham their base for the journey to Cambridge for the degree ceremony on 22 November and then travelled to Liverpool for a performance of the Variations by Alfred Rodewald's Orchestral Society. '… you sounded, you old preacher, gorjus', Elgar told Jaeger. Their London meeting had been brief, and Alice subsequently wrote with motherly concern when sending her translation of parts of the Lessmann article, 'we were sorry your visit had to be so short that evening, we both send our best greetings to you all three, please try & take a little rest'.

The next Sunday Jaeger began writing to Elgar, but was interrupted by the arrival of some musical friends. In resuming the letter he gave a glimpse of some domestic music-making, and found an opportunity to ask for a chamber-work.

We had some Beethoven ('Appasionata') P. F. Solo & Violin & P. F. (Kreutzer) By Jove I quite enjoyed the 'Concert'. after all Sonatas are for the *Home*, not for the Concert Room. I have never heard my dear wife play as she did in the 'Kreutzer' (which she hadnt looked at or heard for 6 years or more.) She was stimulated by a splendid Pianist (Mr. Handel Thorley).[52] We must have some more 'recitals' like that. So please send us a Vn. & P. F. Sonata of *yours*, QUICKLY, please – !![53]

Jaeger was continuing to propagandize for *Gerontius* as much as he could. He went on,

Saw C. Macpherson[54] today. He wanted to see Full score Gerontius, to study orchestration, 'cos he plays the *Prelude* at the 'Service' ('Last Judgement') at St Paul's tomorrow night. If I were not *doubly* engaged I'd go. I told him all I remember about the scoring. He thinks *wonders* of the work; almost as much as A.J.J. I'm delighted the work is, like poison, slowly eating its way into the conscience of English musical life – but it's poison in small doses, and therefore has a *wholesome*, medicinally effective & restoring character or quality about it. I laughed at Thorley last night. He played through nearly the whole of Gerontius & was for ever being startled until he exclaimed, 'Confound the fellow, he is for ever giving one *what one doesn't expect*'.[55]

And on 22 December he wrote to Dora Penny, 'I'm still trying hard to get Gerontius performed in London, but it is almost hopeless. I still hope Wood will do it … '.[56] August Manns had decided to cancel a projected performance at the Crystal Palace because of the complexity of the music, although had given the Prelude alone at the end of October. 'The lofty and impressive music was admirably played, and the piece is so complete in itself that it should be no stranger in our concert – rooms', wrote the reviewer of the Crystal Palace Concerts, presumably August Jaeger himself, in the December *Musical Times*. In the event, the next full performance of *Gerontius* would, as a result of Jaeger's promptings, be given the following year in his home town of Düsseldorf, an outcome which must have given intense satisfaction. And if 1900 had proved an *annus mirabilis* for Elgar, it must have been no less so for Jaeger, who had enthused and encouraged over *Gerontius*, supervised its appearance in print, intervened as its co-creator at a crucial point, and propagandized tirelessly for its wider acceptance and understanding in a detailed analysis which remains the standard work to this day. Seldom has a composer been so well served. In doing what he did, August Jaeger achieved something without precedent in the relations between publisher and composer; his efforts must have bolstered his position at Novello's, for his advocacy of Elgar had been vindicated and his judgement proved right. But Jaeger's devotion had taken its toll, for if it had been a year of success, it had been also a year of much overwork and of repeated complaints of poor health.

Characteristically, alongside his Elgarian preoccupations, Jaeger's loyalty to his other discoveries among the younger generation of English composers continued, as did his keenness to promote them. The November and December issues of the *Musical Times* carried a two-part article – 'A New English Composer' – analysing works by Walford Davies. Jaeger discussed the two violin sonatas, Opus 5 and Opus 7, the Browning setting for baritone and string quartet, *Prospice*, and an anthem for soli and double chorus, with many musical examples in support. Whatever may be the status of this music today – and it is difficult to escape the conclusion that it comes within the 'unfairly neglected' category – Jaeger set out his stall in such a way as to reveal that, at the very least, the works met his own demanding criteria.

> … they do not contain one bar that falls below the highest standard which an artist, taking his art most seriously, could set himself, while there are passages which seem to flash the precious light of inspiration upon us. We have studied the works carefully, but no re-reading can convince us that our first strong impression was too favourable. On the contrary, Dr. Davies's music is not only never written *ad captandem*, but greater familiarity with its secrets breeds but greater love and admiration for it. The more elaborate and serious efforts show the composer's creative gifts at their best: the higher his aims, the nobler the results. This is as it should be, and it is well. It causes us to look upon Dr. Davies more than ever as a composer with whom the nearest future of English music will have to reckon. He has not rushed into print with unripe, ill-digested works. Some of them have been in existence for several years. They must have been put aside time after time for reconsideration and revision. The result is a batch of the sanest, wholesomest, and, what is more to the point, most beautiful compositions it has been our good fortune to see for a long time. The workmanship appears perfect. Padding there is none. Every note seems in its right place, and there are neither too few nor too many. The critic does not question the *raison d'être* of this phrase or the advisability of that passage. Everything occurs as of a logical necessity. This does not mean that the music is not often full of delightful surprises. But when it has become familiar, no other way

> than the composer's suggests itself as possible. This is his triumph, the result of strong intellectuality, of masterly workmanship, of a well applied capacity for taking immense pains. A young heart from which flow warmth and enthusiasm is ruled and kept in check by a cool head. The consequences are a rare conciseness, and an utter absence of 'passion', as the term is understood these days. There is no ranting, no hair-tearing or heart-twisting in Dr. Davies's music. Those to whom Tschaikovsky's 'Pathetic' Symphony represents the summit of all musical art will be disappointed that our young friend has not been influenced in the least by the fashionable pessimism and sensuousness *a la Russe.*[57]

Also in the December number was a review of the Promenade season, which hailed many of Wood's performances as memorable, and welcomed new works by Landon Ronald and Josef Holbrooke, whose contrapuntal resource in the *Variations for Orchestra on Three Blind Mice* was given especial praise. 'More should be heard of Mr. Holbrooke – and at the Queen's Hall', was the verdict. Less enthusiastic was a review of a series of concerts of his own chamber works given by the young and brilliant Donald Tovey. He had been something of a child prodigy, composing from the age of eight and taking lessons in counterpoint from Walter Parratt and in composition from Parry who, however, found that he produced 'sheets and sheets of dull and respectably correct twaddle which he seems to pour out with as much ease as water out of a jug'.[58] Tovey won an Oxford scholarship, and later found an outlet for his abilities as Reid Professor of Music at Edinburgh, producing stimulating analytical writings on the works that he conducted with the University Orchestra. The 1900 concerts blended Tovey's musical and literary efforts, but Jaeger felt that the chamber works were merely cleverly imitative of the German masters whom he idolized. He wrote quite fiercely,

> At some future day Mr. Donald Francis Tovey may look over the programmes of the concerts which he gave at St. James's Hall towards the close of the nineteenth century and wonder how he had the temerity to 'hurl' his works at the public, and at the critics, in the way he has done. He is clever – in fact, highly gifted – and if he bide his time may make a name for himself; for the present, however, he is in the imitative stage, and his powers of imitation are strong. There are themes and developments in his chamber music which sound almost like Beethoven or Brahms, but an attentive listener finds that he has only shadow, not substance; that it is pseudo-Beethoven, pseudo-Brahms. If Mr. Tovey's music were a bad imitation of these masters little harm would be done, but as it is most cleverly formed and fashioned, it may lead many – and among them the composer himself – to accept it as really great. We do not say that the composer lacks originality; for the present, however, it is hid under a Beethoven-Brahms bushel.[59]

Jaeger was careful to keep an open mind on Tovey's future course, but although the composer continued to produce chamber music, concertos and an opera, his true bent was for the art of musicology that he did so much to develop. Many years later Tovey wrote at length to Elgar concerning his *Falstaff*, but found no more favour than he had with Parry and Jaeger. 'I wish people wd. drown themselves in ink & let me alone', Elgar wrote to his daughter.

On New Year's Eve a somewhat out-of-sorts Elgar sent 'My very dear' Jaeger 'one word to close the Century'. Alice herself had invited him to visit over the holiday, and sent thanks for his notices of the music. But complaints against Novello's seemed uppermost in Elgar's mind; with scores of *Sea Pictures* and *Mastersingers* to hand, he was anxious to see full scores of his own works in print. He sent the 'miserable Mal de Mer' score to Jaeger, claiming 'I have given up sending cards'.

> I was afeared you cdn't come here & told my wife it was no time to ask you; but *any* time you can be spared we shall be only too glad to see you. It is very good of you to mention my works as you do – but I take no interest in 'em – if they were to be had in score I shouldn't mind.
>
> Now don't worry about what you said – above all don't recommend me to the firm. They are I know dead sick of me.[60]

Needless to say, it was advice that Jaeger most emphatically ignored.

6 1901: 'I *must* wax enthusiastic over *something* ...'

Elgar's mood should have improved somewhat during January 1901, for Jaeger was overseeing the first printing of the *Froissart* Overture, and inspiration visited him in the form of a new melody, probably that which would be used for the trio section of the first *Pomp and Circumstance* March. Jaeger was given a hint: 'In haste & joyful (Gosh! man I've got a tune in my head)', Elgar told him. Work on the Philharmonic piece, the *Cockaigne* Overture, continued, and on 17 January he conducted a Worcestershire Philharmonic concert consisting largely of English music. The programme included a work by Walford Davies, the *Hymn before Action,* which Elgar thought was 'good & well sung & well received'. Alice wished Jaeger had been there to listen, and sent him the programme book which was presumably the basis of a flattering review of the concert which appeared in the February *Musical Times* under the heading, 'The Worcester Philharmonic Society and English Music'. Alice had implied that the new tune was part of a symphony, and confirmed Jaeger's importance in the scheme of things when she appealed directly to him, 'I LONG for it to be finished & have to exist on scraps – Do write & hurry him, it always does *some* good – '. An excited Jaeger wrote with an Elgarian progress report to Dora Penny on 20 January, 'I think E. is also finishing that Symphony at last. He had the BLUES terribly about 3 weeks ago, but last time he wrote he was joyful. "Gosh man, I've got a tune in my head" he wrote to me'.[1] But the symphony faded from the correspondence to be replaced by mention of a string sextet, which would also fail to materialize. Jaeger leapt to offer to organize a try-over of the work by string-playing friends, together with Isabella, who was recommended with husbandly pride. Although the Jaegers were able to employ a nurse,[2] their regular musical 'at-homes' must have been a welcome change from Isabella's domestic routine, especially now with a second child on the way.

> String Sextet – Eh? Good boy! let me find you six players & we will try it over *here* next time you are in town. I have plenty of *good* players (2 Viole – Hobday & Tomlinson, 2 Cellists T. Werg & Alice Elison) living quite close here. my wife could take one of the Fiddles & we could easily find another. My dear Frau reads *splendidly* & provided she has decent music plays much better than you imagine. Hear her play the Kreutzer, or a Brahms or Grieg Sonata![3]

Jaeger's efforts to encourage foreign performances were beginning to pay off, and he had been deeply gratified to learn just that day that Buths would play the Variations at Düsseldorf in February. 'So there! first performance in Germany in Nimrod's native place. I'm *so* glad,' he wrote, and suggested that the composer attend. He sent thanks to Alice for lending him *Piers Plowman*, the medieval poem which had been Elgar's reading during work on the *Cockaigne* Overture. It had been studied during odd moments at home and on the daily tube journey to the office; presumably Jaeger's gift for languages had helped him to cope with its peculiarites of metre, language and orthography. But in terms of his scant leisure, it had taken second place to the delight he found in his daughter. '*Delightful* Book. I read it in 2d. Toobe night & morning, & here when not writing letters or playing with our darling Babe. She is our greatest Happiness. Such a *sunny* child!'[4]

Dora Penny had to be kept abreast of the Düsseldorf Variations performance – and invited to attend – so Jaeger sent her a postcard that evening. 'Greeting! Variations, not ommitting Intermezzo, at *Dusseldorf* under Prof. Buths on Feb. 7th. I do wish you could go over. Am urging the Dr. to go & hear first performance in Germany. Nice place D'orf!'[5] In the event none of the Elgar camp were able to travel, and on the day of the performance, Jaeger wrote his regrets although looking forward to further hearings of the Variations in Germany: 'We'll go when they do them at Berlin, won't we?'.

There seems to have been no question of Jaeger himself travelling to hear the Düsseldorf Variations performance. Office commitments would have been a factor but also, his finances were in a sorry state. Donald Tovey showed characteristic insight when he referred to the 'unworldly idealism' of the *Nimrod* character in his analysis of the Variations.[6] Jaeger had advanced money on trust, his own and the firm's, to a fraudulent copyist, and was now liable for the work to be made good. He had been in the habit of helping others with loans, and now began to think of securing his financial position by charging for the recommendations that he usually gave as a favour.

> That D—d copyist who did the Sursum Corda Score & who I thought was in sore straights [*sic*] & whom *I helped all I could*, has turned out to be a complete Fraud I fear. He has £6. of my money, (*advanced* on account of some big job he is supposed to be doing for us) & besides he *has 2 Scores of ours* for which we paid £20. & I don't know the rogue's present whereabouts; the work is urgently wanted, & if the fellow is 'perdue' I shall have to get these scores re-done at my expense. I *was* a d—fool! Never again shall I help with money any person. It's ruinous. All over the place I have little amounts standing out which I cant get at. It is too bad, for I am poor myself. That comes of doing people good turns &c.
>
> *I* shall start business too. I shall see whether I cant do something in the Concert Agent line. I get plenty of chances & I dont see why I should spend my time here & my money in stamps for strangers (more or less) trying to get them engagements for nothing. People *often* come to me to recommend singers & players. I shall ask 10% in future as all agents do. I have enough of 'doing favours' for nothing to strangers or slight acquaintances. I'm dreadfully sick over that Rogue though, for a loss of £26 pounds just now is ruinous to me, poor devil that I am.[7]

Perhaps the arrival a couple of days later of a hurried and somewhat informal note from Alice lightened the mood somewhat. Its main burden was of regret at missing the Düsseldorf Variations, but she began by confessing 'Der Tondichter & I have just been playing "Nimrod" as a duet for *Trombone* & piano …' and ended, 'Excuse most curious & unliterary English. The trombone must have scattered my Senses somewhat.' Other items of mail must have brought further cheer. The Variations performance had gone well, and Buths wrote to Jaeger with complimentary press-cuttings and news of his intention to mount an early repeat of the work. A paragraph to this effect duly appeared in the March *Musical Times*. In sending the cuttings on to Elgar, Jaeger referred to the continuing Boer War, saying 'I was so glad to see or hear that the D'orf audience did not let its *political* bias darken its judgement of an English work of art'. Then Henry Wood himself came to Berners Street over a performance of the Prelude and Angel's Farewell from *Gerontius*, which Elgar had newly arranged as a separate concert item, planned for the Queen's Hall on Ash Wednesday. Having at last succeeded in drawing Wood's interest, the canny Jaeger was keen to ensure that the bait was well and truly taken. He sent the original MS score for Wood to study – 'do him good!!' – and made a gift of the printed string parts for marking, 'so that he may do the things again!' Jaeger, with a musician's ear for peculiarities of accent, finished the letter with a delightful portrait in miniature of Brause, Novello's expert German engraver. The *Froissart* full score was causing him problems: 'Brause is schwearing most awful Schwears about the tretful gorrekshuns in "Froissart", poor chap. But he is going aheat as vast as bossible, as ever vos.'[8] Family responsibilities continued to accumulate as Mrs Jaeger senior became ill. '… this morning we found our old mother lying in a heap on the floor of her Bedroom ill with paralysis (partial) or loss of speech! I fear at her age (74) it may prove fatal, or at any rate she will be a confirmed invalid henceforth, poor old thing.' She was indeed to prove a confirmed invalid and a burden to the son she outlived.

Jaeger was able to attend Wood's rehearsal for the Ash Wednesday concert with Elgar, and a bulletin was immediately despatched to Dora Penny:

> February 18th, 1901. Dear Dorabella. Your dear Doctor E.E. is in town & this morning we went together to Queen's Hall to hear Wood conduct the Gerontius Prelude & Angel's Farewell (Kirkby Lunn as the 'Angel'). Oh, Dorabella, the stuff sounded most beautiful, most moving, most elevating. It is the highest thing in English art (musical art) & honestly, I say again it seems to me the noblest, aloofest thing since Parsifal. Wood conducted it with loving care; spent 1½ hours on it & the result was a performance which completely put Richter's into the Shade. I was deeply affected & felt more than I could express to dear E.E. …'[9]

Wood's thorough rehearsal made some amends for the Birmingham fiasco and stimulated Jaeger's admiration for the music all over again. Alice thought the performance two days later 'perfectly played', and next month Wood wrote to Elgar of his intention to conduct the Variations at Queen's Hall that May.

A few days in London gave the Elgars opportunity to sup again at Pagani's, take tea with Jaeger, visit theatres and galleries, catch up on various old friends and make some new ones. Some soon-to-be familiar names from the Elgar saga make their first appearance in Alice's Diary at this time. On 21 February, after a morning going their own separate ways the Elgars '... met at Mr. Leo Schuster's at 1 for lunch. Mrs. Tree, Lady C. Beresford, Rafaels, & L. Schuster sister there ...'. The Schusters and the Beresfords in particular became the nucleus of a new circle of wealthy and influential friends at some distance from Jaeger's own social sphere.

Early in March Jaeger wrote to Herbert Thompson, the celebrated long-time music critic of the *Yorkshire Post*, a colleague who was sufficiently like-minded to be trusted with a fierce onslaught against West and Edwards of Novello's and their musical conservatism. Jaeger also gave vent to thoughts about what he now saw as the shallowness of Coleridge-Taylor's music, and his disappointment with the composer's attitude towards him, although one is tempted to wonder whether the complained-of behaviour was the result of Coleridge-Taylor's characteristic self-effacing shyness. Jaeger was evidently feeling ignored and taken for granted, but this did not discourage him from helping another talented young composer of whom he had a very high opinion, William Henry Bell. Jaeger seems to have persuaded Stanford to give him lessons, and was trying to interest Brewer in his work.

16 Margravine Gardens
West Kensington W.

March 4/01

My dear Thompson

Very many thanks for your letter. Stanford wrote to me re Bell: 'Impossible', but he asked me to send Bell to him with his 'Toil', & since then he devotes 2 mornings or portions of 2 mornings a week to introduce the young fellow into the mysteries of the ancient modes. Bell can't make it out. He had rather a prejudice against C.V.S. but he came back to me with an expansive grin on his merry face, saying: 'I say, Stanford was *awfully decent*!' Since then C.V.S. has been going on being awfully decent and Bell quite enjoys going to 50 Holland Street – composing Kyries and Sanctuses & masses in the mixo-this & that mode, especially as the professor charges the poor fellow nix for his trouble. I say to myself: what can it mean! Of course I felt sure on one thing viz: that C.V.S. must think highly of Bell to devote his valuable time to giving him gratis lessons. Needless to say, because Bell has plenty of the right stuff in him, says something *poetic* &, to a certain extent, unhackneyed, Novellos Editors won't see anything in him, say he 'can't write', is 'crude', can't score &c &c. The idea of 2 bally (excuse slang) English organists sitting in Judgement on a young genius (more or less) like Bell makes me curse dreadful cusses. Bell has written tons of stuff, more *volumes* than West has written pages I should think, but of course he doesn't write in the 'English Church Style!!['] Excuse me, if I said all this before, but I can't write calmly on this preposterous state of affairs, which obtains, alas,! at the chief English publishers. (This quite between ourselves, *please!* But J.E.W. & F.G.E. ruling over the destinies of musical young England *is* a funny idea.)

I'm now trying hard to induce Brewer to try Bell and he seems half-inclined. It is all very well for you to say that Bell's turn will come at Leeds after he has begun to 'go the round of Festivals!['] It is just the *Beginning* which is so darned difficult. One has to move mountains of prejudices and 'reasons' (so called)[.] Brewer followed my advice re Taylor

& he turned out trumps. He may safely try Bell; for though he may lack Taylor's easy invention of *Tune*, he has certainly vastly more *Brains* than the young Blackie, & more Depth & poetic imagination. Why I should bother about these youngsters at all I don't Know. It takes a great portion of my *(few)* spare hours and I get no satisfaction out of the affair except the feeling that perhaps I have done a fellow a good turn.

I fear you won't like Taylor's Leeds cantata much. I leave him severely alone now, for he is too big a celebrity now to ever come near me. He sent me the other day another new choral work to this address without even a letter of explanation. I haven't even looked at it yet. I' ll teach *that* youngster manners yet, *though* his Hiawatha sells like hot cakes. It is I should think the biggest success Novello's have had since the Elijah.

Your remarks on Mendelssohn make me laugh. Why this fury? I daresay living as you do in *the* singing County in England, you have a regular Bellyful of Mendeslssohn every year & this must be somewhat sickening.

You are as bad as Elgar!

By the way the Dr. (EE) was in town the other day & I saw a good deal of him. Have you read anything of his 'Cockaigne' & the String Sextet? I have, more than once. You really must come to London when they do 'Cockaigne' at the Phil. It's big, *important* stuff & full of fun in parts.

But what a chatter-box I am. Forgive this too easy, clumsy pen. Keep my remarks private as far as they effect [*sic*] N & Co. & Taylor.

Parry has just written an 'Ode to Music' words by Mr Benson (son of Archbishop B) of Eton College. We are printing it now. Will be sung at the opening of the new Concert Hall at the College in May.

Very truly, yours

AJ Jaeger[10]

Dont pray think of answering this[.] It requires no answer[.]

No sketches for Elgar's Sextet have survived, and Jaeger may have been just a little too anxious to impress his fellow-critic in saying that he had read them 'more than once'. He was certainly full of news and talk next day, when he met Isabella and Dorabella – he used to say the nicest women he knew had names ending in 'ella' – and took them for a lunch that lasted over an hour, 'we had so much to hear'.[11] Jaeger's efforts to promote Walford Davies through Elgar proved successful when the Worcester Three Choirs committee announced a commission for 1902. It must have been comforting news for Jaeger as he suffered continued problems with his nose and helped Isabella during the final weeks before her confinement. Other initiatives bore fruit with Wood's programming of the Variations as part of that year's London Festival of Music. Once again, Dora Penny heard the news from Jaeger.

April 15th, 1901. By the way, Wood has placed the Elgar Variations in the London Festival Programme. He has just written to me 'How beautiful the Variations are!' *At last*! Brewer tells me he wants to do them at the Gloucester Festival (Shire Hall). 'We' are getting on, n'est ce pas? … The Dr. has just written me a letter in his most Elgaresque style; insults me by saying he would like ½ hour with me, to talk some sense into that German Vacuum! etc. etc. He is a 'killing' person.[12]

Jaeger caught up with Elgar again a few days later, over dinner at the Langham Hotel. Elgar had travelled to London on business, spending some time with

Novello's rival, Boosey, who had agreed to publish *Cockaigne*. Another firm, Schotts, also agreed to bring out another score, the *Sursum Corda.* A disappointed Jaeger had written to Alice, 'Of *course* you will be at the Phil to hear "Cockayne". That's *the* event of the Season to which I am looking forward. I'm only annoyed & *distressed* that Novello's haven't got it ... With E.E. going to Schotts I have nothing at *No. 1* over which I can spend my overflow of enthusiasm. I *must* wax enthusiastic over *something* – it's part of my life.'

On 22 April Isabella gave birth to a son, who was christened Edward Johannes in compliment to two of her husband's musical heroes. In acknowledging the news, Elgar reminded Jaeger of Wood's Variations rehearsal and advised of his intention to seek advice on Jaeger's behalf from Dr Greville Macdonald, a Harley Street ear, nose and throat specialist who often helped singers with vocal problems and who had successfully treated Elgar himself some years previously. The rehearsal went well, and Elgar wrote afterwards to Jaeger how jolly it was 'to see your dear old mug smiling approval'. Wood's workmanlike approach, and the response of the celebrated French musician, Eduard Colonne, one of the other Festival conductors, were breathlessly related to Dora Penny.

> April 28th, 1901. Dear Dorabella, I went to the rehearsal on Friday morning and again yesterday when E.E. turned up, and I can assure you Wood makes these things (Variations) hum. I have never heard anything more daringly, devilishly brilliant & boisterous than Troyte or G.R.S., more gorgeous in colour than 'Nimrod', more dainty and graceful than the lovely 'Dorabella'. I sat next M. Colonne all the time yesterday. He dropped in for a few minutes, but he was at once interested & stayed all the time. He was most appreciative, and from being merely interested & saying 'c'est difficile' & 'c'est charmant' he grew warmer & warmer in his praise & more & more astonished, till 'Nimrod' drew from him an enthusiastic 'Ah' & the remark 'it is the best and very beautiful' (He speaks little English) & Dorabella delighted him immensely. 'C'est vraiment delicieux' & similar expressions came from him & at the end (Wood played that stunning coda superbly) he was quite enthusiastic. When Elgar came down from the platform, C took E's right hand in both his own & made him quite a long speech of congratulation. Elgar was quite touched. The orchestra gave him (E) a splendid ovation, I never heard a better one at any rehearsal.[13]

Elgar was determined to press on with treatment for Jaeger, and arranged and paid for an appointment with Macdonald towards the end of May. As something of a specialist in the problems experienced by singers, Macdonald may have used the larygnoscope, a system of mirrors invented by the celebrated teacher of singing, Manuel Garcia, in order to study the vocal cords. The idea had been adopted by the medical profession and proved invaluable in the diagnosis of throat lesions. In Jaeger's case it is possible that he was at this stage developing tuberculosis of the larynx, which would have allowed the infection to discharge into the bronchial pathway and thence into both lungs, and there was something of an epidemic of laryngeal tuberculosis around this time.[14] Macdonald evidently thought the situation serious enough to warrant surgery, and recommended an operation; after the consultation Elgar went back to Margravine Gardems with Jaeger to break the news to

Isabella, and insisted that he spend a weekend at Malvern to relax before the operation. The continued costs worried Jaeger, but Elgar wrote to offer further financial support. 'As to the next expense we'll talk later: I never borrow anything but have powerful friends & can borrow any amount & will sell my last book, stick & golfball for you, if necessary.'

Just at this time Elgar himself had been offered a holiday in Wales by one of those 'powerful friends', the Liverpool cotton magnate and conductor of the Liverpool Orchestral Society, Alfred Rodewald, an associate of Granville Bantock and conducting pupil of Hans Richter. Rodewald wrote of the walks, rides and fishing that could be enjoyed at his cottage, and of his interest in conducting the *Cockaigne* and *Froissart* Overtures in Liverpool. Jaeger might have been interested to know of his firm's reputation with such an important figure, when the conductor explained,

> Now do me a favour: Please order both orchestral scores at my expense & I will send you a cheque at once for this reason: I cannot stand writing to Novellos without losing my temper ... Send me the scores or order them to be sent here. The brutes do not even allow me the discount I get by going to a common-or-garden music shop on their own publications & as I have the honour to conduct a big orchestra, & do my best to produce **GOOD MUSIC**, do not allow me the discount which the humblest triangle beater would get. But the latter is a 'pro' & I am a blooming amateur.[15]

Jaeger spent some five days in Malvern, where the Elgars made sure that he enjoyed as much fresh air as possible, accompanying the composer to the golf links on one occasion, and walking back from Birchwood Lodge on another. He left Malvern on 28 May, the day before the operation, and returned on 3 June for a few days' convalescence at an hotel. Later that month he returned to work, although Alice's diary makes no mention of him attending either rehearsals or the first performance of *Cockaigne* at Queen's Hall on 20 June, conducted by Elgar himself. No information survives as to the nature of the surgery,[16] but Jaeger's recovery was slow, and he started to worry that Macdonald was keeping things from him. Elgar, many of whose frequent minor indispositions were probably pyschosomatic in origin, responded to Jaeger's anxieties with frank advice.

> Now – I am wearily distressed about your ideas as to your nose, &c. &c. – You really must not let your nerves worry you & go at once to Macdonald & make him tell you things: I shd. think probably your symptoms are the natural sequence of affairs – I fear you brood over C. Woods, or whoever it was, & this is not good for you: now I feel I am a wretch all through & you feel I ought to write yards of sympathy – I *do* sympathise with you most deeply but I still trust it is chiefly worry & fret that causes you discomfort now: anyhow, go at once to the doctor & don't go on fretting over it. – let me know everything.[17]

More positively, Jaeger was able to send news that Julius Buths would produce *Gerontius* in Düsseldorf that December and he forwarded a revised copy of his analysis of the work. Elgar was lavish in his praise, referring to 'acute insight', but made one or two suggestions, in particular concerning Jaeger's use of the term 'ruin' for the orchestral music at *Gerontius's* 'I can no more'. 'The word is *heavy* – too direct', he wrote, once again on his guard against too apparently simplistic an explanation of his intuitive processes.

Jaeger was able to spend more time in the open air of Malvern that summer when Alice invited him and Isabella to have the use of Craeg Lea in company with Buths, who was to holiday in England after collecting his tubercular daughter from her boarding school on the Suffolk coast. The house would be empty while the Elgars stayed at Birchwood. With the Düsseldorf performance of *Gerontius* arranged for later that year, it would be an opportunity to confer, as well as an opportunity for Jaeger to gain strength before further surgery. With careful consideration for Alice's convenience, he wrote to accept.

16 Margravine Gardens
West Kensington
W.

18/7/01

My dear Mrs Elgar,

Your most Kind letter was a delightful surprise to me & I thank you for it with all my heart.

I had already made up my mind to go to Malvern again if I possibly could manage it without ruining myself financially & I had written to Buths that I thought Malvern the very place he wanted. I had also written to Miss Burley (who Knows Malvern so well & is right on the spot) whether she Knew of any place where Buths and I might stay.

She wrote this morning recommending a place near her School to which we might have gone if (provided Buths was willing) we could not have found anything better higher up the Hills[.] But your very handsome offer puts a totally different complexion of the affair. I *wired* your offer to Buths this morning & he has just replied by wire accepting with many thanks, *if* he may bring his daughter, whom he is bound to fetch from Lowestoft. My dear wife will not be able to come, I fear. It would be no Holiday for me if the 2 'Angelicals' came with us & I *must* have another Rest before the Dr cuts & burns me about 'some more.'

My wife will have a month later on at her Home in Yorkshire with her sister. I shall take her there myself, D.V. But I should love to come to Craeg Lea, if I may. I Know the House, & love it & the Hillside upon which it is built.

The question of catering & bed-making is the difficulty. Could a trusty person be found to look after the Bedrooms & prepare a simple Breakfast for us if we two (Buths & I) offered to pay her a handsome fee? Of course you wouldn't care to have *any*body in your House and the choosing of somebody would therefore be a trouble which you in your goodness of heart would perhaps suffer yourself to be put to, if you can find the time & the Dr's illness passes. (I'm sorry to hear of his foot, I suppose it will prevent him from biking & walking, worse luck!) We could easily take our *other* meals at an inn, or hotel, for neither Buths or myself is a gourmand, & if we make 'famose Fusstouren', as he puts it, we shall often be away from Malvern at mealtimes, I daresay. So that difficulty doesn't seem a formidable one. Will you Kindly let me Know what you think of the matter, that I may write to Buths soon.

Malvern did me so much good that I feel sure it will suit Buths also & that he will fully appreciate your exceeding kindness I feel sure. That we shall take the greatest care of your House & all that is therein I need hardly say. We are no Vandals but more or less civilized Teutons. The chance of discussing the Gerontius performance & the

German vocal score (which by the way I received this morning back from the Dr) will be of value, I hope.

Will B's Daughter be a difficulty? I should think not, but of course I cannot pretend to be a judge. Kindly do not hesitate to cancel your Kind invitation if the least difficulty arises. Meanwhile please accept my warmest thanks for your very Kind offer for which I hope I may be able to show myself duly grateful in the future.

With my Kindest regards & those of my wife (who is somewhat better to day, I'm glad to say) to yourself & the Dr[,]

Believe me

Yours very sincerely,

A.J. Jaeger[18]

But matters did not run smoothly. No sooner had Alice issued the invitation than she wrote again to advise Jaeger of the sudden possibility of a more formal 'let' to friends, a welcome addition, presumably, to the Elgar budget. Although he had thoughtfully provided Alice with an *exeat,* Jaeger had already confirmed Alice's offer with Buths. Determined to make the best of the situation, he responded generously.

1, Berners Street, W.
London, July 19, 1901.

My dear Mrs Elgar,

Oh dear! Now I'm in a quandary. You *must* let your house if you get the chance & Buths & myself must find rooms somewhere else. I think it better, after thinking the matter over, to await Buths' *letter* to confirm his telegram (enclosed). I shall then Know how he has planned out his holidays. As for myself I fancy I could in any case only go to Malvern (or wherever it may be) for a week or few days, because I have received (to my *very* great surprise) an invitation from your friend Mrs Baker to stay at Hasfield Court during the Gloucester Festival, an offer which is so delightful that I wish (if at all possible) to accept it. She tells me you twain will be there. So I want to divide my Holidays into two sections. One week or so from the *24th inst,* & then another in September. As for Buths, as I have said, I don't think I can write definitely till he writes & tells me of his plans. I don't even Know yet how long he will be in England.

You see I thought your generous offer too good to be refused & I wired *at once* to Buths & he replied *at once.* We will find some other place either in Malvern or at some other quiet, countryside village-Town. I will tell you more, directly I hear further from Buths. It's a pity he has his young daughter with him, because we could 'gipsy' about so much more easily without her.

Meanwhile you will please ignore us in this puny matter & *be sure to let your House* to your friends' friends. You must *on no account* refuse such an offer just because your generous offer to 2 old duffering itinerant German tynkers was made 24 hours 'too previous' If I had only *also* waited 24 Hours with my wire to Buths it would have been allright. But in *any* case I can make matters straight with Buths, (even if I tell him a Soft taradiddle) & you must not worry in the least about us.

Your own & the Dr's peace of mind & welfare are of greater consequence than our little disappointment. *That* is a mere passing detail & can easily be put right.

I'm warned that if I go to a Country house like Hasfield Court I shall be ruined in *tips* to the Servants. Is that right? If so it is no place for a poor German clerk, which Mrs

Baker Knows I am.

With my Kindest regards and heartiest thanks for your kind thought,

I am

Yours Sincerely,

A.J. Jaeger[19]

That day Buths wrote to Alice with enthusiastic gratitude for the invitation and looked forward to consulting about the German translation of *Gerontius* that he was preparing. He had written to Jaeger in the same delighted terms, and it must have seemed to all concerned that it was becoming more and more difficult to alter the original proposal. Despite having been put in a difficult position, Jaeger continued to take all the blame on himself, although he gently made it clear that finance continued to be a consideration, such that the Hasfield invitation might prove an embarrassment. When he wrote to Alice again some days later the situation still had not been resolved, and a new complication had arisen in the form of jury service. Alice had also forgotten whether she had made it clear to Buths that he would be staying in an empty house.

1, Berners Street, W.
London, 24/7/1901

Dear Mrs Elgar,

Many thanks for your Kind letter. I have just written to Buths once more. Unless I can get away from that Jury business, my plans will of course be completely upset, and I feel so deeply & more & more deeply every day that I have landed you in a quandary through my haste in telegraphing to Buths, that I would at once decide not to come & take a mean advantage of your exceeding goodness of heart, if it were not that Buths writes in such an enthusiastic strain about the prospect of coming to Malvern, meeting you & the Dr, discussing Gerontius & (if I may say so) having me as a companion on his 'famose Fusstouren'. That makes me hesitate to say 'I can't come after all', for I should appear a humbug after nagging the man to accept your most Kind offer & he might never forgive me.

B. ought to know that Craeg Lea is Empty, for in my 1st telegram I said 'Elgar bietet mus sin *beer spehendes* haus an'. Of course, dear Mrs Elgar, if Craeg Lea is after all impossible, *any* other not too awfully expensive Rooms will answer, but what a bother all this is to you. The thought depresses me & I call myself very impolite names & hate myself.

I have decided not to accept Mrs Baker's very Kind offer. I really *must not* spend the money unless the Firm wish me to 'report' the Festival, which is not at all likely. I daresay I shall never again receive such an offer, but poor people must do without other luxuries besides these. And I *am* poor after my operation and other Doctors' Bills.

My love to E.E. What is he so busy on? Anything big? I suggested to Mr. Littleton that the firm gave E.E. a handsome commission for a *Bible Oratorio* (full programme length) & they ask for a few Trios.
Fools!!

Sincerely Yours,

A.J. Jaeger[20]

Jaeger was as always keen to smooth matters for Elgar with Novello's, especially after various recent works had been brought out by other publishers, and he knew of the 'Judas' music that had been used up in *Gerontius*. Over the next few days Alice finally decided to stand by the original invitation to Buths and Jaeger and made efforts to find a maid for them, since the Craeg Lea servants would be at Birchwood with the Elgars until September. Almost immediately on arrival at Craeg Lea, Isabella wrote to thank Alice on behalf of her husband and Buths, both of whom must have felt in some way brought closer to the source of the creative work they so greatly admired. Buths himself wrote of how he wanted to absorb the 'spirit of composition in this workplace'.

> Craeg Lea
> Wells Road,
> Malvern.
>
> July 31st
>
> My dear Mrs Elgar,
>
> How can we thank you enough for all your kindness. It is impossible! Everything is so beautifully comfortable.
> Philips is *very* delightful & nice, & I will do all I can to prevent her having too much work to do. Certainly she must have help in the mornings. We do hope to see you & Dr Elgar very soon.
> Professor Buths & his daughter are also much delighted with Craeg Lea & Malvern.
> The Professor remarked that he never imagined the place would be so beautiful as it is, & he keeps ejaculating Ach! Wie schon! so ruhig! My husband looks his delight, & I think everything perfect. What lovely air!
> I fear you have had great trouble in arranging this for us, & it distresses me. With love from my husband and myself,
> Believe me, dear Mrs. Elgar
>
> Yours very sincerely,
>
> Isabella Jaeger[21]

The party spent time walking the Malvern Hills, climbing the Worcestershire Beacon several times, (no doubt admiring Troyte Griffith's Toposcope design), strolling on the Common near Craeg Lea, and taking lunch with the Elgars at Birchwood. The Jaegers ended their holiday on 12 August, while Buths and his daughter stayed on for a few more days, finally enabling Alice to let the house from the 20th. Jaeger, hopefully feeling refreshed, wrote a letter of thanks the day before their departure. He treasured the visit to Birchwood, but could not resist expressing some first feelings of insecurity over his place in Elgar's life, now that his reputation had begun to be established.

> And now let me thank you & Mrs Elgar from our very hearts for having enabled us through your exceeding kindness to enjoy this delightful holiday at a time when the state of my finances made it doubtful whether I could manage a holiday at all. We have spent happy & delightful days, the most delightful having been that spent at your quiet retreat in the wood the other day. I fear I cannot in future do much for you or your works, for

> you have made a name now which will smoothe your paths for you in all matters. But if perchance you require a somebody in London whom you wish to do aught for you that cannot be settled by correspondence: if I can do anything for you in *any* way, I hope & pray you will let me try to be of use to you & pay off a small fraction of the great debt with which I find myself burdened.[22]

Jaeger decided after all to join the Festival house party with the Bakers of Hasfield Court, where the company included the Elgars, Frederick Cowen and the Pennys. Although he had complained again of problems with his nose, Jaeger was able to participate in bouts of single-stick with the Baker sons, with whom Elgar developed a long-running charade combining Royalist figures with characters from Scott's *Redgauntlet*. A photograph shows him replacing his jacket after a duel by the porch. The Festival programme included several Elgar items as well as symphonies and overtures by Beethoven, Brahms and Wagner. But if Jaeger's presence at Gloucester was in fact to review the Festival for the *Musical Times*, there were no characteristic references to such works in the article which appeared in the October edition. The previous month's number had included the usual 'Festival Novelties' article which is more likely to have been by Jaeger, although much of the music, including works by Sir Frederick Bridge, Charles Harford Lloyd and John E. West of Novello's, was probably not calculated to kindle his enthusiasm. New works by Coleridge-Taylor and Bell were given sympathetic mention, however, and there was also a feature on Bell himself, 'A New Festival Composer'. His academic and professional career was described, together with a résumé of his compositions, including various chamber and orchestral works.

That month saw another major Festival, this time at Leeds. The new Cantata by Coleridge-Taylor, *The Blind Girl of Castel-Cuillé*, suffered from a weak libretto, but the *Enigma* Variations, in a performance conducted by the composer, were reckoned to be one of the great successes of the four-day affair. Jaeger saw the opportunity to plead Elgar's case again with the Littletons, and to persuade the composer to leave Boosey and return to the Novello's fold immediately with a projected Cantata.

> When are you going to send us your Norwich Cantata? Now, you will send *that* to us won't you? You OUGHT to anyhow, seeing what we are doing for Gerontius here & in Germany; & we shall pay you as well as Boosey & Full Scores *won't* be any difficulty in future, I guess. I have had another long talk about you to Messrs Alfred & Augustus Littleton & you need fear no worries in future. They have had an eye-opener over the Leeds Festival & I'm sure they'll meet you in *every way* in future. You know when they *have* taken to a man they'll do **ANY MORTAL THING** for him as in the case of Sullivan & Stainer. Only *understand* each other a little better & all will go like a House on fire & you *can't* deal with a better firm. Think it over & believe me, there's a dear. Our Editors (!!) wont edit *you*! never fear *that*![23]

In fact, Jaeger had covered a good deal of ground in his talk with the Littletons, dealing with all the points which he knew annoyed Elgar, doing everything he could to reconcile him with the firm. The resulting arrangements proved a business success, at least in the short term. And all other considerations aside, Jaeger himself would have found it unthinkable not to be able to play his rôle in new Elgar works as they developed, and see them through Novello's presses. Such a loss would have been a personal blow to him, and might also have diminished his standing in the firm.

There seemed that year to have been a change of editorial policy over the reviews of London concerts in the *Musical Times*. Less space was devoted to them, and the controversial and stimulating tone of some earlier columns gave way to bland comment of merely routine interest, sometimes merely listing the works played. There is little at this time that strikes the eye as being characteristic of Jaeger, although sympathetic if brief comments are to be found concerning new works by native composers such as Frederick Cowen, Arthur Somervell, Landon Ronald, John McEwen and Vaughan Williams, whose Quintet in D was described as evincing 'considerable originality of conception'. Interest in musical activities on the Continent, on the other hand, was reflected in the publication of occasional lengthy articles by Otto Lessmann, particularly an account of the progressive Heidelberg Festival which had taken place in June and which had promoted works by such figures as Richard Strauss, Sibelius, Josef Suk, Humperdinck and Scharwenka. Perhaps Jaeger's tendency to illness that year had reduced his contributions, for the amount of his earlier reviewing suggested that he had been devoting several evenings a week to attending concerts; and perhaps too there was the feeling of battles won over the programmes of the Queen's Hall concerts.

Alfred Rodewald had given the première of the first two *Pomp and Circumstance* Marches at Liverpool, and the first London performances took place under Wood at the Queen's Hall on 22 October, duly bringing the house down. Afterwards the delighted Jaegers treated themselves to supper at Pagani's, and sent an enthusiastic impromptu postcard to Elgar; 'Your SPLENDID marches were the greatest success I have *ever* witnessed over a novelty at ANY concert …'. But the Marches were published by Boosey and a few days later Jaeger kept up the pressure on Elgar by writing again of his efforts to smooth matters at Novello's, particularly as far as finance was concerned. 'Novello & Co can afford to pay you as well as *anybody*, & in future things will be found beautifully "greased" for you. So have no misgivings on that account.' Once again, too, the question of a symphony was raised. Jaeger told Elgar that he had interested Henry Wood in such a work, and further, had secured a written promise from Alfred Littleton for the immediate publication of the score and parts if the work were offered to the firm. Finally he returned to the Marches, confessing to having written a long letter about them to the sympathetic Mrs Baker of Hasfield Court and revealing that the music was having an almost oppressive impact on an easily overwrought sensibility.

> The beastly things are worrying me into an illness. The Tunes, damn them, Keep buzzing in my empty head, & the orchestral effects, harmonies & all your Monkey tricks dance about & within me. The things are splendid & will make your name Known everywhere. Send *us* Nos 3, 4, 5 & 6 of the series *pray*.[24]

With the Düsseldorf *Gerontius* performance planned for late December coming ever closer, the work was very much in mind at Novello's. In the spirit of the firm's

1 Jaeger as a young man. Like Elgar, he liked to dress well.

2 Early days in London: Jaeger with his mother and sisters

3 16 Margravine Gardens, West Kensington

4 Isabella Jaeger: a portrait photograph by Edgar Thomas Holding, 1902

5 Another portrait, with the Guadanigni violin

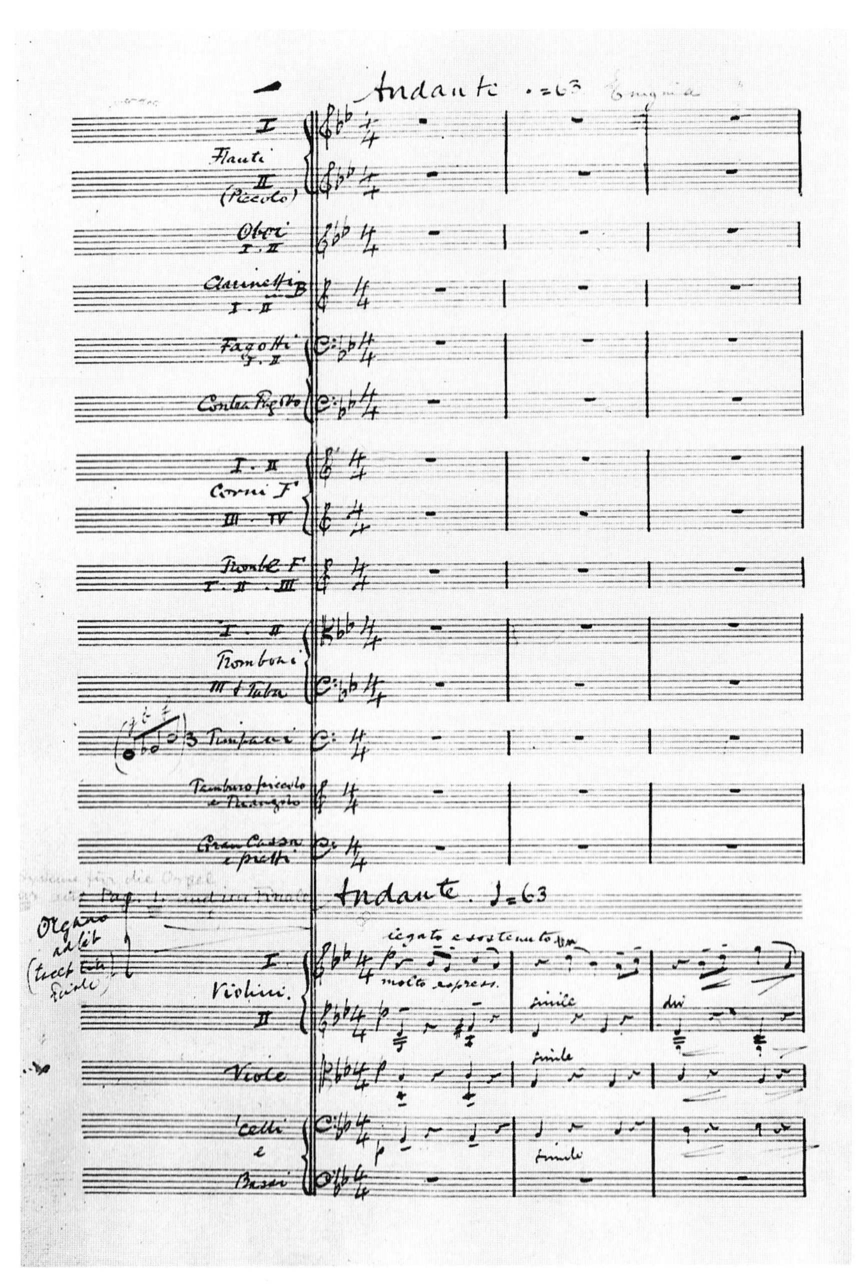

6 The first page of Elgar's Variations for Orchestra, Op. 36. The word 'Enigma' has been added in Jaeger's hand.

7 'My dear Sir Hubert ... ': Parry in middle life

8 Walford Davies

9 Samuel Coleridge-Taylor

10 Horatio Parker

11 Sydney Loeb

12 Jaeger replaces his jacket after a bout of single-stick at Hasfield Court, September 1901

13 37 Curzon Road, Muswell Hill

14 Jaeger, Isabella and the 'bairns' at Ivy Cottage, Honley

fresh start with Elgar, Henry Clayton devised a document to cover the question of royalties on the work once the advance had been covered by sales, and Jaeger had been supervising the production of German language vocal scores using the translation that Buths had provided. The December *Musical Times* gave notice of the performance in an article which also enumerated recent German performances of the Variations in Mainz, Wiesbaden and Berlin, and forthcoming ones in Brussels and Munich; the work was making its way in Europe. In addition there was a translation of a generous notice by Lessmann of the Berlin performance, written for the *Allgemeine Musik-Zeitung*, which spoke 'of Elgar's exceptional talent, of his high aim and extraordinary technical equipment,' and went on to state 'What the work reveals in respect of inventive power, brilliant workmanship, and sovereign command of the means of expression, equals the best which has been produced anywhere – in the way of orchestral variations – since Beethoven.'[25] The verdict must have gratified Jaeger, and the article was introduced as a 'trumpet-blast of enthusiastic appreciation which will, we hope, be heard throughout musical circles of the Fatherland.'

Meanwhile Elgar's name was continuing to attract wider attention nearer home, and he dropped a confidential hint to Jaeger about a Covent Garden commission. Much earlier that year, shortly after the death of Queen Victoria, he had been approached by the Master of the Musick, Sir Walter Parratt, over an ode and a march for the coronation of the new King which was to take place in June 1902. Jaeger worried about what kind of libretto Elgar might use for a possible opera: 'So much good music has been ruined through silly, ineffective, preposterous, dull, unimaginative, &c &c librettos', he wrote, and later advised strongly against any suggestion of adapting *Caractacus*. The example of Coleridge-Taylor, taking on too many commissions and weakening the quality of his output, was also invoked. Neither did some aspects of the *Coronation Ode* find favour with him, particularly the proposal to use the trio tune of the first *Pomp and Circumstance* March as the basis for a song with words specially devised to fit. In explaining his objections he again used a word that would come to be a commonplace of Elgar criticism: 'I say you *will have to* write another tune for the "Ode" ... that drop to E & the bigger drop afterwards are quite impossible in singing ANY words to them. They sound downright vulgar ...'. But with the encouragement of Clara Butt and the approval of the King himself, Elgar would not budge. It may have helped to seal Jaeger's mild disapproval of the whole idea of such a patriotic commission, and of the work itself, although another example of his advocacy paid off when he was able to tell Elgar that Henry Wood was insisting on a fully engraved score of *Gerontius* for a performance he was to conduct at the Sheffield Festival the following year.

Jaeger was again working long hours at Berners Street. 'Night after night I have been here till *10 pm*, to get home tired as a Dog', he told Elgar in mid-December and went on to make an almost frantic appeal over his presence at the Düsseldorf *Gerontius*, in which Jaeger had invested a great deal of personal commitment. Alice had been unwell, and there was a possibility that the Elgars would not attend the performance after all.

I am *distressed* to hear from Buths that you MAY NOT after all go to D' dorf. I say: PLEASE, if you can possibly crawl over the Channel, DON'T disappoint all of us by staying away. It will be a tragedy of disappointment, really. Buths & his choir & orchestra would feel it much & that 'Tusch' which I feel sure they would give you, will never be played. In fact the affair will be robbed of half its glory. Several English Critics are going, not to mention this tinker & even from the business point of view, to come down to sordid earth, it will make MUCH difference to you & *your* works. Even if your dear wife is too unwell to *come* ... I hope *you* will yet come IF *she is well enough to be left behind in good care* ... Do come, there's a dear. Come with me & we'll travel together ... Tell me frankly, as I speak frankly to you ... What will you do? Tell me QUICKLY, PLEASE ...[26]

In the event, Jaeger met the Elgars at Victoria Station and travelled with them to Düsseldorf where they all stayed as Buths's guests. The economy was no doubt welcome to Jaeger, for the expenses of the expedition had hit him hard. Alfred Kalisch had earlier written to Elgar, 'You will be glad to hear that the Jaeger matters are all settled as well as could be hoped. But I fear, poor man, he has found it a very expensive amusement.'[27] Buths himself had done everything he could to smooth matters musical and political, writing to Elgar earlier that month in his quaint English, 'Our rehearsals of your splendid work are in full swing and the admiration of all the singers too. Therefore no fear on account of a different political feeling. I hope the German public will never forget how to appreciate the very art, and your work is strong enough to enforce the acknowledge as a very art's-work, and all the more to win admiration and love by the warmhearted life of your musical expression.'[28] The performance itself, the second full production of the work, took place on 19 December, and was a huge success for all concerned, with the exception of some uncertainties on the part of the Angel which were made up for by the superb artistry of the Gerontius, Ludwig Wüllner. Elgar was given the tremendous reception that Jaeger predicted, marked by a 'Tusch', a congratulatory flourish from the orchestra, and the presentation of a laurel wreath. It was the unmistakable signal of a triumph. The *Rheinisch-Westphälische Zeitung* recounted, 'The composer, who was present but had remained hidden away among the audience at the back of the hall, was so persistently and enthusiastically applauded after both parts that he finally had to appear on the platform and from there bow to Professor Buths and the fine body of orchestral players and chorus singers to show his gratitude to them.'[29] At this point in the proceedings Jaeger, in his enthusiasm, and his determination to ensure that the success immediately became news in England, left the hall to wire an account to the *Times*, no less, which was published the next day. He thus missed the first part of the post-concert supper, and a speech by Buths which praised Jaeger's own rôle in the spread of Elgar's music. Jaeger wrote,

Dr. Edward Elgar's 'Traum der Gerontius' was produced for the first time in Germany this evening at Düsseldorf by the Stadtischer Musikverein, under professor Julius Buths, and in the presence of the composer. The original and beautiful work received a most excellent interpretation by an orchestra of 85, a choir of 300, and the soloists Fraulein Antonie Beel, Dr. Franz Wüllner, and Herr Metzmacher. The chorus had mastered their difficult task splendidly; whether the serenity of the choirs of angelicals or the terrific force of the demons' sullen howls had to be interpreted, they were equally successful. The orchestra produced a series of glowing tone pictures: the Vorspiel especially sounded wonderfully fine in the Kaisersaal of the municipal Tonhalle, which is acoustically one of the best concert rooms in the world. Dr. Wüllner's reading of the part of Gerontius was one of the most artistic and impressive things imaginable. His voice is not remarkable for either beauty or power, but his interpretative gifts are of the highest order. In fact, a better exponent of the difficult role it would be difficult to find. His expression of anguished suffering and fervid prayer, of heavenly peace and sublime ecstasy, were quite masterly and moved the audience deeply. A considerable number of German musicians had come to Düsseldorf especially to hear a new work by the composer whose 'Enigma' Variations have lately been performed in Berlin, Wiesbaden, Mayence, and Brussels, and discussed in the German press. Dr. Elgar was enthusiastically called for after the first part, and at the end he was received with a storm of applause, in which chorus and orchestra joined as well as the huge audience. The orchestra greeted the happy composer with the inspiriting cacophony called a 'Tusch' (flourish), and a splendid laurel wreath of enormous size was presented to him. The greatest impression I received was from the singing of the chorus, which proved the absurdity of the charge frequently made against the composer after the Birmingham performance of 1900 that his work was impossible to render. To Professor Buths, who worked with the rarest enthusiasm and energy, the thanks of English musicians are due and should be ungrudgingly given.[30]

Further ungrudging thanks were due to Jaeger himself, and Johnstone of the *Manchester Guardian* continued his own account of the evening with mention of the grateful speech made by Elgar at the post-concert supper, adding his voice to that of Buths. It was perhaps the only time that Elgar made such an emphatic public acknowledgement of Jaeger, who would remain little-known to the public at large, and the account sought to avoid any misunderstanding over a foreign name by establishing his residence in London. But for Jaeger, once the little boy who loved to follow the marching bands, such praise in the city of his birth must have been sweet.

To complete the account of yesterday's performance I need only add that the concert was followed by a supper, after which Professor Buths made a speech describing the circumstances which had led him to introduce 'The Dream of Gerontius' to the German public. Dr. Elgar responded, expressing his thanks to all concerned in the performance, referring to the profound impression that Dr. Ludwig Wüllner's rendering of the tenor solos had made upon him, and making special acknowledgements to Mr. A. J. Jaeger for his services in calling the attention of German musicians to the oratorio. He laid great stress on his indebtedness to Mr. Jaeger (of London) whom he called the best friend of English music.[31]

Sweet too must have been the *Düsseldorfer Zeitung*'s acknowledgement of the city's rôle in the performance history of the work: 'Düsseldorf may take satisfaction in the fact that though this highly significant work, which was written for the Birmingham Musical Festival and was first performed there on 3 October 1900, will have started its course through the other great German concert halls from here, the composer will always have special ties with the artistic metropolis on the Rhine.'[32] The comparative lack of acceptance of 'serious English music' was noted by the critic of the *Kölnische*

Zeitung, who had attended the first performance of the Variations and played his own part in recommending the work to German conductors.

> It is rare enough that the light of an important new work should shine forth to us from England. Of Sullivan only the immortal and comic Mikado managed to cross the channel, leaving aside his Ivanhoe which was accorded a solemn funeral at the Berlin Hofoper. But of serious music there have only been isolated examples of works that have beaten a path to us. A quartet by Stanford and a few instrumental works by Mackenzie are virtually all that there has been while a productive symphonic composer lile Cowen is still awaiting his call outside the gates of the German Reich. When the strains of Edward Elgar's orchestral variations were first wafted to our ears two years ago at a Richter concert at London's Queen's Hall, we took the liberty of drawing the attention of German conductors to this work, in which the unusual mastery of technique and the splendid tonal colouring made it highly eligible for export.[33]

The Elgars remained in Germany over the holiday period, staying with Buths and then with their timpani-playing friend Henry Ettling at Mainz, while Jaeger returned to Margravine Gardens and a family Christmas. On Boxing Day he wrote to Walford Davies with his daughter's reactions to a seasonal musical offering, and repeated his proud praise of the German chorus at Düsseldorf. There was also some encouragement for *The Temple*, the oratorio that Davies was composing in fulfilment of the Three Choirs Commission that both Jaeger and Elgar had helped him find.

> 16, Margravine Gardens,
> West Kensington.
>
> 26/XII/01
>
> My dear Davies,
>
> Very many thanks to you & Mrs Matheson for your Kind wishes which are most heartily reciprocated[.] Little Miss Bitte-Bitte says the Carol is 'sehr'ubsch', but she prefers 'Schlaf, Kindchen Schlaf', at present. But then she is no critic yet.
>
> I have been to Düsseldorf to hear Gerontius & was *delighted*, as was friend Elgar with all we saw & heard. The work was a *great* success, 2000 people sat still as in a church & drank in Elgars wonderful Strains. And the Chorus sang the difficult work as if it were Childs play. In time, in tune, with feeling, with intelligence. It was *splendid* & we were compensated for the *awful* B'ham experience.
>
> The work is above your countrymen, my boy, but the despised Germans will appreciate it & its Composer.
>
> Elgar was Received with a 'Tusch' & a huge laurel wreath presented to him Coram publico.
>
> To hear him addressed as 'hochverchter Meister' by the musicians who met him was an experience that did him (& me too) good. The work will go round the German Concert Rooms. You mark my prophecy.
>
> What *can* I say about your Temple music? I have only heard it once on the P. F. when it struck me by its dignity, backbone[,] directness & beauty. I cannot go into details from Memory. I'm too stupid for that. Come & play it to me again. Much love!
>
> Ever Yours
>
> A.J. Jaeger[34]

Three days later Jaeger spread himself over a longer and slightly more critical account of the Düsseldorf expedition to Dora Penny, who had not been able to attend. He made a confidential joke about Alice Elgar's reactions to her husband's music, as well as repeating his praise for Wüllner and the Chorus, and repeating too his pride in the ready German appreciation of Elgar's music. He was frank about his frustration at having to socialize with old friends during the interval, when he could have been extending his network of contacts among musicians.

[29 December, 1901]

We travelled to D'orf together & had a lovely passage. Buths and friend met us & we drove to 17 Ehrens Strasse a nice house & a comfortable one. Buths, his Frau Professor & his 2 daughters were as kind as kind could be. On Wednesday morning we went to the first orchestral rehearsal with Soloists. The orchestra of 80 odd was not like Wood's 110 for reading powers or tone, but they answered every purpose & Elgar had not very much to find fault with. Buths, though a man of complete savoir faire is not a great 'interpreter' – I mean co-creator, and there were many passages of which more might have been made as regards mystery, feeling, expression, force, etc. etc. Still, one can't always have everything, & time is an important factor at a Rehearsal.

But directly Wüllner opened his mouth to sing 'Jesus, Maria, meine Stunde kam' we said that man has Brains. And by the Olympian Jove he had Brains galore. He made us sit up and realize that Elgar's intention, & what I had expected when I wrote my much maligned analysis, could be realised by an artist. I never heard such intellectual deeply felt singing. Not that W's voice is wonderful. No! But his Brains and his heart are; & they are more than mere voice in a work of such greatness as this wonderful Gerontius. We were delighted and moved to tears. As for dear Mrs E., you can imagine her state of seventh-heaven gratitude, with eyebrow lifting, neck twisting, forget-me-not glances towards the invisible Heavens! Don't think I am making fun of her! I am not; but you know her signs of deep emotion of the Dr's music don't you?

There was another Rehearsal with Chorus in the evening. The audience (admitted on payment) was quite considerable and the applause ditto. Buths introduced E. to the Chorus, as he had introduced him to the Orchestra in the mg., and everybody seemed in the best of spirits. Then, next (Thursday) mg., there was another Orchestral Rehearsal when Buths filed[35] & E. interfered more frequently to secure readings more in accordance with his conceptions. Then in the evening, the Event. The Hall was crammed full though it was a beastly night (there is no more polite word for it). The Hall is a fine one, and acoustically superb. We (E., Mrs. E., A. Johnstone of the Manchester Guardian & yours truly) sat in the third row of the balcony right facing the Orchestra and we heard marvellously well. Every little detail came out beautifully & I can assure you I have not had such an elevating soul-stirring experience for years as listening under such circumstances to this wonderful music.

The Chorus was perfect, there is no other word for it. The effect of the pp 12 part passages sung dead in tune (throughout the week) was quite ethereal, while the ff tutti were thundered out with imposing force & splendid sonority. They speak of the 'Rhineland tone' among Choruses in Germany & I realized here, where the beauty of tone lay. It is in a remarkable roundness and sweetness in the female voices & by a big sonority in the male. For though the trousered contingent in the Choir was by no means large, the quantity of tone produced by it was quite sufficient, even for the terrific Dämonen Chorus. That masterful piece, which was so completely ruined at B'ham, was given with perfect ease & yet with strenuous dramatic force which one could not possibly realize through studying the music on paper.

Wüllner did not seem in very good voice and he made one serious blunder; but these were only as blots on a summer sun. Elgar was very nearly called after Part 1, & during the long pause (20 minutes or more) he held a reception in the 'Soloisten-Zimmer', where I was told many musicians from other towns congregated to congratulate E. & Buths. I alas! was not there, for I was waylaid by many D'orf friends who all wanted to shake hands & ask questions & stand me Bottles of Hock which I didn't want. In fact, I didn't want them either, but what was I to do? In any case, I missed the chance of speaking to the 'auswartige' musicians, as I ought to have done, & wanted to do. So I didn't bless my D'orf friends exactly. In Part II Wüllner was great, especially in the 'Take me away'. The big Chorus 'Praise to the Holiest' which astonished the German musicians by its monumental architecture, was a masterly performance & the Finale, that wonderful Finale, was another revelation to those who heard it only at B'ham.

Unfortunately the Angel was anything but angelically perfect. But though Elgar suffered sundry twitches & pangs when the Angel threatened to 'fall', the audience could not have realized, thanks to Buths' alertness, how dangerously near collapse the performance came once or twice through this d..... Angel's shortcomings. (By the way, what the *Musical Times* says about her, I did not telegraph). Well, at the end E was enthusiastically called, & though he had to fight his way through thronging crowds of people down the stairs & to the front, the applause & shouts were kept up until at last (the time seemed a small eternity) he reached the Podium. There the Chorus & Orchestra & Organ joined in a tusch & a large fine laurel wreath was handed to him. He asked Buths (so the latter told me) what to do with the thing!

Directly I saw the wreath presented I rushed out, took a cab to the Telegraph office & wired 400 words to the Times. Yes, the Times, the account which you read. How it came about that I wired to the Times is too long a tale to tell here; but in addition to doing E & B & the firm a jolly good turn, I earned 20 Marks! Unfortunately, another wire which I sent to the Central News was much mutilated by that agency & only a few papers thought the event of sufficient importance to give the 8 or nine lines to it.

So much for the English appreciation of High art in music. If this had only been Dan Leno's first appearance in Germany there would have been columns in all the English papers. Ye Gods! You have to do a lot yet to be considered a musical nation. Editors are at fault. After the Concert there was a Supper, but I got to that rather late, because of my work at the Telegraph office. In my absence Buths had made a speech about me, and my inducing him (B) to take an interest in English music, etc. etc.

When I came back at last (about 11.15) I was placed between the Angel and her Sister. (I have never been so near feeling good.) She, the poor Angel, was very depressed, for cruel, wicked Buths had told her during the performance & after she had missed an important entry, that 'es war scheusslich'. Pretty strong that! I said some nice things about her nice voice (it is a nice voice) & the difficult parts & then we became good friends at once. (Of course! you will say.) Well, it was a jolly, most enjoyable evening. Elgar confessed to me that he had never had such an one! He made a nice, quiet, modest speech of thanks & appreciation to Buths, Wullner and me! & I blushed (tried to) as in duty bound; & at 1.30 or so we at last drove home, having spent an exciting, beautiful day.

I wish you & Mrs Baker & a few other English friends had been there to see how my countrymen, my townsmen, honoured our Doctor. It was everywhere 'Hochverehrter Meister' & 'Geehrter Meister'; E's eyes twinkled thereat. On Friday we were invited to Carl Sohn's, a rich D'orf painter. We had a gorgeous feast. Talk of Rudesheimer!! We were 3 hours or so over Dinner, a number of painters & musicians having been invited to meet E. On Saturday, Buths, E, Johnstone & myself went to Cologne to visit old Dr Franz Wüllner, the Director of the Cologne Conservatoire & conductor of the Gurzenich Concerts. He all but promised definitely to produce Gerontius at his first Concert next year.

In the evening I sped homewards. I could tell you lots of other interesting details of our delightful stay at beautiful D'orf, but I must stop. I have sent you a Manchester Guardian giving Johnstone's critique (Very Good!) Next month (February) the M.T. will bring much more about the conspicuous event. The firm appreciate all I have done, the Directors made me nice speeches & have doubled my usual Xmas Box. And now Farewell & say a pretty thank you for this ausführlichen account of our journey. You have never had such a long letter I bet ...

Yours very sincerely

RODNIM[36]

Jaeger deserved his doubled Christmas Box that year, for with the market opened up for sales of vocal scores to the many German choirs, the success of the Düsseldorf *Gerontius* was commercial as well as artistic. On both counts the success was Jaeger's almost as much as anybody's.

7 1902: Kensington to Muswell Hill

As he had promised Dorabella, Jaeger's sortie to the Düsseldorf Telegraph Office also resulted in a bulletin to the *Musical Times*, 'By Telegram From Our Special Correspondent', which appeared in the January number. It covered familiar ground, summarizing Jaeger's hopes for the future: 'It was an evening that will be long remembered, and one that may have a far-reaching influence upon the progress of British music in foreign lands.' That progress was monitored in a paragraph in the same number quoting from press reports of the Wiesbaden and Brussels Variations performances, and there was the suggestion of a further *Gerontius* performance in Germany at the Lower Rhine Festival in May. But meanwhile both Elgar and Jaeger now had to come down to earth again. Elgar felt the return to England after his reception in Düsseldorf very strongly: 'The horrible musical atmosphere I plunged into at once in this benighted country nearly suffocated me', he wrote from Malvern two days after arriving home. Jaeger continued much workaday correspondence with him over details of the printing of the score and parts of *Gerontius*, but kept the question of Elgar's future creative development to the fore by asking the Littletons to consider paying him a regular income. Jaeger himself was continuing in poor health, and it appeared that the operation suggested by MacDonald had been a failure. The news worried Elgar and he revealed the intensity of his concern, offering whatever further help was necessary.

> I'm awfully distressed to hear you are again ill & terribly disappointed that our operation was not finally successful. I wish you all the good things & only wish I could put this right for you; do tell me what can be done & how & when? I think hourly about you & worry about it until I'm sick – which is human but not poetic.[1]

But there was in those days no certain remedy for the disease that was already gradually eating away at Jaeger's respiratory system, and in just three years almost to the day from this letter his condition would become such that the only possible hope for him lay in a prolonged stay in the rarified climate of the Swiss Alps. For the moment Jaeger struggled on through a London winter, although there is a gap from his side of the correspondence with Elgar for some weeks. At last on 19 February Elgar was able to write to thank him for a card with better news, although a few days later he rebuked Jaeger mildly for his compulsive concern over a poor report concerning one of his younger composer protégés. It was only too likely, as Elgar predicted, that Jaeger would spend himself over lengthy correspondence as a result.

> I can't *think* why you worry about what's written in papers – I never see any & don't miss them. You will now have to write eight pages to all your friends explaining that Bell is better than Holbrooke – about which nobody wd. have been in doubt until you call their attention to a foolish article in an unknown paper &c &c &c.[2]

Perhaps there was opportunity for some further chiding soon after, when Elgar spent a few days in London. He lunched with Jaeger at Pagani's, cementing his return to the Novello's fold with the recently composed *Grania and Diarmid* music. Despite his illness Jaeger had managed to produce copy for that month's *Musical Times*, including another longer and more thoughtful review of the Düsseldorf *Gerontius*, and another presentation of excerpts from the reviews in the German press. There was, too, a review of a revised version of Coleridge-Taylor's *Blind Girl of Castel-Cuillé*, which had been seen as a falling-off in comparison with the *Hiawatha* trilogy. The work had been extensively altered and improved, and Jaeger may have been partly responsible. But if his highest expectations of Taylor had proved ill-founded, there were always other stars in the firmament, and at the end of February there was a letter to Elgar reminiscent of the old Jaeger, after a concert of chamber works by Bell and John McEwen,[3] Professor of Harmony and Composition at the Royal Academy of Music.

> Bell's pieces came off well last night, but I was much more interested in a really splendid String Quartet by MacEwen I heard afterwards at the 'King Cole' Club. I was astounded. Such a glorious stream of most impassioned, beautiful *melody*, Strong, unconventional, genuine Melody, treated in the true Quartet Style I haven't heard FOR YEARS. It moved me deeply & I could cry that so gifted & absurdly modest a man cant get a note of his stuff accepted. It's enough to make one swear at the injustice of this world.[4]

Jaeger's position at Novello's, where his judgement counted for so much more than his status might indicate, was becoming increasingly anomolous. A crisis in his relations with the Littletons seems to have developed at this time, all the more hurtful because of the recent vindication of the Düsseldorf *Gerontius*. In writing to thank Alice Elgar for sending a portrait photograph of her husband, Jaeger explained the situation and openly counted on her sympathy.

> I have been quite 'off' writing lately & very miserable because I have had a 'Row' with N & Co. It seems to me they are jealous & disgusted because so many people, i.e. musicians write to *me* & come to speak to me. They seem to want to tie my unworthiness down to mere 'clerking'. Well if they do, I shall leave. I hope I'm a little better than a Clerk who only sticks to his desk & does figures. I wont bother you with any details, but they have taken the pluck & the interest in the affairs of N & Co. out of me, & I' m unhappy.[5]

If there had been complaints that musicians were coming to deal with Jaeger himself more and more directly, rather than with the directors, it was partly a comment on the sheer range of his contacts among composers and musicians of all kinds. He was becoming a focal point in the musical world, and his *amour-propre* would have been greatly boosted by the success of the Düsseldorf *Gerontius*. Perhaps there were times, with the best will in the world, when his enthusiasm became exhausting for others, when his foreign-accented volubility turned into an irritating mannerism and his single-minded campaigns became merely predictable. Moreover, as recent events had shown, he had committed the unforgivable sin of being right, and in his uninhibited, extrovert way, had no doubt let his satisfaction show.[6] If there was little or no prospect of further advancement at Novello's, Jaeger could only ask for the kind of status and respect that he thought his rôle merited. It was a sticking-point, as it had been with Coleridge-Taylor. Jaeger did not leave the firm as he threatened to; the sheer necessity of continuing to support his now extended family dominated the situation. Elgar's next letter, written nearly a fortnight after Jaeger's *cri de coeur* to Alice, refers to the matter having blown over, and it is hard to credit that the management of Novello's could have succeeded in demotivating such a person as August Jaeger for long.

There was too the second Düsseldorf *Gerontius* to look forward to in May, although by early April Jaeger wrote that he was having to spend hours every day over details of the score and parts, now at second proof stage and not expected to be ready until a fortnight before the performance. He had earlier written to Elgar of a new man at Novello's, John Pointer, of whose proof-reading he had a high opinion, but it shows a somewhat unhealthy weakness that even then, Jaeger could not delegate with peace of mind: 'I have gone over the parts & Score sent to-day, after Pointer had done with them, & found all sorts of little things ...', he told Elgar. Jaeger was naturally obsessive over details, of proof-reading as of other things, but it was a tendency that led to stress and in the same letter he apologized for owing several letters but 'I am dog-tired when I get home in the evenings'. He was held responsible for the work of his sometimes less than fully efficient assistants, and seems to have been called to account on one occasion, as indicated in the postscript of a hasty undated note from Elgar, whose relationship with Jaeger evidently did not exclude occasional forays into Anglo-Saxon humour.

> Malvern [day illegible, no date]
>
> My dear Jaeger:
>
> All right dont fidge about 'that correction' – I wondered what ailed Pointer to suggest such a thing & now you tell me you have a 'new man' – I hope P. is still with you, 'as [illegible] a brick' – but don't ee swear – I knew *you* had not looked at it carefully so all is forgiven only I hope Pointer has not left yet.
>
> Much love to you all.
> [Dreary weather
> Good music
> Liver pills
> Calomel
> Income Tax

No Biking
New Boots
Bad golf
& &c

Fill up the life of

Your despised

E.E.[7]

Private

I say : you as chief of yr. dept., suffered (slightly) for the sins of your underlings – which calls to my inferior mind the O.E. proverb
'Sick sheep make a *shytten* shepherd'!

The reviews of London concerts in the columns of the *Musical Times* continued to be more brief and businesslike than in the period of Jaeger's Russian Campaign and there is less of the impact of his personality on them, perhaps another reflection of management control. But several of Jaeger's known enthusiasms shine through otherwise routine pages in the April edition. Henry Wood had played Richard Strauss's *Don Juan* at the Queen's Hall, and the review pleaded the case for performances of more works by the same composer, particularly *Ein Heldenleben*, the title of which was suitably Anglicized on this occasion. Given the composer's technical command, Jaeger was modifying his reservations about orchestral programme music, being prepared to make exceptions for works he thought free of 'extravagances'.

> Richard Strauss's orchestral fantasia, 'Don Juan', was given for the first time at these concerts, and the performance, under the direction of Mr. Wood, was exceedingly fine. The form of the work, the subject which the composer seeks to illustrate in tones, may be open to exception; but there is such skill, such strong character in his music, that one cannot but endorse the opinion of those who regard him as the foremost composer of the day in Germany. To use an oft-quoted yet most convenient phrase: he has something to say, and knows well how to say it. In some of his tone-poems there are peculiarities, extravagances, but of such things 'Don Juan' is well-nigh free. Let us hope that Mr. Wood will soon give us an opportunity of hearing Strauss's 'The life of a hero'.[8]

Meanwhile there was encouragement and practical advice for William Henry Bell after a Philharmonic Society concert back in February.

> Mr. William H. Bell furnished the novelty … by two orchestral tone-pictures from 'Mother Carey', a suite in three movements, representing the parting, absence, and return of a voyager. As the first movement … was not played owing to its undergoing the process of revision, only the sections 'In the night watches' and 'In the Fo'c's'le' were presented. The former of these admirably reflects the gloom of the night watches, the storm at sea, and the grey light of the early dawn. In the second movement much use is made of the sea-song, 'The Arethusa' … This 'In the Fo'c's'le' section would benefit by compression, whereby some of its fragmentariness might be relieved. The work is however, a distinct advance upon what Mr. Bell has hitherto done by its

> clearness of orchestration and restraint from over-elaboration, the insidious snare against which young composers should continually be on their guard.[9]

The question of over-elaboration seemed to be at the heart of a brief and blunt comment on Coleridge-Taylor's three *Negro Fantasias* for violin and piano, recently premièred at the Bechstein Hall: 'Mr. Coleridge-Taylor needs to be cautioned against the complexity which characterises these pieces, and which thereby lose much of the charm and spontaneity of his earlier compositions for the violin.'[10] A performance at the Steinway Hall of a song by John E. West was noted without comment, although an encouraging welcome was given to a new trio by a Royal College student, Frank Bridge. But perhaps one of the most heartfelt comments in that month's notices concerned the weather – one of the London fogs that could make its presence felt indoors as well as out. Of a Royal Choral Society concert at the Albert Hall, Jaeger wrote with justified personal concern, 'The concert on the 6th ult. was greatly handicapped by the fog, which ruled supreme within and without the great building at Kensington, and which affected performers and audience alike by its irritating presence.'[11]

During his working holiday at Cliftonville in August 1900, devoted to the *Gerontius* analysis, Jaeger had encountered another of his London contacts, the composer, pianist and conductor Percy Pitt. After study in Leipzig and Munich, Pitt became the official organist at Queen's Hall, and composed various orchestral works and a *Ballade* for violin and orchestra for Ysaÿe. Later he would become musical director of the Grand Opera Syndicate, and in 1922 would be appointed to a similar postion at the BBC. During that seaside meeting, Pitt had played Jaeger his 'work in progress', incidental music for a play based on the thirteenth-century story of Francesca, daughter of the count of Ravenna, who was given in marriage to a repulsive deformed tyrant, Malatesta of Rimini. She fell in love with his brother, Paolo, and the lovers, being discovered, were jointly put to death. The subject had been variously treated in verse and opera, and by Tchaikovsky in his Symphonic Fantasia of 1876, *Francesca da Rimini*. Now Stephen Phillips's play 'Paolo and Francesca' had been produced in London at the St James's Theatre, and the *Musical Times* review shows every sign of having been written by Jaeger in its well-informed relation of Pitt's incidental music to contemporary developments in European music, particularly the *melodrame* with its subtle psychological possibilities. Once again, a new direction for English music was signposted.

> His music is thoroughly modern, not only in its free employment of polyphony and chromatic harmonies, but in the spirit in which it strives to illustrate the psychology rather than the action of the drama. It deals in a Lisztian and Straussian spirit with ideas as much as with men and women as things … it is enough to show that Mr. Pitt has artistic insight of a rare and subtle kind, and to distinguish his work from most of that which we usually hear. *Melodrame* is much neglected in this country, but in Germany it has recently been undergoing developments of no little significance. The best example of the most modern methods as applied to it is probably Humperdinck's 'Konigskinder' music. And we are told by German critics of the importance, as an attempt to create a new art form, of Thuille's 'Lobentanz'; there is also Richard Strauss's melodrama to

'Enoch Arden' (which somebody might be enterprising enough to let us have in England some day), and in a recent German publication we read of no fewer than seven composers who have illustrated Hauptmann's 'Versunken Glocke'. Naturally enough, the modern *melodrame* is built of leitmotives employed, not so much mechanically, to label the characters of a drama and accompany them whenever they appear, as psychologically, to emphasize their influence on each other and on the course of the action. Thus we hear the motives associated with certain personages when they themselves are not on the stage, and by such means they are made visible to the mind's eye. As far as we know, Mr. Pitt is the first of our composers who has addressed himself to this task with such aims as these, and his success should encourage others to apply to this branch of music the theories which have conditioned the later developments of all other branches of the art. Incidental music has of late years been making enormous strides in our midst. Managers have realised that music can do a great deal to help a play, but they have, so to speak, asked only for help from outside. The music has remained a thing apart, instead of being woven into the very texture of the play itself.

The list of incidental music written by our chief composers at the suggestion of our leading managers during the last few years is instructive and encouraging; but excellent as has been its quality, it has stood on the ancient ways ... Mr. Percy Pitt's music to 'Paolo and Francesca' remains as the first example of a newer style.[12]

Jaeger was present at the second Düsseldorf performance of *The Dream of Gerontius*, again conducted by Julius Buths, given on 19 May as part of the Lower Rhine Festival. It was one of a gradually increasing number of Elgar performances on the Continent which bore witness to the cumulative effects of Jaeger's initiatives in September 1900 in sending Buths a copy of the Variations score and asking Novello's to invite him to the *Gerontius* première. The Festival's three days saw performances of Bach's B Minor Mass, Liszt's *Faust* Symphony (conducted by Richard Strauss), Beethoven's Fifth Symphony and the Brahms Violin Concerto, as well as a Mozart Aria and a Duet from Richard Strauss's Opera, *Feuersnoth*. In such company Elgar's work more than held its own, in a performance enhanced by the greater familiarity of the performers with the work and the distinction of all the solo singers. Jaeger described it for the *Musical Times*.

Of Professor Buths's reading of our countryman's 'meisterwerk' (to quote Richard Strauss) I spoke after its performance at Düsseldorf in December last. That the increased orchestra and chorus, as well as their greater familiarity with the music, added enormously to the effect of the magnificent choral numbers, goes without saying. The work was immediately recognised by the many musicians present from far and near as one of remarkable originality, surpassing beauty, and genuine worth. Professor Buths conducted with a whole-hearted enthusiasm and a conspicuous appreciation of its beauties. The fortunate composer was called to the platform again and again after both parts and cheered to the echo. No greater success, I was told, has been achieved by a new choral work of similiar dimensions at these Festivals within living memory, and a great triumph for English music can thus be chronicled. The soloists were Miss Muriel Foster, who gave a distinguished and impressive reading of the part of the *Angel*, Dr. Ludwig Wüllner, of whom I wrote enthusiastically last December, and can now speak with similar enthusiasm, and Professor Messchaert, a rare artist, by whom, for the first time, I heard the parts of the *Priest* and the *Angel of the Agony* sung with the requisite dignity, pathos, and purity of intonation.[13]

At the end of the third evening's music, a traditional Festival Supper, or Fest Essen, was held. It seems to have been a hearty and prolonged affair – Alice Elgar noted that she did not get to bed until three in the morning – with many speeches and toasts. *The Times* reported an unexpected intervention by Richard Strauss himself, speaking from a unique position of authority.

> A short speech was made quite unexpectedly by Herr Richard Strauss, in which he deplored that England had hitherto not taken her proper place among musical nations, because of the want of Fortschrittsmanner – that is, of men who represent the forward movements in art at any given epoch – ever since the period of England's musical grandeur in the Middle Ages. The creation, however, of a work like *The Dream of Gerontius*, he added, showed that the gap had been filled and that a day of reciprocity in music between England and the rest of Europe was dawning. 'I raise my glass to the welfare and success of the first English progressivist, Meister Edward Elgar, and of the young progressivist school of English composers.'[14]

So the music of an English composer gained the imprimatur of 'Richard II', the composer who was seen as the successor to Wagner himself. Jaeger had the fullest appreciation of the significance of Strauss's celebrated toast.

> With these words the greatest living German composer, Richard Strauss, closed a memorable speech delivered at the 'Festessen', in the Dusseldorf Tonhalle, at the conclusion of the Seventy-ninth Lower Rhenish Musical Festival. The speech, spoken in clear, ringing tones that carried conviction to all who heard it, was sprung upon the assembly as a complete surprise; for the list of official, *i.e.,* expected, toasts had already been exhausted, and everybody, including Professor Julius Buths ... Dr. Elgar, Herr Hofkapellmeister Strauss himself, the soloists, orchestra, chorus visitors, ladies, and others, had already been toasted by more or less eloquent and humorous speakers.
>
> The generous words of the most distinguished living German musician were received with real enthusiasm by the assembled musicians and dilettantes but the few English visitors present were filled with delight at the unexpected great honour paid to their gifted countryman.[15]

At Düsseldorf Jaeger spared no effort to look after the Elgars and help wherever he could, and the composer wrote to Alfred Littleton 'what a *splendid help* Jaeger was & how he made everything smooth & pleasant.' He also admitted '... it was worth some years of anguish – now I trust over – to hear him call me Meister!' The Elgars remained in Germany for a fortnight's holiday, visiting Cassel, Eisenach, Dresden and Leipzig in the company of Alfred Rodewald, who had been at Düsseldorf for *Gerontius.* On returning to London on 4 June they put up at the Langham Hotel for a couple of days and encountered Strauss again, for he was in London conducting several concerts of his own music at the Queen's Hall. That night Jaeger dined with Edward and Alice together with Rodewald and Henry Ettling, the German wine-merchant and amateur tympanist who played his own part in the spread of Elgar's music through Germany,[16] before proceeding to the concert, which consisted of three of Strauss's tone poems. An earlier concert had seen Jaeger's wish fulfilled with a performance of Strauss's setting of *Enoch Arden* for reciter and piano, which he later described in the *Musical Times* as 'charming ... in perfect taste ... every strain is so beautiful in its creative interest and poetic import.'[17]

Back at Malvern, Elgar wrote to thank Jaeger for his *Musical Times* article on *Gerontius* – 'I will read *nothing* now but I made an exception of course for the genial moss-headedness of you' – and commented on the misunderstandings that had arisen over Strauss's speech, which had avoided all mention of English composers of the generation of Parry and Stanford. 'What a fuss about Strauss's speech! too ridiculous & nobody seems in the least to understand what he said or meant. I always said British musicians were several kinds of fool & ignoramus – but this is worse than usual from them.' Jaeger took up the cudgels in the July *Musical Times*, writing as 'One who was present', and sought to act as apologist for Strauss:

> The speech which Herr Richard Strauss made at the recent Düsseldorf Musical Festival in proposing the health of Dr. Edward Elgar and the younger school of English musicians, has been seriously misunderstood in some quarters. He did not say that 'English musicians had not progressed since the Middle Ages' – no man of even average intelligence could possibly say anything so absurd. What he meant, and what he said, was that since the Middle Ages, and at any rate since the time of Purcell, the musicians who at any given time were progressive in relation to other English musicians were yet not as advanced as their most advanced contemporaries abroad, whereas now for the first time England had a school of young composers, with Dr. Elgar at their head, who were not behind the most advanced musicians of Germany. Even this proposition will probably not command universal assent; but it is certainly one in support of which (unfortunately) a great deal is to be said. It is hard to understand why anyone should gratuitously assume that a man like Richard Strauss should go out of his way to talk nonsense.[18]

June must have been a difficult month for the Jaegers, as Isabella became seriously ill just as they were undertaking a house move from low-lying West Kensington to Muswell Hill in north London. In those days this was still semi-rural and the highest point of the city, with attractive new estates boasting imposing double bay and forecourt houses set in wide, tree-lined roads, and a variety of shops in the Broadway. The move in fact marked another step in Jaeger's decline, for it would almost certainly have been undertaken on medical advice, so that he might benefit from fresher air and the exercise readily available in various open spaces nearby. But although there was a direct rail link to central London, distance made travelling an extra burden, and the move may have led to a decline in Jaeger's concert-going and reviewing; before too much longer he would virtually give up London concerts. Yet there was compensation to be found in concerts at the nearby Alexandra Palace, where the choir and orchestra were conducted by Allen Gill, and the Jaegers continued their monthly musical 'at-homes' as before.

With the cancellation of the Coronation at the end of the month due to the King's emergency operation for appendicitis, the première of the *Coronation Ode* was postponed and Elgar was able to enjoy an unexpected bonus of cycling, a favourite form of escape and inspiration for the past two years, around the summer countryside. Negotiations were under way for another big choral work, *The Apostles*, for the next

Birmingham Festival, and as with *Gerontius*, the Chairman of the Festival Committee, G.H. Johnstone, was dealing on Elgar's behalf with negotiations with publishers. For Jaeger there was only one possible outcome, and he sent a forcible reminder of the efforts that had been made on the composer's behalf. '... I sware; Demmie! if your next big Choral work goes to Booseys I shall curse the blue from the Sky, as we say in Germany, & hate myself for ever having exerted myself to make Gerontius known to Buths & to Germany (through him). Demmie!, I say once more.' No doubt Jaeger exerted what pressure he could on the Novello's management, for he might well have known that when Elgar spent a few days in London in July, Arthur Boosey met him on several occasions. Johnstone was asking a thousand pounds and a royalty for the work, and this Novello's eventually accepted, although the final agreement was not made until early the following year.

During that stay in London, Alice had noted in her Diary, 'E.E. with Mr. Jaeger to be photographed.' The photographs were taken by the distinguished painter and photographer Edgar Thomas Holding (1870–1952), who had been a neighbour of Jaeger in Margravine Gardens. He was a member and later Fellow of the Royal Photographic Society and exhibited for many years, and his studies of Elgar, held by the National Portrait Gallery, have become classics. In addition to his portraits of Elgar and his family, Holding also photographed August and Isabella Jaeger, providing the best formal images of them that have been preserved.

Elgar left London, without Alice, to go to the Bayreuth Festival, attending performances of *The Flying Dutchman*, *Parsifal*, *Rheingold*, *The Valkyrie* and *Siegfried*. Jaeger, who would no doubt have given a great deal to join him – there is no record of him going to Bayreuth – remained behind to tend Isabella, whose illness had necessitated an operation. His own health was again poor, and he was experiencing eye problems in addition to the usual complaints. On his return Elgar wrote with affectionate concern over the condition of both partners, and concluded '... *do* have your eyes seen to & anything else that wants patching up or revising in your dear old body.' Isabella's convalescence was slow, and a fortnight later Elgar again wrote to sympathise and to offer insistent further help for Jaeger himself.

> We hope your wife is progressing as well as you could reasonably wish: it is a sad & great trial & we deeply sympathise with you all. I *wish* you wd. get your eyes seen to & other things: I shall have to rush up & seize you again – I trust with better results than before.[19]

Jaeger was able to tell Elgar that Ludwig Wüllner wanted to sing *Gerontius* again, this time at Cologne, and was hoping that either Henry Wood or Elgar himself would conduct. It would be another landmark performance in Germany. But Elgar was keen that Jaeger should be present at a performance planned to be part of that year's Worcester Three Choirs. It would be the first in a Cathedral acoustic, albeit with alterations to the text, much as Jaeger had warned and predicted. 'Look here you must come to Worcester & hear what Gerontius *might* be – the building will do it,' he wrote, and then '*Do* make Alfred L. pay you for coming or something or offer to 'boom' somebody in the M.T. if they'll fork!' In the event the Elgars arranged that Jaeger should be part of their Festival house party at Castle House, College Green; he duly arrived on the Saturday before Festival week, delighted to be there. That day there was a rehearsal of *Sursum Corda* in the Cathedral, no doubt reminding Jaeger of his Sunday tube journey on the 'Sewer Line' some years before. On the Wednesday, after the orchestral concert at the Public Hall, he dined with the Elgars, Atkins and Alfred Rodewald at the Star Hotel; another member of the party was the wealthy American Samuel Simons Sanford, Professor of Music at Yale University. Elgar conducted the *Gerontius* performance on the Thursday, an occasion made more solemn by the death of his mother some ten days before. Alice wrote her impressions in her Diary; 'Most beautiful, most wonderful in Cathedral. Prelude never to be forgotten. Vast audience wonderful rapt attention. Soloists too wonderfully good & impressed ... a most wonderful day to have had in one's life. D.G.' But according to the *Musical Times* review, the weakness was again in the chorus, who 'began wonderfully well; but the tremendous strain of the work told somewhat upon them in the end.'[20]

Richard Strauss's music made its first appearance at a Three Choirs Festival when Ivor Atkins enterprisingly mounted a performance of *Tod und Verklärung*, possibly as a result of urgings by Jaeger, whose further influence was heard in the major choral novelties of the Festival, the third part of Horatio Parker's *St Christopher* and Walford Davies's *The Temple*. The American composer's music had continued to find a ready welcome in England after the initial success of *Hora Novissima* at Worcester three years before. Hereford had commissioned a work for 1900, the complete version of *St Christopher* would be heard at Bristol after the Worcester performance, and Norwich had also commissioned a work, *A Star Song*, for its own Festival that year. Another major biographical profile of the composer appeared in the September *Musical Times*, referring to his latest work, an organ concerto, and describing the ideal conditions that Parker enjoyed as Professor of Music at Yale, with a four-month vacation every year, and a sabbatical every seven years. *St Christopher* received a generally complimentary mention in the *Musical Times*, but the reception accorded the Walford Davies work was more critical. The best that could be said by the reviewer was that the Oratorio was 'clearly earnest, careful, and conscientious. Let us regard it as a stepping-stone to higher things.'[21] Davies had worked hard to rise to the Festival occasion that Jaeger had engineered, but the length, structure and orchestration of *The Temple* revealed the inexperienced composer and the rehearsals, conducted by the diffident Davies himself, had not gone well. H.C. Colles was present at the performance and described the occasion in his biography of Davies.

> On the day everyone 'played up' (to use the sporting vernacular) extraordinarily well, and much of the work had its intended effect. Mme Albani led the narrative sections with a surprising amount of dramatic energy, and that scene of the consecration of the Temple which had first inspired Walford to the task was the most stirring moment in the narrative. The big choral numbers too did not fail in their effect. Any unprejudiced person could perceive that the choral writing was masterly and that there was a strong lyrical feeling in the big solos, baritone and tenor. *The Temple* was in fact all good music,

> and some of it was quite evidently great music. A.J. Jaeger, on whose judgement Walford relied very strongly at this time, disappointed him by blurting out something to the effect that after all it had sounded better than he expected, cold comfort to a man who had just put every ounce of energy into bringing to fruition the concentrated effort of two or more years.[22]

Colles, subsequently Editor of two editions of Grove's Dictionary and music critic of *The Times*, had formed a strong friendship with Davies as his counterpoint pupil at the Royal College of Music in the 1890s; on the advice of Parratt he then proceeded to Worcester College, Oxford as an organ scholar. Colles was a deeply religious man with a close interest in Church music, another member of the English musical 'establishment', perhaps, with whom Jaeger would have shared little real artistic affinity. But Colles was close to Davies, and if he overvalued *The Temple*, his rather loaded account of Jaeger's reaction to it and the composer's resulting hurt at a vulnerable moment would have had some basis in fact. It may be that Jaeger did not have quite the instinctive rapport with Davies that he had with other figures. Perhaps, too, Walford's apparent shyness had led Jaeger to modify the usually uncompromising criticisms he was capable of making of a work in progress. In his Christmas letter to Davies the previous year, Jaeger had referred encouragingly to the work's 'dignity, backbone, directness & beauty', after one hearing (and had written as far back as 1897 of 'your fine Oratorio,' although it is not clear if this work was *The Temple*). Now, some weeks after the Three Choirs performance, Jaeger made brief mention of the matter with emphatic advice over the orchestration.

> 1, Berners Street, W.
> London, Sept 24 1902.
>
> My dear Davies,
>
> Kindly look at – and try by writing & scratching out – the 2 enclosed papers & say which one you would like, *if either*! We will then quote. The 80 lb paper (marked 80) costs more than twice as much as the other.
>
> I have meant to write to you but have been too busy travelling about (I have only just come back). Your work has had a very mixed reception to be sure, and personally I found the Oratorio too long & too lacking in contrast to be grasped easily. But I have in no way lost faith in your powers, *on the contrary*. This is all I can say now. But one word more: NEVER again use a *Euphonium*. It sounds *beastly* in an orchestra & *doesn't mix* with Horns *at all*. It was the greatest blot on your orchestral Score at Worcester.
>
> Ever yours
>
> A.J. Jaeger[23]
>
> I hope to have a chat with you soon.

Colles himself considered that Jaeger had neglected to devote proper attention to the work during its preparation.

> His criticisms were justified as far as they went, especially about the euphonium. I can remember it 'plobbing' along and adding weight without dignity to the too numerous fortissimo passages. Walford profited in future by Jaeger's much italicized strictures.

The complaints of excessive length and of the lack of contrast were also merited. They were what any newspaper critic writing an account of the first performance for next morning's paper would feel bound to say. But as a considered commentary from a friend who had had the work played over to him in private long before it was printed, and who had been concerned professionally with seeing it through the press, such remarks seemed superficial, to say the least of it.[24]

Colles went on to suggest major cuts in the work, and concluded,

If Walford had been content with a scheme of this kind the Festival Committee would have got the hour of music they asked for, the choir would easily have learnt the four big choral numbers assigned to them, Jaeger would not have been bored, Joseph Bennett would have been denied his gibe, and everyone would have realized at once that the Three Choirs Festival had brought to light a new composer with something of his own to say and his own way of saying it ... As it was, however, the 'mixed reception' meant that like so many works of the nineteenth century *The Temple* was put on the shelf and never looked at again by conductors of the greater choral societies or heard by anyone outside the walls of the Temple Church. If Jaeger had looked into it deeply enough to make a practical suggestion and had then shown the result to his friend Julius Buths, he might have laid the foundation of a second European reputation for an English composer.[25]

But whatever the undoubted merits of much of the music of *The Temple*, the whole nature of the work was in fact far removed from that of *Gerontius*. Davies was a distinguished organist and choirmaster, and it was inevitable that *The Temple* would belong essentially to the English Church tradition that Jaeger despised. Many of the press reviews of the Worcester performance included phrases that gave the game away: 'Laid out on established lines ... testifies to the composer's sincerity and intellectuality ... solid and substantial ... scholarly as well as interesting ... erudite musicianship ...' But the fullest if most subtle account of the weaknesses of *The Temple* was provided in a review and brief analysis of the work which had appeared in the September *Musical Times*. If it was by Jaeger, as it has every sign of being, it would go some way to explaining why he had not criticized the work in depth to the composer, for he would have known that such criticism was pointless. The whole premise of an oratorio in the English tradition was anathema to Jaeger, and he knew that no amount of criticism and advice would enable Davies to produce genuine music-drama.

... when I heard that this clever young composer had chosen for the central idea of his new choral work, the inception of The Temple by David and its building by Solomon, my first thought was, 'How is it possible to invest such a subject with musical and human interest, without which an Art-work is foredoomed to dullness? On further thought, however, the possibilities of the subject opened up, and I rather expected that the composer had made his work a vehicle for the painting of a picture of Oriental magnificence ... So one would hardly have looked upon it as out of place had Dr Davies presented us with a glowing piece of Oriental picture-making, brilliant with local colour, setting to luxuriously exotic music words which tell of the most magnificent of Oriental monarchs. Yet the composer has not allowed himself to be led into what many an English critic would consider a pitfall to be avoided, but has rather chosen a form for his work that is, I believe, much more acceptable to the majority of British ears and susceptibilities, I mean the much more austere and rigid mould of the 'oratorio'; for

'The Temple' is oratorio pure and simple. For the most part Dr. Davies's effects are produced by fine though rather complex choral-writing, interspersed with narrative and arias for the solo voices.[26]

Jaeger pointed out the secondary nature of the orchestra's role, and referred to a theme introduced in the overture and repeated later in the work, as 'the nearest approach to *leitmotiv* that the work affords.'[27] In going through the work he made his points over again in describing the eleventh number, a setting for male chorus, 'We will go into the tabernacle of the Lord.'

The situation, though not the music, is strongly suggestive of 'The Procession of the Ark' in Mackenzie's too rarely heard 'Rose of Sharon,' and we would have pardoned Dr. Davies here if he had allowed himself a little local colour as did Mackenzie in his work; but the composer has evidently set his face strongly against such treatment, deeming it, perhaps, to savour more of the opera-house than the cathedral, so that we have to be content with a thoroughly English setting of the words, a setting that once more proves the abundance of the composer's technique, rather than the exuberance of his imagination.[28]

With some degree of reading between the lines, it is easy to appreciate the force of Jaeger's thinking and the irony of some of his phrases, although the points had all been put in such a way that the minimum of offence would be taken by the composer. The article concluded,

To sum up this rather discursive though inadequate analysis, we have in Dr Walford Davies's new work an impressive and scholarly composition, imbued with deep earnestness of purpose, and never for one moment calculated to outrage the susceptibilities of an English oratorio-loving audience, yet, by its sound musicianship and clever, massive contrapuntal writing, calculated to call forth the admiration of the musician.[29]

Davies summed up his own philosophy in a letter about the oratorio to Herbert Thompson.

I hold a presumptuous belief that Opera and Wagner has damaged our wits while they enriched our language; that they have had (temporarily) vicious influence on the highest abstract forms; and that the Bach of 1985 will write symphonies not symphonic poems, oratorios not dramatic somethings; or – better still – new and undreamt of abstract choral works, of the lineage of Bach, Beethoven & Brahms.[30]

Elgar continued busy after the Worcester Three Choirs, for he conducted another performance of *Gerontius* at the Sheffield Festival at the beginning of October, together with the delayed première of the *Coronation Ode*, which was repeated almost immediately at Bristol. Jaeger was unable to be present at either event, and the nature of his understanding and advocacy of *Gerontius* is all the more evident when compared to the approach of the critic who provided a review of the Sheffield performance for the *Musical Times*. The chorus had lapsed in intonation in one 'treacherous place',

... but may this not be regarded as an accident due to atmospheric conditions, to nervousness, and to the exacting demands made upon the singers by the difficulty of the music? Such risks should be guarded against, even if the composer has to make some modifications in his score. But as if to more than atone for this shortcoming – which no one could have regretted more than the sensitive chorus-singers themselves – the Demons' chorus was rendered with such fiendish snarlishness as to be almost too realistic ... (One has just the feeling while listening to this section that the scene might better be depicted orchestrally).[31]

Jaeger now complained to Elgar of problems with his digestion.

... it's all wrong & for a fortnight I havent been able to run, or walk fast, or sleep properly for pain round my heart. My doctor says nothing but indigestion of an acute type. My stomach is blown up like a balloon & presses against my heart & lungs, & every breath I take is like a dagger into my side. Lively! ... May you never have such an attack. It's fiendish. Of course I cant eat a decent meal, hungry as I am.[32]

A week later there was a gossipy letter about Henry Wood, a person about whom Jaeger had some personal reservations, apart from his earlier advocacy of Russian music. Long-term overwork, with heavy concert and festival programmes in London and the provinces, together with teaching, had led to a complete breakdown of the conductor's health.[33] Jaeger could not help comparing his own situation with that of one whom he regarded as a 'grabber'.

Isn't it sad about Wood? I'm not surprised though. Two years ago I told him he would be an old man before he reached middle age, unless he gave himself more Rest. He has been burning the Candle both ends & in the middle too & now he is a wreck & has to be massaged every day to get rid of his (partial) paralysis of the legs. They give out here that it is Influenza; but it is much more serious than that. I'm *very* sorry for him & yet There was another would-be monopolist, like Newman. That the Gods fail not to punish these 'grabbers' fills me with a sort of unholy joy, *though* they punish me too, who am not a grabber, I hope, (not brains enough!) But fancy a strong young fellow like Wood having Paralysis![34]

Jaeger was the last person to see that his own overwork might be one of the factors contributing to the gradual deterioration of his own health.

The *Coronation Ode*, with its overwhelming final number, continued to receive further performances after Sheffield and Bristol, with two hearings in London on 26 October, followed by a further performance four days later at a Queen's Hall Promenade Concert, with orchestra and military band, which Jaeger attended. Within the next ten days the work would have two more performances, at Leeds and London. Of the London performance on 31 October Alice wrote in her diary,

... E rehearsed Coldstreams on arriving. Mr Jaeger to dinner with us & then to Promenade Concert. Immense audience. Overwhelming enthusiasm, Newman had to make a speech & say E. wd. conduct Ode again next Sunday. Yells of delight ...

But Jaeger himself had earlier expressed doubts about the wisdom of fitting words to the trio tune of the first *Pomp and Circumstance* March, and mistrusted the patriotic fervour over what was after all an occasional piece. His misgivings were expressed in a letter to Parker concerning the printing of his organ concerto. The meticulous Jaeger had discovered many errors after the score had been passed for publication.

1, Berners Street, W.
London, 10 Nov 1902

My dear Parker

I'm awfully sorry, but I must send you another proof of the Score of your Concerto, and of the Band parts because there are sundry *Queries* in them which only the Composer can answer. But I also wish to draw your attention to the fact that, as I expected, dozens of mistakes have been discovered in the score, *passed* by you & Mr West as *correct for the press Yah!* Mr. Littleton (Augustus) asked me to print the Score some weeks ago, but I thought I would just wait till the Band Parts had been read with it. Lo! and Behold the wisdom of Augustus! I'm glad now I disobeyed Mr L. for once. Aren't you? I hate turning out a Full Score of a good work with a lot of mistakes in it. David J. Smith *also* discovered a number. These are incorporated in Wests remarks.

And how are you & yours? Well, I hope, & very happy in your American Home, *sweet* Home. What a pity you couldn't be at Norwich for your 'Star Song'! I didn't hear the work at Rehearsals, being too busy here; and the Criticisms were contradictory so that one couldn't form an opinion of the work obtained. [*sic*]

Elgar has 'knocked 'em' in the Queen's Hall with his brilliantly *effective* but by no means great 'Coronation Ode'. *Six* times within 4 weeks to audiences from 3000–5000 people who *howled* at it. Oh dear, when will people take to a man's *best* work & not shout themselves hoarse only over the *weak* stuff he has written. For I can't call this Ode strong Elgar, though it sounds so effective[.]

Does Henry J. Wood Know of Your Concerto! If not, I'll ask him to do it at the Proms or Symphony Concerts after Xmas. *Tell me*, For I won't worry him if you have *already done so*. He is ill at present.

Goodbye & my Kindest regards to Mrs Parker & yourself

Ever yours

A.J. Jaeger[35]

Walford Davies made a policy of introducing as wide a variety as possible of devotional music in his weekly services at the Temple Church, including movements from works by Handel, Haydn, Brahms and Schubert, and he made too something of a speciality of including Bach Cantatas whenever he could. He was now keen for Jaeger to enjoy the music one Sunday, and issued an invitation, but Jaeger sent his apologies together with an account of his day at home with the children. Davies replied with a superb musical jape on Jaeger's 'Nimrod' music, entitled 'the dear A.J.J. at home with his bairns,' and a delightful suggestion of horseplay with Miss 'Bitte, bitte.'[36] More seriously, he concluded with an unconventional view of the Variations finale.

Nov 10th. 1902
W. Hampstead.

My dear J.

You were much better employed yesterday than coming to the Temple; I am so glad I didn't beguile you away from so delightful a Sunday at Home.

'Der liebe A.J.J. zu Hause mit seinen Bairns'

repeat ad. lib.
then P.T.O. subito

He rolls on to the floor, and Bitte, bitte requires him to do it again.
I saw you at the Symphony Concert. I wonder whether you enjoyed it as much as I did. Elgar's Finale is grand & TOO long, you sinner[.]

thine affectionately,

H.W.D.[37]

Two days before this letter, on 8 November, Elgar had conducted the Variations at Queen's Hall. Davies's doubts concerning the finale of the work, extended at Jaeger's suggestion, were later echoed, albeit in different terms, by Tovey, who thought the movement 'tub-thumping'.

> A report is now current that Elgar originally ended the Variations quietly, and that this Finale was forced upon Elgar by more experienced friends. If this is true, for Heaven's sake let every effort be made to recover the original Finale. There is always the possibility that Elgar himself may have found it inadequate; and in any case the present Finale has enough humour to entrap the humourless. I fell badly into the trap myself when I first heard its solemn organ-strains with their facile descent into prestissimo semibreves. But we do want to know how Elgar rounded off the work before he was induced to put a brass hat on it instead.[38]

Wood made his welcome reappearance at Queen's Hall early in December, sharing a concert with Richard Strauss, who conducted the English première of *Ein Heldenleben*. Some days later Macpherson's Psalm was duly performed at the Worcester Philharmonic Concert, although Granville Bantock took Elgar's place as conductor. Elgar asked Jaeger to make sure that F.G. Edwards made some mention of the concert and Macpherson's Psalm in the *Musical Times*, and sent local reviews. He also recommended the work to Hans Richter. Jaeger wrote of hearing a new string quartet by Bell, and took the opportunity to nag Elgar again over the projected sextet. He dealt with various other more or less routine Elgarian matters, including a three-part arrangement of 'Praise to the Holiest' and the *Greek Anthology* partsongs. He also helped to prepare a major *Musical Times* feature on Richard Strauss for the January 1903 number. But a problem arose over Parker's Organ Concerto, and Jaeger seems to have had little thanks for his conscientiousness in arranging for second proofs. There was an unexpected performance of the work in the offing in the States, and the printing was being carried out in Germany. Jaeger, through no real fault of his own, was in the middle, and once again Parker needed to be pacified.

1, Berners Street, W.
London, 2/XII 1902

My dear Parker,

I'm sorry to hear that you are in such a fit over your concerto. I hope you will agree that it *was necessary* for you to see the proofs of the Score again, & also the parts. Up to the moment of writing the proofs have not reached us (Tuesday 6.30 p.m.). We telegraphed yesterday to Leipzig (Geidel) to print a copy of the Score & *8. 8. 5. 6. 6.* Strings & 1 Set of 'wind' *at once* & to post them *to you direct* as early as was possible. They ought to leave Leipzig *tomorrow* (Wednesday). You never said how many Strings you wanted! I hope I have made a pretty good guess. We did not Know either that you were going to perform the work in Boston. I had a vague idea that performances were 'coming off', but had no *details*. Why did you not warn us? The parts & Score which you will receive will of course be 'spotty' as you call it. You will have to make them correct as best you can. I don't envy your conductor (Gericke?). But what else could we do? It will be an expensive Luxury printing that one Score & the parts. When done with I think you had better return all the parts & Score to Mr Gray, New York.

Mr Clayton wishes me to tell you that by letting the first performance of the work take place in America you have forfeited the *English performing* rights; and he is not sure whether the Copyright *also* is not lost!

Henry J Wood has *just* come back after a long illness (nervous breakdown). I will speak to him about the Concerto when I get a chance.

Good luck to the performance at Boston & may the many 'Spots' not prove a bar to the Success of the work.

Sincerely yours,

A.J. Jaeger[39]

Prof H.W. Parker Mus Doc
Newhaven
U.S.A.

'Spotty' parts notwithstanding, Parker's Organ Concerto received its first performance that month. With Christmas fast approaching, Jaeger received a cheerful 'brandy-saucious' letter from Elgar, delighting in some splendid presents, including the Encyclopaedica Britannica and Wagner's complete Prose Works. He remembered the Düsseldorf visit of exactly a year before, and was gearing himself up for intensive work on *The Apostles*. A peacock butterfly was inhabiting a chrysanthemum in his study, and he told Jaeger, 'just fancy sitting in this Study surrounded with flowers & a *live* butterfly at Xmas – this music's going to be good I can tell you.'

In a letter of seasonal greetings, Jaeger responded suitably, although the *Coronation Ode* was at the back of his mind.

> A Happy Xmas & New Year to you & your dear ones! May the future put plenty of Big ideas into your dear Head to make us poorer mortals happy & lift us out of ourselves & out of our narrow world into higher, purer spheres where we can forget & hope. 'More heart & soul & Geist & less "effect" for its own sake' may be your motto, for *then* you are greatest, & we thank you most & bless You, we poor Erdenwurmer.[40]

Excited by the prospect of the new music, especially after having seen part of the *Apostles* libretto, Jaeger concluded his last letter of 1902 by asking if he could visit Malvern to hold Elgar to a promise to play him the work. 'Supposing I should be staying in your neighbourhood next week, would You carry out your promise, if I came over for a day? Tell me, thou wizard of the Malvern Hills.'[41] His enthusiasm for the new music was entirely understandable, but the labours involved in preparation for its first performance the following October would bring him to the point of physical collapse.

8 1903: 'Let someone other than Jaeger give answer!'

Jaeger began 1903 with a welcome change, a 'long promised' visit to Ivor Atkins at Worcester. In a tactful letter to Alice he complained of neuralgia of the eyes and went on to ask if he could include the visit to Elgar which he was so keen to make. He went to lunch on the first Sunday in January and took an afternoon walk with Elgar and Troyte Griffith, who found a room for the night for him near his own house at Lower Wyche as Craeg Lea was full. Jaeger returned there for breakfast next morning, and went on his way to College Yard; he was later able to assure Alice that the 'bright cold weather' had conquered the neuralgia. No doubt there had been opportunities to admire the new Encyclopaedia Britannica in its revolving bookcase, and, more importantly, to hear the music from *The Apostles* which Jaeger was so keen to get to know. There might have been a chance for him to express satisfaction that Alfred Littleton had agreed terms for its publication with George Johnstone, who was again negotiating on Elgar's behalf. This time there would be no repeat of the misunderstandings over *Gerontius*, and that month final agreement was reached on a figure of £500 on submission of the manuscript, a further £500 after the sale of 10,000 copies of the vocal score, and a 6d. royalty per copy on the sale of further vocal scores. It was Elgar's biggest financial return so far,[1] and would enable him and Alice to begin to live the life they dreamed of.

But the première was only some ten months away and a mountain of work remained to be undertaken on the construction of the libretto as well as of the music. The Prologue was sent to Novello's towards the end of January. Jaeger was keen for Buths to provide a German translation so that the work could be engraved in both languages. Elgar was not able to supply a full text of the libretto at that point, and Jaeger, anticipating problems, promised that if necessary they would expect Geidels, the Leipzig engravers, to complete the score in three weeks.

Elgar sought inspiration in cycling, a hobby he had taken up in the aftermath of the composition of *Gerontius*, and the rides continued throughout February and March while Jaeger fretted over Buths's slowness in dealing with the translation. He was again working such long hours at Berners Street that his children hardly saw him, and was still having to attend to correspondence at home.

> We are getting so busy now in my Deptt. that I cant get through my correspondence & must scribble to distinguished composers at Home, with my wife & baby girl, bless her pretty face, at my side. *She* ought to be in her little Bed, but she walked downstairs with naked feet, & staring eyes, to 'see Daddy'.[2]

Early in February Elgar experimented with a hired free-wheel bicycle, and decided to buy one to replace his original machine, the fixed-wheel Royal Sunbeam nicknamed 'Mr. Phoebus'. Alice remembered that Jaeger had expressed interest in cycling, and her husband wrote him a jocular letter offering the old machine, concluding 'Gosh! Augustus darling! you might write some music on it!!' Jaeger accepted the gift gratefully, adding his own touch in describing his friend as a 'Deus cum machina'. His doctor thought the exercise would be beneficial for the 'nasal organ'. Jaeger continued anxious about his health, complaining of two recent scares when he felt himself becoming faint. There were many quiet roads around Muswell Hill, and his young friends Bell and McEwen had promised to teach him. He was going to fewer concerts every month, he told Elgar, and would use his Saturday afternoons to take exercise instead. Jaeger seems not to have become a successful cyclist, although Elgar advised him not to give up under a month's hard work, and subsequently offered to pay for lessons. Jaeger looked forward to the bicycle as offering a new hobby, something to think about 'instead of bothering about helping young composers'. He could not refrain from venting his spleen, perhaps in the bitterest terms yet, over the continued frustration he was feeling when trying to promote talented young composers at Novello's. His latest discovery was the 24-year-old Cyril Scott, a Cheshire-born composer and pianist who had studied in Germany and whose output up to that time included symphonies and chamber music, much of which was later withdrawn. But Jaeger's high estimation of William Henry Bell remained undiminished, and he ranked his latest choral music next to Elgar's own.

> ... I fight an uphill game from which I shall now retire. Lest West & the firm stick to their Cathedral friends & tenth rate mediocrities. The best of the Talent in England has to *prostitute* itself before it can find grace in the eyes of N & Co. The young men must write Anthems & Partsongs, all as easy & stereotyped as possible, before J.E.W. will take to them. Their *real* work is ignored. It is as easy for a Camel to walk through the needle's eye as for an original work by a new man to be recommended by our 'Editor'. My latest recommendation has been young Cyril Scott. I failed, but Broadwood, Wood, Forsyths & others are taking him up. This youth of 22 has *great* talent, I am sure. Of course his work is still immature, but he is worth looking after. But West won't see it. I have had a great disappointment over a Choral work of Bell's which I sent to Mr Johnstone of B'ham (at his J's suggestion). I feel *quite sure*, that excepting yourself there is NO one in England who could write a work so strong, individual & *English* as this 'Song of the Sea'. Of course it is *very* different from what you might do with such a poem, but it is also *very* different from what the *old* fellows could do. When will Festival Committees look at works that were *not* 'composed to order', but out of the composers' sheer necessity? My parcel *had not even been opened*! *No* musician at B'ham looked at it. But I daresay some of the old Fogeys have some 'commissions' in the Festival programme? Next time I see Richter I'll just mention it; not that

> I expect any good Result. The thing takes only 25 minutes & the stuff is 'real good', I think ...[3]

Jaeger knew that he was riding a familar hobby-horse but he could not restrain himself from spilling his feelings, which reflected total commitment to his self-assumed rôle, rather than a mere professional concern. It was the kind of situation that made him feel a failure, so complete was his involvement. 'I feel kind of disgusted with myself & everything ...', he continued. Soon he was able to report to Elgar that a piano quartet of Scott's had scored a success in London, in terms which emphasized the extent of the rivalry with West: 'That is another feather in my cap versus J.E.W. &c!' Such was his belief in Scott that the following month Jaeger paid for the publication of his *English Waltz*. 'I must make some money somehow, (or lose it!)', he told Elgar. Scott later remembered Jaeger's initial efforts to encourage Novello's to publish the piece, and the terms in which they declined.

> I had also made another acquaintance in the publishing world, Mr A.J. Jaeger, for some time head of the printing department in the firm of Messrs Novello. But although he tried to persuade the readers of that long-established firm to interest themselves in my work, he did so without success. 'Mr – ' I have forgotten his name – 'considers your compositions too licentious,' he told me when explaining the fruitlessness of his efforts. 'Still,' he went on, '*I* believe in you, and intend to publish that English Waltz of yours at my own expense – it will, of course, appear as a Novello publication, but the copyright will be mine.' Mr Jaeger carried his project through, and the only *bravura* piece I have ever written appeared in print ...[4]

The piece became a vehicle for Percy Grainger who featured it in a lengthy concert tour he undertook with Adelina Patti. Scott became a prolific composer of dramatic, orchestral, choral and chamber music, as well as something of a literary figure. His treatment of melody, harmony and form marked him out at one time as an advanced modernist, and although in later years he seemed somewhat dated, his music awaits proper reappraisal. Bernard Shaw told Scott on one occasion that he was the only composer of the younger generation in whom he could detect a style, and on another reported a conversation with Elgar when Shaw had said to him, 'Why, Elgar, for a British composer you have become quite daring in your harmonies of late.' Elgar replied, 'Yes, but don't forget it was Scott who started it all.'[5]

Work on *The Apostles* continued meanwhile, alongside the stimulus of two *Gerontius* performances in the Midlands in March, and plans for a further performance in London; the work also received its first American performances that month. Amid cycling attempts and dealing with the first proofs of the *Apostles* vocal score, Jaeger found time to be present at a concert given by the Bach Choir in the Portman Rooms at Baker Street. It was the first concert under Walford Davies, who had succeeded Charles Stanford as conductor and whose growing reputation had recently gained him a commission to compose a work for the Leeds Festival of 1904. The Choir had evidently suffered something of a decline, as Jaeger noted mercilessly in a letter to its new conductor.

37 Curzon Road
N

29/11/03

My dear Davies,

Congratulations on the Leeds Luck and the Bach Choir Boom. The former is *splendid* & I hope you will rise to the occasion in a *fine* work.

As to the Concert last night, it would have been really enjoyable if you had poisoned (pro tem) that Tenor before the show began. He made me roar at first & then I wept. The granddaughter of Jenny Lind also was an infliction of a vicious Kind. She can't sing Bach any more than I can. Your men in the Chorus haven't any voices & the quality of their tone is sepulchral. The ladies, bless their 'youthful' ardour, sang quite well, *in spots*, & now & then the tone colour was distinctly nice & agreeable. But the orchestra was the best & you got them *at last* to play Bach with *expression*, which is something to thank you for. The cantatas are beautiful, especially the second one, which moved me much.

Parry went awfully well & was *very* enjoyable. On the whole I thought the show encouraging & worth persevering with. You will do more with them than C.V.S. did, for you will make old J.S.B. live & breathe & smile & weep. So 'Gluck auf'!

Your little service shall reach you next week *certain*. We have had to put every man Jack on Parry's work, to keep the Albert Hall choir going & the Corrections (Parry's) have been awful. But we are now out of the wood, I hope & then H.W.D. We shall rattle the things off quickly, & print in 'no time'. So have a *little more* patience & we shall 'make up' in fine style.

It is late & I'm tired. I must go to Bed

Ever Yours

A.J. Jaeger[6]

The new Parry work referred to was his Symphonic Ode *War and Peace*, to his own libretto, the first of a series of works reflecting a consciously idealistic, ethical philosophy. The piece was dedicated to the dead of the Boer War, and was first performed at the end of April that year at the Albert Hall, conducted by the composer. Parry had composed and scored the 135-page work against a looming performance deadline amidst a full programme of work at the Royal College of Music, and its printing was not finally completed until three weeks before the première; the choir had been receiving the work in instalments of one chorus at a time from week to week. The stress over its printing had taken its toll of Jaeger, who complained in a letter to Alice Elgar, 'I'm nearly off my head with the *Rush* & anxiety over this thing.' But he was able to reassure her that with the Parry Ode out of the way, better progress would be made with the engraving of the *Apostles* vocal score, which had now reached the Mary Magdalene section, the third scene of Part 1.

Towards the end of April Jaeger characteristically embraced another opportunity to promote English music in Germany, this time that of Parry, who was far less well known in Europe than Elgar or Stanford. The Duisburg Music Society was to celebrate its 50th anniversary in May, and was – possibly at Jaeger's suggestion – preparing *Blest Pair of Sirens* for inclusion in a special festival to mark the occasion. The English masterpiece would be performed alongside works by Bruckner and

Strauss, and Jaeger was determined that the busy Director of the Royal College of Music would find time to take up an invitation to conduct it. A request from Duisburg for a programme photograph gave Jaeger opportunity to launch the necessary campaign.

37 Curzon Road,
Muswell Hill
N.

20/4/3.

Dear Sir Hubert,

Dr. Walter Josephson of Duisburg writes me an *urgent* request for a Carte de Visite photo of you, to reproduce in the programme & 'Festschrift' to be published in connection with the Duisburg Festival (which, as you may remember, is apropos of the 50th Anniversary of the foundation of the Society). Now I can't find a carte de visite photo of you; can you put me on the track of one of a fairly recent date? I should much like to please the good people who are introducing your glorious work into the Fatherland. R. Strauss's promised Choral Work 'Tailleferre' could NOT be got Ready in time. So yours will be the *only Choral* novelty. The other novelty will be Bruckner's posthumous (9th) Symphony.

You really *must* go over & be present. You can leave here at 8 p.m. & get to Duisburg by midday next day. You could leave there the following day in the afternoon & be back in London by 9 a.m. You see it takes *no* time. I shall *most* likely be there & you can *order me about* if I can help you at all. (I am not sure whether you speak German).

Oh yes! *You really must go.* Why, You are always travelling about England conducting your work, why then not please those Good Germans? They will make you feel at Home; Rhinelanders *can* do that. Ask Elgar!

Sincerely Yours,

A.J. Jaeger[7]

Even my dear wife who sends her Kind remembrances says 'You REALLY **MUST** go'.

Despite this plea, Parry remained unmoved and would not commit himself to the Duisburg concert on 24 May. A new college term began on 7 May, and Parry noted in his diary for that day that it had taken the best part of an hour just to open and glance at his accumulated mail. He had an Oxford lecture to prepare for the following week, a new work, *Voces Clamantium*, to compose for that year's Three Choirs Festival, and his usual routine of committees and evening engagements. The pace of his life frequently took its toll of his health, and several times that month he reported feeling 'fearfully fagged', 'horribly tired & stupid', or just 'dilapidated'. Novello's had not published *Blest Pair* in full score, although they seemed to be making a special effort to do so and Pointer visited on the second day of term to look over the revised score. Some three weeks after his first letter, and with just ten days to go before the Festival, Jaeger tried again.

37 Curzon Road,
Muswell Hill,
N.

13/V/3.

Dear Sir Hubert,

I am going to Duisburg after all, (I have been invited by the Committee) as representative of the firm. In fact, Mr Alfred Littleton is *very anxious* for me to go. He has charged me – in case you go too – to place myself *entirely at your disposal* IF I can be of any service to you either on the journey or in Duisburg. So there! Of course I don't Know, nor does Mr. Littleton whether you *want* any of my 'Services', much less of my company; but if you do not speak German, and are a stranger in the Fatherland I *might* be of use to you. In that case pray command me; I shall be happy to be able to do aught for you, though, on the other hand, I have absolutely not the faintest desire to inflict my Services & person upon you if you *don't* want'em. I'm not such an ass, I hope. And now we all hope devoutly that you *will* go. It would be a terrible disappointment to the Committee & especially to Dr Josephson & the Chorus if you stayed away, while your going would, I feel sure, give English music a tremendous push uphill *abroad* (which it wants badly, don't it?) If Oxford Examination papers keep you, why – take 'em with you, & do them in the train; there's plenty of time going & returning.

It is an exceptional occasion & surely for once you may be allowed to take exceptional liberties with your 'work'. The Committee are inviting *all* the Conductors of big Societies in Rhineland & Westphalia (Steinbach, Buths, Schwickerath, Henbuer, Haym, Rentor-Müller &c &c &c). They can do much for your music & English music generally: So once more – **DO** go!

Pray, Pardon the length of this epistle & pardon my worrying persistence!

Yours Sincerely,

A.J. Jaeger[8]

Parry would have received this letter on his return from Oxford for his lecture in the Sheldonian, and it does seem to have persuaded him to make the journey to Duisburg. Now there remained only the travelling arrangements for Jaeger to advise over, in a further letter – a manic semi-comedy of alternative train times; his scrutiny of the timetables was as meticulous as his proof-reading.

37 Curzon Road,
Muswell Hill.

15/5/3.

Dear Sir Hubert,

That's Better! Eppur se muove!!
Of course you *could* – an you would – leave Victoria (8.25 p.m.) or Liverpool Street Station on Saturday *night*, arrive at Duisburg about 11.6 on the Sunday morning (too late I fear for the Rehearsal of the 'Sirens'); and leave D'burg Monday at 6.35 in the MORNING (!) to arrive here in London about 7.15 in the evening. But why in the name of Heaven such a fiendish Rush?

May I propose to you leaving Victoria *Friday morning* 9.28 arrive at D. about 12.30 at night, and attend the Rehearsals & concerts &c on Saturday and Sunday, not to forget the Festessen (Dinners) &c which always play a great part in these German Festivals. They'd never let you off the 'Festessen'. So prepare & Beware. Of course if you absolutely MUST spend Friday at the College, you could leave on Friday night 8.25 arrive at D'burg at 11.6 on Saturday morning. It would look a little funny to arrive after the festival has virtually begun, wouldn't it? They have invited you for the whole Festival, have they not? And you ought to hear a Rehearsal of the Sirens. So do go on Friday morning or Thursday night, won't you?

I must in any case leave in time to be in D'burg on Saturday morning & if possible I should arrive there Friday night. I'm taking young Brooke with me (son of one of our Directors); he knows German fortunately. Kindly let me know what you decide & PLEASE let the Committee Know. They can't understand your silence, Josephson tells me. So I have explained both to J & to the Commitee how *fearfully* pressed you are. *Any other man* in England except yourself would ask his friends to do his work for him for a few days. YOU *will* do it yourself even under these quite exceptional circumstances & perchance disappoint those good D'burg people terribly.

Sincerely Yours,

A.J. Jaeger[9]

So Parry took himself to Thomas Cook's and organized tickets to Duisburg for himself and his son-in-law Harry Plunket Greene, who was engaged to sing in the Festival, although he disregarded Jaeger's advice and travelled on the Saturday, arriving after midnight. Jaeger, Brooke and a member of the Committee met him and they sat up 'drinking German beer till long past 1', Parry remembered, and he felt 'very ragged' the next morning. He was not happy with the arrangement of the orchestra at that morning's rehearsal, and was dissatisfied also with the Choir, but afterwards Jaeger took him, Brooke and Plunket Greene for coffee at a restaurant in some nearby woods where they wandered for a while; Parry found it a 'very pretty place'. The performance of *Blest Pair of Sirens* that evening went much better than anticipated, despite coming immediately after Strauss's *Tod und Verklärung*, and Parry received a very warm reception marked by the presentation of a wreath when he appeared on the platform to acknowledge the cheers and applause. The four-hour concert was followed by a two-hour wait while the Hall was prepared, and then, as Jaeger had warned, the Festival Supper began. Many speeches were made and Parry's health was toasted several times, and he remembered the enthusiastic participation of 'the chorus girls who trooped up to the high table to drink with me. Didn't get to bed till 3'. He signed autographs innumerable and Josephson's toast in his honour was greeted not only with a threefold 'Hoch' but by an enthusiastic 'three cheers' in true English style. The next day, perhaps at Jaeger's suggestion, the composer and his son-in-law spent a few hours in Düsseldorf on their way home. They spent some time sitting in the gardens – 'very pretty' – and looking at pictures, 'mostly extremely bad'. Parry arrived back at Kensington Square just after eight o'clock on the Tuesday morning, snatched a few hours' sleep, and was off to the College just after midday for a busy afternoon of work, including an Associated Board meeting which went on until beyond eight o'clock that evening.

For his part, Jaeger, who had complained of feeling unwell to Alice before setting out, reported to Elgar on his return that he was 'dead beat & must go home. I had *1* hour's sleep last night.' But he was pleased with Parry's success, which had vindicated the whole venture, and he told Elgar that *Blest Pair* had been given a better reception than *Tod und Verklärung*. Jaeger's feelings for Parry and his music were rekindled. 'I wish him all success for I like the dear old, noble Fellow,' he wrote, and his estimation of *Blest Pair of Sirens* remained high. The work was 'what Josephson called it in his toast to Parry, an *Oasis* in the Festival. It was the only work which really *thrilled* & *elevated* me. And I have Known it for nearly 20 years! Not a bad test!' The German press echoed Josephson's praise of *Blest Pair*, calling it 'a valuable work', 'a pearl among English compositions', and stating with pride that it was 'not difficult for Germans to accept the good from whatever direction it comes.' Jaeger retailed these plaudits in a biographical article about Josephson for the July *Musical Times*, which also contained a review of the Duisburg Festival under his 'special correspondent' by-line. In an otherwise straightforward account of the history of the Duisburg musical society, together with reviews of the Haydn, Handel, Beethoven and Wagner works which had been performed in addition to the Parry and Strauss, Jaeger reserved his criticism for the Bruckner Ninth Symphony, which had been given its first German performance. After one hearing, Jaeger could muster little enthusiasm, writing 'His last symphony is a disappointing work, but it must not be forgotten that while writing it Bruckner was practically dying ... The first and third movements are laboured; there is restless striving without attainment ...'.[10] He held the *Scherzo* in higher estimation and admitting that Bruckner's music was little known in England, was sufficiently interested by it to drop a broad public hint to Wood, who he thought 'may perhaps one day perform the symphony, and then will be a convenient moment to write a detailed account'. Jaeger had earlier mentioned to Elgar that he was going to write to Brewer to suggest the work, with its *Te Deum* finale, for the Gloucester Festival the following year. The suggestion, if made, was not taken up. Wood did in fact programme Bruckner's Seventh Symphony during the 1903 Proms, but it was not a success. 'The public would not have it,' he wrote. Perhaps they enjoyed more the significant amount of new British music that the conductor played that season, including works by Bantock, Elgar, Boughton, Holbrooke – whose student works had often received encouraging notices from Jaeger – and Cyril Scott, whose Symphony in A minor was given its first performance.

Jaeger had been able to report to Elgar at the beginning of April that the vocal parts of Part 1 of *The Apostles* were all engraved, and he pleaded for as much fresh manuscript as possible in order to expedite the printing of the work. Elgar had still not completely finalized the libretto and held out little hope for the combined English-German version, arguing that the difference in price would make two copies essential. It was becoming evident to him that time would not allow for the work to be completed, and that the original plan for it would have to be curtailed. Towards the middle of May Novello's promised an anxious Johnstone that the Birmingham choir would soon have half the Oratorio to begin rehearsing, but found themselves having to ask Elgar exactly what that might consist of. There had been difficulties too in finding soloists for some of the demanding rôles, causing further delay, and Elgar was forced to write to Novello's to explain his proposals for recasting the work, reducing it by almost half. Part 1 would now end with the Mary Magdalene scenes, rounded off by a new chorus, Part 2 would cover Judas and the Ascension, and a brief concluding Part 3 would use the sketches for Peter. But by the end of June the Birmingham people still had nothing to work on and Jaeger wrote to Elgar begging him to minimize proof-corrections, which necessitated time-consuming alterations to the plates; some advance copies were essential for rehearsal purposes, he argued. The precedent of the *Gerontius* debâcle three years earlier was very much in his mind, and Elgar now decided to omit the proposed Part 3, and end the work with the Ascension. To Littleton he repeated his dissatisfaction with many of the available singers, and reported a bout of eye trouble, in further support of his decision. There remained the orchestration to be dealt with, a task which Elgar could always achieve easily, and which he began on 28 June. Jaeger, along with all involved, must have breathed a sigh of relief at the belated decision on the final shape of the Oratorio. But another mountain of work now loomed, for he had agreed, somewhat anxiously, to furnish an analysis in time for the première in mid-October. Despite their earlier differences of opinion over some aspects of Jaeger's *Gerontius* analysis, the composer had pressed his friend to undertake the work. It would help Jaeger to some much-needed extra income, and the sympathetic approach he knew he could count on would reassure Elgar after the uncertainties he had experienced.

At the beginning of July the Elgars went to Wales to stay with Alfred Rodewald at his holiday cottage near Bettwys-Y-Coed. Work on the orchestration continued there and Jaeger received the first 48 pages of full score at Berners Street after a week, together with an invitation from the genial businessman-musician to join the party. Elgar suggested that it would be a good opportunity to work together on the analysis, realizing perhaps that such an arrangement would be an ideal way of ensuring some degree of control, and by way of further encouragement passed on a message from Rodewald emphasizing the lack of 'Black beetles (clergy)'. Jaeger replied with a reluctant refusal and his first, enthusiastic response to the *Apostles* score.

> … *much* heavy, weary work keeps me here & though I think I *should* have a chat with you about the Analysis I fear I must alone flounder along through the Labyrinth of your creation. I say, last Sunday for the *first* time (!) I went for the thing; I spent about 4 hours on it &, O Lor!, you made me sweat with 'Entoosm' as dear old Hans R. calls it. Why, you *wretch*, this is even more wonderful than Gerontius, & I shall have to buy a Revised, up to date Lexicon for my supply of adjectives. Really, there is nothing in music like this & I am frightened out of my wits when I think of that analysis which nevertheless I am *burning* to do as well as I, with my amateurish outfit, can do it. The Prologue is marvellous & the temple Scene made my hair curl and my back crumple up like a tomcat's on the warpath. I have no time to go through the whole of Part 1 & tell you how the stuff knocked me in the eye page after page … As regards your scene just to hand, it looks

wonderful, *wunderbar*. That opening! & 'that there' Temple stuff with Shofar, antique cymbals, colour most gorgeous & new, effects most astounding & bewildering, organ! &c &c Oh! my poor analysis.[11]

Elgar so strongly felt the urgency of the need for collaboration over the analysis, that he wrote to Littleton to ask for Jaeger's release from Berners Street so that the work could go ahead. Permission was granted and Jaeger must have been delighted at the prospect of an opportunity to work closely with a man he idolized over his newest work, so far from the confines of 'hot & smelly & dirty' London. He duly took a train for North Wales, where he remained for some twelve days. Elgar continued with scoring and proof-correcting, and Jaeger made progress on the analysis, but there was time for both men to enjoy something of a holiday as well. Rodewald's occasionally unreliable motor-car was a centre of attention and various expeditions and walks were undertaken amongst the rugged scenery; card games occupied the evenings. Alice recorded a private performance of the new Oratorio in her diary for 18 July.

Mr. Wilson, Richter's Choir Master came about 12.30. After lunch E. played his 'Apostles' music to him, Rode & Jaeger in the room & A. some of the time. A. felt & Mr. Wilson sd. it was an aftn. that would be remembered & I think, written about – Most marvellous music. Each listener deeply affected & intensely moved & excited. Mr. Wilson sd. he felt quite paralysed – there was nothing like it. Very nice day altogether.

The following day cannot have been such a nice one for Jaeger, who accompanied Rodewald's friend Gordon Chapman in giving Wilson a lift on his return journey. They failed to return and the weather was poor. Alice and Edward became 'more wretched and anxious, wandered up the road in the rain & listened & watched.' The car had broken down and Jaeger stayed the night at Corwen after spending several fruitless hours helping Chapman to repair it. He sent a telegram to reassure an anxious Alice and spent the rest of the day in Chester. Jaeger seemed none the worse for the misadventure, although Rodewald's motor became nicknamed 'The Shover' on account of the amount of pushing it required. But a bout of ill health followed immediately on his return to London. He complained of weakness and fatigue, classic symptoms of tubercular infection, and sought his doctor's help yet again. The prolonged absence from Berners Street inevitably brought problems, as did the polluted London atmosphere. He complained to Elgar,

I found this office in a *dreadful* mess of work & have had no time to write, feeling always very tired out & limp in the evenings. My nose & Tummy are giving me dreadful trouble & last night I lay awake till 2 a.m. oh dear! To return to London, dirty, filthy stuffy London after a delightful Holiday in a *clean* air is awful. I shall get over the effects of the sudden change in a few days I hope.[12]

Shortly after his return, Jaeger wrote to Walford Davies who had sent the libretto of his Leeds work, a cantata based on the 16th century morality play, *Everyman*. Jaeger had discussed it while at Bettwys-Y-Coed with Elgar, who felt very strongly that it was unsuitable for setting, a view that Jaeger did his best to discount. In his letter,

Jaeger made some apt probings concerning an appropriate musical style for its setting.

37 Curzon Road
Muswell Hill
N.

[Undated]

My dear Davies,

I am back, as you will see, all too soon for a real refresher after weary months in a stuffy office, none too soon for my dear wife & children, who missed me, & whom I missed, even in the excellent company & in the most lovely country in which I found myself. I will not now waste time discussing Wales, & Elgar's 'Apostles', since it is Sunday & I have many letters to write before I retire for the night. I wish to say a few things about the Libretto which you sent me & about which I had no time to write at Bettwys. We motored (splendid sport!) & tramped everyday & in the evening those wretches E.E. & Rodewald made me play 'Bridge' which I *hated.*

Well, I have had a careful look through 'Everyman' & am *puzzled.* The thing is so peculiarly naive & quaint that everything seems to me to depend (in the musical setting) on the manner or style in which you will treat such a subject. I am no respecter of 'Taboo'–subjects, as Elgar is. He tells me that he has seen 'Everyman' acted & knows it thoroughly and that he has been written to by *dozens* of people asking him to set the play or subject to music & that he holds *most* strongly that the thing is unique, & *COMPLETE in itself*, & should *not* be handled by a modern musician. He says even the best music that the 20th Century could produce would ruin the play (or 'poem') & that any attempt to musically illustrate it is doomed to failure.

Now I hold no such views because I cannot look upon the Play with the poets' or mystics' eyes as Elgar does. Nor do I feel the reverence for mediaeval mystery plays that he seems to feel. I am a plain, commonplace person. Elgar's views I can therefore ignore, though I thought you might like to Know them, since Elgar is undoubtedly one of the brainiest men of England besides whom I feel an utter ignoramus & a fool.

To return to 'Everyman': it is certainly another of the very sad subjects, dealing with Death, of which you composers are all too fond. That it is quite an exceptional poem of this particular kind I readily allow; but the fact that God Himself is introduced (though you set His words for Chorus) adds to the solemnity of the work.

I take it there will be only one number in which a bright note can be struck, so that the work must needs be fearfully solemn & severe. That I fear will interfere to a certain extent with its general acceptance, while I fear also that very many in an ordinary, common or garden audience will see only Material for ribald jests in the strangely child-like language. That there is power in the poem & beauty of a quite exceptional Kind I allow & if these qualities can fetch similar high qualities out of your well of musical thought the End will justify your daring step, your leap in the dark. Only, what style will you adopt? Sham mediaevalism or ultra modernity with the richest orchestral effects on your palette or what? You see I am puzzled, and though I am sorry You have chosen so sad a subject (most unconventional though it be) I can (pace E.E.) quite foresee that a most impressive work can be produced therefrom. But personally I dont believe in imitation archaic music. Since you are so bold as to tackle such a strange subject I wonder whether you will be bolder still & set it in your own *individual* way & not by aping (pardon the ugly word) a defunct style. Tell me that. Meanwhile I return the libretto herewith.

Elgar's Apostles are his *most original* & I fancy (but am not yet *quite* sure) his most beautiful work. Come round one Saturday afternoon & I will show it to you. I am just beginning my analysis for the B'ham Festival. (I wish I had finished it!)

Good night. I'm very tired. Much love

Ever yours

A.J. Jaeger[13]

An apparently tactful degree of uncertainty about an Elgar work expressed by Jaeger to another composer became something of a habit in later years, and he had not of course yet heard a proper performance. But he seems to have harboured genuine doubts about parts of it. He wrote to Elgar of 'a *fearsome* progression' in the 'Turn you to the Stronghold' chorus, and went on to describe it as 'crude,' a word which rankled with the composer for some time. There was a host of further minor points that Jaeger's careful eye noticed, but Elgar was usually adamant against any changes and stuck to his own judgement; there was to be no rôle for Jaeger in this work as there had been in *Gerontius*. Jaeger took the responsibility on himself.

> I wouldn't alter Anything in your Apostles for the world if you think your original idea is quite O.K. I only draw your attention to things that strike my critical eye & ear & appear to them as little specs on the Sun (or moon). But I do not dare to write until I have *got quite used* to the things that worry me, for I know your stuff is so confoundedly original & unconventional that they *require* getting used to.[14]

At this time the symptoms of Jaeger's gradually developing illness, combined with a necessarily hectic pre-Festival period at Berners Street – especially relating to the new Elgar work – were beginning to have effects. 'I am nearly dead,' he wrote to Elgar. 'Haven't felt so seedy for years. I sometimes wish I *were* dead & had done with all illnesses & worries. Never to have a day, *not one* day of a wretched life free from illness is *awful*!'

By mid-August Elgar had sent the final portion of the full score and Jaeger telegraphed congratulations and then wrote from Berners Street with his first estimation of the whole work. He was careful to include a warning over its initial reception, and if the letter began with a characteristically emotional response, his overall reaction was more considered and less ecstatic than that for *Gerontius*.

> I'm steeped in your music just now & have no thought for aught else. I spend odd half hours upon it in the morning & wipe my eye when nobody is looking. The beauty of the music moves me to tears & the longer I study the work the more & the greater Beauties I find. 'The Apostles' are certainly your maturest & greatest work; the certainty of touch & style displayed throughout is wonderful, & the feeling of the most touching heartsearching kind. But it is all so original, so individual & subjective that it will take the British Public 10 years to let it soak into its pachydermal mind; unless of course the 'story', being known by everybody, will carry the work along, assisted only by the prima facie '*effective*' parts of the music. As for the poor critics (the duffers amongst them I mean), they will be *bewildered* I fear. But all this can't affect you. I believe that by the time you have completed Part III You will have given to the world the greatest oratorio since the 'Messiah', though this seems a rash statement to make, & time alone can prove the accuracy or futility of such a 'guess'. Anyhow, I know (in oratorio) nothing in which

> consummate mastery of technique is allied to such deep feeling, pure & holy; such mystic revealing of hidden truths, such chaste beauty of thought as I find in the Apostles. And then the strength & manliness of other parts, the convincing force of your proclamation of the Faith that is within you are superb & astounding. So you will believe I sent my congratulations this morning with a full heart overflowing with gratitude to the master to whom I owe so much of beauty & of inspiring, ennobling thought. I wish I could & *dared* do justice to the work in that wretched analysis![15]

Jaeger's work on his analysis continued throughout August, with many early morning hours and late nights devoted to the task. He told Winifred Norbury that it needed 'eight weeks' hard study, spending every spare morning, 4–7, and evening, 10–2 (or 3) on the difficult task.'[16] Despite a protest from Elgar, the remuneration from Novello's once more proved disappointing. Initially indeed Jaeger had appeared less than fully enthusiastic about the undertaking, citing lack of time and characteristically doubting his fitness for it. He admitted feeling frightened by the idea of attempting to analyse a work which he felt much harder to understand than *Gerontius*. Elgar offered help with the theological aspects, and was determined that Jaeger see the work through: '*you must* do it', he wrote, before he arranged the working holiday in Wales. Jaeger for his part was pleased with an opportunity to 'make a few pounds,' although his ultimate reward for many exhausting hours of work would merely amount to the equivalent of a week's wages.

His temperamental inability to do anything other than throw himself wholeheartedly into the analysis resulted in a booklet of over 60 pages, containing 92 musical examples – 64 of which he gave labels – as well as the entire libretto. Each scene was dealt with in order, its text coming first, followed by a few bars of the appropriate motives set in a text containing explanations of various related features, often spread over several pages. It is therefore difficult for the eye to scan the material in such a way as to relate motives to particular points in the story, especially as, once again, Jaeger derived his own names for them. The scope of his intentions meant that Jaeger was sometimes unable to see the wood for the trees. With material of such length and complexity, it would have been better to adopt the suggestion he had made over the *Gerontius* analysis, for the title or number of a motive to be inserted next to its appropriate line in the text. Such an approach would have been familiar from various German analyses of the Wagner music-dramas, some published by Novello's in translation,[17] in which the emphasis tended to be limited to naming the various motives and tracing their reappearances in order to show how the music illustrated the text, although questions of musical development and structure then became secondary.

Faced with coming to grips with a complex, extended work, and with his own everyday pressures to cope with in addition, Jaeger played for safety and based his own approach on these lines. He sought to label every theme he could, even for example a three-note figure that Elgar had inserted above a version of the 'Gospel' motive in the Prologue. Elgar sensibly commented, 'I should not call that theme (?) anything. It only adds to the sort of "life of the passage" – gives it more sort of "movement"'. But Jaeger, determined to explain everything, insisted on giving the brief counterpoint the status of a motive, and labelled it 'Preachers', presumably for no other reason than its combination with the 'Gospel' theme. In describing it he could only use the language of supposition.

> A dignified phrase of three notes is superimposed ... it appears to be connected with the idea of the preaching of the Gospel, and later in the oratorio characterizes the Apostles as PREACHERS. It is evidently derived from the first bar of the orchestral accompaniment to the words 'The spirit of the Lord is upon me'.[18]

Anxious for Elgar's approval, Jaeger sent him a portion of the analysis in a version fair-copied by Isabella. The response was kind – 'it is *superb* as a piece of informing dissection & you hit off every idea & feeling of mine' – although he then asked for less praise and fewer adjectives. Elgar's letter crossed with one from Jaeger enclosing a list of questions; on one point he seemed close to complaining that the music did not fit the framework he was creating in the analysis.

> Tell me, is that ghastly thing on page 71 last line which afterwards comes in 3 muted Trumpets & strings (page 72 top line) the '*Sin*' theme? I call it that, but are the fearful progressions in the Fantasy p 76 &c the *inversions* thereof?
>
> The chromatic melody line is allright, but the Harmony don't answer to the description, does it? It *ought* to have some connection with the '*Sin*' motif, but I won't say so unless you say it's allright. And what *does* that ritornello (in 6/8) pages 73 &c signify? I have spent hours trying to think of something & *cant*. It *eludes* me completely. And may I consider the pppp chords on page 107 the '*Sin*' theme differently harmonized, but gently enfolded by the *Mary's consolation* theme (Bass) and the 'yearning' theme (*though* the *intervals* are not the same as usual) and thus made to finally disappear? Or is this a farfetched 'Fantasy'? let me know *soon*, there's a love.
>
> You see I dont want to guess & then have to do it all over again. I have so little time (only from 4 or 5 to 7.30 in the mornings!) and Sundays. I shouldn't really have taken on the job: its too big for a very busy man like me, much as I love it & *eager* as I am to do it.[19]

In his reply Elgar was anxious over the hours that Jaeger was spending over the analysis. 'Now, Moss,' he wrote, 'nobody can do it like unto you, but you must not do too much.' The composer went on to deal with the various questions, although he was characteristically uneasy in attempting to 'explain' his creative processes, adding to one answer the rider, 'You need not say a 10th part of this – 'tis what I feel'; however, Jaeger largely paraphrased his words for the analysis, despite this reservation.

Another anxiety came to preoccupy Jaeger when towards the end of August, Elgar wrote of a decision to cancel the tenancy of Birchwood Lodge, the woodland cottage to the North-West of Malvern which had become an essential retreat and inspiration and where so much composition and orchestration had been accomplished over the last five years. Jaeger had visited it during his Malvern holiday with Buths two years before, and instinctively feared for Elgar's creative well-being in the wake of its loss. He leapt at a possibility of securing the cottage for the future.

> I'm sorry you have to give up Birchwood Lodge. Is it *for sale*? A friend of mine wants to buy it, if possible, & if he can afford it (I'm sure he CAN)! to *present it to you* (between ourselves). Do tell me, & I'll tell him. I hope it will 'come off'? Who is the Landlord? Do you care sufficiently for it to wish to *Possess & own it? Do tell* me at once. I'm speaking *Seriously*, REALLY.[20]

Elgar sent '10,000 thanks,' and promised to enquire into the matter, saying that he would like to end his days there. But nothing more seems to have been said. Proofs of the *Apostles* analysis reached Elgar at Hereford during the Festival, where he had enjoyed the company of Walford Davies. In writing to Jaeger, Elgar was now noticeably more direct, saying that he had marked out some of the names of the motives, that he thought too many names confusing, and that he felt it was sufficient for the principal motives only to be named. He had evidently taken the opportunity to discuss the growing problems over the analysis with Walford Davies, who offered help. Elgar went on to suggest, 'Do talk it over with W. D. who very shyly said something about casting a fatherly eye over your technical remarx: you have my full permission (!) to consult him', although no record of any such consultation has been preserved. A week later Elgar wrote again with two major points of criticism, although he was careful to preface each one with a compliment.

> Your 'stuff' is A.1. & I am delighted. I have altered a few places. Don't insist on the Faith part of the forgiveness in Mary M Scene (end) – the words of Christ mean a good deal more than mere Faith as interpreted literally by dissenting folk of a low type & your remarks may be understood in this limited sense: I think it's innocuous as I've left it.
>
> Your Judas scene is splendid – I should have liked a reference to the way a proud sinner at last confronted with the result of his sin is swayed by all sorts of feelings – prompted or suggested by the psalm he knows so well – ending in blasphemy & despair. I don't like *Plot* – it (that theme) figures more the man of action – and it staggers about at the end in a ghastly way.[21]

If Elgar was intervening more and more to polish the analysis, Jaeger had already told him to 'hack it about as you will, I shant have any feelings in the matter'. In Jaeger's defence it can be argued that his analysis was written to introduce a long and complex work to a public which he thought would need '10 years to let it soak into its pachydermal mind'; the provision of an analysis with many readily identifiable musical examples would make it easier for people to grasp the new work. Jaeger did the best he could for the first audiences of all three of Elgar's major choral works; it is not entirely his fault that his analyses were taken to be complete, fully authoritative statements of the composer's intentions in later critical assessment.[22] It also cannot have helped that *The Apostles* was composed without a coherent overall plan, libretto and music evolving together; as Ernest Newman wrote, 'no solidly built work of art can be put together in this way'.[23] The same writer put his finger too on the work's fundamental difference from *Gerontius*, Elgar's midnight-oil strivings to express theological niceties that Jaeger could not be expected to grasp fully. 'Truth to tell, the Apostles *as* Apostles are rather dull dogs, and one is always glad to see them go … the oratorio is at its best when clear issues of human feeling are treated of in the music, and at its worst when the merely theological element comes uppermost.'[24]

Jaeger's life at Berners Street continued meanwhile on all too familiar paths. He wrote to Elgar that he could not count on being able to attend the *Apostles* première on 14 October, and that he had offered his analysis to the Editor of the *Musical Times*. The reaction was such that he felt 'Edwards *hates* my enthusiasm, I KNOW. Old ass!! *I* don't mind.' He also railed at the critics of the *Times* and the *Yorkshire Post* for their praise of Coleridge-Taylor's new Hereford Festival work, *The Atonement*; 'Heavens! Where *are* critics with taste?' Taylor's work seems to have attempted to mix operatic and traditional oratorio styles with a result that was unacceptable, even irreverent, to the Cathedral audience, and in fact its general critical reception was poor. (The composer was hurt and never composed again for the Three Choirs Festival; later he was to write to Nicholas Kilburn rather bitterly of the 'dishonest newspaper criticisms, many of which I found were written in the neighbourhood of Berners St *a fortnight before* the Hereford performance'.)[25] Jaeger concluded the letter to Elgar with a touch of risqué humour.

> Do you know this?
>
> Mary had a little Watch
> She swallowed it one day,
> And now she's taking Beecham's pills
> To *pass the time away*.
>
> Strikes me as rather funny.[26]

In reply Elgar offered to set the doggerel, and savaged the Coleridge-Taylor work which he would have heard at Hereford. 'Taylor's work was a disgrace to any civilised country: the utter want of *education* is the curse of this chap.'

Earlier there had been a little light relief for Jaeger when he took Dora Penny to lunch and on to the Hereford Festival rehearsals at St James's Hall. She remembered, 'The gallery was full of interesting people – composers waiting to rehearse their own works, soloists, conductors, and musicians of all sorts. As we came through the doorway he remarked: 'Someone should announce us: "Nimrod and Dorabella!" All faces would be turned this way!'[27] That afternoon the pair listened to Elgar rehearse the Variations.

From about mid-September onwards the *Apostles* analysis having been finalized and sent to the printers, Jaeger's next urgent priority was to ensure the production of orchestral parts in time for rehearsals, the first of which was to take place in Manchester on 5 October. On 23 September he was able to report to Elgar that the string parts had been sent to Leipzig for engraving and that several copyists had been engaged to work on the wind, brass and percussion parts; all would require correcting. Jaeger saw trouble coming and cautioned Elgar, 'Having to split the stuff up amongst so many copyists makes me a bit nervous, but I hope we shall get through in good time if only we Keep our nerves & Tempers & do not precipitate things, See?' Four days later Elgar had finished dealing with corrections to the string parts but complications arose over the hand-copied horn and clarinet parts, where the copyist Dodd (who had worked on *Gerontius*) had omitted the special signs Elgar had devised to show *ritardando*, *accelerando*, and *largamente*. Jaeger, despite his own advice to Elgar, became decidedly jumpy as he asked the composer to come to London to check the parts on the spot, as he had for *Gerontius*.

> I'm nearly off my head with the Apostle's parts. Look here: are you coming to town to check these parts (interalia)? Meanwhile I am having all the *Duplicating* seen to. Dodds omission of the R – A – is an AWFUL business. How could he be so stupid?
>
> To get them all in now means putting several men on the job to do nothing else, but I cant do much until I get the parts back from the Duplicators. The Rush will be terrible during the last few days ... but the thing *must* be done.[28]

On the eve of going to London for soloists' rehearsals, and after a day of Chorus rehearsals at Birmingham, a becolded and somewhat bemused Elgar could only return Jaeger's advice.

> I'm sorry the parts worry you, I can't think *why*? Your men must be jolly slow ... I'm *not* fearfully busy at all – just left this time blank to correct parts & where are they? oh, where?? I don't know how I got this fearful chill, but it is a bad 'un. Don't worry take Bile Beans Felsnapthah any thing only preserve Nimrodic Calm – it doesn't matter a straw if the Oratorio is never heard. Yah![29]

Jaeger made a dash to Paddington Station to catch Elgar as he was about to return to Malvern after the London rehearsals on 2 October, and handed over sections of the score and revised woodwind and brass parts for further checking, although there was no time for him to explain that Dodd would now have to be sent to Manchester if required for further work at the orchestral rehearsals there in four days' time. The last-minute pressures were overtiring all concerned. 'I can't get a note more out of Dodd,' wrote Jaeger, 'He says he is completely done for and must rest for a day.' Next day, amid a collection of exhausted copyists, Jaeger sent Elgar at his request the remainder of the score and parts, some still unfinished. There was little let-up for Jaeger. Elgar asked Augustus Littleton to send him to the first full choral and orchestral rehearsal at Birmingham on 9 October, 'in case anything is wanted – alterations and additions'. Meanwhile the orchestral rehearsals at Manchester had proceeded without mishap. '*Wonderful* to hear orch. for 1st time, most splendid,' thought Alice, 'Glorious orchestra Gr. impression'. And she promptly and kindly telegraphed the news to Jaeger, who confirmed his presence at Birmingham in a brief note. 'No time for more tonight,' he concluded, 'I have had an *awful* day again.'

Jaeger, 'full of delightful anticipation,' according to Alice, travelled to Birmingham on 8 October, dining with the Elgars and Edgar Speyer, who had heard of the new work from Jaeger at one of that summer's Strauss Festival concerts in London. The next day Jaeger heard the sounds for the first time as choir and orchestra rehearsed *The Apostles*. Alice again confided her delight to her diary. 'Mr. Spier [*sic*] breakfasted with us & Mosshead. Splendid rehearsal the faithful band assembled, *wonderful* hearing chorus &c for first time – & wonderful impression seemed to be made on all ...'. Jaeger returned to London the following day, but travelled to Birmingham again on the eve of the première, dining with the Elgars and Alfred Rodewald in an atmosphere of intimate, pleasurable anticipation. However, Jaeger's inexorably declining physical condition, weakened by months of stress and overwork, caught up with him to deliver a cruel blow: he suffered a collapse on the morning of the first performance of *The Apostles* which confined him to bed. He was thus unable to be present on an occasion to which he had contributed so much. It was a harsh injustice. Alfred Kalisch later related how the sufferer's hotel was almost within earshot of the Town Hall, and how he spent the morning with the vocal score in his hand, 'trying to imagine he was listening to the performance. After it was over he had quite a levée in his bedroom of friends who came to tell him all about it, and to sympathise with him in his deprivation.'[30] John West of Novello's told Elgar, not altogether kindly perhaps, how he had spent time before his train '... chatting with poor Jaeger. Wasn't he unfortunate? His disappointment was most pathetic!'

Jaeger was unable to go into the office for some time. Remembering the recent rehearsals they had attended together, he sent Dora Penny a copy of the Birmingham programme containing his analysis, inscribed 'Nimrod to his neighbour across the Double Bar, with Kindest regards'.[31] Elgar had visited Jaeger in his hotel, and later remembered seeing him at the station as they both left Birmingham, '... I did see you with an immense cigar', he wrote, for, at this period, Jaeger was a smoker. It was not until a week after the missed performance that Jaeger was able to write to Elgar a long, personal and unhappy letter which showed that he had been brooding during his unaccustomed inactivity over such things as the effect the success of the new work might have on Elgar; he could also not resist expressing again some doubts over the music itself.

> Bless you for sending me a dear letter though you are so pressed by admiring congratulating friends. Whatever you do: If you get conceited I'll come and spank you & put your dear noble nose on all the pages which I cant & wont & never shall get used to in them there 'Apostles'. They are precious few I admit & they simply show that you are mortal. 'Homo sum' even you, the great artist must humbly confess. I was much & deeply touched by your kindness in coming to my grubby bedside in B'ham & the many tokens of love & friendship proffered me, during those days of pain & disappointment, by many dear friends quite recouped me for *the great* disappointment of my life. Fancy my not hearing that first performance after all. It is evident I had been burning the candle at both ends & in the middle too for weeks past; the excitement of the 'from-hour-to-hour-getting-nearer-to-Oct-14th–11.30a.m.' kept me up till *nearly* the appointed hour, & then swish! came the guillotine upon the small of my back. Well I'm much better now, though still pretty stiff. The weather is all against me.[32]

Jaeger's account of the causes of his collapse emphasized the effects of his excitement as well as the overwork, and for someone with his highly wrought temperament, the emotional was always going to be at least as important as the physical. It might be an example of what some medical authorities thought of as the 'tubercular personality'. His visceral responses to music had been emphasized to Alice earlier that year, when Jaeger confessed, 'I want something *fresh* now to wax enthusiastic over, to get cold shudders down the Back, & drops of perspiration on my brow ...' Jaeger continued the letter with characteristic worries about events at Berners Street in his absence, and confessions of feelings of inferiority to other critics with 'university &

Bible educations'. In conclusion, he dwelt again on his dissatisfaction with his position at Novello's, and his financial situation. His basic pay of five pounds a week seems to have remained unchanged since the rise he had been given five years before, while the hacks who produced endless programme notes were able to make twice that. To cap it all, further family sinecures on the Board of Directors were being created.

> Many thanks for your sister's sweet message ... tell her I cant buy any more presents for my babies as I have hardly enough to pay my 'rint'. At Nov. & C. I seem to stick at my present miserable wage & no 'rises' loom in the distance. With 4 directors' Sons just Entered into the firm & all no doubt requiring big salaries to keep them in luxury & idleness (more or less) there is precious little chance for a man like me there. When I see men like Webb[33] & Harvey make £10 a week & more with their scribbling I swear to myself & despair of ever making even two thirds of that. But thats a beastly personal growl & I apologize. Still, a clerk's life is a brilliant one as regards prospects, & no mistake.[34]

By the end of October Elgar had received £ 500 from Novello's, as stipulated in Johnstone's agreement with the firm. It was a sum roughly equal to Jaeger's basic wages for two years, and on the strength of it the Elgars were preparing to spend the winter abroad.

Jaeger's Birmingham Festival article for the *Musical Times* necessarily offered a vivid account of the music of *The Apostles*, with examples of its *leitmotiven*, rather than a review of the performance itself, although it would seem that Jaeger was able to do justice to performances of the works featured in the succeeding days, one of which was Bruckner's *Te Deum*, being given its first English performance. Evidently Hans Richter had taken the hint contained in Jaeger's account of the Duisburg Festival. Jaeger's *Apostles* review, like many others, gave attention to Elgar's use of *leitmotif*; in doing so, however, he did not shirk from expressing some of the doubts he harboured.

> Of the libretto nothing need be said in this place, since it has already been dealt with by more competent hands in previous issues of this journal. To deal with the music in anything like adequate detail would require many pages, for its newness is evident in almost every bar, and a treatise would be needed to do justice to the mere technical part of the composer's masterful workmanship. Dr. Elgar's most striking development since 'The Dream of Gerontius' lies in his complete surrender to the Wagnerian method of using the Leitmotif. The Oratorio bristles with representative themes; they are employed with a freedom which rivals that of the deftest of post-Wagnerian composers. In carrying out his design he has not, however, been consistently successful. There are a few isolated passages where the Leitmotif has been a fetter rather than a help to his imagination, so that the music, and especially the vocal *melos*, seems to flow somewhat haltingly.[35]

The reference was to Elgar's tendency to fit words to instrumental melodies for which they were not originally intended. The nature of Jaeger's criticism gave the lie to the chorus of disapproval that had arisen in the press over his *Apostles* analysis. The 'humble Analyst' was unrepentant. 'Aren't the papers pitching merrily into poor me for that analysis!' he wrote to Elgar. 'I don't mind, if *You* don't. I don't withdraw a word.' Talbot of the *Manchester Guardian* had been the most outspoken, panning Jaeger's whole approach and going to the heart of the matter as far as the naming of themes was concerned.

> ... it is to be noted that the *Leitmotif* system, which has always had great attraction for Dr. Elgar, is here employed with an elaboration and an ingenuity which can hardly be paralleled in the works of Wagner himself. The enthusiastic critic who, through the unsuitable medium of an analytical programme, has done his best to alienate the public from the work by the absurdly lavish eulogy which he bestows on its every detail has discovered an immense number of representative themes and has duly labelled them with appropriate titles, although it is doubtful how far this has been done with the composer's sanction.[36]

It was perhaps not Jaeger's fault that his analysis, intended as a separate item needing special study, was reproduced *in toto* in the Festival programme for the day, along with Barry's notes on the Brahms Fourth Symphony. The *Athenaeum* praised Jaeger's enthusiasm but considered it out of place, and agreed with the *Guardian* over the appropiate style for programme notes. 'His enthusiasm we heartily admire, for that quality is not common; but it outruns discretion in programme-notes, which should abstain from comment, favourable or otherwise.'[37] The *Birmingham Daily Post* echoed and developed the theme; it was felt that an audience should have the right to make up its own mind.

> ... the work is so large in design, so full of detail, that the description fills more than sixty pages in the programme book. And here we venture a word of protest. Such study as we have been able to apply to 'The Apostles' causes us to admire this published 'appreciation,' to admire the skill and insight of the writer; but we think far too much is said therein for a programme-book. It may be argued that a general audience is not capable of arriving at a just conclusion in regard to an elaborate composition, and needs guidance. This may be so, but it is the inalienable right of the public to be the judge of anything submitted to it, whether in art or other matters. And, in the long run, the judgement of the public is true. Now this 'appreciation' rather interferes with the freedom of the audience, and renders the work of the critic more than usually unthankful and irksome.[38]

The reactionary Fuller-Maitland of *The Times* also had his say. Unlike the critic of the *Athenaeum*, he used the very word 'enthusiastic' as a criticism in itself.

> ... it is abundantly evident that a great deal of the first two parts of *The Apostles* is but an index to that which will occur in the third part. Indeed, we are told so by the extremely enthusiastic analyst, who in his programme notes has labelled some hundred or more themes[39] and *leit-motifs* many of which can only attain their full significance on the completion of the oratorio. How enthusiastic this writer is may be judged from his opening sentence, in which he declares the advance of Dr. Elgar from his *Lux Christi* (1896) to *The Dream of Gerontius* to be 'as astonishing in its way as that of Beethoven from his second symphony (1802) to the Eroica (1894)'.[40]

Jaeger's capacity for enthusiasm and sheer uninhibited feeling, those 'ardent and mercurial' qualities which Elgar understood, could thus cause affront to English middle-class standards of proper behaviour as reflected in the musical world. He must have been accustomed by this time to negative reactions at Novello's but to be so publicly vilified by his fellow-critics was a novel experience. After the hours of work and worry that the analysis had cost him, for such small reward, its poor reception was very hard to take. Its demands on the reader, even the professional critics, were great; Canon Gorton, who had produced his own 'The Apostles: an Interpretation of the Libretto' told Elgar, 'Jaeger's admirable work will only aid the learned, I might do something for the unlearned.'[41] But ultimately Jaeger was concerned only with Elgar's reaction – 'I don't mind if *You* don't'.

At the end of October Jaeger was able to send Elgar welcome news of future performances of *The Apostles* in Germany under Buths and Steinbach, who wished to produce the work at the Cologne Lower Rhine Festival the following Whitsun. He continued the letter with specific suggestions for improvement over two major musical points of concern in *The Apostles*, but Elgar would concede nothing apart from the addition of a pause mark in one passage. There had been an edge to Jaeger's approach. '... I know nothing now. Blackburn is the only Critic now, because he *never* finds *anything* to criticize, Eh??' But Elgar replied, as he always did, that he never read the critics.

At the beginning of November the Jaegers went to spend a few days at the new Wimbledon home of the Holdings, who were evidently musical. 'My wife has just played your *Salut d'amour*, *Chanson de nuit & Chanson de matin* & our Hosts are delighted,' wrote Jaeger to Elgar on 3 November.

That day Alfred Rodewald also wrote to the composer, on whom he had lavished support and affection. He was looking forward to a Manchester performance of *Gerontius* that month under Richter, and the proposed Cologne *Apostles*, but had been feeling unwell. Jaeger had been invited to visit him, and the triumvirate would attend the Manchester concert together.

> I'm going to Cologne next Whitsun Tide. Hurrah! I only thought that if you come here on the 14th Nov. you would meet old Nimrod & we could go to Manchester on 19th for Gerontius. I'm in bed, bad attack of flue, but really thought I was sickening for typhoid. But fever has left & I shall get all right. Love to Alice.[42]

But the influenza killed him just a week later, on the day that an apprehensive Elgar had rushed to Liverpool to be at his bedside. The sudden, unexpected loss shocked and upset both Elgars deeply, especially Edward who reacted in an almost hysterical way, walking the streets of Liverpool in a daze, weeping in his hotel room and writing to Jaeger to remind him of the happy time they had all shared in Wales. 'I am heartbroken and cannot believe it. God bless him,' he wrote. 'He was the dearest, kindest, *best* friend I ever had. I don't know how I write or what I've written – forgive me. I am utterly broken up.' And Alice herself wrote, 'I cannot express our grief & my dear E. is utterly overcome, they were devoted to one another & it feels as if such a great piece of sunshine had gone out.' Jaeger's reaction was as openly emotional as Elgar's, and as closely self-observed, although he did not miss an opportunity to recommend a musical response from the composer. Alice later considered that the suggestion came to fruition in the slow movement of the Second Symphony.

1, Berners Street,
London,
W.

10/X1/1903

My dear Elgar

This is awful! I move as if in a dream & *can't* realize the truth. Good God!, that this dear, strong man should be snatched away from his friends like this, cannot be true. I was stupefied when I got your dear, sad letter for I had hoped that his magnificent constitution might fight a victorious Battle with Death after all. But I'm told that this fell disease is fatal more often in the case of strong men than with comparative weaklings.

I have in my pocket a letter addressed to him who is now gone. I wrote it last Sunday; a lively letter which I didn't post because I had no stamp. It seems to be burning a hole in my pocket & yet I don't like to tear it up. I *can't* realize that he is dead, *dead*!

My warm sympathies go out to you who knew him so well & loved him so dearly; I am sorry for you, for it's no use, nor is there need to be sorry for him. Oh dear.

He was a *new* friend to me, but I took to him from the first, & liked, aye loved him, as I admired him. His good nature, his enthusiasm, his love of you whom I love, his great kindness to poor me. These entwined themselves round my heart & I felt deeply how dear he was becoming to me. I could cry as I *have* cried.

You must get back to work, dear friend & find in your music relief; You must tell us in your music what you dare not say, dare not, because your grief is too deep & great. Work is the only remedy against such ills as this fearful loss. So when you have put him to his last rest, go back to work.

My love to you & kindest regards to Mrs Elgar & to both of you my heartfelt sympathies in this dreadful irreparable loss.

Thine ever

August Jgr[43]

It was perhaps fortunate that preparations for the imminent Italian holiday distracted the Elgars from their grief. They spent time in London purchasing necessities and dining with friends, including Frank Schuster and a member of his circle, the art critic Claude Phillips. There was discussion of a possible festival of Elgar's music at Covent Garden the following year; 'beautiful to think of,' wrote Alice. When her husband went to Manchester for *Gerontius*, Alice remained behind to be entertained by Jaeger. She visited the Berners Street Offices from where she was able to watch a 'procession of King & Queen of Italy. Beautiful sight.' That evening he took her out to dinner, followed by a visit to the theatre to see a German play, 'Zwillings Schwester'.

Next day Jaeger contacted Parry with a rather last-minute invitation to a performance of his *Judith* at the nearby Alexandra Palace conducted by his friend Allen Gill, plus a brisk reminder of other, later work that remained to be seen through the Novello's presses.

1, Berners Street, W.
London.

Nov 20 1903.

Dear Sir Hubert,

They are doing your 'Judith' at the *Alexandra Palace* tomorrow night at 7.30. Can't you come & hear it? They sing *very* well & the performance is sure to be enjoyable. The good people would *love* to see you there. I fancy you have never been so far North into the Suburbs of London Eh? Allen Gill conducts, one of the best Choir trainers in the Kingdom, & a good lot of soloists incl. 'that blessed Agnes' (Nicholls) will do justice to your fine music. Heavens! It seems only a year ago since I sang by the side of friend C.L. Graves in the first London performance in St. James Hall. DO come & shed [*sic*] the light of your kindly, dear countenance shine upon us benighted Northerners. [*sic*]

I shall be there in any case, & if you can't come, will send you a line to say how the work fared.

DON'T (PRAY!) trouble to reply to this impertinent suggestion.

Don't forget 'History Primer'
" " Birds March
" " English Symphony
" " Cambridge Symphony
" " Organ arrangements
" " original organ compositions
&c &c &c.

I feel almost inclined to commiserate with you, because those Kind Gloucester people want another *new* work. Let them do the splendid Te Deum & allow you to devote your time to clear up arrears (as per above) a little! Why not? Why *won't* they leave you alone for once & give You rest?

With my Kindest regards

Yours Sincerely,

A.J. Jaeger[44]

Jaeger reviewed the performance for the December *Musical Times*, praising this time not a new composer, but an emerging choral society in north London.

The Alexandra Palace Choral and Orchestral Society is rapidly winning for itself a high position in Metropolitan musical circles. Next to the Royal Choral Society, it is now the largest permanent musical organization of its kind in London. The existence and success of this Society is one of the foundations for hope that after all the conditions of things chorally in London is not so bad as has been dolefully painted. Here we have 500 enthusiastic choralists, wholly recruited from North London, and a competent amateur orchestra of nearly 100 players – which at concerts is augmented by thirty or so professionals. These forces meet for rehearsal in one of the large rooms of the Palace under highly favourable circumstances, and are enabled to give their performances in one of the most commodious halls in London, where there is a magnificent organ and an ample orchestral platform. What more could be desired? An inspiring conductor and an appreciative audience! The former the Society enjoys in the person of Mr. Allen Gill, whose alertness, skill and experience have placed him in the front rank of oratorio conductors. As to the audience, that too seems forthcoming.

The mettle of the Society was well tested on the 21st ult. by a performance of Sir

Hubert Parry's oratorio 'Judith'. In a work of this type the choralists have splendid opportunities. It is gratifying to report that the Alexandrists rose fully to the occasion. It may be said that the voices did not exhibit the ring and resonance one hears somewhere even farther north. Certainly there was often fine vigour in the attack and a satisfactory assurance in the execution. In short, the whole performance was painstaking and creditable, and proved the capacity of both the choral and orchestral resources ...[45]

As if in defiance of the reviewers who had savaged his *Apostles* analysis, Jaeger could not resist making play with the 'farther north' phrase, originally used by Elgar to the great irritation of the London critics, in a published letter to Canon Gorton: 'some day the press will awake to the fact ... that the living centre of music in Great Britain is not in London, but somewhere further North.'[46]

It is perhaps to be hoped that both Elgar and Jaeger would have been amused by an account of a performance of *The Dream of Gerontius* which took place shortly before Christmas somewhere a good deal further east. The work received its first Australian performance at Sydney Town Hall on 21 December, and in reviewing it the independent-minded critic of the *Sydney Morning Herald* was determined not to be overly impressed by its reputation. Once again the analysis came in for obloquy, with the integrity of both Elgar and Jaeger thoroughly called into question.

... The oratorio itself is devotional but gloomy, and in spite of some melodious phrases the solo music must be summed up as ungrateful. Wagner's influence is shown in the employment of motives, of which Dr Jaeger, in his analytical notes to the book of words, enumerates more than thirty. The importance of the instrumentation, which is paramount, should also be noted. Regarding the work as a whole, it must be pronounced dull. Hence, once more, our gratitude to Mr Delany and the orchestral forces so ably led by Mr Rivers Allpress. But for their art-enthusiasm, the first performance in Australia of Elgar's oratorio might have been delayed for years, and in that case we should all have been 'bursting in ignorance' of a work which the great body of English writers have trumpeted forth as likely to rival the immortal efforts of Handel. In the meantime we shall adventure the prediction that the London press will gradually withdraw from this untenable position. The new oratorio, composed for the Birmingham Festival of October, 1900, and rendered last year at the Roman Catholic Cathedral, Westminster, by a choir from North Staffordshire has not yet been produced by a London choral society, nor will it be performed in that way until March, 1904. This delay might not have meant anything. After hearing the work, the conclusion to be drawn is that it means a great deal. At this far remove from the centre of action, conjectures can but be of a hazardous character, yet it should be reasonable from the course of events to suppose that Dr Elgar is not only a musician of undeniable talents, but also a smart business man. Reference has already been made to a masterly analysis of the oratorio by the eminent musical critic Dr Jaeger. It is erudite, amazingly detailed and of immense length. Also it has to be added that it is from the pen of a writer who is intoxicated with admiration for Dr Elgar. Either because he was commissioned to make this analysis, or for pure love of art and hard work, Dr Jaeger prepared this pamphlet in such good time that it was ready for distribution at the Birmingham Festival already mentioned. That is to say, the entire audience, including all the journalists had this amazing eulogy of Dr Elgar's oratorio placed before them as a guide to the work. The question which must always remain unanswered for a few years is this – 'Had this fact any influence upon the press opinion of the hour, and in that way upon the public opinion of the day?' Because Jaeger's talent must not be underrated. His analyses have long been celebrated, and very properly so. What is more is that it is so complete and shows such a minute study of the music (from the viewpoint of a rapturously enthusiastic Elgarite), that after reading it is impossible to write a line about the work without trespassing upon the ground it covers.

Before leaving this subject, which is important also because many who were present last night left the hall with the book in their possession, it may be useful to quote one of the many instances in which the voice of honest commonsense is forced to protest against the finely-worded comments of the eminent but too partial Jaeger. It is at the point where Gerontius died, and the 'Miserere' theme (p 19) 'vanishes into space, its last chord unresolved, the prayer finished, as the immortal soul of Gerontius takes its flight to God.' Then follows the bass solo of the Priest, and we are instructed (p 29) 'As the sunshine suddenly flooding an erstwhile darkened sick room is welcomed when the patient is well, so the bright, sonorous chords, which annouce and support the Priest's words "Proficiscere, anima Christiana", are welcomed.' Not at all. Pure, authoritative, misleading Jaegerism. Whatever the chords are the whole effect of the solo is inky-black, 'a darkess that may be felt,' a gloomy piece of declamation which possesses some element of grandeur, indeed, but taken as a whole is so frightfully lugubrious as to be almost ugly. And the new oratorio is flooded most gloriously with 'sunshine' of this kind! Similarly, there is a learned note on p 45 concerning the bass solo of the Angel of the Agony, to the effect that the composer shows 'an exquisite effect in spite of a flagrant violation of the rules against consecutive fifths, and proving once more that a master of his art can step boldly outside the pale of restricting rules to produce the intrinsically beautiful.' 'But no,' cries the reader, who has an ear for melody, and the courage of his opinions, 'this is not beautiful. I know little of your consecutive fifths, and care less, but I do know when an aria is uncouth and inexpressive from a vocal standpoint, and I am listening to such an aria now. The 'intrinsically beautiful' is just exactly what I do not find.' Very few readers will dare to say this, unfortunately, because they cannot help seeing that the writer of the Notes is a learned musician, and it does not occur to them that he may also be a violent partisan. This at any rate is the only conclusion we can come to after listening most carefully to the new oratorio. Just as Berlioz's 'Faust' and Braham's [*sic*] 'Song of Destiny' when first produced here but a few years ago exceeded in emotional power and beauty all that we had dared anticipate, so equally do we find 'The Dream of Gerontius' clever and learned, but very rarely inspired and in no wise exciting to the emotions.

... Chorus and orchestra, the former with an especially weird 'ha-ha-ha' ... triumphed over the difficulties of the colossal 'demon ensemble'. 'We are approaching a cloud [*sic*] of demons and hear their distant howls (p 29). A scene of great power, remarkable boldness, and wild grandeur commences and holds us in its grip.' Thus Jaeger. But does it? Or is it merely clever and superior pantomime music? Does it, for example, as a pure piece of 'theatricalism', come anywhere near the final movement (in the Hall of the Mountain Troll) of Grieg's 'Peer Gynt' suite? Let someone other than Jaeger give answer! One other triumph of the united forces must be mentioned, namely the Choir of Angelicals in the tremendous setting of Newman's own unrivalled hymn, 'Praise to the Holiest in the Height.' The composer touches greatness at this point, and is genuinely inspired by the majesty of his theme. The interpretation was magnificent, and after the sudden silence which follows the fff close the enthusiasm was so insistent that the whole had to be repeated. Unfortunately two or three really fine pieces of music will not redeem a dull work.[47]

Elgar continued to see to *Apostles* proofs from Italy, while hoping that he might be able to devote himself to the composition of the Symphony. In the first flush of holiday enthusiasm, he invited Jaeger to join the party; if the weather was poor, the domestic conditions were evidently first-rate.

> Our Cook is an angel: do come out – it seems *so easy* to come & so difficult to go back – & have a meal or two – What matters the Mediterranean being rough & grey? What matters rain in torrents? Who cares for gales – *Tramontana*? we have such meals! such wine! *Gosh*! … We are at last living a life.[48]

As Elgar must have known, the expense of the journey and the need for further leave of absence from Berners Street made it out of the question for Jaeger to accept, and he was unwell yet again during December. Such an invitation might serve only to underline the growing gap between the composer and Jaeger and other friends in England who were not 'living a life'. But there must have been comfort for Jaeger in Elgar's concluding tribute, 'I can't believe all these great Germans are doing my music: is it true? I think it's a dream[.] I hope you are pleased, old boy, anyhow.'[49] He seems to have been too ill to answer, and two days after Christmas Elgar wrote again, fearing that he had been overworking, and anxious for news: 'This is only to wish you all a most happy new year & many, many more.' It was in fact the last new year for some time that Jaeger would not have to face the prospect of embarking on foreign visits of his own, considerably less enjoyable than Elgar's.

9 1904: Remission and Relapse

For Jaeger the beginning of 1904 brought painful developments at the *Musical Times*, and a growing feeling of insecurity over his relationship with Elgar. The continuing incompatibility with F.G. Edwards had been festering towards some kind of crisis, and there seems to have been some uncertainty over Jaeger's future as a staff writer; again he wondered whether coaching singers would be a more enjoyable way of supplementing his income. Then, with doubts exacerbated perhaps by the sheer distance between them, Jaeger accused Elgar of failing to correspond with him as much as with other critics such as Bennett, Pitt and Kalisch. Elgar robustly but affectionately denied the charge, and went on to confide over his failure to make progress with his symphony during the Italian holiday, although he hoped to produce a concert overture for the proposed Covent Garden Festival to be held in March. He returned to England at the beginning of February, staying with Frank Schuster in London, in order to accept an invitation to dine with the King and conduct the first *Pomp and Circumstance* March afterwards. Jaeger came to lunch that day, bringing some of the newly engraved full score of *The Apostles*, and the next day he received the first part of the new overture from Elgar, who then returned to Malvern. Jaeger wrote to advise him to discuss openly with Littleton an exclusive publishing contract which had been mooted, and then went on to apologise for a lapse of confidentiality over the non-appearance of the symphony; another glimpse of Jaeger the gossip, especially in the company of fellow-critics.

> I say, it seems that Baughan did get the news about *no* Symphony from *me*, NOT from Kalisch. I am sorry, but we were talking about the disappointment in store & I said more than necessary, I dare say, & though I said that You '*don't wish the news made public*' YET, B. abused the Confidence. I thought that perhaps Kalisch & he had agreed to publish the news simultaneously, but Kalisch does not seem to have been guilty of that.
>
> My trop de zèle, as usual! Really, a Journalist has no soul & no conscience. I am very sorry for my misdeed.[1]

A week later Jaeger wrote again to ask for more score of the overture for the engravers, and went on to recommend a string quartet by John McEwen, whose 'big & fine' piano sonata was also going through the firm's presses at that time. 'Mac is the most modest man in creation, a dear fellow,' he told Elgar. 'I'm delighted he has at last had a real success ... I "discovered" him (as regards this firm) & am proud of him.' McEwen's quartet had been published by Novello's, and was given a half-page advertisement in the February *Musical Times*, which also contained a supportive review, identifying certain 'Scottish' elements in the music.

> British music was strongly represented at the first of this year's concerts at St. James's Hall on the 7th ult. by a string Quartet in A minor, from the pen of Mr. John B. McEwen, and a set of six 'Pastorals' for voices, pianoforte, and string quartet, by Dr. H. Walford Davies. Both works proved masterly efforts as regards workmanship, and of more than common interest on the score of invention and effectiveness. Mr. McEwen, a native of Glasgow and a Professor at the Royal Academy of Music, is but little known as a composer. Those acquainted with his music, however, think highly of his gifts, an opinion which the Quartet under notice is calculated to strengthen. The work is of generous dimensions, especially as regards the first and last movements, and the idiom throughout is unmistakably Scottish. The themes are fresh, strong of mien and bold of outline; they all have a sound backbone of rhythm. Their treatment, at once elaborate and interesting, is full of healthy, vigorous life, and at times even of a ruggedness which suggests 'Caledonia stern and wild' as the 'meet nurse' of the composer's inspiration. Effective contrast to the composer's strenuous mood is presented by the beautiful, romantic slow movement (an uninterrupted stream of spontaneous melody), by the *Trio* (a capital tune assigned to the viola) of the bustling *Scherzo*, and by the long-drawn sentiment of the second subject in the *Finale*. The Quartet is a serious and valuable contribution to modern chamber music, and as such deserves a warm welcome ... Dr. Walford Davies has selected the texts of his 'Pastorals' from some beautiful poems by Fletcher, Greene, Dekker and Andrew Marvell. He is frankly modern in his setting of these old-world lyrics, and the poetic refinement and deep thought there is in him he has poured into his music with the happiest result. If Dr. Davies's themes lack the robust strength of Mr. McEwen's, there is about them a quiet beauty and appropriateness ; and throughout the cycle his music shows many masterly touches with results that are delightful. Four of the poems are set for four voices, and these are likely to prove the favourites, for they are charming in the best sense of the word. Two Dialogues, one for contralto and baritone, the other for soprano and tenor, show greater originality and strike a deeper note than the Quartets, but a first hearing left us in some doubt as to their spontaneity. Dr. Davies obtained some beautiful effects from his novel combination of voices and instruments ...[2]

Walford Davies had been much in Jaeger's mind, for on the same evening as his apologetic letter to Elgar, he sat down to write what must have been a difficult letter to the composer. Davies had evidently been pressing for a frank opinion of his work and seems to have felt that Jaeger had been neglecting him. The letter mixed blunt honesty over *The Temple* with tactful support and encouragement.

> 37 Curzon Road,
> Muswell Hill. N.
>
> Feb 11.04
>
> My dear Davies,
>
> Pardon my procrastination. (I am always begging your pardon for this sort of thing) I have had an extraordinary spell of hard work at 'No. 1' & can't break the back of it at all. Mr May is away ill, work is accumulating all round me, I get no assistance – it is maddening. Now to make matters worse as regards this would-be reply to your letter, I have left that letter of yours in my Office Coat, & I must trust to my poor memory if I want to give you an answer.

Well now imprimis: Don't talk nonsense about my 'dropping' you. I have always admired your art for its many sterling though 'severe' qualities, & admire it as much as or more than ever, especially the 'Temple', in which I believe thoroughly, while sincerely deploring its wretched fate which permitted its ruin (temporary I hope) by an inadequate, perfunctory performance. Now you ask me to tell you sincerely what I find wanting in that big work. Well, to *me* it is wholly satisfactory, though it cannot & never will (I fancy) *overwhelm* me as the Apostles & Gerontius have done. Your creative gifts strike me as falling short of that supreme power which moves me to tears of exultation in [illegible] (You come nearest to it in 'Prospice'). You are not yet a true pathfinder discovering *new* realms of Beauty. You lack the faculty of *real originality* of melodic invention, which amongst English Composers only Elgar has. Your effects (You will hate that word) are also on more stereotyped lines than is good for you *if* you wish to attract the attention of the 'musical world'. 'Nothing new to say' is a damning criticism & it is levelled against many a worthy musician. That *'newness'* is generally looked for in the thematic invention rather than in new forms &c.

Thus on the one hand you seem to me to give too little to those expecting greatest originality, while on the other hand your music cannot, it seems to me, appeal to those simpler folk who want what *they* call 'tune'. Your 'tune' is not of the 'popular' Kind. Hence a large section of would-be musical people would call your music 'dry'. A great many of these good people call the greater portion of Gerontius 'dry' also. So your music, fine, noble, dignified stuff though it be, appeals fully neither to (the majority of) 'critical' cusses who want Wagners or Bachs always, nor to the uncritical asses who want their 'tunes'. In these days few, *very few* critics will believe that work like yours needs attentive and repeated hearings, just as Brahms' earlier works did. This is an age of hurried impressions & hurried criticisms. I have ALWAYS found this [:] the more intimately I know your music, the more I admire it, & the more it affects me wholesomely & beautifully. I still have *patience* with works that come from the brain of a deep thinker like you, & my patience *always* gets rewarded. The question which worries me is whether you can wait till the public, amongst whom there must be many like me, will give You the reward of a due recognition of your genius & whether publishers will issue your works if they are not 'taken up'. You see, a publisher is ready enough to try a new composer, but when commercial success does not attend his 'speculations' he can't be blamed for hesitating over further ventures. But meanwhile you will & must go on in your own sane, straight way & do your best & leave the rest to the future.

Pardon this long rigmarole I hope it isn't quite as nonsensical as it might be, considering the tired out state of my noddle. I have had an *awful* day! if you won't come & play your Everyman to me, I must come & hear it at your House, but God wot when that will be. Next Saturday I *must* go to hear Pitts Songs at the Symphony Concert, but I hope to be back here about 5–5.30.

I say, Edwards hacked my M.T. notice of your Pastorals *shamefully* till I don't recognise it.

I must speak to Mr Alfred L. about the 'Temple' when I get a chance. I don't think the music of the spheres would drag me from my house on Sunday *afternoons!* Sorry to have to confess it. But I do appreciate my Sundays with my bairns.

Goodnight, dear Davies,

Much love to you,

Ever yours sincerely & admiringly

AJ Jaeger[3]

Another pressured period at Berners Street was building up, with continued work on the engraving of the *Apostles* score and parts as well as the new overture and other music to be prepared for the looming three-day Covent Garden Festival. Jaeger wrote to Elgar that he hoped for a 'close time' of six months in which to deal properly with the next big work, and mentioned how he had been unable to resist sampling part of a *Gerontius* performance at the Queen's Hall on his way home after a long day.

> I dropped into Queen's Hall for 20 minutes last night (after working here till 10). A *magnificent* House, every seat taken; uninspiring performance I thought, though the Choir sang 'nicely' ... We sold 100 Scores & 750 Analysis last night. I wish to goodness I had a 1d royalty on my stuff![4]

Elgar sent the final portion of the *In the South* manuscript to Jaeger on 22 February, some three weeks before the première. Inevitably another last-minute saga began to develop. Elgar, anxious to expedite matters, asked for the parts to be ready in a week, an impossible target and one which upset Jaeger. 'Don't frighten us again for noddings. It's bad for our nerves & livers,' he wrote, and was unable to resist making a point concerning the coda of the new overture. He went on to ask for a spare ticket so that he could make sure of hearing its first performance.

> Why the Divel have you a *silent Bar* in your Coda (Overture)? You WILL play pranks with Your Kodas. Foolish boy!, unsagacious neophite! Weber, Beethoven Wagner Knew better. It's never too late to do the wrong thing, however. But that there overture looks Dem fine allee Samee... I say, IF the C.G. people give you any tickets which you *cant* do with remember poor 'Nim'. I really can't afford to pay & I *should* like to hear at least the *overture*. You have no poorer friend now ...[5]

Somehow the orchestral parts of the overture were available for the first rehearsal in Manchester on 9 March, even if some had not been fully corrected. The clash with preparations for a Leeds *Apostles* – for which Jaeger had engaged another seven copyists – had been unfortunate. Once again he proposed a 'close season' for Elgar's next work; 'the present method is Bedlam, to be sure!' In addition to supervising the work on the parts, Jaeger had much to do in liaising with various figures connected with the Leeds and Covent Garden Festivals, and was continuing to spend so much time at Berners Street that he hardly saw his children. He summed it all up in a brief undated note to Elgar.

> I am still in my senses, but that there Festival & the other Apostles performances are driving me cracked. I am arranging for copyists galore, telegraphing wildly all over London & Suburbs, interviewing R Newman (Re Leeds performance) C. Garden Librarian, writing & wiring to Forsyth, Embleton, Schulz Curtius, Neil Forsyth, holding conferences with A H. L. Pointer, Brause, Copyists &c &c
>
> Oh my *poor* head ... To night I see 'Little Mary' for a change.[6]

A week before the unprecedented Festival was to begin, and with interest in Elgar developing to enormous proportions, Jaeger wrote to say that he had been asked to write a book on his music for a royalty of sixpence per copy. He was tempted, and spent some weeks considering the proposal. But he must have realized that such an undertaking would mean even greater inroads on his time and energies, with likely ill effects on his health. Then he went on to voice worries over the possible effects on Elgar of the social side of the Festival; 'You *will* have festive times next week! Don't let 'em spoil you,' he pleaded. Elgar protested, perhaps a little too much, with a formal note to 'Mr. Jaeger', to the effect that his position now warranted throwing him over, and that all familiarity between them should cease. But then,

> Now, you old moss, read the other side ... What an old frump you are! – whenever anything of mine is to be done you beg me not to be conceited & not to forget my old friends &c.
>
> ... *You* are an old *PIG* & deserve some such letter as the unfinished one on the other side – anyhow you always seem to be *expecting* it: be assured you wont receive anything of the kind from me. There is no fear that I shall forget anyone.[7]

The historic three-day Festival took place in mid-March, with performances of *Gerontius* and *The Apostles* occupying the first two evenings, and a mixed concert on the final evening including the new overture. The Elgars stayed with Frank Schuster at his Westminster house, and during the heady period of the Festival rose higher socially than ever before. They extended their acquaintanceship among Frank Schuster's circle to include the MP Charles Stuart-Wortley and his wife Alice, the daughter of the painter Millais, whom Elgar found deeply sympathetic and who was gradually to take on an inspirational role in his life. They also attended dinners and receptions along with various members of the aristocracy and diplomatic service. The King, who 'gave E. a nice smile' at the Levée held on 14 March, attended the first two evenings and the Queen all three – after the final performance, which concluded with the first *Pomp and Circumstance* March amid 'immense enthusiasm', she 'sent for E'. Two days later the Elgars met Arthur James Balfour, the musical Prime Minister, at Lord Northampton's. Matters concerning copyright were discussed, and the question of a knighthood for Elgar – anticipated and perhaps privately feared by Jaeger – was explored. Jaeger seems to have been able to attend the Festival throughout, and Elgar made a point of visiting him at home one day, his first sight of the Muswell Hill house ('your pretty home'), while Alice took in a private view and made calls. The gesture was appreciated. 'It *was* good of that dear Edward to come & see us last Saturday & I appreciate it greatly', wrote Jaeger from Berners Street to Alice, and earlier, although 'half dead with a cold' and anxious to get home to bed, he had told her with justifiable pride, 'I guess there were few really more *gratified* men (or proud men) in the audience there than myself who have had faith for many years in E. & have spoken up when things looked desperate here.'

Once again Jaeger was keen to be helpful over German performances of the new work, but Elgar was anxious to avoid complications and wanted to keep his own hands on the reins. Ettling had brought word that his friend Weingartner would like to give the prestigious first performances of the overture in Berlin and Munich, and Elgar told Jaeger bluntly, 'don't go suggesting it in Deutschland to other folk until Weingartner has been to London.' Perhaps he was mindful of Jaeger's occasional lack of control over his tongue, and earlier in the letter he had pointedly referred to a rumour that the future symphony would be premièred at Essen. Jaeger pleaded innocence – 'However that Rumour come about *I* certainly *never* suggested such a thing' – but went on to suggest that it might be better for Elgar himself to conduct the first German performance, especially in the Rhineland, unless Steinbach were to programme the work for the Lower Rhine Festival. Jaeger concluded the letter by asking for the MS score of the overture to be returned and, never one to lose an opportunity, referred to some music of McEwen, evidently still much in his mind. 'I sent You yesterday McEwen's things just to show you that this quiet, modest fellow is capable of doing better Work than those Anthems which he wrote for us under protest more or less.'[8]

Jaeger expected certain moral qualities of his young composers, and there seems to have been no risk of a falling out with the 'quiet, modest' McEwen such as had occurred with Coleridge-Taylor, whose path – teaching, accompanying, adjudicating and conducting all over the country – now hardly crossed with Jaeger's at all. Wider prospects were opening up for that composer in the United States, where his achievements were becoming an intense focus of admiration and pride among the coloured community. A Coleridge-Taylor Society had been formed in Washington, consisting entirely of coloured singers, and later that year he would conduct it during an historic and inspirational American tour which took in five other cities and culminated in an audience at the White House with President Theodore Roosevelt.

There was occasion now for Jaeger to write to Dora Penny, who had been unable to be present at the Covent Garden Festival because of her father's disapproval of 'musical entertainments' during Lent (she wrote later that the Elgars seemed quite hurt, 'and Mr. Jaeger thought it extraordinary'). He confessed to her his emotional reaction to *The Apostles*, shared with Mrs Baker, wife of 'W.M.B.' and the kind hostess of the Hasfield Court house party some three years before. He was able also to proudly claim that his analysis of the work had been entirely vindicated, especially with a change of mind on the part of Talbot, the *Guardian* critic; and the Elgar book project remained sufficiently alive for him to seek to lighten the load by asking Dora's help with it.

37 Curzon Road,
W.

27/iii/4

My dear Dora

... Why the Beelzebub didn't you come to that unique Festival? ... They played you beautifully & the audience liked you hugely. They liked me too, though they only murmured approval, that particular audible sigh of approval which often means more than applause. They applauded You, though. The new overture is beautiful & new, & shows a surer touch than almost anything else I know of E.E.'s. The Apostles impressed me tremendously though nothing 'came off' as the composer meant it. The acoustic defects of the theatre were too great. I sat near dear Mrs. Baker, & we twain cried silently & shyly over the marvellous beauties of the various scenes. You don't consider me a softy or an old woman, because I can still be moved to tears by the happiness of letting such beauty 'creep into my ears' do you? I say, that analysis of mine isn't a bad guess at things. I have without a performance anticipated the effect & beauties very correctly, though I say so ('cos no one else does). Even the 'Guardian' critic, Talbot, after pitching frightfully into me in October confesses that things sound quite different now (after he has studied the work, doubtless with my analysis – read his remarks!) I smile. Ask dear little Mrs. E. She must have been in the 7th Heaven of Happiness. Such swells they met, from the Queen downwards. A great time for E. E. and some of us who have believed in him and fought for him (I had to fight hard for him at Novello's) are happy. I have been asked to write a book (chiefly critical) on Elgar. Will you help me? I hope to see something of you when you come to town. Meanwhile kindest regards to you and Miss Danks.

Ever yours

NIMROD[9]

Jaeger remained steadfast to the cause in the aftermath of the Festival. When Elgar complained of a flood of begging letters, he saw his fears being realized: 'I want to drown all people worrying you with letters & things You ought to be left alone with your work: you have enough in hand for 10 years! When will You do it if these fools & Rogues & snobs worry you so? I am jealous for your work's sake.' And he spread himself in a long review of the Covent Garden concerts for the *Musical Times*, although predictably enough it was shortened by the Editor. 'Friend Edwards has "cut" me again quite furiously,' he told Alice. 'He *is* an erratic. I daresay it *was too* long, but then – we haven't had many such Festivals!' It was just this point, together with the question of national pride, that Jaeger emphasized in the introductory paragraph of his article.

A triumph for English music! In these words may be summed up the unique event which stirred musical London on the 14th, 15th, and 16th ult. Who could have ventured to prophesy a few years ago that an English composer's music would draw crowded and brilliant audiences to Covent Garden Theatre on three consecutive evenings? Not Dr. Elgar's firmest friends, not even the staunchest champions of his genius would have dared to think the time so near when the Metropolis of the British Empire would pay him this great, this unprecedented homage. The event – unique, let it be noted – was more than a local celebration. From all parts of the country visitors flocked to do honour to England's foremost composer, and their Majesties the King and Queen by their presence gave expression to that pride which Englishmen the world over must feel in their great compatriot.[10]

In dealing with the performance of *The Apostles*, the first in London, Jaeger repeated and extended his earlier claims for the work, now stating that it was above *The Dream of Gerontius*. Anxious for its continued reception, however, he concluded with a repetition of his earliest fears about the readiness of audiences to make efforts to understand it.

Jaeger treated the *In the South* Overture, 'a treasure amongst recent additions to orchestral music', to a brief analysis, and was allowed enough space for six musical examples featuring the main melodic material. The last of these was the famous viola solo, 'the tune,' Jaeger thought, 'which, unless we are much mistaken, will make the fortune of the Overture.' He spoke of the 'great charm of this lovely melody' and went on to correct the comments of the Festival programme-note writers over its origin.

> We may here correct an error into which Dr. Elgar's fondness for a joke has led the writers of the excellent analyses for the third concert programme, Messrs. Percy Pitt and Alfred Kalisch. Their statement that 'the tune is founded on a *canto popolare*, and that the composer does not know who wrote it', is misleading. The tune is Dr. Elgar's own, and he has every reason to be proud of it after it has been greatly admired as 'An Italian Folk-tune.'[11]

Kalisch responded with a joke of his own, which Jaeger evidently took more seriously than was intended. It set off a burst of letter-writing, as Kalisch affectionately explained to Elgar.

> Dear Jaggers has been very excited & wrote me eight pages telling me not to be thin skinned. I had told him I should have a gory revenge because he has said in the Musical Times that Pitt & I had allowed ourselves to be misled by the jests of one Elgar. He (Jaeger) thought I meant it (my threat) seriously. He is quite calm now, & his pulse was normal again yesterday. Where should we be without our only Nimrod?[12]

Jaeger's article gave an account of the ovation accorded Elgar at the end of the final concert, and his summons to the Royal Box, and concluded with a prediction that might have doubled as a disguised, intimate warning.

> Thus ended an occasion unique in the history of English music – a one-composer Festival so successful in nearly every way that all who took part in it may look back upon it with pride and satisfaction. To our distinguished composer however it will be but the most powerful incentive to continue in his own individual way, and add fresh and still more beautiful works to the rich store which is the present proud possession of his grateful countrymen.[13]

Elgar continued to show particular consideration for his friend when he could. When the expected London visit of Felix Weingartner took place, Jaeger benefited to the extent of two circle tickets for the noted conductor's performance of *Gerontius* at the Queen's Hall on 9 April. He took Isabella and they had tea with Elgar and Kalisch at the Langham Hotel after the performance. Alice Elgar had remained behind in Malvern, 'very mis', as she confided to her diary, and so Isabella penned her a tactful letter. Isabella's enthusiasm for Elgar's music was second only to her husband's and her responses equally emotional; whatever her letter lacked of his style and fluency, was made up for by its warmth and sincerity.

> 37 Curzon Road,
> Muswell Hill,
> N.
>
> April 10th [1904]
>
> My dear Mrs Elgar,
>
> We are both wishing so much that you had been at yesterday's performance. It was wonderful! That splendid chorus simply surpassed itself! My husband wept tears of

absolute joy – so did I. The 'Kyrie' was most exquisitely sung – the lovely sounds stealing into the air in an almost unearthly quietude.

And the magnificent 'Praise to the Holiest' bursting forth like a great wave of joy. It was perfect.

But there is nothing in all music like 'Gerontius'! Yesterday's performance was a revelation. The Demon Chorus made me shudder. The Tenors & Basses absolutely snarled. Mr Elwes was very beautiful in the way he interpreted – if *only* his voice were a little stronger & richer.

Of course Mr Davies sang with great conviction, but he does not move one as one longs to be moved in such a glorious part. The lady who sang the 'angel's' part was *quite* inadequate! – one could only hear her singing with the remembrance of how that most exquisite music *can* be sung. It warmed one's heart to see how enthusiastic the chorus were when they saw Dr Elgar. They rose & shouted & clapped madly – & they only stood for him, not for the conductor or anyone else. But one quite understood their feelings. Dear Mrs Elgar I can never put into words my great admiration for your great husband.

Anything I can say seems so unworthy of him so – to him – I say nothing, – but still I do so wish you to know a little of what I am feeling & maybe you will find words for me to tell him?

Yesterday's triumph was glorious. With my kindest greetings,

Believe me

Yours Very Sincerely

Isabella Jaeger[14]

P. S. We had tea with Dr Elgar after the concert, & it was a most delightful time. My husbands [*sic*] sends his kindest regards & asks me to tell you he sent a copy of 'Gerontius' to Lady Thompson yesterday.

Shortly afterwards Jaeger confirmed to Elgar that Weingartner would give the first performances of *In the South* in Munich and Berlin, and could not resist adding, 'Weingartner is clamouring for that there E.E. *Symphony*'. Meanwhile the composer, mindful of his responsibilities to the younger generation of composers, wrote from the Athenaeum, to which he had recently been elected partly at Parry's instigation ('You *are* getting on. What more *do* you want?' teased Jaeger) of his efforts to persuade the Leeds Choir to take up Macpherson's Psalm. Jaeger for his part concerned himself with preparations for Steinbach's forthcoming production of *The Apostles* at Cologne in May. But he had displeased Alice by something he had written or said concerning the work, and she charged him with 'not following the development' of her husband's genius. 'I feel quite "hurt"', he wrote to Elgar at the beginning of May, and summoned Wagner to his aid. 'I cry with Marke: "*Nix* das! Tristan; Dein, Tristan, *mir*"!?' and he continued with a totally fair vindication of himself: 'I thought I "followed" the Apostles pretty well. Has any critically reliable person appreciated it more & said so in more honest words? (I don't count hysterical sentimentalists who would Rave in similar terms over Perosi if he came along again, dressed in priest's garb.)' It was not the last time that Jaeger's honesty over his own responses would provoke a strong reaction from Alice, and it may not have been entirely coincidental that a week or so later he announced his decision not to proceed with the suggested 'chiefly critical' book on her husband's music. But there was some light relief to hand, for he was able to conclude with something of a wink, 'Dear Dorabella is in town once more enjoying her sprightly self,' and he was able to take time from the office to spend an afternoon with her on 10 May, when she noted in her Diary, '... lunch with Nimrod at Paganis. Wagner concert Queen's Hall. Tea at Buzzards.'

Jaeger was pleased to be asked to report for the *Musical Times* on the Cologne performance of *The Apostles* which took place under Steinbach on 22 May as part of the Lower Rhine Festival. Elgar had earlier been unwilling to go but Alice thought that at the first of two rehearsals which they attended, Steinbach 'gave a glorious reading'. That evening Jaeger, Harold Brooke and the German conductor Hehemann dined with the Elgars, and there was the usual round of celebratory suppers and speeches throughout the Festival. Jaeger had also attended the two rehearsals, and earlier on the day of the performance sent off, perhaps rather dramatically, a wire with the first of two brief articles for the *Musical Times*. In it he recounted, with a justifiable pride, his rôle in the performance history of *Gerontius*, and looked forward to what he called the 'second chapter'.

> When, in 1902, Dr Edward Elgar's 'Dream of Gerontius' was introduced to these historical Festivals by Professor Julius Buths, in Dusseldorf, I drew attention to the unique character of the honour done hereby to an English composer, and ventured to hint at the far-reaching results that might safely be expected to accrue from the great and immediate success which our composer's beautiful work achieved before a severely critical audience. Those results were not long in showing themselves. A gratifying revival of interest in the 'Dream' in England, and a most welcome, new-born and wholly beneficial spirit of emulation amongst English Choral Societies were the first-fruits of that 'famous victory' in the Rhineland ... This evening the eighty-first Festival of the Lower Rhine commences with Dr Elgar's 'The Apostles', and to judge from two complete rehearsals which I have been privileged to hear, the work will be given an exceedingly fine performance. The Festival is under the direction of the municipal Kapellmeister, Generalmusikdirektor Fritz Steinbach, of Meiningen Orchestra fame, whose enthusiasm over the English novelty is gratifying to hear. 'Es ist mir eine wahre Wohlthat gewesen, das Werk einzustudieren' (it has been a downright boon to me to rehearse this work), he remarked after last night's final rehearsal. 'There is something about it,' he continued – 'You know, *here*!' (slapping his broad chest in the region of the heart.)[15]

Of the performance itself, Alice wrote 'Great audience. Gorgeous performance. Great enthusiasm E had to go out on platform after 1st part & 2nd great impression D.G.' The overwhelming reception accorded Elgar was not lost on Jaeger and neither was the quality of Steinbach's large orchestra. Once again, he could feel vindicated and his feelings were, characteristically, perfectly evident physically. The next day, Alice thought he looked 'quite pink with happiness', although the flush could have had more sinister causes. The customary postcard was duly despatched to Dora Penny.

> Dear Dorabella
>
> We had a magnificent performance of the Apostles. The orchestra (150) especially was gorgeous & for the first time within my experience realized *all* my anticipations (as

expressed in my analysis). E.E. was called out after part 1 (a RARE honour here) & TWICE amid great enthusiasm at end. The chorus was excellent & soloists at least quite adequate. Mrs E. & E. are delighted.

Yours

NIMROD[16]

It was the best performance the work had yet been given, one that the composer would remember all his life, especially in regard to the quality of both orchestral and choral tone colour. Jaeger told Ivor Atkins it was 'immensely finer than any I have heard yet. The work had a *splendid* success.'[17] Elgar wrote to Littleton of the performance, and explained that he had with difficulty persuaded Jaeger to stay another day so that he could find time to talk to the busy Steinbach. Meanwhile 'our special correspondent' made reference in the *Musical Times* to the municipal subsidies available in Germany; this reference was not lost on Elgar, who would advocate such support in one of his Birmingham lectures.

> Of the performance I can but repeat in the most emphatic manner that, a few trifling mishaps excepted, it was superb, and that Herr Steinbach proved himself a great conductor by the way in which, without any sort of hint from Dr. Elgar, he managed to realize the composer's intention; the orchestra playing was a pure delight from the opening note to the last, and the true value of the orchestration and its tremendous importance as a great factor in the composer's scheme were fully appreciated. Every point was clearly brought out, and I heard beauties and effects which I have never heard before. It simply showed once more what an enormous advantage a conductor of a municipal subsidized German orchestra with unlimited chances for rehearsing has over his colleagues in England. Herr Steinbach's orchestra was a revelation. What Sheffield did for the choral portions of 'Gerontius' in London the other day, that Cologne has done for the orchestral score of 'The Apostles'.
>
> The chorus sang with sureness, beauty of tone, and depth of expression. They produced, with the huge orchestra, the most astounding climaxes, the like of which I have never heard in a long experience. No wonder the composer was delighted therewith ...
>
> After this unique performance I repeat once more what I have already, on two occasions, stated as my conviction, viz., that 'The Apostles' is a great work.[18]

Thus, hopefully, Alice was mollified, particularly perhaps when shortly afterwards Canon Gorton wrote to her, 'I had an interesting letter from Mr. Jaeger – who I am thankful to know was at the Lower Rhine Festival – and whose heart rejoiced at what he heard.'[19]

Meanwhile Jaeger was taking in hand the printing of Parry's Three Choirs commission for that September. *The Love that Casteth out Fear* was another ethical cantata, emphasizing the power of God's love over frail mankind, and it seemed to show the influence of *The Apostles* in its use of a mystic semi-chorus. A letter to Parry at this time seems to show that even his works were not always necessarily produced at the firm's expense, and identified the orchestrator of Sullivan's 1886 Leeds Festival work, *The Golden Legend*; presumably Jaeger had been encouraging Parry to delegate his scoring in order to reduce his workload.

1, Berners Street, W.
London.

June 11th 1904

Dear Sir Hubert,

Many thanks for your letter. We are proceeding with the Engraving. Mr. Littleton will no doubt write to you on Tuesday whether the Firm will take over the work. No doubt they will, but I thought it best *not* to wait for that decision! I return to you M.S. from 'Act III' to End. Kindly Return it in sections directly you have done the scoring of such sections. We may at any moment find a chance – as other work is being cleared off – of putting *more* engravers on your work. Meanwhile we will do our utmost to Keep you busy with proofs.

I suppose you couldn't send me a fair (fairly fair) copy of the 'Book' or merely a list of *Bible references*, so that the Engravers could turn to the Bible for the words? It will *save them much time*. They are mostly Germans & have to battle with your M.S. of the *words* more than the music M.S.

You are *too* conscientious over your Scoring. Why, Sullivan's 'Golden Legend' was largely scored by Hamilton Clarke,[20] as *we* Know very well *here*! No one thinks the worse of S. for that! And He wasn't as busy as you are!

However, it is just like 'C.H.H.P.' to see differently in such matters from the rest of the world & we all honour you for it.

Yours Sincerely,

A.J. Jaeger[21]

There seemed little chance of a significant break from routine for Jaeger, who in answer to a query from Elgar said he had no plans to take a holiday that summer and had turned down another invitation from the Holdings at Wimbledon. Instead, he intended to stay at home, play with the children, and work. Not surprisingly, perhaps, he later told Elgar, 'I have the Hump badly.'

He was cheered, however, by the announcement of Elgar's long-expected knighthood, an honour which Jaeger himself had foretold. Enjoying his break at home, Jaeger was able to wire congratulations from the Muswell Hill Post Office soon after seeing the announcement in the national press on the morning of 24 June:

Muswell Hill 9.28 am rec'd 10.10 am

To Sir Edward Elgar Craeg Lea Upper Wyche Malvern

Happy and delighted beyond words thousand congratulations upon honour most nobly earned.

Moss Nimrod Jagpot August[22]

Five minutes later he sent a second message on behalf of all the Jaegers, to Alice, to acknowledge her own rôle in the success.

Muswell Hill 9.33 am rec'd 10.35 am

To Lady Elgar Craeg Lea Upper Wyche Malvern

Sincerest congratulations to our dear Meister ['s] best truest friend and sturdiest helpmate Hoch sollt Ihr Leben Dacapo dreimal hoch

Nimrod family[23]

Alice replied immediately to thank 'one of the very warmest & best of friends & his Frau Gemahlin', and concluded 'E. is gone to the Golf Club but will write soon'. It was a week before he did, by which time the Elgars had moved to an imposing house at Hereford, Plas Gwyn. Meanwhile Jaeger wrote to Alice with repeated congratulations and a description of the Jaeger household's first reaction to the news of the honour.

> ...You know how happy I am to see one honoured by his King & Country, in whose gifts & great qualities of head & heart I have believed for so many years. May you both live long, happy years to enjoy the honour. Nobody that ever Received a similar honour can have deserved it more thoroughly, for no one can have lived a life more earnestly devoted to the highest & best & purest in life & in art.
>
> We were all *jubilant* when I opened my paper on the morning & read out *the* news. I jumped up from my chair, & leaving my breakfast in the lurch, rushed to the Piano & played *the* Tune in 'Pomp & C. No. 1 in D'. The Bairns marched around the Table, the grown-ups sang, & my neighbours, who had read *their* paper, Knocked on the wall in Rhythmical approval & sympathy. *Such* doings![24]

During the year Jaeger's position as a writer for the *Musical Times* had not suffered as much as he had feared and the battles with F.G. Edwards did not always go against him. The July number saw space allotted to him for a further article on the Lower Rhine Festival, together with a book review, a new departure. Jaeger returned briefly to *The Apostles* at the beginning of the Festival review, emphasizing the success of Steinbach's rendition of the orchestral part, as important in this work, he felt, as in *Tristan* or *Parsifal.* He continued with mention of various works, one of which in particular receiving a performance that made a special impression.

> ... we heard a glorious performance of Bach's 'Brandenburg' Concerto, No. 3, played by thirty-six violins, twenty-four violas, eighteen violoncellos, and twelve basses. The last movement was actually encored! and no wonder, for I can only repeat it was phenomenal, not on the score of jumboism suggested by the number of executants, but on artistic grounds, viz., tone, finish, and spirit. The audience were delirious with delight, and over Bach![25]

Jaeger concluded with the music of the third concert, which as well as works by Wagner, Haydn, Schillings, Bruch and Weber, featured the *Taillefer* of Richard Strauss.

> Dr. Richard Strauss's 'Taillefer', a ballad for soli, chorus, and orchestra, was the great attraction of the third concert. It is laid out on would-be popular lines. The voice parts are comparatively straightforward and diatonic, but in the dramatic situations the orchestral writing is as complex as ever. The music bounds along with the strepitous swing of 'Don Juan' and 'Heldenleben' towards the climax, for which the poem was evidently chosen by a composer who loves to work in the Ercles vein. This is the scene of the 'Battle of Hastings'. I will not try to describe it, but content myself with the remark that, compared with this 'Battle of Hastings' the battle of Charlottenburg – otherwise Strauss's studio – in 'Heldenleben' is the merest lullaby.[26]

Jaeger's doubts about Richard Strauss, gradually increasing with the passing of time and the appearance of increasingly gargantuan tone-poems, particularly the

Symphonia Domestica of 1904, were further aired in a letter to Emily Harding, a friend of the singer Muriel Foster, the original Mary Magdalene of *The Apostles.* They had travelled together to Cologne for the Festival, and presumably Jaeger had made Miss Harding's acquaintance there. Her father, a retired Birmingham solicitor, was a governor of the University and an active supporter of local music; he was a friend of Richard Peyton and would have a hand in the negotiations leading to the offer of the Birmingham professorship to Elgar. Later that year, Strauss himself would stay with the Hardings while conducting in Birmingham, and he must have been the subject of conversation at Cologne. Jaeger followed up with a copy of the *Musical Times* containing his Festival review as soon as it was in print, accompanied by a letter on *Musical Times* stationery which included a comparison of Elgar and Strauss, together with mention of one of Elgar's notable weaknesses as shown in *King Olaf* and *Caractacus.*

THE MUSICAL TIMES
Established 1844
(Published on the First of Every Month)
1, Berners Street, W.,
London, July 2 1904

Dear Miss Harding,

I send the 'Musical Times' with my little article on Cologne, Elgar, Strauss etc. You will see I was wide-awake enough in 1896[27] to scent a 'big' man in R. Strauss and wondered whither he would lead us. Nobody could have been more enthusiastic after a *first* hearing, I fancy. But where he leads us *now* I refuse to follow him. His *beauties* I appreciate as much as anybody (e.g. the marvellous 'Love Scene' in Heldenleben) but his *outrages* I won't listen to any more [.] I don't see why I should. And his jokes! Oh! those chestnuts! (the third time one hears them they *are* old chestnuts, are they not?) I want to know nothing about his aunts and uncles and his baby.[28] My own babies are *much* more interesting *to me.* Really it is playing the fool with art in spite of what dear little Kalisch says about a *general application* of his (S's) ideas. And his example to the younger, less talented fellows is awful in its effect, as I said.

I swear by Elgar though he *can't* write love music. All *his* love scenes are 'bread and butter miss' cum 'college Boy' calf-love scenes, though nice enough music. But E's oratorios are great and *elevating*, pure and ennobling, and that's what we want, or what *I* want from Art (with a capital A). R.S's technique is a marvel and he carries everything before him with that alone. Elgar could never give us the 'rush' of unbridled passion which we find in Strauss, hence his music will never appeal to the amateur and the uncultured as his German colleague does. And therein lies Strauss's danger I fear. He leaves too little to be treasured at the 10th, 20th hearing. I doubt whether such red hot outpouring of the lava that burns within him won't result in the usual, natural phenomenon, that the lava cools and only a waste of cold *ashes* remains. Qui vivra vivra! I may be wrong and R.S. may be calming down into a more philosophic, thinker's mood. His aberrations of taste may be forgotten and forgiven, and as he grows older, and has enough *money* to keep him quiet (He's all for making his thousands now!) he may *wish* to write for the future. He *must* know that *lasting* work is made differently, and he *can* produce it and he will.

I hope you can read my 'drefful' lecture. Pardon its length and Langeweile. Yours very truly

A.J. Jaeger[29]

I have marked all my little things in this month's MT to prove my bona fides, i.e. to show that I don't speak as a *Raw*, new-baked journalist.

One of the 'little things' to which Jaeger proudly called Miss Harding's attention was his review of the first volume of Max Kalbeck's monumental biography of Johannes Brahms, one of his musical heroes from Düsseldorf days. The lengthy piece would be spread over three issues, and faithfully summarized Kalbeck's narrative from the point of view of a devoted sympathizer; there never had been any difficulty for Jaeger in maintaining enthusiasm for both Brahms and Wagner. The final paragraph concluded in eloquent and characteristic mode; the image of genius struggling against adversity was one which always appealed.

> ... this biography is one more recital of the hard fight for recognition which genius has to face. Brahms can never have been considered a revolutionist, and yet the story of his early life, as told with hitherto unobtainable amplitude in this excellent work, differs but very slightly from the tales of the world's callous indifference to some of his great predecessors and contemporaries. It is the old tragi-comedy of the distrust, stupidity, and malice of the many who ignore and deny, and of the sweet recompense found in the devotion of the few who love, and, loving, understand.[30]

Hubert Parry, meanwhile, had been working on the scoring of *The Love that Casteth out Fear*; as always, against time and against a full timetable of College and other commitments. During the first week of July alone, he took the chair at a committee meeting of the Folk Song Society, spoke at a public meeting at Queen's Hall about the Musical Piracy Bill (' Mackenzie made a very boring speech, Elgar a very foolish one and "Stephen Adams" a vile one', he noted) spoke at a ceremony of the Royal College of Organists and again at a dinner afterwards, went to the funeral service for Watts at St Paul's, and attended a College Council meeting and an evening College chamber concert. Socially he had spent the weekend with friends of his wife's at Buckhurst ('an unpromising looking party – who turned to at Bridge directly after dinner'), although matters had improved on the Sunday when they motored over to Penshurst ('interesting pictures ... place itself a marvel of its kind') and 'turned to' at music after dinner with Parry playing accompaniments. Other less enjoyable musical experiences occurred that week as well, such as when he returned from the Watts funeral to find 'a lady with a prodigy waiting for me, who took ¾ of an hour to dispose of'. To cap it all there had been earlier in the week 'a tiresome woman ... from Australia with a prodigy son to be heard. He turned out a feeble youth. Mother with a long story about someone having maliciously poured oil into his violin to prevent his making a good impression on me! – Wild twaddle.' Parry told Jaeger of these pressures on him, and received something of a lecture in return.

1, Berners Street, W.
London, July 6th 1904.

Dear Sir Hubert,

Poor man! I grieve for you & your worries. But you allow Yourself to be *victimized* by every busybody who has the impertinence to intrude upon the privacy of your study, so to speak. You are *too* Kind & goodnatured & complacent, You won't let anybody help you! I wish you could display some wrathful temper & drive out these people with a whip & a few strong words. Not too bad!

Many thanks for sending the pages with Rehearsal letters. You didn't send *all* we wanted, but enough to suit our *urgent* need. Kindly see that these Rehearsal letters are inserted throughout the work before you Return the proofs.

If at all possible I will endeavour to get off part 1 to the 3 Choirs in time for the Singers to go through it before meeting at Gloucester for a general (combined) Rehearsal. But it will require an effort, wherefore kindly Return all proofs as quickly as you can under your exceptional circumstances.

Also Kindly send us an instalment (however small) of the *Full Score* for the copyists to start on. One of them is now *free.*

I note your instructions re the *English* Title for the work. As regards the Adelaide affair, it will take some time to elucidate such a matter. However, we will try.

Yours Sincerely,

A.J. Jaeger[31]

Two days later, Parry duly sent a bundle of corrected proofs to Berners Street, a task he called 'a truly fearful racket'.

If Parry at that time was plagued with overwork, Elgar had his own problems, complaining to Jaeger about his finances, strained by the move to Hereford. He spoke of taking violin pupils again, and busied himself with various potentially lucrative arrangements of the *Canto Popolare* from the *In the South* Overture, which work Jaeger was analysing for its forthcoming performance at the Three Choirs Festival; he asked Isabella to advise over the bowing and fingering of the string parts. The Variations, five years on, had brought in just eight pounds, he told Jaeger, and claimed to feel no incentive to devote time to big works. Jaeger sympathized and once again bemoaned his own lack of resources. Then he somewhat pointedly reminding Elgar of the presence in London of the wealthy and generous Samuel Sanford, Professor of Music at Yale University. Sanford, who had been at the 1899 Worcester Festival with Horatio Parker, had given Jaeger a fine gold-mounted stick, and was intending to present Elgar with a Steinway piano. 'Dont rub him up the wrong way', wrote Jaeger, 'he is a good fellow at Heart & means you well.' He was careful, too, to make sure Elgar approved of his *In the South* analysis '... cut out what is wrong. Dont mind my feelings – I havent any, *except a desire not to misrepresent Your meaning.*' Elgar had very little fault to find, but allied himself with Jaeger over an introductory reference to Richard Strauss; 'I do not think I should put that about Strauss at the beginning – not necessary – S. puts music in a very low position when he suggests it must hang on some commonplace absurdity for its very life.'

With no major work under way, there was no very extensive correspondence between Elgar and Jaeger that summer. Towards the end of August, Jaeger was able to announce that he would be coming to the Gloucester Festival – drawn by the Overture – and would be bringing Isabella, who had never experienced a Three Choirs meeting; further, in a complete change of plan, he would after all be taking a holiday, going to Germany for a week with Holding. At Gloucester the Jaegers introduced Professor Sanford to the Elgars, and would have heard, among other works, the *Prelude and Angel's Farewell* and *The Apostles* as well as the *In the South* Overture, the Brahms Requiem and Granville Bantock's Rhapsody for Chorus and Orchestra, *The Time Spirit.* Afterwards they went to Plas Gwyn to stay with the Elgars for three days, arriving on the same day as Sanford's Steinway. Jaeger probed about the Symphony, but was disappointed. Various excursions were undertaken together, although when Edward and Alice went to Mass on the Sunday, the Protestant Jaegers 'walked about', as Alice wrote in her diary, reflecting, 'Gott sei Dank to be Katholiken'.

Shortly afterwards Jaeger wrote his first surviving letter to Sydney Loeb (1876–1964), whose friendship was to prove greatly supportive in the difficult times which lay ahead. Loeb's German Jewish forbears had come to England, like the Jaegers, to escape the Bismarck factor, and his father Sigismund had married an English girl. Sydney received a classic English education at Harrow, where he was a near-contemporary of Winston Churchill, and grew up to become a connoisseur of the arts and music. His extant engagement diaries of the years from 1901 to 1920 tell of close acquaintance, not only with London's musical life, but with the intellectual and political world also; he attended Fabian lectures and suffragette meetings, and several times sought out, and recorded, the conversation of Bernard Shaw. But music came first. He attended all kinds of orchestral and chamber concerts and song recitals, and became a discriminating judge of singers, on one occasion lunching with Parry at the Royal College of Music to discuss the inauguration of a singing prize. Sustained by a comfortable and apparently undemanding Stock Exchange career and blessed with a gregarious and generous nature, Loeb led a busy social life. Like Elgar, he sat for William Strang, and was a member of the U.B.Q. Club. He cultivated the friendship of many well-known musical figures, especially singers, frequently entertaining them and other friends to post-concert suppers at some of London's best restaurants, especially Pagani's. Marie Brema and Emmy Destinn were two celebrated singers with whom he enjoyed longstanding friendships. A specially bound autograph book – signed and admired by Elgar on the day of the *Apostles* première – gradually came to include dozens of famous names. Sometimes he would squeeze gossipy accounts of his conversations with the great into the pages of his tiny diaries:

> 11 June 1907. Gala performance – Puccinin & Tosti wrote their names. Called on Puccini (letter from Destinn). He was a perfect dear. Thought Strauss not equal to Wagner & was not contented with staging at Covent Garden of Butterfly. Said they wanted a stage manager with authority [–] which was impossible [–] to speak to Caruso about his acting. Had been to Bayreuth heard Parsifal & Meistersinger [with] Van Dyck & Reichmann. It did not hurt him to cut his works for the gala. As Wagner had to, why should not he![32]

Loeb took up photography as a hobby and became an enthusiastic and accomplished practitioner, snapping his idols in an extensive series of refreshingly informal photographs, subsequently mounted in handsome volumes. But his greatest love was for opera, and the diaries tell of attendance at many performances of works by Verdi, Puccini and Richard Strauss. However these pale into insignificance compared to his total of Wagner performances. Loeb's diaries show that he attended virtually every Wagner performance in London for a period of 19 years, clocking up 50 *Mastersingers* and 63 *Tristans*, together with many *Ring* cycles; sometimes he would take in two complete cycles in successive weeks. Able to undertake frequent continental travel, he had attended his first Bayreuth Festival in 1896 for the first Ring revival there for 20 years. He became a regular follower of the Festival, and his devotion to the Wagner cause gradually gained him entry to the Wahnfried family circle and the friendship of Hans Richter. Many of his most memorable photographs were of the Wagner family and their entourage of singers and musicians, and were taken around Bayreuth and in front of the Festspielhaus during Festivals. Loeb's closeness to the Wagner saga would be sealed in 1912, when he married Mathilde, Hans Richter's youngest daughter. He maintained a regular correspondence with the retired master-conductor until his death in 1916, exercising some diplomacy during the Great War when Richter's repudiation of his English honours and degrees upset many friends and supporters; one in particular, Marie Joshua, was so affected that Loeb, calling on her one day in February, 1915, noted that she 'refused to read Richter's letter'.

Some months previously Loeb had paid one of several visits to Elgar at Severn House, and he noted a revealing fragment of their conversation: 'Called on … Elgar. He sent his love to Richter & said he much regretted he had not waited until he was better informed (re Dr's degree). He said he was very strong with the orchestra but weak in character.'[33]

But back in 1904 Sydney Loeb had been travelling extensively in a Europe that was enjoying pre-war conditions as if they would never end. He spent Easter in Paris, attending performances at the Comedie Française and collecting autographs while cultivating the acquaintance of various artists, actors and musicians such as the celebrated Réjane. Towards the end of July he set off again, this time for his annual walking holiday in Switzerland, taking many photographs and participating in a tennis tournament with fellow guests. An encounter with a Wagnerian fellow-passenger on the journey out had resulted in a lively discussion concerning the merits of various singers, which he duly noted in his diary. 'Friday 22 July. Left London by 2.20 train for Adelboden. Between Boulogne & Amiens had heated argument with a Yankee who abused Frau Wagner & looked upon Nordica as an ideal Brunhilde.' But once arrived, there were some delightful moments:

> Wednesday 27th July. Played tennis in the morning. Afernoon: walked across the brook beyond the Scherntanne, as far as a meadow where saw 8 little piggys in the house with their mother. Had my first glass of goat's milk at the Scherntanne rest. Saw it milked.

Early August saw him embark on a leisurely journey to Bayreuth, via Interlaken, Lucerne, Zurich and Nuremburg, where there was a performance of *Parsifal* to be enjoyed. Loeb attended two further performances of the work at Bayreuth, together with two performances of *Tannhäuser* and a *Ring* cycle. He took photographs, including some of Cosima Wagner herself, many of which he later had specially mounted and bound for Hans Richter, with whom he walked and talked. He was invited to Wahnfried and met two of the Wagner daughters, and the memorable summer continued as Loeb took in further Wagner performances in Munich and Frankfurt, crossing Jaeger's path, on his return journey. He arrived back in London at the beginning of September, anxious to have his photographs developed: 'Monday 5th September. Sent 14 day films to Austins.' Given their shared backgrounds and musical tastes, and the wide range of both men's contacts in the musical world, it is likely that the friendship between Loeb and Jaeger had been a longstanding one. Shortly after his return he wrote with news of his travels and photographic exploits, together with an invitation to lunch. Jaeger's reply revealed the extent of his working commitment to the *Musical Times* and his continued interest in an Elgar symphony.

37, Curzon Road,
Muswell Hill,
N.

21/9/4.

Dear Loeb,

Alas! I cant come to lunch with you on Friday. It is 'Musical Times' Proof Reading Day & I cant absent myself from the Printing works for more than ½ hour or so. And even on other days I am pressed for time, for one of the young fellows in my office is ill (operation – appendicitis!) & I can ill be spared. So forgive me. But I mean to go to the Promenade concert tomorrow (Thursday) evening to hear myself in Elgar's 'Variations'. I leave at 6, & then take a modest cup of tea at Slaters. Oxford Street (near Peter Robinson.) Can't you join me there? or at the Prom. (Box office say 7.45–7.55). I could take you in (grand circle) for noddings mit mein Season (*Press*) Ticket. You can telephone to me at Novellos (I forget our number, but it's in *the* Book, – you know). Kindly let me know *before 4 p.m.*

Yes! I was in Frankfurt & drove with a Friend to see the sights. Why didn't you 'eave 'arf a brick at me? We might have had some fun together. But I forgot, there are no 'arf bricks lying about in nice clean German Towns.

Bring your schnappssots along! Fancy schnappssotting Cosima! You are a devil of a dook!

Very Sincerely Yours,

A.J. Jaeger[34]

My wife & I spent some days with the Elgars. I fear me that Symphony is as far off as Ever!

Some days later Jaeger wrote to Elgar with news of a further disappointment with the *Musical Times*; an offer of his *In the South* analysis for the October number had been rejected in favour of a reprint of Grove's much earlier article on Mendelssohn's *Scottish* Symphony. He went on to write of his correspondence with Granville

Bantock, whose music with its Oriental influences must have been almost as antipathetic to Jaeger as that of the modern Russian school.

> The Gran Ban writes me thumping letters about my depraved taste in music. Ye Gods! He is certainly welcome to his Camel bells & the Tom Tomming of the Keepers. The mighty Gran Ban (long may he wave, dear old fellow!) seems to want only one kind of muscular, Billposter music. I told him I like Gerontius some, THOUGH the In the South (a *very* different kind of music) lifted me out of my seat.[35]

And the gossip continued as Jaeger irrepressibly recounted his reaction to Bantock's exhortations to the Three Choirs organists.

> He (The Gran Ban) told Brewer that he & Br. & Atk & Sin 'have the music in the Midlands in their hands & *must do something for it.*' I said to Brewer: 'a Simple matter; of course you will perform each other's music.' Br. blushed & smiled & this *morning came in & begged* copies of *the Gran Ban's* male voice *partsongs*! I thought that funny & roared pp ma dolce e con gran espressione like your Trombones.[36]

Early in October Jaeger was able to report that there were plans at Berners Street to send him abroad on a tour of 'Elgar Propaganda', and although the idea was not put into practice, his excitement must have been great. But Walford Davies was not forgotten when Jaeger travelled to Leeds for the day to hear the first performance of *Everyman* at the Festival, together with Holbrooke's *Queen Mab*. The new Davies work achieved a far greater success than *The Temple*, and Jaeger dashed off a brief note.

> My dear Davies,
>
> Just a *word* to congratulate you from my heart upon your *remarkable* success & to thank you for your beautiful, deeply impressive work. I could not say much at Leeds, & have been too frightfully busy since then to write. I will do so soon (tomorrow perhaps) meanwhile *Excelsior*!! & Gluck auf zut kuhnsrau Flug!
>
> Ever yours
>
> A.J. Jaeger[37]

He followed up with the promised letter, dealing first of all with the availability of some of Davies's earlier music published by Novello, originally at the composer's expense; *Everyman* was also to be published by the composer himself, through the printer Riorden at an address in Poland Street. Jaeger went on to write of the feelings of vindication that the success of works by Davies and Bell brought him, and of the consequent victory over his 'critic friends'.

> 1, Berners Street, W.
> London
>
> Oct 12, 1904
>
> My dear Davies,
>
> Many thanks for your Kind letter. Just now I have only time to tell thee: we have sent 100 'O little Town of B' & *50* only Sonata in E minor and only 1 soiled copy of

Prospice because we *haven't any* left, as You Know. We have only *13* copies of the Sonata left & only *64* of the 'Little Town'.

If you wish any of these works reprinted kindly send your *orders*. But why, oh why no P.F. Edition of Prospice! The beautiful work *must* be made Known and you *cannot* expect any Singer to always engage a String Quartet to sing the piece. So 'buck up' (Everyman's language – in London) with that P.F. arrangement.

I say, there is a *splendid* notice of Everyman in to-days '*World*' written by Mr James, (an excellent critic). If that doesn't make you conceited, nothing will do it. I laugh now at my critic friends, those who have laughed *at my Davies enthusiasm*, in view of my M.T. article of 4 years ago! & would see nothing in you but Dulness, 'larned' dulness!! these Johnnies never see the lion's claw in a young composer. And I shall laugh at Elgar & Cowen with whom I *quarelled* [*sic*] 3 years ago (at Gloucester) over Bell (W.H.) because I stuck up for his *great* gifts & they 'saw nothing in him'. W.H.B. came to my home last Saturday & played me a Symphony 'Epithalamium' (after Spencer) for *Small* orchestra (mirabile dictu!) so beautiful *& happy all through*, that I cried with sheer happiness & joy over the beauty & the healthy, sane optimistic feeling displayed throughout.

Well, England is waking up *with a vengeance.*

I *must* send a copy to Prof Buths of 'Everyman'. He will like it muchly. Come & talk some. I want to criticise your work a little and give you a tip or two.

I say I called at Riordan's [*sic*] yesterday. Oh what a place. A Lady can hardly go to such a publishing place[,] a 'shop'.

No more just now.

Ever yours

A.J. Jaeger[38]

Walford Davies replied that day, ordering a characteristically impractical number of copies of his *Prospice* score, and sidestepping the issue of a piano arrangement. He mentioned a symphony project, sparking off a confidence from Jaeger over his continued close interest in such a work from Elgar.

1, Berners Street,
London.

Oct 13 1904

My dear Davies,

Many thanks for your letter. I say! 250 copies of a *Score* like 'Prospice' is a deuce of a lot! *Do* you mean it? I should think they will last you 10 years. Really, do Singers *buy* such scores? I doubt it. That first 100 were largely *given* away, were they not? if I am wrong, I apologize. Of *no* work of ours issued in score do we ever print more than 100 at a time. So you may imagine I am surprized at your order. I know of course that there's no Vocal (P. F.) Score (worse luck!) but even then I doubt whether you can sell 250 *Scores* in ten years, however fine the work may be (and nobody could think more of it than myself!) So explain yourself and *make that P.F. arrangement* you *wretch*. Why even Brahms' Requiem is arranged for the P.F. Then why not Prospice?? Come & discuss the thing. Come to my house on Saturday & I'll have a long talk 'at' you! Elgar's Symphony is 'off' again, I only wrote to him about it last night. That you too have one on the stocks[39] is FINE news!

Is this the beginning of the End of Pessimism in music? Theres a *Revolt* in progress, and a healthy sign it is. I welcome it with Joy & hope in my heart.

Ever yours,

A.J. Jaeger[40]

Work at Berners Street at this time seems to have been confined to routine matters, including the *Canto popolare* arrangements, the French translation of *Gerontius* and the provision of the correct percussion instruments for *The Apostles*; Jaeger personally visited Hawkes the instrument makers over the 'antique cymbals'. With no major Elgar work in progress, and no prospect of the Symphony, there was no focus for enthusiasm, and the old complaints about the firm and the *Musical Times* Editor resurfaced. He told Elgar,

> ... all day I am doing *Junior Clerk work* at No. 1 & am getting sick of it, I can tell you. I can't get any assistance & had thought I had proved myself capable of doing better work for the firm. But only *one man's* advice is ever sought & followed at No. 1 & that is the jokist of the M.T., ye Gods! ... I have proposed to the said jokist to print my Analysis of the Overture in the M.T. as a sort of 'Review' of the Full Score. I know his answer beforehand, but did it as a joke.[41]

Perhaps in compensation, Jaeger was not short of ideas. He made a suggestion that extracts from *The Black Knight*, which he felt to be neglected, could be arranged as an orchestral piece for a proposed LSO concert, although Elgar showed only lukewarm interest and the project was never undertaken. But another proposal, born out of the Cologne Brandenburg Concerto performance, would have historic results:

> I'll hope You can write the Symphony orchestra a short new work. Why not a *brilliant* quick *String* Scherzo, or something for those fine strings *only*? a real bring down the House *torrent* of a thing such as Bach could write (Remember that *Cologne* Brandenburger Concerto!) a five minutes work would do it! It wouldn't take you away from your *big* work for long. You might even write a MODERN FUGUE for Strings, or *Strings & Organ*![42]

Jaeger's most direct interventions over Elgar's music had hitherto been confined to suggestions for improvements to work-in-progress. This time, in characteristically incandescent terms, he hit on the framework for the overall conception, style, form and instrumentation of a work yet to be written. It was a classic example of how Jaeger could play the role of catalyst, as Ivor Atkins would aptly describe it. In his programme note for the first performance of what became the *Introduction and Allegro for String Quartet and String Orchestra*, Elgar wrote that he had conceived the idea of writing a brilliant string piece during a Welsh holiday in 1901, but the sketches he made that year of what he called the 'Welsh tune', based on distantly heard singing across Cardigan Bay, are accompanied by notes which seem to show that the music was intended for woodwind instruments, and another layout of the tune with the beginning of a piano accompaniment was for Alice to find words for it. Jaeger's idea provided a context and a purpose for what might have remained unfulfilled possibilities, and he found words to describe it which might almost be guaranteed to stimulate Elgar. The evocation of Bach's name and the memory of the Cologne Brandenburg Concerto performance would count for a good deal, and so too would the 'torrent' image, invoking associations with the natural world and particularly with the rivers that Elgar loved. The whole idea was a stroke of sheer intuitive imagination on Jaeger's part, born out of his capacity for excitement and exhilaration, specifically reflecting the heightened awareness of the tubercular sufferer. The suggestion found its mark in every respect, for the final idea of a work for strings and organ remained with the composer and was most poignantly taken up in the *Sospiri* of 1914.

Three days later, Jaeger wrote to Sydney Loeb, accepting a dinner invitation. It was an unbuttoned and gossipy letter, showing something of that side of his character which Dora Penny described as racy, and Elgar as mercurial, but again there may have been something almost pathological in its almost frantic gaiety. Once again Tchaikovsky and Wood came in for condemnation, Jaeger having been unable to sit out a performance of the *Manfred* Symphony, and there was discussion of the relative merits of the singers Muriel Foster and Marie Brema, whose daughter Tita Brand was to be a fellow-guest.

37, Curzon Road,
Muswell Hill
N

31/X/04

Dear Loeb,

Many thanks for your letter. I shall be delighted to dine with you on the 15th inst at 7.45 o' the clock, & I'll bring a huge appetite with me & a thirst that would rejoice a Heildelburg student on a hot August day. What more *do* you want? Get thee hence, then, tempter, & replenish thine ginger beer & Appolonaris Cellars, (are there 2 ps or 2 l's, I forget) & cease thou not from cooking joints & pasties & 'Baron' of Beef à la Sir Hubert Parry Mus. Doc. from this day forth unto the eve of the 15th of the moon. Mine shall be a gargantuan Hunger & a Falstaffian thirst, all ad majorem Loebi gloriam. So Perpend!

And you too, Brutus, wented & heardest that *beastly* 'Manfred' thing? I heard it twice before & *loathed* it, so I thought I'd give it & myself another chance, in *case* I was stupid or biassed the previous times.

But, bless your astral Soul, I loathed it more than ever, and before that Inferno in the last movement commenced I ran away, the while the great Mrs. Newmarch of the gerrand Russian School eyed me contemptuously. Poor Wood, what an ass he is making of 'hisself' beating the air, & contortioning his lovely body & rolling his wild, frenzied cock-eyed orbs over this Russian Billposter music! As if that stuff could impress a musicloving thickheaded German? Why, it wouldn't frighten a silly cow nor a Thibetan [illegible]

What *do* you mean, to suggest that I dont like Mme. Brema & sa fille Tita, yclept Brand? All I say is, that I prefer the handsome Muriel as the 'Angel' in our friends Gerontius. I used to admire Mme. Br. *greatly*, but even an idolator like unto ye cant affirm upon oath that her voice & method are like unto what they used to be. As for Mle. Tita, I know nothing about her. I have only heard her once, in Grieg's thing – whatdyoucallit? I daresay she is totally charming & wholly clever & I am utterly unworthy to meet her. I shall abase myself before her beauty & her genius – provided the ginger beer cometh forth in abundant barrels. Farewell! Expect me on the Tuesday of thy choice.

Yours Sincerely,

A.J. Jaeger[43]

Jaeger's evident healthy enthusiasm and appetite, while characteristic of the elation often experienced by tubercular sufferers, may also have been the result of an 'exercise cure' which he was following at this time. He recommended it to Elgar, who was able to report early in November that it had done wonders, and that he had stopped taking 'physic'. Jaeger for his part wrote of being able to enjoy Sunday morning romps with the children in Highgate Woods, after sticking religiously to the exercises every morning. '... I can honestly say I feel another man & much fitter for work,' he told Elgar.

Neither man's well-being seems to have been disturbed by Josef Holbrooke, who characteristically complained that the piano arrangement of *In the South* had been undertaken by a certain Schmid and not an Englishman such as himself. Elgar treated the occasionally exasperating Holbrooke sympathetically, and Jaeger continued to take a fatherly interest in him. Some weeks later when the young composer took on the financial burden of marriage, he told Elgar '... I ... expect to have a tough time of it now, but I could not live any longer alone like a wild man. I'd give some'at for a professorship too! Jaeger is giving one all sorts of weighty warnings![44]

As the year drew to a close, there was further correspondence with Parry, mainly over the second edition of his *Summary of Music History*, which Novello's had originally published in 1893. The antediluvian printing methods of the time caused problems for publisher and author alike.

1, Berners Street, W.
London

23/XI/1904

Dear Sir Hubert,

I approach you once more with apologies & regrets! Our Printers are not happy *yet,* alas. They say that you have some more pages of paste-up proofs which they want back. Without them they don't know where certain newly-set pieces of type are to be inserted. There's a Dilemma! I daresay I could find the proper places by carefully reading the new matter & comparing it with the Book, but it isn't safe of course. If you can't find any more 'paste-up – page proofs' could you mark on enclosed galley-proof against the place where it is to be inserted? page – line – &c.

Once more I am truly sorry to have to worry you again, but what can I do.

P. S. Oh! *Pardon*!! I see that there's only *one line* which they can't trace. The one re Brahms. I daresay you could place that easily.

Yours Sincerely,

A.J. Jaeger[45]

There were plans afoot for Novello's to publish two of Parry's symphonies, No. 2 in F Major, the 'Cambridge', dating from 1883, and No. 3 in C Major, the 'English', of 1889. Both works had undergone revision, and Parry evidently felt that they had reached a final enough form for publication, although the firm would not fund the production of both works.

1, Berners Street, W.
London.

26/XI/1904

Dear Sir Hubert,

Many thanks for letter & proofs. I hope we can go ahead now at last.

Yes! we *can* get that full Score out by February if we can start on it very soon. It *may*, however, be necessary to Send it to Leipzig to be engraved. *There* they can put 20 men on such a piece of work at one time. However, perhaps Mr. Brause can do it here. I *hope* so. Yes! the idea was that if you paid for the Cambridge Symphony the firm would pay for the English ditto, & that arrangement still holds good of course. But *where* IS that English Symphony??

So send the Cambridge along!

Miss Daymond has at last sent us the M.S. of the P.F. arrangement of the Radnor Suite.

Yours Sincerely,

A.J. Jaeger[46]

The newly engraved scores would appear over the next two years. A further letter to the composer, now busy with his biography of Bach, advised of more proofs of the *Summary of Musical History*, and complimented him on the College production of Gluck's *Alceste* at His Majesty's Theatre, the first in England, which Jaeger attended and enjoyed. He went on to apologize to Parry for his non-appearance at a Patron's Fund Chamber Concert at the Aeolian Hall held a few days later, where of sixteen new student works performed, the highest acclaim was won by William Hurlstone's Piano Quintet.

1, Berners Street, W.
London.

Dec 7th, 1904

Dear Sir Hubert,

The 'Summary' is getting on slowly. I thought we could print straight away, but alas! the printers propose sending you further proofs of the contents (Index) & plate proofs of all new pages & *amended* pages. We shall never get this book out; & meanwhile the orders are coming in fast & angry protests from disappointed customers are reaching us daily, even from Australia! (I am not exaggerating.) I hope you will very Kindly do your utmost to let us have *everything* back as soon as ever possible.

Yes! Alcestis went extremely well & I was delighted, *though* N.T. & her husband-tenor looked so *un*greeklike. But She is a very gifted girl. The thing quite impressed me & I spent a much longer time in the theatre than I should have! Unfortunately I was prevented from coming to the Aeolian Hall last night. That concert would have just ruined me.

Kindly lets have the Symphony soon. Are the wind *parts* to be done too? I could place *them at once.*

Yours Sincerely,

A.J. Jaeger[47]

And then, amid such day-to-day business, with its problems and pleasures, the dark shadow fell.

There would seem to be little evidence up to this point that Jaeger had experienced any serious degree of poor health during the whole of the year; for one thing, there had not been the long drawn-out stress of a major Elgar choral work to oversee through publication and analysis. He seems to have been well enough to maintain some journalism, to enjoy the holiday with Holding and attend several of the music festivals; there had been the apparently successful exercise cure, and the *joie de vivre* of his last letter to Sydney Loeb. But all the time the insidious progress of Jaeger's condition had continued, for the tuberculosis bacterium can grow slowly over long periods of time, with periods of remission. The damage to his lungs now reached a crisis point. He became ill again that December, probably suffering a prolonged haemorrhage, so serious that his doctor recommended immediate departure for a sanatorium cure in Switzerland. In the days before antibiotics, only rest, rich diet and pure air would provide the best hope of respite from the disease and a possible cure. It was a long-drawn out, uncertain and expensive business, and it meant that Jaeger would have to leave Isabella and the children, and his work at Novello's, although crucially they were generous enough to continue his salary. He would have to sacrifice his participation in London's musical life, and his proximity to Elgar and the flock of younger composers on whom he lavished encouragement. He would be completely out of things. Elgar understood. 'I was looking forward to much talk with you over past schemes, present schemes, & above all, *future* ideas,' he wrote from Frank Schuster's London home on 16 December, on his return from ten days of performances on the continent. 'Well this must wait until we meet.'

But Elgar was not to meet Jaeger before the departure for Switzerland, although he and Alice stayed on in London until 20 December, enjoying various social gatherings and taking in various theatres and art galleries. They mingled with friends in Schuster's circle, including the Stuart Wortleys, the Beresfords and the art critic Claude Phillips, and there were dinners at Cheyne Walk, the Savoy and one of Schuster's clubs, the Carlton. Fritz Volbach was a fellow-guest, and conducted performances of his *Rafaelle* at the Royal College of Music and Brahms' Fourth Symphony at the Queen's Hall. Elgar was 'much thrilled' at the latter, Alice noted. On 18 December the Elgars enjoyed a performance of *Dream Children*, dined with Richard Strauss and then went on to receive guests at the Concert Goers Club, 'shaking hands with some 350?' Alice thought. But Elgar did find time to call on Jaeger's new acquaintance, Archibald Ramsden, President of the U.B.Q. Club, and discuss the plight of their friend.

And plight it was, for the Swiss sojourn added financial worries to the burdens of serious illness and family separation; despite the continuation of his salary, Jaeger would have to face many extra expenses. It must have been an anxious Christmas, as the parents explained to two children under five that they would not be able to 'see Daddy' for a long time, and Jaeger wound up his affairs and occupied himself with detailed calculations of the costs of travel and subsistence that he faced. Meanwhile Isabella and the Jaeger ladies no doubt busied themselves in organizing the overcoats, warm woollen underclothing, socks and thick laced boots that the patient would need, bearing in mind perhaps the decree of the Reverend W. H. Otter, in his *Winters Abroad*: 'It is of the utmost importance to invalids to be thoroughly protected against every kind of chill from the top of the head to the sole of the foot.' But despite all such precautions and preparations, news of the sudden death at the age of 43 of Arthur Johnstone, the *Manchester Guardian* music critic, would seem a most unhappy augury.

Part Two

1905–09: Prisoner of Hope

'I'm only waiting from day to day for the time when I get confined to Bed, never to rise again. When I think over it all, and realize how beautiful life is & what work I might & could do & what intellectual beauty (E's Symphony) there is still bought forth by men of genius – and how very soon I shall be dead to it all, dead to family & friends & Sunshine & green fields and Symphonies & quartets & poetry & pictures & all that makes life the great thing it is, then my heart feels heavy, heavy as lead, and tears flow readily.'

10 1905: 'This Godforsaken, lonely Hole'

Early in the New Year Jaeger wrote of his financial anxieties to Elgar, who replied that he felt sure the firm would prove helpful, as in fact they were. Then he continued starkly, seeming to face the worst for both of them, 'This is no comfort, &, indeed, it is impossible to say anything under the circumstances that does not appear foolish or at least jejune.' Elgar had reacted almost hysterically to the sudden death of Alfred Rodewald less than two years before. Now, faced with evidence of Jaeger's decline, an honest and calm refusal to resort to platitudes was perhaps the greatest compliment he could pay his friend, even if it was, at the same time, part of a process of self-insulating withdrawal from an impossible situation. Jaeger's winter journey would also have had deeply personal resonances for Elgar because of his early love for the musical Worcester girl, Helen Weaver. The engagement had been broken off, possibly due to religious differences, and subsequently Helen's lungs became affected. Her stepmother had died of pulmonary tuberculosis, and in October 1885 the girl left England for good for the beneficial climate of New Zealand. Other friends were thought of during the final busy few days before the start of Jaeger's new life. There was what she would describe as a 'sad letter' to Dora Penny, and a farewell postcard to Walford Davies.

> 7/1/4 [*sic*]
>
> Dear D –
>
> I'm off to Davos Platz for *3 months* in a few days. I *may* be away even longer. So Goodbye & Auf Wiedersehen. Wish me *luck*, I need it. Say goodbye for me to your friends at Segenbalm. I cannot possibly come round. *Too* much to do to clear up.
>
> Ever yours (with a heavy heart)
>
> A.J. Jaeger[1]

Next day Jaeger wrote to Elgar, confirming Novello's liberality. But then, in the wake of Elgar's recent socializing in London, he continued with some blunt honesty of his own.

> I worry over your *muse*, for I fear greatly we shall get less & less out of you. This is the danger of success artistic & social! (especially social, of course). I grieve over it, & so do

all those who most sincerely love & admire you. We know you *must live*, but England *Ruins* all ARTISTS ... much devoted love ...[2]

Rosa Burley wrote of how on one occasion Jaeger beseeched her 'almost with tears in his eyes' to discourage some of the social friendships with wealthy people that success had brought Elgar and which he seemed keen to foster. Even the strong-minded Miss Burley seems to have shrunk from that task, and Jaeger himself seems to have have geared himself up to attempt it only at this point, as a kind of parting shot. No reply from Elgar is extant; perhaps his true response is to be found in the work he would soon undertake on the string piece that Jaeger had suggested.

Meanwhile friends were mobilizing to bolster Jaeger's financial position. Archibald Ramsden sent a cheque for £20 through Elgar, saying 'we cannot afford to have good men like him laid on the shelf', and 'it will find him some comforts, and may help to gave him peace of mind'. John McEwen, whose piano sonata Jaeger had given a substantial review in that month's *Musical Times*, sent £15 but Jaeger felt he could not accept it. Elgar wrote to Novello's proposing that Jaeger be asked to provide analyses of the early choral works, more perhaps for the sake of occupation than anything else, but the suggestion was not taken up. Two days before his departure, amid last-minute preparations at home and at Berners Street, Jaeger wrote his warm thanks to Elgar and Ramsden, affirming that his mind had indeed been set at rest over financial matters, although he admitted dreading the long journey he was faced with. Hoping to take Elgar up on a thoughtful offer, he added 'Send me your "theme" to shorten the journey! Do!' Even on the day before his leaving, there was one final business item to be dealt with, a hurried postcard response to a query from Walford Davies.

[10/1/05]

Dearie D.

Yes! you *can* sell a certain *arrangement* of a thing apart from the original version of which you *retain* the copyright.

Awful haste

Yours

AJJ[3]

Off *11 a.m.* tomorrow. Victoria Station Goodbye

And so next day the family farewells were said and the journey begun. Amid other preoccupations at Plas Gwyn, Alice spoke for all concerned in confiding her hopes to the Diary: 'January 1905 T. Hughes busy with E's portrait. A & C to Mrs Battiscombes to tea. Moss started for Davos – Trust will return well.'

Davos – the word means something like 'back of beyond' – is in the Graubunden Canton of eastern Switzerland, and Jaeger could have reached it after a two-day journey by train, coach and sledge via Dover, Calais, Paris, Basle, Zurich and

Landquart. He seems, however, to have managed to stop off at his beloved Düsseldorf, even now making a call on Buths on Elgar's behalf; soon he would meet up with one of the conductor's daughters, stricken like himself, at Davos. The main village, Davos-Platz, lies some 5200 feet above sea level at one end of a long valley sheltered from wind on both sides by mountains whose lower slopes are clad with larches and pines, and wide enough to allow a maximum amount of sunshine even in winter. At the other end a large lake feeds a stream, the Landwasser, which meanders along the whole ten miles of the valley; in summer months its green meadows are clothed in a massed brightly-hued abundance of soldanellas, gentians, anemones, buttercups, campion, heartsease and polygonum. But Jaeger would see little of this beauty, for it was the winter months that were considered beneficial to health. The November and December snows clothe everything in snow several feet thick, producing the cold, dry, dustless air that had given the area a developing reputation as a health resort.

The beauty of the environment, and its apparent success in ameliorating pulmonary consumption, attracted various well-known literary figures over many years, including John Addington Symonds, Robert Louis Stevenson, Conan Doyle, Thomas Mann, James Elroy Flecker and Llewelyn Powys. It was however an earnest anonymous author, one of the earliest English residents, who provided one of the fullest, if somewhat highly wrought, descriptions of the Davos Valley in winter.

> The flowers that decked the valley in June and July are replaced by the blossoms of winter – splendid snow crystals – strewn about the meadows with no niggard hand – before whose prismatic hues the fairest petals of summertide grow dull. The snow too in many places assumes the forms of a fairy forest, the intricate network of foliage outrivalling the most delicate of exotic ferns. Or again, the crystals combine to produce the appearance of a thick, rich fur. Often, too, when the heat of the sun has partially melted the surface, this freezes again into a glittering crust, and many a southern slope – now and then a whole mountain side – looks as though attired in a bridal array of sheeny satin.
>
> The winter appears to the greatest perfection after a recent fall, when each tiny branch of every fir-tree is covered with a complicated lace-work, and there is then a lightness, a brightness, and a freshness about the snow, which it loses when it has settled down into a compact, solid mass. But, viewed at any time, the scene is a magnificent one. Dark and stern on the hill-sides, darker and sterner by comparison with the white landscape around them, stand the solemn pines, in grim and stately array, while far above tower the dazzling summits of the mountains, among which a few, too rocky and too rugged for the soft covering to rest upon, rise up black and bare against the sky, in bold contrast to the smoothly-rounded forms of the cupola-shaped hills besides them. The western hemisphere is brilliant turquoise, but to the east the heavens display a colour of deep violet, and the intensity of the hue goes on increasing as day advances – till it reaches its richest tint, just before sunset. The evenings are grand beyond description. One scarcely knows whether to give the preference to the moonlit nights, when the whole valley, and the most distant peaks that bound it, are seen as clearly as by day, flooded by a gentle chastened light, which defining the contours, conceals insignificant details, that often lessen the general effect – or to the darker evenings, on which myriads of stars shine with a brilliancy undreamt of on the plains, while the 'milky way' is one long gleaming network, and the planets hang like great lamps in the firmament.
>
> If the nights seem strange and startling to natives of lower levels, the days must

> astonish them still more. The sunrise is superb, when the orb of day, with no envious clouds or vapours to mar his glory, slips suddenly from behind the mountain, like an enormous ball of fire, and shoots his golden darts through the sombre silent forest, transfiguring the pine-trees on the glowing ridge into brilliant, mysterious forms, clothed with a transient illumination of ghostly, silvery light.[4]

But his surroundings find little reflection in Jaeger's letters from Davos. Indeed it would be entirely understandable for an exiled invalid to feel simply imprisoned in a narrow, monotonous, stifling corridor. Tchaikovsky himself had visited an ailing friend at Davos in 1884, and Jaeger might have been grimly amused to know that the composer studied Byron's *Manfred* while there, before embarking on the composition of the programme symphony that he abhorred so much. But he would surely have understood and trusted the verdict on the *genius loci* that had filtered through Tchaikovsky's highly-charged sensibility. 'In spite of the scenery being so grand and magnificent,' he wrote to his brother Modest, 'it is sad and mournful here. My heart contracts from sorrow, and all I want is to leave as soon as possible.'[5]

In theory there was plenty to occupy the patient. Alongside the increasing number of residential sanatoria, there had developed a large English community, with its own consulate, chaplain, lending library, newspaper and various clubs and societies. Social and sporting activities were highly organized, with events of one kind or another – dances, fancy-dress balls, tableaux-vivants, symphony concerts, sweepstakes, curling, skating and tobogganing competitions – held almost daily. Jaeger, more interested in communications with the outside world, would have been reassured to know that 'letters and newspapers, posted in London, are punctually delivered on the third day'. He would write to Isabella every day, even if no more than a postcard; like many patients at the beginning of their stay, Jaeger was instructed to do very little. It might seem an ideal recipe for depression, with nothing for his mind to focus on apart from the life that had been left behind, the separation from friends and family, from Elgar, and from London's musical life. And extra costs were accumulating all the time.

Jaeger was able to stay at one of the most luxurious Davos establishments, the Hotel Buol, which boasted electric light, a lift and central heating, and where full board in a room without balcony could be had for six francs and upwards *per diem*, 'attendance' being 50 cents extra. The dining hall, lined with portraits of past members of the Buol clan, a long-established and distinguished Davos family, gave on to a reading room and then to a billiard room, where the less active guest could while away his abundant leisure time. Various 'promenades and excursions', including mountain ascents, were available through the hotel for the more hardy. Jaeger would have needed to 'acclimatize' at the beginning of his stay, for the rarified air could initially cause breathlessness and feelings of oppression. After the first week he wrote to Elgar that he had been forbidden any sport and was allowed a little slow walking only, and he complained of bad dreams, expense and boredom. It was taking him time to feel settled in what he described as 'this Godforsaken, lonely Hole in the – the d— Alps', although he altered the 'lonely' to 'lovely'. He went on to elaborate the reason for his visit to Buths, whom he had interested in a new orchestral work from Elgar for the forthcoming Lower Rhine Festival. Replying on 21 January, Elgar ignored the idea completely, merely telling Jaeger to 'just roll round & get fat & well. I cannot write a letter at this moment because I am full of *business* (alas!)'. That day, a Saturday, had seen Parry go into the Royal College of Music, to deal with what he described as a 'considerable lot of business', but characteristically he found time to think of Jaeger. 'Wrote to Jaeger at Davos Platz & sent him a cheque, the poor fellow having broken down badly.' Parry seems to have avoided direct mention of Jaeger's tuberculosis, a condition which would have had associations of the deepest sadness for him, as for Elgar. Both Parry's mother and sister had died as a result of it.

Before the end of January, Elgar was able to report progress on 'that string thing', and soon Archibald Ramsden was able to report to Alice that he had received 'a most cheery letter' from Jaeger, as the Davos air now began to work its magic of well-being and exhilaration. In the middle of February Elgar, with the *Introduction and Allegro* finsished, found time to write and keep Jaeger informed of various doings – Parry's award to him of an honorary degree at Oxford, his forthcoming Birmingham lectures, more Steinbach performances, a possible American trip. In connection with the latter, Elgar wrote of financial support for Jaeger from Professor Sanford of Yale – and from himself.

> Now: I wrote to S. S. Sanford & I hear from him – a most kind & affectionately worded letter – & you must let him do all he wishes to do – in case, that is, that he wishes to do more. This I beg you for all our sakes: I did not offer to send you anything because I think you know that anything I have is yours![6]

Finally, there was a suggestion as to reading matter – Merejowski's lengthy examination of the creative mind in his novel *The Forerunner*[7] – and an encouragement to 'send a p.c. sometimes – never mind a long letter'. Alice wrote the next letter, at the beginning of March. She sent news of the forthcoming premières of the *Introduction and Allegro* and the third *Pomp and Circumstance* March, of performances of the Oratorios, of the Oxford visit, and of her husband's latest escapist outlet – oil painting. She concluded with quiet, purposeful reassurance, 'I do hope you have good accounts from home & will be restored there strong & well – You shall have all the news I can send you, best remembrances. E. is out or would send his love.' Later that month Jaeger received a letter from Hubert Parry, and in return he seized the opportunity to thank a benefactor – a matter about which he was always conscientious – and to indulge himself in a long, gossipy letter. There was good news about his health, although a further visit to Davos was possibly necessary; but more than anything else, Jaeger was able to talk about matters musical in England, over which he showed himself to be well informed. Once again he pleaded Bell's cause, and continued on familiar ground with comments on the standards of German orchestral playing compared to those in England, and a snipe at one of the leading English critics.

Hotel Buol,
Davos,

20/3/5

Dear Sir Hubert,

I have just received your Kind letter. Strange coincidence – or telepathy! –: I saw my Dr on Saturday (my Birthday) & as he gave me a very good report I said to myself 'I must *now* at last write a line to dear Sir Hubert to tell him the good news'. At that very time (it was about 12.30 Central European time) you were mayhap writing to me! I feel ashamed of myself now because I did not write before, though I did not mean to write *until* I could tell you some *really satisfactory* details about my progress.

Well: Dr. Buol examined me at great length, & was very satisfied. Before I could ASK him any questions, he burst out: 'That's good, you are much better & going on capitally, the right lung is virtually *healed*, & the left one doing well'. His finding tallied with my 'feeling', for I am a different man from what I was 8 weeks ago. I have still to be quiet: walk leisurely, abstain from 'climbing' or *running* upstairs. But I sleep well, *without any coughing*, have no fever – in *fact* I feel as well as, or better than, I have felt these last ten years. This does not mean, of course, that I am cured already. The left lung may yet take several months, and I *may* even have to return to this valley next winter to complete my cure. After seeing how greatly I have already benefited I do not look forward with any dread to returning here, even if it comes to spending our little savings. The hope of being able to commence life afresh (Just this complaint, according to Dr Buol, and *old* neglected ones) with my lungs healed (though reduced in quantity) has put enough courage into my Heart to enable me to brave another winter here, another enforced (and perhaps longer) separation from my dear wife & Bairns & from friends & work – & *music*. I shall *not* of course tell my firm anything about this (nor my wife) until the Dr's final report, for I may of course be able to start working & continue to live in London *without* having to come here again. So 'mum' is the word at present.

Anyhow, dear Sir Hubert, I can assure you that my stay here has already benefited me greatly & I hope much from April & May in Switzerland – I need not say that the *absence of any worry* on account of *financial difficulties*, a state of mind to which the kindness of friends, including your dear self, has so greatly contributed, has been one of the prime factors in my 'cure'. For the weather has been *beastly*. The famous Davos Sun has been playing truant in the most disgraceful way. The percentage of sun*less* days has been unprecedentedly large: out of 75 days we have had 40 on which snow fell (often for 2 or 3 days & nights continuously) & we have had altogether over *15* METRES snowfall this winter! Sunless days without snow, but with a grey, murky sky, & often with wind have also been numerous & *perfect* days without a fleck of cloud in the sky (like *to-day* – at last!) have been most rare. We poor 'lungers' would all have progressed better if we had had more sun, the air is lovely, dry & clear & free from dust, of course.

And now let me express an ardent hope that you, dear Master, & yours, are quite well. That you are fearfully busy, cela va sans dire because you *always* are, & wouldn't be happy if you were not. I read of your success with your 'Clouds' music,[8] & congratulate you thereon.

Is not to-day & tomorrow the C. Williams Concert at which the Cambridge Symphony will be done? I have told my wife to go & tell me all about it, for she wrote that she would like to hear the work. She is *very* partial to your music: loves its strength, directness, & loveable humanity. So I hope she will go & enjoy herself to her heart's content. She told me that Elgar sent her a ticket for his concert the other day & that she had a quiet cry when it came to No. IX ('Nimrod', of the Variations which is 'me') which the orchestra played most beautifully. Elgar wrote to me about his Oxford degree day & how 'dear Parry was in great form'.

I hope you liked young Bell's work (Epithalamium) the other day & thought it not unworthy of my 'entoosm' (as dear old Hans Richter called it). I love the thing, though I have only heard it on the P.F. To *hear* his score has been an *enormous* help to Bell & we may expect even better work from him now, and I have no doubt that my faith in him (now 6 years old) will yet be justified.

B. Gardiner seems to have made a hit, though from the *look* of *his themes* (I have a programme) I can't imagine his work being better as regards *invention* (after all the main thing) than Bell's. Bell's great fault is a certain loquaciousness, which he must curb. I am glad Sir Ch. Stanford had a good success at Düsseldorf.[9] I hear he was there with Lady Stanford. I haven't yet heard from Prof. Buths (his young 2nd daughter is at Davos) as to his Lower Rhine Festival programme. I know he is *fearfully* busy.

I have just received a letter from my sister in law, with [a] cutting from a Huddersfield paper describing your *great* TRIUMPH there with 'Judith'.[10] I am *delighted*, for I *love* 'Judith' & remember with pleasure 'our performance' ('Novello' choir ages ago – is it really 19 years?) The work of Dr Cowards Chorus seems to have been of the supreme, ideal excellence – due to C's brains & enthusiasm, AND MANY *rehearsals* – of which I had a sample in the rendering of the *orchestral* score of Elgar's 'Apostles' at Cologne, under Steinbach last year, when all my expectations were FULLY realized, and my analysis, pace J.A. F-M & the 'Times' justified. You in England *haven't heard* the 'Apostles' yet! For even the composer can't 'fetch out' his score with 1 or 2 rehearsals, the utmost you English musicians can get for your orchestras. 'Judith' seems to have for the first time been *fully* REVEALED, even to your astonished self (I read your speech!) Thus F. Steinbach will one day 'reveal' the 'Apostles' to Elgar's countrymen. You can tell J. A. F-M this with my Kind regards.

Meanwhile he is at liberty to pitch into my analysis ad. lib. I don't mind, for I am convinced of the accuracy of my estimate of that big work.

But now I must close for the sun is burning my back (I am writing this in the open air!) Uncomfortably crisp & I might get Sunstroke! Pardon a long scrawl, perhaps you *may* find time to read some of it, & yet think no evil of me.

With my Kindest regards,

I am ever your devoted,

A.J. Jaeger.[11]

Jaeger's pent-up critical energies also found an outlet about this time in a brief article he wrote about the music of Max Reger, second only to that of Richard Strauss in popularity in Germany, and the subject of partisan controversy despite its reliance on traditional forms. Jaeger's piece was probably largely culled from various German newspapers and reviews, and would appear in the May *Musical Times.* He drew attention to an example of musical 'spelling' somewhat in Schumann's style in one of Reger's works, and concluded with a broad open hint, 'Who will be the first to introduce the young master to an English audience?'[12]

A week after the letter to Parry there was another letter from Alice (who acknowledged that Jaeger would be 'vexed & disappointed at not having heard for so long') containing news of the all-Elgar concert with the London Symphony Orchestra which finally fulfilled Jaeger's vision of the 'great rushing torrent' of a work for strings. The brief, pedestrian notice accorded the concert in the *Musical Times*, while complimentary enough, was patently not by Jaeger, the 'great fugue such as Bach would write' becoming merely 'another interesting feature'. The absence of any review or analysis of the *Introduction and Allegro* by Jaeger is a sad lack. In fact the work had proved difficult for the audience to understand at first hearing, although Alice's account was glowing. Isabella had evidently been issued with firm instructions to be present and report back to her husband, and Alice apologized for not seeing her, 'having a severe cold myself & many social functions'. Elgar too had not been well, for in addition to the London rehearsals and concert, there had been the demanding and busy period of final preparation for his controversial inaugural lecture as Peyton Professor of Music at Birmingham on 16 March. 'Edward's love & hopes that you are better,' she concluded, but Elgar himself wrote briefly several days later, on 3 April. He praised their mutual friend the critic Alfred Kalisch for his accurate reporting of the inaugural lecture, and went on to point out how he had recognized the serious efforts of Walford Davies and Holbrooke, both protegés of Jaeger.[13] He promised to 'write soon', although this was not evidently until 29 May, when he added a three-line note to another letter from Alice.

Jaeger's stay abroad was prolonged beyond the three months that had been his original sentence, and his treatment continued to be only partially successful. Dora Penny received a postcard in May to the effect that he was leaving Davos and travelling to Lucerne, where Isabella would meet him to accompany him home after their five-month separation; the message was, 'I am not quite Healed, alas!' At the end of the month he sent a card to the Elgars from another Swiss resort, Glion, and Alice replied with news of their imminent departure to America for a stay of several weeks. Elgar added his three lines. 'My dear Jaeger: I am so sorry not to write fully but I have really nothing to *tell* you: I wish you all good & a very happy return home. We shall meet on our return from the good S.S.S.' A week later Elgar sent a short letter to Jaeger, thanking him for letters which do not appear to have been preserved. Jaeger sent messages to Sanford, and mentioned an operation that he had been advised to have for nasal problems. Elgar responded with good wishes for its success, and mentioned a similar operation undergone by a Malvern friend – 'he's doing finely but it was a much more severe business than yours – such comfort you'll say.' The letter concluded with one of Elgar's self-dramatizing poses. 'I have no news of myself as I have for ever lost interest in that Person – he ceased to exist on a certain day when his friends interfered & insisted on his – It is very sad.'

The invitation to America had come from Sanford himself, the dedicatee of the *Introduction and Allegro*. Elgar received an honorary degree at Yale, with Horatio Parker presiding at the organ, and attended various social engagements. But the aim of the visit was also to make preliminary arrangements for a further trip the next year, when Elgar would conduct at the Cincinatti Festival for unprecedented remuneration. Jaeger probably viewed the whole affair with some disapproval as a potential interruption to composition, but it was part of a chain of events originating in Europe, for the Cincinatti conductor, Frank van der Stucken, had first met the Elgars at Steinbach's Cologne *Apostles* the previous year.

On the day of the Elgars' voyage to New York, 9 June, there was news of Jaeger's operation, which had been performed at a clinic in Lausanne. Alice sent a card from the boat before departure – 'thankful to hear opn. over. We trust & pray you will now speedily recover' – and immediately on arrival at Professor Sanford's house, she wrote to Isabella, whose wifely concern over a sick husband was something with which she could fully identify.

Fifty-Two Hillhouse Avenue,
New Haven, Conn.

16 June 1905

Dear Mrs Jaeger,

We arrived here about 12 today & think you & Mr Jaeger will like to hear we have arrived all well. The voyage was most *delightful.* E. was rather ill & miserable for the first day but after that enjoyed it & looked *so* much the better for it.

Our kindest of hosts met us at N. York where we stayed the night Saturday & came on this morning. It is a *charming* house & there are great Social & Yale functions going on this next week. Our dear host was deeply concerned to hear about yr. husband's sufferings, we do *trust* he is getting on as well as possible & that you are cheered by steady improvement. I know well what you must have suffered in *his* sufferings. Do send us a P. card & I trust with good news of him.

It is intensely hot, they say the 1st hot day, but they do not expect it to continue – & here it is fresh not the intense *steaminess* of N. York. It is wonderful the feeling of life & Enterprise in this country, very attractive E & I feel it so far –

The harbour of N. York & river scenery are magnificent. No more today this is only a little word in hopes of having an answer of good news, E. is downstairs with our host, I know they wd. both send messages, did they know I was writing.

With love

C.A. Elgar[14]

Excuse haste from heat & fatigue

Jaeger now sent Hubert Parry a full report of his operation, a prolonged and painful affair under partial anaesthetic, which attacked the 'disgusting & most exhausting nasal trouble' by drilling through the mouth and nostril into the sinus cavities in order to drain them. The surgeon was of the opinion that the lung trouble stemmed from the sinus condition, and that further visits to Davos might be unnecessary; Jaeger responded to the new hope with elation. Parry himself had suffered a collapse earlier that year, and as a result had reduced his workload and taken an extended motoring holiday.

Clinique Mermod,
Villa Chameny 2,
Lausanne.

27/6/5

Dear Sir Hubert,

Pray do not think me a callous Brute because I never replied to your last very kind lettter, a letter which you had absolutely no business to write to me, seeing that you were both fearfully busy – as usual – *and* far from well! You should *not*, dear Sir Hubert, waste your precious time upon me, least of all under such sad conditions. I was *awfully* sorry to hear of your Breakdown & hope very sincerely that you are restored by now & able to resume the work which you love with such an unselfish selfsacrificing love. English music cannot spare you for long!

I will not waste your time with a long letter, but must just mention my excuse for not replying sooner: I have been in this Clinique for a long time now. Prof. Mermod performed a severe operation from which I am now slowly recovering. I have had for years disgusting & most exhausting nasal trouble which 2 London specialists failed to cure (& failed to correctly diagnose!) This trouble got no better even in the beautiful Davos air, and when I heard of a famous & very reliable specialist at Lausanne, I made up my mind to contact him. So when my wife came out to fetch me home we found our way to this Clinique & the Professor soon gave me absolute proof of the fact that the trouble was caused by the right lung chest cavity.[15] I had to bear 2 minor operations & then one morning at 7 o'clock I was called down into the operating room & then the dapper little Professor gave me 'a regular doing' *without chloroform*, though one injection of morphia was given me & the gums were cocained. He chiselled one hole through my mouth into the aforesaid cavity, cleaned the latter with sharp edged long little spoons (*very* painful) then chiselled another hole through the nostril into the same cavity. I was four hours & a quarter on the operating table & though I didn't howl or wince, I swore some & lost a few pounds through the agony & sweat which flowed freely from Head & Chest. Ugh! it wasn't jolly exactly. The next few days were wretched, but now I am getting on nicely and on Thursday Professor Mermod says I may leave to spend a week somewhere else to recuperate a little. Then, at last, we shall start for Home, where we mean to arrive Saturday week. Prof. M. believes that my lung trouble was caused by my diseased nose & is of opinion that it may not be necessary for me to return to Davos next winter. I devoutly hope he may be right. If only a quarter of the beneficient results come true which he has promised me as the outcome of the operation, I shall be truly grateful to the little man & thank the stars which led me to him.

Now I won't keep you any longer, but with renewed heartfelt thanks for all your kind interest in my weakly body, your help, sympathy, and the COMMAND that this is ON NO ACCOUNT *to be answered* – since I hope to go to a College Concert with a view to presenting myself & shaking hands with you, I am, Dear, good Sir Hubert,

Yours Sincerely & devotedly,

A.J. Jaeger.[16]

My wife who suffered more from my operation than I did, sends kindest greetings & thanks.

Both the Elgars and Jaegers returned home during July. Jaeger showed himself immediately keen to pick up the threads of their working relationship by suggesting poems for setting, asking for a copy of the latest *Pomp and Circumstance* March and raising the question of the next Oratorio and its analysis. Towards the end of August he wrote to Elgar regarding the proofs of a piano duet arrangement of the *Introduction and Allegro* and sending news of a forthcoming performance of *The Apostles* at Düsseldorf under

Buths. Novello's decision to publish for the first time the original version of the Introduction to Act Three of *Tannhäuser*, the subject of his 1898 *Musical Times* article, must also have given Jaeger pleasure.[17] However, he had consulted his doctor to find that a return to Davos was considered necessary, although the medical advice was not unanimous; such uncertainty was a customary part of Jaeger's ordeal. He wrote to Elgar from Berners Street,

> I saw My Dr (Schofield) last night; He says I have done *splendidly* at Davos, but that the left lung is not yet quite right, & I ought to return to D. next November. Dr Buol at Davos told me the same thing, but the Professor Demieville (Lung Specialist) at *Lausanne* said I was quite fit to return to England to work. Needless to say I am fearfully depressed over Dr S's (a *very* capable & honest *friend*) finding & yet I know that to get ever *quite* well & safe from that terrible disease, that 'damned spot' (between the 3rd-4th Rib) *must* be healed up.
>
> I haven't dared to tell anybody here yet.[18]

'Keep up your spirits, you old dear, & all will be well,' advised Elgar gamely, and did what was in his power to help by inviting Jaeger to be his guest at the forthcoming Worcester Festival, which in addition to performances of the Oratorios and the *Introduction and Allegro*, would see him granted the Freedom of the City. 'I say, You *are* being "honoured" past belief & beyond all precedent,' wrote Jaeger. Then, with his usual tenacity: 'But what of that Symphony? I daresay it is *still* in the Clouds, or in your Brainbox. I wish I could lift the veil surrounding that much talked of & long expected Symphony.'

Despite being less than fully restored, Jaeger had thrown himself back into his rôle of committed encourager and advisor to the younger generation of composers, keeping open house for them.

> I have seen a great deal of J. Holbrooke lately. He comes to my House frequently (*uninvited*) & we play Beethoven Symphonies (P.F. Duet) together. He is actually coming round to the extraordinary view that there's something in B's Diatonic Harmony & modulations. He is now anxious to write a Symphony *in Form*. There is hope for the young Bounder yet. For he is a *Bounder* in many ways, & lately I have had occasion to write him two such letters (quite dignified, without any abuse) as he quite humbly (!) confesses he has never received before. Mr A.H.L. & AJL & Mr H.R.C *can't bear him*, and I have had a *very* heavy job in getting some of his things accepted. And then, when N & C won't do exactly as he likes, he writes *me* a rude letter in which he insults the firm. By Jove, I gave him 'what for', and told him some truths about his lack of manners *generally* (He *insults* all who cross his path, publishers, critics, musicians &c). He wants a lot of Educating yet before decent people put up with him & his cockney vulgarisms & 'ganuin'[19] impertinences. He is a brilliant fellow in many ways, but his character is that of a money-grabbing, *greedy*, objectionably loquacious *Jew* (I believe he *is* of Jewish descent) He is now writing *for money*, he confesses, & the Norwich (or is it Bristol) 'Bohemian Song' contain stuff which is distinctly written to please the gallery. (There is one *poem* – the *words* I mean – by himself, all about a Drum, which becomes dumb rummin' tea-tum!) And the 'Jugendsunden', some of them *quite* unworthy of his present reputation, which he now brings forward to make money prove him the reverse of a true artist. I advise him to burn or drown them like first puppies, but he won't, & so I spend hours pointing out utterly false accentuations in his texts &c. &c And oh! how *slovenly* he is in every way![20]

Jaeger concluded this letter rather sourly by pointing out that, through Elgar's help, Holbrooke would get a Birmingham commission – 'Lucky Dog!' For his part, he would help Bell – 'poor, splendid young fellow' – all he could. Jaeger felt that Bell was a man of '*sterling, manly* qualities', unlike the slovenly Holbrooke – and Coleridge-Taylor, presumably, with whom the breach, some years old now, seems to have been permanent. In the wake perhaps of his American tour of the previous year, Taylor was beginning to move away from European sources in his music, producing that year his *Twenty-Four Negro Melodies*, *Variations on an African Air*, and the *Five Choral Ballads*, settings of Longfellow verses on slavery. In response to another commission for incidental music, this time for Stephen Phillips's *Nero*, he succeeded, much as Jaeger might have predicted, in producing attractive light music essentially at odds with its subject. Jaeger's interest in Holbrooke at this time was remembered by another visitor to Muswell Hill, Havergal Brian.

> I was spending a week-end with the late A.J. Jaeger at his home at Muswell Hill for the purpose of playing my manuscript works to him. Jaeger's sympathies were with young English composers: he considered Holbrooke the most gifted. After I had played to him my setting of the psalm *By the Waters of Babylon*, Jaeger said he would like Holbrooke to hear it. In response to a message, Holbrooke arrived during Sunday afternoon on his bicycle with his pockets stuffed full of manuscripts. I played to him and he played to me. Of the works he played I have never forgotten the impression made on me by his song setting of Edgar Allan Poe's poem *Annabel Lee*. I still regard it as one of the finest of English songs ...[21]

Holbrooke had achieved an important position in English music – recognized by Elgar in his inaugural Birmingham lecture – since his symphonic poem *The Raven* had been given at the Crystal Palace in 1900. Two further orchestral works were produced during 1904, and his *The Bells* would be given alongside *The Kingdom* at the Birmingham Festival of 1906. He became a prolific but uneven composer, whose many orchestral and chamber works, operas and concertos have fallen largely into neglect. After their meeting at Curzon Road, Brian and Holbrooke developed a somewhat uneasy relationship, but helped each other from time to time. Brian became the dedicatee of a set of orchestral variations by Holbrooke, and as a journalist, reviewed his music sympathetically; Holbrooke provided an introduction to his patron, Lord Howard de Walden, and offered copying work from time to time. Brian was also to recall Jaeger's help that year to another young composer who was producing music of great promise, the Hallé cellist John Foulds. Jaeger persuaded Novello's to bring out his *Variazioni ed Improvvisati su una Tema Originale*, Op. 4 for piano, his first published work, announced in the July *Musical Times*. The same number also carried advertisements for several works by Theophil Wendt, another young composer Jaeger had earlier encouraged by asking Elgar to allow him an inspirational visit to Craeg Lea.[22] When Brian once asked Jaeger if he had his eye on 'any other original talent like Elgar', it was Foulds's work that Jaeger sent him. Earlier Elgar himself, possibly at Jaeger's instigation, had asked to see the score of Foulds's large-scale choral and orchestral *The Vision of Dante*, and had commented to the composer, 'It is a work of festival dimensions and scope. Don't you know anyone of power on any of the committees? It is very difficult to get in without influence.'[23] On this occasion, Elgar seems to have made no offer to take up the cudgels as far as the Three Choirs Festival was concerned.

The Elgars were keen that Jaeger should have a special place at the Worcester Three Choirs that year. Towards the end of August, the composer wrote to Alfred Littleton to appeal for his release from Berners Street; 'It wd give us the greatest pleasure to see him. We wd. do anything to have Jaeger with us!' They met at the London rehearsals on 5 September, together with Rosa Burley, who had been invited by Elgar. Jaeger's almost reckless resumption of his previous level of activity, together with continued anxieties about Elgar, were already taking their toll. Miss Burley noted that Jaeger's cure had 'all too obviously failed' and remembered that it was on this occasion that 'he begged me to try and separate Edward from some of his newer friends'.[24] Two days later, with Alice busy preparing in Worcester, Elgar remained in London with Professor Sanford who had come over for the Festival, and joined a lunch party of 19 at Pagani's. The American visit earlier that summer looked as if it had paid off, for in addition to an agreement to conduct at the 1906 Cincinatti Festival, there had been another offer of £2200 plus expenses to conduct a series of eight to ten concerts, no doubt to Jaeger's horror.

Jaeger arrived in Worcester on the Monday of the Festival week, joining the Elgars' house party at Castle House, College Green; Frank Schuster, Julia Worthington, a new American friend, and Canon Gorton were among the fellow-guests. It was a heady week for Elgar, his family and friends; the first Worcester Festival since his knighthood for the piano-tuner's son. On the Tuesday Jaeger would have been among the audience at the Guildhall to see him awarded the Freedom of the City and County of Worcester, subsequently joining the procession to the Cathedral – '*lovely* sight brilliant sunshine in old picturesque streets,' wrote Alice – for a 'very hushed & wonderful' performance of *Gerontius* conducted by Atkins, the work supplanting *Elijah* from its time-honoured position at the beginning of the week. The next day he would have heard the *Introduction and Allegro* for the first time, and on Thursday Elgar conducted a performance of *The Apostles.* Alice thought it a 'beautiful performance, wonderful hush & awe,' and noticed 'many weeping'. Ivor Atkins had been determined that the Festival should do appropriate honour to Elgar's music and it occupied virtually a quarter of the whole programme. Jaeger enjoyed other items too, including the Fourth Symphonies of Beethoven and Brahms, the *Mastersingers* Prelude, Parry's *De Profundis* of 1891, and Strauss's *Don Juan* and *Tod und Verklärung.* His characteristic uninhibited enthusiasm for the latter work amid English proper behaviour was remembered by a musical friend who would later help him devotedly and who would become another favourite 'ella', Arabella Wright.

> … I first met him in 1905 at the Worcester Festival & so well remember at supper at the Atkins' after a performance of 'Tod und Verklarung' him jumping up & crying 'Ach, but it takes one up to heaven', & I responded inwardly, but with the usual English reserve didn't jump up & let myself go as I should have liked to. From them on till his death we were fast friends …[25]

The week was a triumph for Atkins, whose own *Hymn of Faith* had been given its first performance, and who had been so keen to see something of Jaeger that he pressed him to quit the Elgars for a night to stay at College Yard. On the Friday, after some hesitation, Elgar finally decided to accept an invitation from Admiral Beresford, one of the new and rather disreputable friends who worried Jaeger so much, to join Schuster in a month's cruise with the Mediterranean fleet, and prepared to catch the 2.45 train. Jaeger joined fellow guests as the house party quickly gathered to see him off, and on his return home wrote to Alice of how Elgar's success had vindicated his own judgement and support. But he was careful to give Alice herself first place and could not avoid drawing a contrast between himself and 'other friends'.

> Yes! it was a remarkable & wholly enjoyable Festival experience, & I thank you once more with all my heart for so kindly letting me enjoy the prized privilege of joining your House party. I am convinced your other friends could not have appreciated the Honour more than, if as much as the ever devoted old mosshead, Japot, Jaggs, Nimrod! I fancy even you, dear Lady Elgar, could scarcely feel deeper joy & gratification than I do at the wonderful rise of our dear E.E. & the phenomenal growth in the appreciation of his great works. It warms my heart, & makes me happy (& also *proud*) to have been one of those, who, like yourself, have believed in his genius for so long, & fought the good fight for his recognition staunchly & fruitfully through good & evil hours. The triumph is *yours* no less than his![26]

Whatever his private doubts may have been about the Mediterranean cruise as a potential interruption to composing, Jaeger put the best possible construction on it, although he was unable to resist a warning about the next Oratorio, with the Birmingham Festival already looming for the next year.

> That Edward has safely arrived in Greece delights me. What impressions will crowd upon his wonderful Brain as he nears Athens & beholds from afar the Acropolis which stands – even in ruins – for all that is greatest & noblest in art & History. The journey will stimulate him & his creative faculty tremendously, I have no doubt & he will return strong in health & brimful of ideas. Only! – What about 'Apostles Part III' for B'ham next year!? I begin to fear me that we shall hope in vain to see our soaring expectations fulfilled.[27]

After the Festival excitement, Jaeger went down with a bad cold but was still able to join Elgar and the sympathetic Julia Worthington for tea at the Langham Hotel on 12 October, the day that Elgar returned from the cruise. At Berners Street Jaeger was supervising the belated engraving of the full score of *Caractacus*, and in response to a special request from Alice he helped provide some linen portfolio cases so that she could arrange and store her husband's precious sketches. He also enjoyed preparing a six-column preview for the *Musical Times* of Parry's *The Pied Piper of Hamlyn*, a commission for that year's Norwich Festival and a project which had been mentioned in one of Jaeger's earliest letters to him of ten years before. But Jaeger's mind must have been more on his own imminent departure for Davos once again, and in particular on the problem of obtaining the expensive heavy outdoor coat that his doctor had recommended; much of the treatment consisted in sitting outside, absorbing the pure air. Elgar, visiting Novello's at the end of the month, heard of the difficulty and appealed to Frank Schuster.

> ... I passed thro' town yesterday & saw poor dear Jaeger. He has told no one yet but he must return to Davos at once. Now the doctor tells him to bring a fur coat to lie out of doors in. It does not matter how old or shabby it is as he doesn't want it to show off (poor dear) but only to slumber in out of doors when he is in Davos. *Don't* trouble at all but perhaps amongst your many motoring sort of people there might be such a thing. If not – and you must on no account worry about it – I will manage somehow, but send me a line *soon* about this.[28]

A newer friend was also deeply concerned about Jaeger's condition, Canon Charles Gorton, founder of the Morecambe Festival, the long-established choral competition which did so much to raise standards of singing over the whole country. Jaeger's influence had been felt here, too, for he had suggested that the Festival Executive set 'O Death! Thou Art the Tranquil Night', a demanding eight-part unaccompanied part-song by Peter Cornelius, a composer with Düsseldorf connections,[29] as a test-piece for that year's Festival.[30] The May *Musical Times* had featured a short biographical article on Cornelius, considering his style 'deeply expressive, with a tendency to sombreness, relieved by finely wrought-up and thrilling climaxes. The music is often extremely difficult. Strange, weird chords, discords hard to hold, sudden contrasts of distantly related keys are frequent and provide stiff problems for the ears and voices of the most experienced singers.' Other Cornelius part-songs were adopted by the Blackpool Festival. 'O Death!' with a translation by Gorton, appeared as special supplement in the *Musical Times*, which carried emphatic advertising for a wide range of choral music by the composer. Once again, Jaeger seems to have sensed a business as well as an artistic opportunity.

Gorton wrote of his anxiety over Jaeger to Alice, summing up Jaeger, and his employers, in memorable words: 'I am much concerned about the news about Jaeger, to whom I am greatly attracted. A man among a thousand. So different from the wooden people who run the concern & pocket the proceeds. He seems like a razor often used to cut cheese.'[31]

During his visit to Berners Street, Elgar had spoken sympathetically to Jaeger about compositions by William Henry Bell the young composer had sent him for criticism, probably through Jaeger's negotiation. 'I have just had a note from A.J.J. who tells me that he has seen you & that you spoke to him about the work I sent you,' wrote Bell, and went on to thank Elgar for the offer of a personal meeting, something of a minor triumph of diplomacy on Jaeger's part. Elgar became preoccupied with further Birmingham lectures, a conducting tour and with work on the new Oratorio, and the meeting seems not to have taken place, but he wrote to Bell with suggestions and advice over a choral work, *The Call of the Sea*, later in December. In a grateful letter of thanks, Bell showed himself a true disciple of Jaeger. '... you are the first to find anything good in it at all. People seem to prefer sentimentalism to vigour & morbidness to health ...'.

Meanwhile Jaeger had made his preparations and departed for Europe in his continuing search for a complete cure. He would have had to gear himself up to ask his employers for another extended period of leave, and harden himself to the prospect of further separation from Isabella and his beloved bairns. Frank Schuster parted anonymously with his own fur coat ('You are an angel ... ten thousand thanks', wrote Elgar) and Alice wrote with the best of intentions, but somehow rather sadly,

> ... I want to say how it is my *heartfelt* hope & wish that you will return home completely restored & that yr. dear wife will be able to bear yr. absence with something approaching to cheerfulness – with that, I trust, happy prospect to look forward to. I know it is very dismal for you both but trust it will be better this year & perhaps you will be able to find some little recreation – [32]

It must have been more and more difficult for even the most thoughtful and tactful of friends to find something new to say; no doubt there was a firm handshake from Hubert Parry, who visited Berners Street on 23 November, 'to say goodbye to Jaeger who goes abroad again tomorrow'. Lausanne seems to have been Jaeger's first destination, presumably the clinic which had given him such hope during the previous visit, but this time the results were not so satisfactory. With her husband besieged by work on the lectures and the Oratorio, it fell to Alice once more to do what she could; again, she placed her trust in some 'recreation,' and offered sisterly sympathy for Isabella. To Alice, there could be no greater hardship than for a wife to be separated from her husband.

> ... We were very sad to find you were still kept at Lausanne & distressed to hear you had again been suffering. It must indeed have been a most wretched time & made yr. separation from yr. dear ones much worse to bear. I do hope by now you are at Davos & will soon feel better & then if you can have some of the recreations that wd. help to pass the time, we trust by the Spring you will have made splendid progress ... I do hope Mrs Jaeger & the babies are well, I do feel so much for her having to be separated but hope all will be well & no more exile necessary another Winter. Edward sends his best love & every good wish – he is sorry for all your weary trial you have been through – [33]

And so after disappointment at Lausanne, Jaeger returned, no doubt with a heavy heart, to Davos. The *Courier* of 8 December entered his name on the guest list for the Hotel Buol, whose clientele was worldwide. Fellow guests included the three Paton Smith sisters, Vera, Nellie and Hilda, from Kiev – unlikely as it may seem; Monsieur and Madame Robert Lemonon, from France; Herr Boymann from Wiesbaden; Mr Christophidis, from Trieste, and Miss Lindsay Andrews and governess, from Sussex. For many the seasonal return to Davos was the occasion to renew the friendships that inevitably formed in that small enclosed world, for people often returned year after year. Some did not, of course, and their absences would be noted. Others in the last stages of tubercular illness managed the journey to Davos, and expired once there, despite all expectations. But the managers of the various 'hotels' could be relied upon to make the necessary funeral arrangements in such a way as to cause the minimum inconvenience to other guests.

15 Jaeger and Alfred Rodewald at Bettwys y Coed, 1903

Nimrod had better look to his laurels, for the Shover took Nancy out for a ride the other day, but the best joke is, that a young admirer of hers who evidently knows something about music drew the Shover into a musical discussion — [illegible] waxed enthusiastic about the modern school as exemplified by you & Richard Strauss & was [illegible] as an authority. — Love to you all

16 Elgar driving 'the Shover' at Bettwys. A postcard from Rodewald: 'Nimrod had better look to his laurels ... '.

17 Jaeger and Alice Elgar at Cologne, 1904

18 Jaeger with an unidentified companion, Cologne, 1904

19 Jaeger, by Edgar Thomas Holding. Jaeger inscribed a copy for Dora Penny, 'EE's No IX "Nimrod" to his sempre "Scherzando" neighbour 'DORABELLA' with sincere regard & great admiration, (for EE's MUSIC) LONDON 29.XI.02'.

20 Sydney Loeb's 'schnappssot' of Cosima Wagner at Bayreuth, 1904

21 Muswell Hill Broadway, *c.* 1905

22 Isabella Hunter in later life

23 'This Godforsaken, lonely Hole ... ': Jaeger at Davos

24 The Davos Valley

25 The Hotel Buol

26 Davos propaganda, from *The Courier*, 20 December 1907

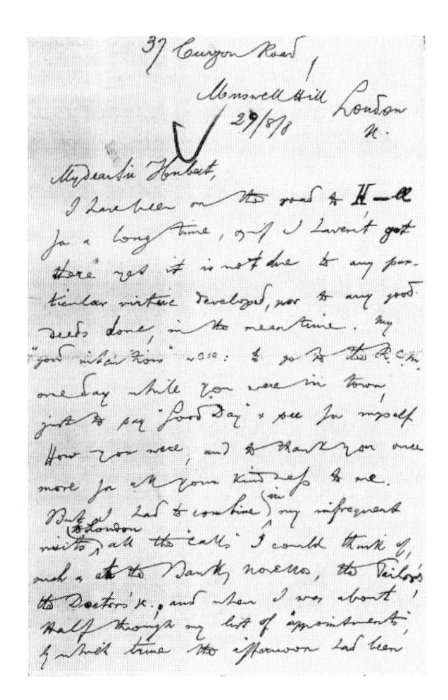

37 Curzon Road
Muswell Hill
London
N.
29/8/8

My dear Sir Hubert,

I have been on the road to H—ll for a long time, & if I haven't got there yet it is not due to any particular virtue developed, nor to any good deeds done, in the meantime. My "good intentions" were: to go to the R.C.M. one day while you were in town, just to say "Good Day" & see for myself how you were, and to thank you once more for all your kindness to me. But I had to combine (in) my infrequent (London) visits all the "calls" I could think of, such as at the Bank, Novellos, the Tailor's, the Doctor's &c., and when I was about half through my list of "appointments", by which time the afternoon had been

27 'I have been on the road to Hell ... ': Jaeger's letter of 29 August 1908 to Parry

in that purgatory through the nights. How can a man fight against that sort of thing?! Well, I'm a weakling to write like this.

I feel honoured by your request to say something on Hereford work in the M. T. But, my dear good friend, I can make *no* promise in my present state of collapse. I may be dead in August, when I suppose the stuff should be ready for the press. And I may in any case be unfit to undertake as task such

will require a great deal of study to enable me to get right inside your music. Forget not I'm a mere amateur. At present the task frightens me & I'd rather say "no". I'm so feeble in body and mind. Better ask Colles who is a better musician critic & journalist than old Nim.

I must stop for I'm exhausted with this exertion of writing. Please thank Mrs Mathieson very heartily for her kind letter which I was happy to receive. My dutiful respects to her, & my love to you, dear P. Davies

Ever
A. J. J.

28 Jaeger's last letter to Walford Davies, written three weeks before he died. 'I can make *no* promise in my present state of collapse. I may be dead in August … .'

29 Poster for the Jaeger Memorial Concert

11 1906: '*Please* not lose heart'

Throughout January the *Davos Courier* publicized the varied sporting and cultural activities that might have offered the 'recreation' that Jaeger had so earnestly been advised to seek. He seems to have spent some time skating, and would presumably have noted the weekly 'Symphony Concerts' given at the Belvedere Hotel. That for Monday 8 January was to feature Grieg's second *Peer Gynt* Suite, Dvořák's *New World* Symphony, and two cello solos given by a certain Herr Berthold. If he had read the comments of the anonymous critic of the *Courier* about a concert given by the Davoser Kurpakelle earlier in the season, Jaeger might however have had second thoughts about attending.

> Every year since the inauguration of this orchestra by the Curverein these concerts have become more and more successful and popular, and both the Curverein and the orchestra itself are heartily to be congratulated on this auspicious commencement to another season. Herr K. Kunzell still wields the baton, and works most enthusiastically … The playing on Monday, especially when one remembers that this was the opening concert of the season, was most creditable. As to the programme of this first concert, it is to be remarked that the Conductor (contrary to his wont) made a rather ambitious choice for the opening item. This was Beethoven's 5th symphony. It speaks well for the composition and form of the orchestra that they came through the ordeal remarkably well. The audience accepted the first two movements in a cool and critical spirit, but were moved to fairly enthusiastic applause by the finishing strains.[1]

The writer concluded by announcing the next concert as a 'Wagner Evening'. Perhaps this gained more than 'fairly enthusiastic' applause. But such concerts may have done little to improve Jaeger's morale. He would have been cheered to know that Alice Elgar, in a letter to Isabella, told her that 'my husband is *very* hard at work, I think you will love the new tunes'. He would have been cheered, also, to be the recipient of proofs of the new Oratorio from Novello's. He told Isabella, who in turn told Elgar, who wrote immediately, somewhat in embarrassment, on 26 January. It is his first preserved letter to Jaeger since that of 3 November the previous year. '*Heart friend*,' he admitted, perhaps a little guiltily,

> I have been very evil in not writing to you but I had not the heart to do so. *To-day* we hear from Mrs Jaeger that you are seeing the proofs of my new thing: I did not dare to suggest that you *should* see them & I dare not send my own sheets, so – I could not write. I am so delighted to know that the firm send the stuff on to you. So far it is the best thing I've done *I know*: remember it's not piano music & won't sound well on a tin kettle.

We are really so glad about your skating & know it must be a pleasure & a great help in many ways for health as well as recreation.

I was delighted to see Bell's works which he kindly sent to me: & I have done what I can in the way of recommendation but people *are* so *difficile.*

I must now go on with my work – but I have been *bursting* to write to you for a long time.[2]

Elgar mentioned in this letter nothing of the difficulties which were surrounding the composition of *The Kingdom.* In truth he had made inadequate progress with the work, and April and May would see him at the Cincinnatti Festival, a prolonged interruption. The composer began to quail at the mountain of composition that had to be climbed before the October Birmingham Festival, and already arrangements had to be put in hand for the engagement of soloists and the German translation. He became ill and depressed – a newspaper report spoke of a nervous breakdown – and was ready to withdraw, but Alice took determined charge of the situation. She negotiated confidentially with Elgar's doctors, the Festival authorities, and with Alfred Littleton, with the result that a shortened version of the work, approximately half the original plan, was accepted.

In January, Hubert Parry had written to Jaeger most generously offering to bear the expense of sending Isabella to join him at Davos, and Jaeger, discouraged from writing letters on medical advice, only now replied with guarded news of a positive verdict on his lungs – although another sinus operation at Lausanne remained a possibility – and a rueful and confidential account for Parry's private amusement, of an embarrassing and painful incident during his first attempt at tobogganning. The lively, racy side of Jaeger's nature was not entirely suppressed, and the escapade had involved an 'Irish lady' and some scions of the English aristocracy, a class which Parry often viewed with something approaching contempt.

Hotel Buol,
Davos.

9/3/06

Dear Sir Hubert,

Forgive me, I beg of you, my great sin of omission. Long ago I should have replied to your very Kind letter of January last; but apart from the lamentable Fact, that we 'Lungers' here are the laziest set of people on God's Earth, and consider letter writing an abominable nuisance, (our Doctors 'command' us to write as little as possible,) I was afraid to communicate with you lest I should be sorely tempted to say something resembling an acceptance of your most Kind suggestion as to sending my dear wife out to Davos to keep me company.

That was a tempting bait, for I have missed & still miss her greatly. But dear Isabella has had to earn money in London while I spent it here in my idle way, and besides, the Children claimed her time & care, especially since my little Boy has not been well. So I can but thank you from the bottom of my Heart for your Kind thought & let my Wife continue to give as many fiddle lessons as she can secure, & to count the days & hours till the time when I return to our little house on Muswell Hill. She has been *very* brave throughout this anxiety & suspense, & I hope she will be equally brave *if* I have to go to

Lausanne once more on my way home, to undergo further operations, as I greatly fear I shall have to. My nasal trouble, though GREATLY relieved, is not quite removed, and seeing how greatly Professor Marmod has relieved me, I am in hopes that he may cut & chisel some more & virtually cure that part of my wretched anatomy. Only, don't *please,* say a word about this, as I have not yet told either my wife nor my firm of my intention to go to Lausanne. If Prof Mermod thinks another *big* operation (like last year's) necessary, I fancy I shall say 'nay', & defer the horrible ordeal to a more congenial (?) time. We shall see. As regards my lungs (Pardon my going to such lengths in describing my state of Health) I am very happy to be able to tell you that my Doctor examined me a fortnight ago & told me that he could hear no more 'noises' in them, & might therefore consider them *Healed.* What exactly that means for the present & for the *future* I cant say, but anyhow, I rejoice exceedingly to have reached the goal which I set out to reach. Of course, I cannot yet leave, & at once face English weather & Berners Street work in the treacherous Spring time. I shall remain here till early April anyhow. It depends on my Doctor's Dictum when I may leave Davos.

As a sportsman you may appreciate my account of my *first attempt* at *Tobogganning,* & how We came down, at a *lightning* speed (2 on a Toboggan, an Irish lady & myself) & crashed into a Bobsleigh with the result that *I* sprained my right foot TERRIBLY (its a wonder my leg wasn't smashed into smithereens!), suffered a week's abominable pain (48 hours' real agony included!) & much discomfort & suffering (– especially during massaging twice a day! –) ever since. Even now I have to walk in the street with the aid of 2 sticks, though I am nearly allright. I *am* an unfortunate pig! The disgusting part of the business was the fact that We were 'enjoying ourselves' on the 'Buol Run' at the back of this Hotel, a 'Run' which is well Known as a regular *Children's* run, where a Bobsleigh (beastly, heavy machines!) was never seen until that afternoon. Moreover, the owners of the infernal thing (son & daughters of Lord Balfour of Burleigh!) were on the wrong side of the 'Road', at a bend, where every toboggan *must* have run into them; and they did nothing to 'clear out', & make room for us, though we shouted 'Achtung' with all our might. '*Damn* & confound the people', I have said many a time in my pain. If you happen to know this particular Lord Balfour of Burleigh, you may give him my love & tell him I am ashamed of his children & that I have a good mind to send him on a bill for £1000 damages, to repay me for loss of dignity & [illegible], much pain, Doctor's & masseur's fees, medicines &c &c.

Once more, Damn them! But wasn't it unlucky to be thus punished for trying to enjoy myself for once in a way. My first (& most likely last) Toboggan Ride! my wife & my Firm *don't know* the *cause* of my 'sprained foot' (that sounds very innocent, so don't give me away, I beg of you.) I *promised* dear Isabella I wouldn't Toboggan! See how I got punished for disobeying my dear, good wife. 'Serve him right', you will say, yet *I* don't think so.

I hope that you, dear Sir Hubert, are keeping as fit as your troublesome heart & your surfeit of work will let you. Are you at work on anything large? I see that there are many interesting concerts & things going on in London. Heavens! How I miss music & 'being in the swim'. I starve here, musically.

But I have already wasted too much of your precious time with my twaddle. Forgive me & believe me to be, with my kindest regards & all best wishes for your Health & work,

Yours very sincerely,

A.J. Jaeger.[3]

Amid the usual pressures of indifferent health and official duties, Parry was working on his commission for that year's Hereford Three Choirs Festival, *The Soul's Ransom.* He had also revised for a second time his 1893 *Overture to an Unwritten Tragedy,* given at the Queen's Hall during February. Generous as ever, he replied to Jaeger's letter on 15 March with a cheque for £25.

Jaeger continued to offer his reactions to the *Kingdom* proofs, and seems to have been critical of the final chorus of the first scene, 'O ye priests!' Alice responded with a magisterial reprimand, coloured by her awareness of Jaeger's agnosticism as well as her determination to keep all mention of the matter from her husband. Also remarkable were her specific injunction to Jaeger not to speak to others of the new work, and her reference to the opinions of 'real musicians'.

> I think yr. surroundings &c must have depressed you when you wrote –
> It is curious that that Chorus did not fire you, it works up all who have heard it to a great pitch of excitement – & I think you might have given E. some credit for his really fine literary taste & poetic feeling in his selection of words – If you cannot feel the Sacerdotalism of any *Church*, there is the eternal priestdom of Elect Souls in all ages, who have stood above the lower minds & dragged them up; to those who believe by religion, & to others by art, literature & pure & noble character & aspirations; so instead of 'Matthias' meaning nothing to us, it is the type of Everything wh. can still infuse heroism, self sacrifice & great thoughts into all who are not dead to such things –
> Wait to judge of the new work, & especially to *remark* to anyone on it, till you have heard E. play it – all those who have, & all those have been real musicians think it the most original & the greatest thing he has done. He is very very busy & has much to think of, & so soon to start for America so *please* not remark on anything I have said – He is better I am thankful to say but the strain of the work is very great for him & makes him very easily worried – He wd. send his especial love I know, did he know I was writing.[4]

As if to ward off any reply from an incorrigible writer of letters, and to finally put Jaeger in his place, she concluded, 'This does not want *any* answer – I shall *really* not have time to read letters till we start – Please rest & not write.' Honest criticism had always been the accepted currency between Jaeger and Elgar, indeed it had on several occasions spurred on the composer to reach heights of which he might not otherwise have been capable. If the sheer distance of separation had inevitably done something to change the relationship between them, Alice's over-reaction might only have added to Jaeger's gradually developing feelings of neglect. But, ignoring Alice's advice, he did respond, with praise for the Pentecost scene and the hurtful incident – to all intents and purposes – was over. And Jaeger, like Elgar, had 'much to think of'. In writing promptly to thank Parry for his cheque, he revealed that Professor Sanford had also given generous help, as had other friends. Financially there seemed little immediate problem. But as far as his health was concerned, he had been confronted with some ominous news.

> Hotel Buol,
> Davos.
>
> 20/3/06
>
> Dear Sir Hubert,
>
> I hardly Know what to say to you after your last Kind letter enclosing the 2nd generous gift. I mentioned to you some months ago that Prof. Sanford (formerly of

Yale) had been Kind enough to send me £100; and that sum, together with a nice present from my firm I thought might, and I still think *may* pay my expenses here, if I am permitted to leave Davos soon. I was therefore more than lucky, to have received as much help in the *second* year of my 'recruitment', as I did in my first. My friends have indeed been most good to me, and I have been greatly touched by their tokens of friendship & goodwill & by their display of practical sympathy in my trouble & great anxiety. A heavy portion of my anxiety, viz that connected with the heavy expense of a protracted stay in this expensive place Was generously lifted off my mind by my friends, and I could thus devote myself to 'curing' with that 'easy' mind, that absence of 'worrying' which our doctors say are *necessary*, but which are not easy to 'cultivate' when one is spending more than one is earning. Now I don't mind telling you quite candidly, dear Sir Hubert, that I *purposely* mentioned Prof Sanford's £100 to you lest you, in your exceeding goodness of heart, should imagine that I was greatly in need of money wherewith to pay my Exs, and perhaps think of helping me again, as you very kindly did last year. I meant to suggest that after receiving Prof Sanford's gift I was really 'well off' & in *no* need of further Help! And now you have done that which I meant to prevent, and I feel as if I accepted money under false pretences in Keeping your Cheque. However, I may, if I have to go to Lausanne, have to incur yet further heavy expenses in Doctor's fees, 'Clinique' Charges &C; expenses which may bring me far beyond the sum which my American friend & the Firm have given me, and your gift will thus prove a *real & great help*. I therefore accept it with the deepest gratitude, & I only wonder how I can ever do anything to prove how greatly I appreciate your Kindness, or to show by deeds how gladly I would do something in return for it.

22/3/06. I was interrupted here, & since then I haven't felt well. Now my Doctor this morning tells me that I have 'gone back', & that he can again hear 'some dry noises' in my left lung. This is *very* depressing news, & shows the uncertainty of our so-called 'cure' here. If I can thus be set back here in Davos, what may not English weather & work do for me?

Well, I must hope for the best & continue my cure. But I do so with a *very* heavy heart, – doubly heavy after my 'rejoicing' of the last few weeks.

Goodbye, dear Sir Hubert, & once more a thousand thanks!

Ever yours sincerely & devotedly,

A.J. Jaeger.[5]

In what he referred to as 'the hurry of departure' for the American engagement, Elgar sent a brief commiseration over the setback, offering hopes and prayers for improvement. 'C.H.H.P. is an angel as ever. God bless him!' he continued, and then repeated his own earlier offers. 'If you *do* want anything you know all that's mine is yours, so go ahead.' Working together, albeit at a distance and under Alice's watchful eye, over *The Kingdom*, had brought back something of the old relationship, as shown by another letter to 'Dearie Moss' over the offending two bars in the Prelude. Elgar praised Jaeger's 'unerring instinct', although claiming that the bars were never really intended to go in, being there only as a reminder of the design of the movement.

Understandably downcast by the news about his lungs, Jaeger had after all used Parry's gift to enable Isabella to join him at Davos; no doubt Jaeger's sister Joanna – 'Donnie' – something of a trusty family factotum, helped look after the children. Two months later, back at Muswell Hill, he wrote Parry a letter of thanks and expressed his conscientious determination to return to work. There was news too of a medical report which Jaeger was determined to regard as hopeful, although he was fully aware of the likely effects of London's polluted air.

37 Curzon Road,
Muswell Hill.

Sunday 6/5/6

Dear Sir Hubert,

Here we are again! My wife & I arrived last night from Switzerland & were delighted to find your Kind letter to my wife. Since I wrote to you last, & felt wretched in consequence of the 'set-back' in my cure, I have had my dear Frau with me. I couldn't stand the separation any longer, under the depressing circumstances, and so I decided to use your most kind gift for the purpose for which I fancy you chiefly wished it used. Her presence at the Hotel was a great comfort & help to me, & when I left I received what I believe I may consider a *good* report from Dr Buol. And now I am anxious to get back to regular work, to do something for my living, something that might perchance repay my firm in a small way for their kindness to me. (They have paid my full salary all the time and presented me with £25 additional, and my usual Christmas Box, which latter I could not consider to have deserved, seeing I worked only for 5 months last year!)

My wife enjoyed her stay at Davos very much & feels all the better for it. At present we are both a little affected (disagreeably affected) by the sudden change from the pure atmosphere of 5500 feet above Sea level to London's murky air. But we shall soon get used to the old 'style' again & perhaps even wax fat on coal dust & other impurities in the oxygen we inhale. Anyhow, we are both very deeply grateful to you, dear Sir Hubert, for having given us the Chance of having the month together in beautiful Switzerland. We shall never forget your Kindness.

I hope I may soon have a chance of seeing you, & I trust I shall find you well & in as high spirits as usual, in spite of the overwork to which you seem to be for ever condemned. We both send our Kindest regards & warmest thanks & I am, dear Sir Hubert

Yours, very sincerely & devoted,

A.J. Jaeger[6]

Picking up the threads of ordinary life again, no doubt there would have been some accumulated back numbers of the *Musical Times* to be perused. February's number contained reviews of new songs by Holbrooke, McEwen and Walford Davies, which would have been of interest, together with mention of a volume of *Old English Organ Music* edited by John West, which might not. Jaeger's own voice had been sadly missing from the concert reviews, of course. The March edition provided a rather predictably English account of a performance of Strauss's *Don Quixote* at the Queen's Hall.

> ... the symphonic poem 'Don Quixote' by Richard Strauss – Richard the Second, as he is sometimes called – amply satisfied the desires of the extremists. 'Don Quixote' displays Strauss's marvellous talent in exuberance. It is said to be his most characteristic work, and certainly we can conceive of no one else writing anything as perplexing, astonishing and, we are bound to add, at least occasionally fascinating. How far imitative effects such as the bleating of sheep and the sound of the wind, – a good many

composers have regaled us with orchestral storms – and how far extraordinarily persistent discords are legitimate means of art expression will never be finally settled, but it would seem to many, even of those who endeavour to suppress bias and who strive to appreciate novelty, that as to this Strauss does not leave much scope for posterity.[7]

It gave Jaeger's detested 'jokist', F.G. Edwards, the notoriously punning Editor, an opportunity to offer this in another column:

Overheard at Queen's Hall, after the recent performance of Richard Strauss's symphonic-poem, 'Don Quixote':
He. What did you think of the sheep music?
She. Not at all bad: but how many bleats are there in a baa?[8]

More to Jaeger's satisfaction would have been a review in the April number of a performance of *The Apostles* at the Alexandra Palace under Allen Gill, offering a musical vindication of his decision to live in the area.

This Society continues to flourish under the directorship of Mr Allen Gill. It has become now an important factor in the musical life of the metropolis. It is boldly and ably managed, and as a consequence has attracted the cream of North London choralists. A curious newspaper-born convention regards Muswell Hill as not London proper, and so what goes on there is stamped as suburban, and consequently as necessarily not important. Yet for millions of Londoners it is easier to reach the Alexandra Palace than it is the Albert Hall. The most recent achievement of this Choral Society was a performance of Elgar's great work 'The Apostles', which was given on March 10. The interest excited may be measured from the fact that the audience numbered 4,000 persons.[9]

The same number included extracts from press reviews of performances of the same work in Germany, probably found by Jaeger himself, together with mention of a concert 'devoted to his own creations' mounted at the Bechstein Hall by Cyril Scott.

Elgar had found time during the American visit to make some progress with the orchestration of the new Oratorio, but on his return to Hereford at the end of May continued composition became blocked. He fell ill and Alice's anxieties – and protectiveness – returned. A short break in Wales saw some progress, but the shock of a heavy fall on some wet stones put an abrupt end to the holiday and caused a further setback. The fate of the work seemed to hang in the balance once more and Jaeger was again the recipient of some direct and repeated hints from Alice over the next few weeks '... he is of course dreadfully worried about his work being late ... we must not hurry him or any thing ... I prevent anythg. possible from worrying him ... he has worried so much over it so it is better not to write about it to him ... please have a little more patience & all being well, the new work will be about his best, and in time convincing even to pagans, but you must PLEASE not worry or hurry him in any way ...'. Still, he was able to send part of the orchestration, begun in America, to Novello's on 8 June.[10] Jaeger was asked to write the analysis,[11] but the degree of his creative involvement in *The Kingdom* was much less than in the previous oratorios. His own reduced energies, together with Alice's warnings, may have led to this but even so, despite all the delays and problems over the work, Elgar was able to resume its composition and scoring with a phenomenal certainty of touch. The result was a work with no musico-dramatic weaknesses whose reputation stands with, or even above, *Gerontius* in the estimation of many. Amid various more or less routine comments on minor matters of tempi and orchestration, perhaps Jaeger's only contribution was the suggestion that the phrase 'and the patience' from the soprano solo in Scene IV, 'The sun goeth down', be repeated for emotional effect; the idea was adopted and gave scope for a typically Elgarian sequence.

Flashes of the old relationship between Jaeger and Elgar did continue to appear in their correspondence that summer. '... I played thro' Variatn No. 9 – written by one Ass to the glorification of another old duck: you will never be more *dearly* idealized than that – better perhaps but not so sincere,' wrote Elgar in July, finding it easier perhaps to relate to the music than to its increasingly invalid subject. He dined with Jaeger during a visit to London at the end of the month, and wrote later, 'It *was* good to see you again & your dear, old, *earnest* face, bless you!' Their meeting had included some discussion over the *Kingdom* analysis at Elgar's suggestion, for he must have anticipated a repetition of previous problems. Elgar made sure that Jaeger was equipped with a suitable commentary to help with points he wanted mentioned, but was unable to prevent Jaeger's predictable anxiety over the naming of motifs: 'As to naming themes we'll see to it,' was Elgar's only comment.

As before, Jaeger undertook the work in his free time and the strain quickly began to tell on his weakening constitution. By 15 August a crisis had arisen such that Alice noted in her diary, 'Heard Moss cd. not finish Analysis – very concerned.' Two days later she was able to record that he had changed his mind, with arrangements belatedly being made for him to continue working on it at home during office time. He accepted, too, an invitation to stay with the Elgars at Hereford to go through the analysis, staying for three days towards the end of August. Alice met him at the station and thought he looked far from well, and Elgar, determined that Jaeger should have something of a break, persuaded him to stay another day after he became 'very poorly' with what was described as lumbago. Alice looked after him, hiring a carriage and taking him on something of a countryside tour one afternoon while her husband was out cycling. '*Lovely* afternoon – Mr J. slightly better', she noted. The fresh country air must have been welcome, for during that month Novello's began to move offices from Berners Street to the sumptuous and imposing surroundings of new buildings in Wardour Street, and Jaeger blamed the inevitable inhalation of dust during the process for a serious inflammation of his lungs. In writing to Elgar with news of the new address, Jaeger put the Oratorio first.

> ... I *may not* be here to morrow or Wednesday because I *must* finish that Analysis which worries me. I have only about 40 [pages] more to do, – the most impressive, *Holiest purest* portion of the work. Those last 30 or 40 pages are marvellous, dear man, & as uplifting as anything I know. Ever thine, with much love ...[12]

But that same day he wrote sadly to Alice with news of his doctor's reaction to the latest setback – early retirement. She responded immediately with determined sympathy and proposals for the future.

> Plas Gwyn
>
> 4 Sept 1906
>
> Dear Mr Jaeger,
>
> I cannot tell you how much I feel for you & Mrs Jaeger in this trial about your health, but you must *please* not lose heart. In doing what the Dr orders we trust, D.V. that your health will be really established & *then* your gifts & talents will find some new path wh. will make all well for you & yours, but I know how painful it is for you if you have to leave Berners St, & what a terrible loss to music lovers. Meanwhile you may be sure the many friends you have befriended are [illegible] thinking of you & your sad worries – & not forgetting.
>
> Forgive haste. I have so much to think of just now. E. is in London as no doubt you know – We are so glad of this coolness. With love to Mrs Jaeger & again all sympathy,
>
> Yours truly,
>
> C. Alice Elgar[13]

She wrote also to her husband, away from home at Three Choirs rehearsals, and he added his voice to hers:

> Alice tells me you write sadly of yourself to her – well I can only say how sorry I am that you are depressed & wish with all my soul I could cheer you. She does not tell me *what* you say but I shall learn that tomorrow, Only for the moment be assured that anything we can do shall be done to our last coin. Bless you.[14]

Parry too got to know of Jaeger's predicament when he called at Novello's on 6 September, to find the moving still going on. 'To Berners St about band parts. Found the shifting of the establishment to Wardour St going on. Paid Jaeger a long visit. He very low & upset. The doctor having given him an ominous report of his condition,' he noted in his diary.

There was no question of Jaeger attending that year's Hereford Three Choirs Festival, and he seems to have been recommended a seaside holiday at this time in order to benefit from some fresh air. In the middle of the Festival week Elgar wrote to say that he had received proofs of part of the analysis, adding 'you shall not be bothered with it'. It seems a considerate decision, and Jaeger's state of mind at the time and the nature of his letters, may perhaps be gauged from Elgar's concluding paragraph: 'I will not go into your private affairs now: I only say do not worry yourself but do all you can to get better & don't tell us we can't understand or sympathize because, of course, we know that already: you old Moss. Love from all …'

But Elgar also made use of the opportunity of having the final form of the *Kingdom* analysis easily under his control to alter it significantly. It is the shortest of the three, and only some 29 of the 78 music examples have titles. In a somewhat despairing farewell letter to Hubert Parry written towards the end of September, Jaeger claimed that he had not wanted to undertake the analysis in the first place, and laid the blame for the deterioration in his condition entirely on the office move. He also expressed concern over Parry's own health, for the composer had long been experiencing heart problems and had collapsed unconscious at a recent Three Choirs rehearsal.

37 Curzon Road,
Muswell Hill.

27/9/6.

My dear Sir Hubert,

I called at the College to-day to say Goodbye once more, but alas! you were at Gloucester. I'm off for another 6 months 'Holiday' (How I *loathe* these 'Holidays'!) early next week. My lungs are bad again – worse they are than before, – and I shall have to make another desperate attempt at getting 'cured'.

And all through that wretched moving business at No. 1 Berners Street, when the filthy, 20 years old dust choked my 'tender' lung & at once set up inflammation of a bad Kind. My expectoration has been *much* worse than ever before. Oh dear, what a dreary business it is & how despairing.

I have not yet decided where to go. I shall consult some German Doctors in Düsseldorf (my native place) & then do that which they think best. The Firm has once more given me 6 months leave of absence on full pay. They are *very* good to me. Your Kind letter will be attended to allright. I was glad to hear that you had a good performance. I heard some good reports about your work.[15] (I don't know it yet, alas, having been away from Home for sometime, and altogether too upset to look at *any* of the festival novelties except Elgars which I was *made against my will* to 'analyse' for the Festival.[)]

Well, I must close & go to bed.

Goodbye, dear Sir Hubert & good Health to you. Keep well! English music cant afford to see you ill as you were a short time ago, at Hereford.

I leave England with a very heavy Heart. Heaven Knows how I may feel six months hence[.]

I'll let you Know occasionally *if* I make any progress towards recovery.

Very Sincerely & devotedly Yours

A.J. Jaeger.[16]

Both Elgars wrote briefly to send their good wishes; earlier Alice had sent a postcard about the first orchestral rehearsal for *The Kingdom*, describing how the band had broken into spontaneous applause. As with Hereford, there was no question of Jaeger being able to attend the Birmingham Festival, and the première of the new Oratorio. His absence marked a further step in a gradual decline which may be traced directly in terms of the works he had done so much to support, for he had been unwell at the *Gerontius* première, and confined to bed in his Birmingham Hotel during the first performance of *The Apostles*. On the eve of the *Kingdom* première all he could manage was to write further letters of farewell. One was to Walford Davies, who had called at Curzon Road while Jaeger had taken the children on a Sunday outing.

37 Curzon Road,
Muswell Hill.

[Post Mark Oct 2 06]

My dear Davies,

I was so sorry I missed you yesterday. The day being so lovely I went for a walk & Tram ride to Whetstone with the Bairns, & did not return till 1 p.m. I never expected You on a *Sunday morning*, but felt sure you were on Church Duty at the Temple. I am very annoyed I was wrong. To morrow Tuesday I shall be in Town till the evening, to say Goodbye to many people, visit my Tailor, &c &c so don't come, unless you can manage to do so in the evening after 7. I wish I could come to You, but I must avoid railway travelling wherever possible. If I don't see you ere I go (Wednesday or Thursday) I'll now say good bye & good luck & good Health to you & 'Auf Wiedersehen'.

Ever yours, devotedly

A.J.J.[17]

To Dora Penny Jaeger sent a promised copy of his *Kingdom* analysis, with some account of its treatment by both Elgar and Littleton.

37 Curzon Road,
Muswell Hill N/

2/X/6

My dear Miss Dora,

Here is my wretched analysis, written under great difficulties (of ill health). I hope you may find *some*thing in it to interest you. Of course you can't – in fact nobody can [–] guage [*sic*] the qualities of work by Elgar from the few quotations in an analysis written by a Duffer like me. My stuff was knocked about by Elgar & my 'governor' after I had passed the proofs for the press – to take out some of my 'appreciatory' remarks, and in this process of bowdlerizing two words have dropped out & other bad things have happened for which I'm *not* responsible. So forgive *me* these 'faults', anyhow. The thing was *much longer* originally.

I'm off tomorrow or Thursday for another 6 months stay abroad trying to 'get better'.

I have been *very* bad, but am picking up again. I fear I shall not have time to say Goodbye to you & your dear Mother & sister; I'm very busy 'getting ready' – writing innumerable letters, amongst other things.

But I remembered my promise to send you my analysis, and here is the little thing.

Goodbye now, and *keep well, you* & Your dear ones, – That's the main thing; nothing else seems to matter!

With my kindest regards to your dear mother [,] Your sister & your kind, good self

Very Sincerely yours

A.J. Jaeger.[18]

'How & where are you … you never send a word as to yourself,' wrote Elgar in mid-October, and Jaeger, who had been disinclined for yet another return to Davos, responded with news of a new cure based on naked open-air cold baths and exercise, which he was undergoing at a a centre in the Rhineland. 'What a drastic cure!' wrote

Elgar, '*how* I should like to join in it: we would skip together in fine form. – dear old boy, I hope you are getting on well: it seems very lonely with you away and all the good Americans gone home … Love to you now & always …'. It was the warmest-toned message, albeit as another addition to a longer letter from Alice, that Jaeger had received from Elgar almost since he had been forced to spend time abroad. To Parry he wrote an account of his exercise cure and accompanying diet, a regime completely different from that at Davos; once again he was able to hope, for he was feeling fitter, and had even been assured that there were no signs of tuberculosis. Isabella was nevertheless preparing to take up a singing career with an eye to the future, and with a flash of his old generous enthusiasm, Jaeger recommended Marguerite Swale, her teacher, for a position at the College.

bei Inspektor Hermes,
Repelen, bei Moers,

Rheinland (Germany)

November 20/06

My dear Sir Hubert,

I know you will have been too busy with your 1001 engagements & worries to give a thought now & then to a certain A.J.J. who is spending a happy time (this is wrote sarkastic) far away from everyone & everything he loves & cherishes. I don't mean to say that I don't 'love' my Fatherland; I do, – but this God-forsaken village, where there isn't even a lantern in '*the*' street (there's only one) to show us the way o' nights, I cannot take to, or 'cherish', though the 'cure' which I am going through is doing me good, I believe. I read an English paper occasionally & see your dear name, & my thoughts fly to London & to you & other Kind friends whom I'd rather see & speak to than any angels that Heaven might send down for my consolation & entertainment.

How are you? I do hope your Health is Keeping in good order & that you are 'fit' for your important work in England's Art-world. I hope also that the various compositions which Novellos had in Hand when I left London, are finished & published, or nearing completion, anyhow. Wish I were there, to superintend things, as I have done for so many years.

I will not bore you with particulars of my cure here, but just to show that it is not a 'coddling' affair, I will tell you that twice a day (8.30 & 3) I take cold Baths *in the open air*, as cold as the pump in the 'Park' (so called) draws it from the ground. Afterwards we run about, *wet* & *stark naked*, until the wind and our hands (rubbing our bodies) have dried our skins (*no* towels are used). Then we go through some gymnastic exercises & breathing operations, all as we stand stark naked in the open air. With the temperature at 2–5 degrees Celsius, & the water several millions below nowhere, the thing isn't exactly a Bath 'de luxe'. However, I feel very fresh & fit (though tired) after them, and they, together with a strict vegetarian diet *without alcohol*, *tea* or *coffee* are setting me up a bit.

I can't say how long I shall be able to stand the drastic cure. Soon the weather will be *too* severe & then I *may* go to Davos once more & see what that dear (in more than the sentimental way) place will do for me. I'm told by the medical authorities here, and I'm told this in the most emphatic manner, that I'm *not* 'consumptive' & have *no* tuberculosis. Certainly I have not, & never have had any of the symptoms of tuberculosis, e.g. high temperature, night sweats, 'claw' nails, wasted 'mice' on my hands (or what do you call the soft thick part of the Hand at the bottom of the thumb, inside of the Hand). I hope therefore that I may get rid of my phlegm, which chokes my chest & makes me cough. Were I consumptive I'd been long ago in my grave, I have coughed so much. Instead, I can now *run* (canter) 9–10 times as far round the park as when I came here, & my lungs stand it quite well. In fact, I'm doing the *exact opposite* of what Doctors in Davos order. *There*: *quiet*, little movement, slow breathing. *Here*: I run, & I also exert my lungs with the cold baths, the pumping on my body afterwards & the breathing exercises. Enough of this!

My dear wife is now taking singing lessons, & you won't be surprised, will you? when one day you will see in the papers 'Mrs A.J.J. took the part of so & so in the oratorio – '. She has, & always had a good voice, which sings *dead* in *tune*, she is *very* musical, as you know, & her splendid teacher, Miss Marguerite Swale, says she will do very well, and very soon too. I have always told my wife she ought to have been a *singer*. Her voice moves me easily nigh to tears, it is so pure, & unaffected & *sweet*. Now my working capacities are growing less through ill health, *some*thing must be done, & I hope Belle – meaning my wife, may be able to earn a few Pounds. Her fiddle still brings in *some*thing, but it is too little to be of much use to me & my family. Alas! that I am compelled to rely on my wife's earnings to Keep up a decent Home! If I don't get well this time I can't expect Novellos to keep me, & then? I *dread* the future.

By the way, Haven't you room for a really excellent, very particular & *very* capable singing teacher? I would recommend Miss Swale *strongly* to you. She has trained amongst others, Miss Edna Thornton, Mr Charles Tree, & she 'coaches' Miss Percival Allen, Ella Russell, & Miss Gleeson-White; was for a long time Marguerite Macintyre's accompanist & 'coach' (travelled with her through Russia & Germany, and helped her with all her Covent Garden work.) My wife says she Miss S is teaching the Tenor part of your 'King Saul' at the present moment to some Tenor who will sing in the work at Halifax under you &, she also taught Miss Allen the work, who is also singing at Halifax.

Miss Swale was trained at Berlin Hochschule & Liège, is an excellent Linguist & musician, plays P.F. remarkably well & has had 20 years' experience in teaching singing & coaching. Really, she would be an acquisition to the College staff. When you do want a teacher, do send for her & learn all about her qualities. I have known her for many years & have sent many people to her, who were all highly pleased. Mr Alfred Littleton's daughter in law Mrs Harry Littleton who went to Miss S. at my advice, told me she learnt more in one lesson from Miss S. than elsewhere in a dozen lessons. And my wife (who, at the College, had a few lessons from Mr Lather, I believe,) is quite enthusiastic about her, *though* Miss S. is 'so *very* particular'.

I believe Elgar Knows the lady & her doings too; so if you dont value my opinion you may like to hear Elgar's, who isnt a fool (like me) exactly. Or Best of all, let her give a lesson before you & judge for yourself! Her address is

Miss Marguerite Swale,
120 F Portland Street, W
London

Pardon my championship of this friend of mine; but I seriously mean it when I say that she would be an acquisition to the Staff of any music School. Also pardon a long letter. Keep well, dear Sir Hubert, & *spare* yourself for the future.

With my Kindest regards, I am yours very sincerely

A.J. Jaeger.[19]

At the very time of this letter Parry's own health problems were mounting once more to a crisis. He became unwell while conducting the Halifax *King Saul* on 22 November; 'heart tottering on complete collapse all through,' he noted, 'just staved it off by going steady & not exerting myself.' An Oxford lecture a week later proved a similar ordeal, and on medical advice Parry took a long holiday, travelling to Italy after Christmas, and spending the whole of the month of January in Mortola, Genoa, Florence and Pisa. Jaeger meanwhile, braced by the Repelen cure, returned to London in December, once more determined not to miss Christmas with his family.

Jaeger's interest in Peter Cornelius – whose part-songs the *Musical Times* had advertised in October – had continued with a lengthy review of a two-volume edition of the composer's letters, diaries and poetry, spread between the September and December issues. It was Jaeger's major contribution to the journal that year. Cornelius would have been of interest through his associations with the great – Liszt, Berlioz and Wagner – but he was as well a writer-musician with Düsseldorf connections, and an archetypal Romantic figure to boot.

> ... His is the usual story of a genius-gifted composer's struggle for recognition which refused to come, or at any rate to provide the wherewithal of an independent existence until Cornelius had reached the middle-aged period of his life ... Most of his compositions ... went the round of many publishers' offices only to be returned or forgotten ... Cornelius was one of those artists who, knowing in what direction their strength lies, spend the greater part of their lives waiting for something to turn up which shall enable them to exercise their particular gifts to their own fullest artistic satisfaction, and meanwhile refuse to turn their hand to other work – uncongenial perhaps, but neither difficult nor degrading – which would secure for them something like independence.[20]

It had been Jaeger's good fortune that he had been able to combine the exercise of his 'particular gifts' with the securing of 'something like independence', at any rate since the beginning of his employment with Novello's sixteen years before. But the progress of his illness was now such that all this would be taken from him before another year was past.

12 1907: Dum Spiro Spero

... I wrote this dance-poem[1] in 1847, at a time when the bad state of my health had already advanced to a serious degree but had not yet cast its grim shadow over my spirit. At that time I still had some flesh on me and some paganism in me, and I had not yet been emaciated down to a spiritual skeleton now awaiting its final dissolution. But do I still really exist? My body has shrivelled so much that almost nothing is left but the voice, and my bed reminds me of the tolling grave of the magician Merlin, which lies in the forest of Brozeliand in Brittany, and tall oaks whose tops shoot up to heaven like green flames. Ah, I envy you, dear colleague Merlin, these trees and the fresh breezes blowing through them, for there is not a single green leaf rustling here in my mattress-grave in Paris, where early and late I hear only the rattling of carriages, hammering, scolding, and strumming on the piano. A grave without repose; death without the privileges of the dead, who need not hand out money and write letters or even books – this is indeed a sad state of affairs. Long ago my measure was taken for a coffin, and also for an obituary notice, but I am dying so slowly that it is all gradually becoming as tiresome for me as for my friends. But patience – everything has an end. One fine morning you will find the booth closed where so often you were entertained by the puppet show of my humour.

Heinrich Heine, postscript to *Romancero*[2]

After Christmas Elgar undertook another American visit, with performances of the *The Apostles*, *The Kingdom* and the *Enigma* Variations. The printing of the *Kingdom* full score was under way at Novello's, no longer under Jaeger's eye; the proofs were given to Elgar just before his American departure by Harold Brooke, a Littleton nephew who had been moved around the Firm in order to take up some of the work of the Publishing Department. And after a Christmas at Muswell Hill spent 'as happy as a sandboy', Jaeger also resumed his travels, returning again to Davos. Once there his condition worsened considerably; he was confined to bed with a fever and was even forbidden to speak for a time, a real hardship to such a man. Despite a course of injections,[3] there was continued confirmation of the presence of tuberculosis in throat and lungs, to add to Jaeger's financial anxieties and his worries over his family's future and the condition of his elderly mother. Sanford had made a princely promise of financial support, but it failed to materialise when he left unexpectedly for home as the result of an unexplained upset at the previous year's Hereford Festival. Novello's continued to be generous, as did Parry. Far from home, unwell and depressed, with no one to talk to, Jaeger trusted Parry, who may now be seen as filling the void increasingly left in Jaeger's life by Elgar's gradual withdrawal, with a long, frank and detailed letter. For the first time he showed some anger and bitterness over the lack of response from some of those he had helped, he now realized, at the cost of his health; he referred in particular to Sanford, who had made a princely promise of financial support which failed to materialize.

Hotel Buol,
Davos,
Switzerland.

11/3/7.

My dear Sir Hubert,

Your Kindness to me exceeds all bounds, and I don't Know how to write to thank you. I was much moved by the thought that, though so ill, you wrote to me from Italy. Believe me, I thoroughly appreciated that Kind thought of yours, though I was very, very sorry to hear that you were so unwell, & had derived so little benefit from your stay in the land 'wo die Citronen blühn', as poor Mignon sings. I'm greatly relieved to read in your last letter that you have once more 'picked up'. What a constitution & what recuperative powers are yours, fortunately!

I could not reply to that Italian letter, because I was really too ill. A daily, pencilled Post Card to my wife was all I could manage. For over a month now I have been confined to Bed (where I write this) by a most awful ('ganz colossaler', as my Dr calls it) Bronchial Catarrh, *& fever*, and this enforced idleness in Bed, & the fever have undone all the great good that the Repelen cure, Spartan though it was, undoubtedly did. For, when I was in London at Xmas, I felt as happy as a Sandboy & as strong as I have done for *many* years. True, I coughed, but that did not worry me much; for I felt so strong generally. However, when I got here, my voice went completely during the first week. I went to my Dr about it and he gave me a great fright by telling me my throat was *tuberculous*, & that, moreover, my lungs were *worse* than last year. I couldn't believe my ears & *would* not believe his statement about my throat; & so I went to a throat specialist, who opined that the symptoms which he saw *need not* prove the presence of Tuberculosis. A month's treatment by him (during which I had to emulate the Trappist monks & speak to nobody – a great trial to a chatterbox like me) I got my voice back, to my great relief. Shortly afterwards this wretched Catarrh got hold of me, & for two weeks I could hardly get breath. My Windpipe rattled & spluttered like a savage motor-car waiting impatiently outside your front door. The fearful strain of coughing, day & night soon caused my voice to go again, though now it is returning, since I cough less, & fancy that I have, with much poulticing, & Sweating, cold-compressing, & medicine-swallowing, broken the neck of mine enemy, who has so long held me in his iron grip.

Of course, this wretched thing has greatly added to my sufficiently 'considerable' expenses, – what with two Doctors, medicines, attendant for my elaborate Sweating Bandages & subsequent cold rub-downs, 'Service' in my Bedroom, (which alone costs me Fr. 12.50 a week!) &c. &c. So you will understand how greatly & deeply I appreciate your renewed generosity which prompted your sending me another cheque. I accept it with deepfelt thanks, and believe me, dear Sir Hubert, with a feeling of distinct *relief.* For, as I wrote to Mr Alfred Littleton last Friday, I had (before the receipt of your Cheque) only between £70 & £80 Cash at the Bank remaining (I can't name the exact sum without seeing my Pass-Book). When that is spent, *nothing* remains for us to do but to sell some of my dear wife's shares (she holds about £700 worth). A heartbreaking thing to do, & one that leads to the workhouse. But we must live & eat, & we must spend what there *is* to spend, & ignore the future. True, the Firm pays my salary (£5 (!) ENTRE NOUS a week is all my princely pay!). But I reckon that will cease at the End of this month, which is the end of my '6 months' leave'. After these six months are over, Mr Augustus Littleton told me, (again; *entre nous!)* that they could do no more, but would 'reconsider the situation'. Can you imagine my state of mind, in view of these circumstances? Heaven Knows when I can work again, though I am even now eager to take up again the work at N & Co which I love. Of course N & Co *may* continue for a little longer to pay my salary, though I cannot hope or expect it. They have been very Kind to me so far, and a Business isn't a charitable institution; maybe they consider they have done quite enough & more than enough in return for the splendid work I have done for them (I say that without wishing to boast, but I *know* what I have done for them all these years!) Business is Business, and I might easily have entered a firm which would have treated me not half so well. Mr Alfred L. told me at Xmas that they were 'Very fond of me', & he is a dear, Kind man. Alas! he is not alone – there are 4 other Directors!!

I left England in October with a light Heart, in *one* respect, for I had been told that Prof. S. Sanford (who you may know, is – even in 'Sovereigns' – a millionaire twice over) would see to it that for a whole year I need not worry about financial matters. You Know he has been kind to me before, & the idea of accepting more from a man so enormously rich as S.S., one who called himself (on a Photo I have at Home) my (don't laugh!) 'persistently admiring friend' (!!), & who wrote me the most kind & charming letters promising generous help in my trouble – I say the thought of accepting money from such an one did not upset me. But alas! S.S. left England suddenly without saying goodbye to me or other friends, and I have not heard a word more about that golden promise! Something, Somebody upset dear S.S. at Hereford Festival. I can make a shrewd guess, but won't say nuthin'![4] And so *I* am the loser, and am eating away my small remaining pile of savings, soon to reach the rock bottom; & then – a 'Future' that will prove a terrible 'Present' for me & my wife & Bairns & my 83 year old mother. For I cannot say, of course, how long I shall be 'getting well', or 'Kicking the Bucket'. I have undergone a Tubercular-injection cure, but that had to be discontinued when the catarrh arrived, & the *fever* with it. And so I have lost precious time that should have been devoted to a continuation of the injections. I have been *most* unlucky in every sense, and, – sans phrase – your letters have been the only bright spots on a generally black background – unless I except my wife's tales about the doings & sayings of my little rascals at Home. (By the way, my boy, aetat 5, is *very* musical. He loves sitting at the Piano, inventing little phrases, & Harmonising them in different keys, with occasional crossing of the Hands, so that the 'tune' is played in what he calls the 'dark' (Bass) of the P.F. The 'treble' is the '*Light*' to his mind. He has never been taught a note yet.)[5]

My sister tells me that she replied to your Kind telegram asking for my address. My wife happened to be at Gloucester, where she played at one of Brewer's organ recitals in the Cathedral. She earns a guinea or two occasionally, but Oh! *so* rarely considering her really great talent. Had she not been, as is now, the most modest, as she is the most lovable of women, she ought to, & would, have done well. She is most anxious to find work, to relieve me, while I'm ill; but oh the difficulty of finding work – pupils, or Engagements – for there's nae luck about our House, except that we are devoted to each other.

How I have worked (in my own spare time at Home) to help people in every way I could, making myself ill with writing & working till past the midnight Hour, night after night – and how few have ever moved a finger to do *me* a Kind turn, or my wife. You, for whom I have done *nothing*, have been Kindest to me, & the thought of it moves me to tears, such as only a beautiful thought – in this case of a beautiful action on the part of Great Britain's noblest master, – could force into my eyes.

I must close, dear Sir Hubert. Pardon the long, ill-written screed. It has helped me to Kill another tedious day in my matress-grave (as Heine called his Bed). It has done me good to pour out my heart to you & I feel sort of soft & warm about my heart as I think of your goodness. Perhaps you will forgive my occupying so much of your time? (I only hope you won't find my fist illegible).

I was sorry to read that Lady Parry also has been unwell, but trust you will both keep better & enjoy the coming Spring (which *may* find me near the Italian lakes).

The weather here has been *very* bad. It began to snow & 'blizzard' Thursday night & has never ceased. *Over 5 foot of snow* have already fallen. It's awful!

With my Kindest regards I am
dear Sir Hubert
yours ever sincerely & gratefully

A.J. Jaeger[6]

I see in the Musical Times that your Songs are out at last, but NOT your Violin Suites, nor the Symphonies. Ye Gods!!

Physically and emotionally Jaeger was at his lowest point, with time on his hands to look back over the course of his life and illness, to relate the two together and to realize the degree to which he had sacrificed himself. A month after his letter to Parry, he repeated his bitterness to Dora Penny, and did not shy away from expressing his feelings as to the main cause of his decline. 'I have worked terribly hard for E.E. and ruined my health over it very likely … I have never loved & admired a man more, made myself more a slave for any man out of sheer enthusiasm …'[7] Walford Davies had also been keeping in touch, and had sent a copy of his children's Cantata, *Humpty Dumpty*. Jaeger replied in desperation from Davos, with Heine's phrase continuing to haunt him. Early retirement from Novello's was now an imminent reality, as the destruction of his lungs continued.

28/4/07

My dear D.

Many thanks for letter & H.D. which latter is *delightful*. I can't write a letter; much too weak & feverish. I appreciate your cynicism; but you need not fear: I *shan't* take 20 years to 'cure', and relapses I have every few weeks [.] Can you men in good or fairly good Health realize (and you *bachelors* especially) what it is to be exiled for months; to long oh! so much! for one's dear *children*, one's wife, for work, friends & all that makes life worth living? here I lie on my 'Matratzen – Grüft', getting weaker every day; I can't go for walks, I can't write letters, I can't work; I cough & cough & cough & my lungs & my life disappear in big chunks. Day & night the Oh! *so* wearisome process continues. 'Pluck', 'patience' – Words, my masters! My poor wife & Bairns! My wife is trying desperately to get work to keep our Home together. In a month or two my salary will cease to be paid & I have to accept a 'Pension', Mr A.H.L. tells me. Have *you* ever faced such a pretty situation? I shall leave next week for Lippspringe.

Ever yours

A.J. Jaeger[8]

Don't be too hard on me

Taking the latter injunction to heart, Davies replied promptly, successfully negotiating the task of writing a morale-boosting response. Jaeger's fever lessened and once more he found new hope for a cure, this time through taking the waters at a Spa town. Davies received a postcard with the new address.

Davos
Monday 6/5/07

My dear Davies,

Many thanks for your Kind letter, which cheered me greatly. What a pity 'H Dumpty' couldn't be given! When I played it through I thought it was rather difficult not so much in the notes to sing, but in the taking up of cues, rapidity of action &c. I suppose they will give it next year? I'm sorry to hear Canon Gorton is ill. My Fever having abated somewhat & the weather being mild, I mean to leave Davos on Wednesday morning for Lippspringe. I shall go via Munich, & as I'm sure the long journey will exhaust me (I'm very weak) I shall very likely stay there a day or two (*not* in Bed, I do hope). My address in Lippspringe will be:
Dr Brackmann's Sanatorium
Lippspringe, Westfalen, Germany.
The move is quite a 'speculation', for I cannot of course say whether the waters at L. will do for me What they did for a cousin of mine, who was cured of the wretched disease. I live in Hopes, for I have still a fair fund of recuperative powers, I believe. Now I wonder (entre nous) what my Firm will do for me in the way of that promised 'pension'. Whether I can live on it, however humbly. I can never again work at N & Co.

Love!

Ever yours,

AJJ[9]

Correspondence with Dora Penny also continued. She confessed that she had begun to dread that Jaeger's health would never be better, and knowing how depressed and downhearted he could become, she set out to cheer him, continuing the rôle she had played in Elgar's life. ' If I could do nothing else for him I could at least write and tell him everything I could think of which might amuse him,' she wrote, 'and finding that it did so was reward in plenty.' Jaeger sent her a postcard from Lippspringe after one such letter. He had taken a timely opportunity while in Munich to hear the legendary Joachim, a direct link with Mendeslssohn, Liszt, Schumann and Brahms, and a frequent visitor to London over many decades. The elderly violinist would die a few months later.

Dr Brackmann's Sanatorium,
Lippspringe,
Westfalen.

18 April, 1907

Many thanks for your kind letter which has been forwarded to me at the above address, where I hope to stay for two months or so. I'm delighted to hear you feel well after your splendid Holiday. Strange! I very nearly went to the Italian Lakes. What a joke if we had met and Oh, what a surprise! I'm here to drink the waters which are supposed to do the lungs good. Nous verrons! I came via Munich, where I spent three days (& heard the Joachim quartet – poor Joachim. He really can't any longer.) I liked Munchen muchly & had a nice time, though quiet (very) naturally. When I'm allowed to by my Dr, I'll write you a letter. Meanwhile be a good child & send me the promised continuation of your delightful screed.

Ever yours,

NIMROD[10]

Back home in Hereford, Elgar was working at part-songs, another *Pomp and Circumstance* March, and the *Wand of Youth* pieces; there was no major project under way, and he wrote to Jaeger of his lack of interest in music and his preference for pipe, bicycle and countryside. Jaeger sent warm 50th birthday greetings at the beginning of June, and Alice responded carefully. Already there had been a further crisis for Jaeger, despite the new doctor and the new treatment.

> Edward is writing hard, so I am going to send a few lines & thank you for him (& myself) for yr. cards & all yr. good wishes for him on his birthday. You have written him such *beautiful* wishes in such beautiful words, it touches us very deeply.
>
> Your cards make our hearts ache to think you are still so unwell, & still having to stay in exile. We do trust & pray you are recovering from this attack which must have been so dreadfully anxious & trying for you & that the new Dr & treatment will soon have some good effect. *How* glad we should be for better accounts, I cannot tell & I am sure you know –[11]

Elgar added his own usual postscript, referring to the American performance of the Variations; 'how I did make "you" sound in Chicago ... I shed a tear over it.'

Jaeger returned to Muswell Hill during August, suffering after the fatigue of the journey. He would not go abroad again, and his retirement from Novello's was now an accomplished fact. The firm awarded him a pension and Isabella, well-prepared, took over the rôle of breadwinner for the extended family. Elgar met Jaeger at the London Three Choirs rehearsals on 5 September, and went on to conduct performances of *The Kingdom* at Cardiff and Leeds. At Cardiff he heard Parry's Symphonic Poem *The Vision of Life*, a setting of words written by the composer which summed up his series of idealistic ethical works, and recommended the work strongly to Jaeger. 'I say! that "Vision" of Parry's is *fine stuff* & the poem is literature: you *must* hear it some day,' he wrote in a very short letter, which he concluded with disarming honesty, 'This is only to bring my love – I've really nothing to say.' Parry himself sent Jaeger a copy of the *Vision* vocal score, and in a reply which had to be written over a period of several weeks, Jaeger offered criticism, focusing, as he so often seemed drawn to do, on the work's Coda. His critical faculties were languishing unused, and Novello's had not been keeping him in touch with new works.

37 Curzon Road,
Muswell Hill,
N.

14 Oct 07.

My dear Sir Hubert,

I was so delighted to receive your Kind letter, though I felt so strongly that you, most worried of men, should not have spent your precious time in writing it. I always have told you that I expect no reply to my screeds, or a Postcard at the utmost, if a reply is *necessary*, which was not the case in this instance. But I have learnt from you, that the busiest men always find time for a Kind thought & action. O si sic omnes! I have myself tried all my life – since I have been in a position to be able to help people – to act upon your principle, & I have followed your shining example, whenever possible, in the face of the greatest pressure. And I know that I have experienced much happiness afterwards from the thought that a Kind word or a helping hand at the right moment was appreciated. So I hope that you were not cross with me, at any rate, because I wrote to you about my having left Novellos.

For the copy of your 'Vision' my heartiest thanks. No, Novellos are *not* flooding me with their novelties. In fact, nobody there thought of me in connection with the new works written for the Festival, and published by them. Thus soon one is forgotten in these fast moving times! I did think & hope that *some*-one at N & Co would have remembered me & thought that I might like to see the Festival novelties in which they must have known I would be very much interested. But no such luck! Now I have 'protested', they have promised to think of me in future. I wonder how long that promise will be remembered.

Elgar had told me in a letter how splendid your new work is – music *and* words – '*they* are literature', Elgar wrote to me –. So far, as I have not been in a P.F. playing mood, – I have only studied the poem which *is* fine and after my own heart. We 'workers' owe you thanks for it.

18/X/7. I have now had a good go at the music and I am deeply impressed with it. It seems to me certainly one of the very finest of your works, though these are now so numerous that it is difficult to carry in one's Head a ready-made critical estimate of their value (– in one humble opinion) for comparison with any new work from your pen. But I have no doubt in my mind that the 'Vision' stands in the very front rank of the noble & elevating utterances with which you have enriched the realm of British thought. Strange!, playing the work through time after time, I have the feeling that the Coda (final Chorus) is not so convincing & upsoaring & 'crushing' as other final climaxes in others of your works of a similar nature. As if you had been driven to a 'hasty' End by lack of time. The End is there (page 106) long before I expect or want it, & the utmost summit of your accumulative powers, where one Knows: *there is no 'beyond'*, seems never reached. Am I a fool? I seem alone in this feeling, for the critics who heard the work are enthusiastic about the final chorus, & opinions seem wellnigh unanimous, that you have done little that is finer. Yet, since your 'form' is always to me so satisfying & astonishingly beyond cavil by clowns like unto me, that this time, when I feel *un*satisfied I ax myself the question I put above: Am I a fool & have I grown weak in intellect as well as in Body? I look forward to hearing the work somewhere, when I hope I shall get a truer, correcter impression of a masterpiece.

1/X1/0. Oh dear! Here I am still at it, finishing this screed. I called at the College one day when I felt comparatively well, but you had flown to Highnam, I was glad to hear, to get some rest. Since then I have had another relapse, into Fever & a week or so in Bed. Curse it! Now I'm as flabby & feel as weak as I have done any time these last 3 years.

I will not prolong this letter. I'd sooner destroy [it] & write another, shorter & more sensible one; but alas! I don't feel equal to that. So Kindly excuse my rambling rigmarole & *do* send me the 2 Suites for Vn & P.F., as you very Kindly suggested. I shall very much like to study them with Mme. Isabella.

I hope you feel refreshed, & better than you did when you wrote your letter from Leeds, for which once more heartiest thanks.

Now N.B: *This requires* NO *kind of answer*! So I BEG of you, don't carry the screed about with you, to let the thought of having to write to me worry your greatly troubled & worried mind. You have too much to do with your 1001 engagements & friends. PLEASE do not reply, or I shall feel guilty of having been yet another straw to break your brave back!

Send me the Suites & that will be sufficient answer. My wife & I send our Kindest regards, & I am as ever, yours devotedly & gratefully,

A.J. Jaeger.[12]

To help financially, Novello's agreed to buy Jaeger's copyright in his *Kingdom* analysis. In writing his grateful thanks to the firm's secretary, Henry Clayton, Jaeger felt well enough to ask to undertake some reviewing. He was under another new doctor but was continuing the Repelen regime of vegetarian diet, cold-water and air baths and open-air exercise. He was coughing but free of fever and characteristically optimistic, if now with the added, irrational hope of the tuberculous, the 'spes pthisica'.

37 Curzon Road,
Muswell Hill [,]
N.

Oct 16/07

Dear Mr Clayton,

I enclose Copyright-assignment & receipt for Cheque (£21) for the 'Kingdom' Analysis, and need hardly say, how greatly obliged I am once more for the Firm's largess [*sic*]. At the same time I do wish you would have allowed me to *prove* in the 'practical' way I proposed, *how* deeply grateful I am for all the firm have done for me.

It would have filled me with a sense of satisfaction & a certain 'pride'. But I suppose I must not indulge in such dreams; and when I make up my Bank Book (I have just finished doing so!) I have to come to the sad conclusion that perhaps such 'satisfaction' & 'pride' would be misplaced in a poor fellow like unto myself. So I will once more thank your Firm most sincerely for their Kindness. Candidly, I don't think the 'Kingdom' Analysis worth £21, especially after Elgar knocking it about in the way he did. But – comme vous voulez!

I certainly feel somewhat stronger [–] can take longer walks, eat heartier (vegetarian) meals, and enjoy my cold bath & subsequent air-bath (windows & door wide open) & exercise (wet & naked) more. But I still cough a good deal. But then my new doctor told me I should have to do that for some months yet – a cryptic utterance, which may mean anything! Well, I cough away & hope that's the right thing. I have no fever, sleep pretty well, on the whole & – hope on. Dum spiro spero.

I mean to call at No 160 [Wardour Street] one day soon & then I may perhaps have the pleasure of seeing you. And I hope I may find you in good Health.

Yours, very faithfully & gratefully

A.J. Jaeger[13]

My Dr wants me to do some light work at Home. Can't I do some reviewing for the M.T.?

Elgar, too, was helpful, insisting – against Jaeger's strong protest – on making over his own rights in all three of the analyses. Creatively there was little to engage him at this time, although Alfred Littleton, with whom Elgar was now dealing directly in Jaeger's absence from the firm and who had become something of a family friend, was asking him for a Marching Song, something it is difficult to imagine Jaeger doing. But the ripples of German nationalism were beginning to be felt even then, ultimately resulting in 'Der Tag', as Jaeger foresaw, although he did not live to see the Great War begin. Other projects under consideration were the final form of the piano *Allegro* he had composed for Fanny Davies some six years before, and a setting of O'Shaughnessy's poem *The Music Makers*. But Elgar was waiting for the stimulus of another winter in Italy, this time at Rome, where he arrived early in November.

Meanwhile, Jaeger had received the two Violin Suites that he had requested from Parry, one of them, the second in F major, dedicated to him. Once again a lengthy letter of thanks, interrupted by the onset of fever, took him several weeks to finish. In a heightened emotional state, he explored the Violin Suites, revealing in the process his intense personal responses to music. He found points of comparison between Parry's music and that of both Brahms and Wagner. Jaeger also took the opportunity to extol the melodic strength that he found in the orchestral works that Parry had largely abandoned with the E Minor Symphony of 1889, in favour of the long and unequal series of choral compositions that he had produced in response to festival commissions. He returned to the weaknesses of the finale of *The Vision of Life*, which Parry was now intending to revise, and related his involvement with the finale to *Gerontius*. If Parry's fresh examination of the *Vision* owed something to Jaeger's promptings, then so too perhaps did his return to instrumental music in the shape of the extensive recasting of his Fourth Symphony, and the composition of such works as the Symphonic Fantasia *1912* and the Symphonic Poem, *From Death to Life*.[14]

37 Curzon Road,
Muswell Hill,
N.

November? [*sic*] 1907

My dear Sir Hubert,

Very many thanks for your letter of the 9th and the 2 Suites. We have had a good 'go' at them & are delighted with both, *though* my P.F. technique is not equal to the demands made upon it by the dashing Scherzo, (Presto capriccioso) in the first Suite. I'm self-taught, hinc illae lachrymae! We expect Miss A. C. Fry at our House one day soon, & then I shall get something like an adequate performance. Meanwhile, I revel in such movements as my wife & I can play (of course my wife can play them all, but I'm rather handicapped). On the whole I prefer the second Suite & for that reason I am glad that you have so very kindly put your & my name on that. The two Slow movements are splendid, especially the second ('Retrospective'); and the middle section in 3/2 time is not only one of the most beautiful things you have ever uttered, but in mood, – deeply felt resignation or longing, most affecting. When I first played it, my heart opened out like a clenched fist under the impulse of a warm friendship or love welling up in the heart. (I know that Goethe uses a simile like this in a letter to Zelter, after he (Goethe) had listened to some good music at Carlsbad or Teplitz). I thought of Dante's famous lines:

'Nessun maggior dolore
che ricordarsi del tempo felice
nella miseria'

True, the prevailing note in this short & beautiful section is not sorrow; but then I have always held that in a musical reproduction of the mood of these lines there should be a perfect blending of the 'tempo felice' with the 'misericordia', thus producing the exquisite tenderness tinged with longing which I seem to recognize & which holds me enthralled in these lovely few Bars.

Your 'picture', when writing down this strain may have been something quite different; but I feel music very acutely & always 'feel', however vaguely, *some*thing of the composer's meaning, I *fancy*.

Of course it is dangerous work, this guessing at a composer's meaning, and one can 'come an awful cropper' as they say in the classics. By the way: as regards 'mood' (and slow tempo, – but in *nothing else*, –) your beautiful idea recalls to my memory the Coda of the slow movement of Brahms's third (it *is* the third, is it not?) P.F. Sonata:

(so much like the End of Hans Sachs's first monologue!)

I quote from memory, an *amateur's* memory! – so pardon any errors.

I see that the 'Musical Times' in reviewing (*such* a Review!) your Suites describes 'Retrospective' merely as a 'graceful' movement! Of all the futile, inadequate & silly epithets for such a movement! I fancy I know the 'gifted' writer of this 'Review' (& of the greater part of the paper). He *is* a fine Judge & no mistake. I asked N & Co to let me do some reviewing for the M.T. You see I'm conceited Enough to think that I am also a Judge), but I never received a reply to that request.

I cannot & must not go through the Suites piece by piece and bore you with my precious 'opinions'. They will be nothing to You, for an artist Knows full well the value of his work. But there is not a movement which has not given us great pleasure & a deep satisfaction, and more and more so as we play through them again & again (generally on Sunday afternoons.) There are pieces, like the 'Dialogue', which grow upon one with each fresh hearing & unfold new beauties to us.

By the way, I have often thought, dear Sir Hubert, and I think so again, after making the acquaintance of these two fine Suites, that you really reserve your most beautiful, *innermost*, deepest & tenderest thoughts for your instrumental compositions. I think of the 4 Symphonies – especially their Slow movements – and the classic breadth of the long-drawn melodies there to be found. *There* your muse has time or opportunity to 'expand' into long, spacious melodies & no restriction is placed on your imagination by 'words', which – since you never repeat a syllable – seem to me to put a bar in the way of your melos growing into the long melodies I love in your Symphonies &c. I do not forget the exceptions (e.g. 'O may we once again') which anyone Knowing your Choral works well could bring forth as arguments to refute my view.

By the way, you have surely written a piece of programme music in the 'Scherzo' (Presto capriccioso)? What is it all about? An exciting motor-ride with 'hoot' obbligato (and a Fine for 'furious driving' as the End??)

Dec 19/7 I wrote most of the above long ago, but was prevented by Fever from finishing the lengthy scrawl. I have indeed spent much time with that unwelcome companion in my Matratzengrüft. The weather – raw, clammy & in turns foggy & windy – has been much against me, and I feel rather 'so – so'. I go only for *very* short walks, if I go out at all.

And now I have to acknowledge the receipt of & thank you warmly for your letter of the 10th inst. How very Kind of you, & how like C.H.H.P. not to take umbrage at my remarks about the 'Vision of life!' That you think of recasting the finale is very interesting news, & I shall be looking forward anxiously to the new version. I fancy some of the (to me) unsatisfactory effect of the movement is due to the orchestral interludes which recur even up to the penultimate page of the Vocal Score. They seem to me to *cut into* the climax & spoil the accumulative strength of what should be the crowning glory & the convincing, inevitable 'final word' of a splendid work. May the Muses inspire you so happily that another such triumphant Final Chorus as that in 'Blest Pair of Sirens' will be the result. (I mean 'triumphant' in the sense that the composer triumphs over all difficulties, and writes *the* one, great, the only possible & convincing coda.)

Did I ever tell you how, in 1900, I had an awful fight with Elgar over the Finale to 'Gerontius', & that – though we nearly broke our Friendship – I caused him to *recast* that beautiful movement & write the famous passage (orchestral) suggesting the approach to the throne of the Almighty, & the frenzied outburst 'Take me away'. These *did not exist* in Elgar's M.S. I have a set of proofs of the original setting.[15] Very interesting *now*, but very dull, *I* thought. I have been a *cruel* (private) critic to Elgar ever since we have been friends, I fear.

My wife is now building up quite a nice teaching connection, chiefly singing, in Gloucester. We shall have to move there if she goes on! Will you *ever* find time to read all this? I hope the Xmas Holidays will give you some much needed rest & restore Your Health as much as ever you can. Forgive all this longwinded chat. We send heartiest Xmas greeting & I am, dear Sir Hubert, as ever, yours most sincerely & gratefully

A.J. Jaeger.[16]

Isabella's Gloucester teaching connection took up two days each week and had been found for her by Herbert Brewer, one of the many musicians who had been given opportunities through Jaeger's support at Novello's and the *Musical Times*. Her success would have cheered him during the rigours of a London winter, his first at home for some years. He was bound to stay indoors as much as possible, but would have been tempted to make a special effort to attend Wood's rehearsal of the first *Wand of Youth* Suite for its première at Queen's Hall on 14 December. The day before, Dora Penny had spent the afternoon with him, and wrote of it later,

> I was terribly sad and shocked at the change in him and it was a very great effort to me to forget it and try to be amusing and cheerful. I could not help realizing that the end was fast approaching. Dear 'Small German' (as he used to call himself), what a tragedy this was! Such a brilliant brain and such quick wit and understanding of people and things, such fine enthusiasm for genius, expressing itself in a torrent of words! I had to do my full share of talking that day though, as talking made him cough and it was a cough that shook him.[17]

Alice Elgar wrote from Rome to commiserate over London fogs and to describe her husband's explorations in the historic city. Jaeger's heart would have leapt when he read on to find that the composer was at last focusing on the Symphony, the work that he had wanted so much and asked for so many times, and awaited for nearly ten years now, ever since the 'Gordon' proposals. Earlier in June while working at the *Wand of Youth* pieces, Elgar had stumbled on what Alice described as a 'great beautiful' tune, which he would use as the motto-theme for the Symphony, his most extended abstract orchestral piece to date, and in that sense the greatest challenge he had faced, as both he and Jaeger knew. They both must have feared that it was by no means certain either that the work would be successfully achieved, or that Jaeger would live long enough to hear it. Alice wrote with determined reassurance, 'I TRUST you will hear the Symphony, yet, & many times.' Music alone might sustain Jaeger through his sufferings; the longed-for Elgar Symphony, above all, would offer him a future.

13 1908: The Road to Hell

Jaeger's leisure enabled him to indulge his love of correspondence – even if Isabella had sometimes to act as his amanuensis – and many letters of this period have survived. Sydney Loeb had continued his sympathetic interest, and the rapport between the two became such that this correspondence in particular was to prove a rich vehicle for many of Jaeger's most intimate thoughts about Elgar and the Symphony. Correspondence continued also with Walford Davies, the content of whose new song cycle *The Long Journey*, for bass voice and orchestra, came in for some criticism of a distinctly worldly-wise kind, although Jaeger seemed as determined as ever to bolster Davies's morale. He revealed fears that he was no longer fully in Elgar's confidence, and probed over his progress on the Symphony; Alice had written with news that Elgar had been unwell.

37 Curzon Road,
Muswell Hill,
N

5/2/8

My dear Davies

I see Parry has resigned his Oxford Professorship. Are you going to be a candidate for the Post? You are just the sort of man for it, (I nearly said the *only* man), or is a University Training with Knowledge of Greek &c a sine quâ non?[1]

I could not go to the Palace on Saturday. Too unwell. My cough is very bad just now. We *all* have had colds & mine settled in my chest – of course – with dire results I'm now choked with Bronchitis.

I say, you need never lack the feeling of *confidence in yourself.* I am sure – *more than ever now*, – that you will do great things in music. Your *imagination* seems to me to be expanding its wings splendidly lately, & your things have a beauty (first amongst the things making up that idea of 'beauty' I place *melodiousness*, & serenity & strength & fire that augurs for *splendid* work in the future[)]. Only *work* & don't '*sketch*' only as Elgar seems to be doing now. Its all 'sketches' with him & no finished work, I fear. I wonder *what* he is busy on. Hasn't he told you lately?

About your song cycle: It has struck me that I cant remember the subject of *Love* being referred to in the songs. Now Man's life without Love, which rules the world & is mightier than aught Else, *is no life*! Be your attitude towards la grande passion ever so 'platonic', you cannot surely write a long cycle dealing with life & *ignore* Love!? I should VERY much like to hear your views on this matter, & I'm VERY curious.

When are you coming again? I feel very lonely. Nobody has been for weeks (– except a few *ladies*.)[2]

Ever yours

(Excuse scrawl)

A.J. Jaeger[3]

Davies accepted the invitation, and played and sang *The Long Journey* to Jaeger. Once again there was eulogistic praise, with Brahms – whom Davies had met the year before his death – as the point of departure.

37 Curzon Road,
Muswell Hill,
N.

22/2/8

My dear Davies,

I'm still under the influence of your splendid songs. They are the finest thing you have done, I verily believe, & I can honestly say that nothing of the Kind (song cycle) that I have heard these many years has moved me so deeply, not since Brahms 'Four serious songs' touched me to the quick when I first listened to them. How long is that ago? Heavens! How time flies! I have *not* heard many of the cycles that have of late years made their appearance in public, but I fancy I may safely say that I doubt whether there was one amongst them possessing the qualities of delicacy, grace, strength, lightness of touch, melodiousness, deep pathos, dignity, exaltation &c &c (all made more wonderful by superb workmanship) that I admired in Yours. There is one remark I want to make; and seeing that I only listened to the songs once without reading music or words, you must not be cross or misjudge my motive, if I say aught foolish.

Thinking back & pondering over my 'sensations' as I listened to you I have an idea in my head, that the sudden dropping into the 'conversational' tone in 'Top of the Hill'[4] (As *I* walked &c) is perhaps an Error of judgement on your part. It struck me as peculiar this 'As *I* did this and that', as You sang it. I confess I forgot whether any of the other Songs have the same characteristics but I fancy they don't. (I except 'Sweet Joy'[5] which doesn't matter, coming as No 1 after the 'Prologue')

Think it over, whether 'Top of the Hill' isnt *de trop* in your Scheme & call me not a traitor. I *mean* well, as you Know.

Another thing: when you publish, print *2* final numbers, – (that sounds Irish) – I mean 2 versions of the final poem, one for the singers who *have* breath & voice left for your splendid coda!

Love & Devotion to you!

Ever yours

A.J.J.[6]

Early in April he wrote to Dora Penny, and she preserved an extract from the letter with items of musical interest, including a first mention of Jaeger's response to the part-songs that Elgar had composed in Rome, and his interest in Debussy's *Prélude à l'après-midi d'un Faune*. But there was also another pathetic expression of his feelings of exclusion from the Elgar circle, and his anxiety to know of work in progress.

One of the letters I did manage to write was to Elgar who sent me proofs of his five new part-songs, which I suppose you have seen by now? They are splendid, are they not? The first one, 'There is sweet music here' is an exquisite composition, a perfect Gem, a masterpiece worthy of E. at his best ... I wrote Ivor Atkins a card the other day asking about his programme for the (Worcester) Festival. He wants to do Debussy's 'Apres-midi d'un faune'! Oh! if the 50,000,000 Worcester parsons knew the lewd, impossible poem on which this music is built! There would be an outcry and a show of Holy Horror! Debussy is a thorough Décadent &, well, – he must be a pig to choose such a poem to be inspired. Music is coming to a fine pass to need such crutches to keep it going. All the same I like the piece – as music – very much.

I say, what *is* Elgar composing now? You, as Keeper of the Archives *must* know, surely. He never tells me now, the wretch. I am glad you are coming to London soon. Ja! I do hope you will come and see me. I will try if the weather will let me – to get a little stronger by then & so we can have a long chat.

Ta Ta. Very sincerely yours

A.J. Jaeger.[7]

Later that month Jaeger heard from Sydney Loeb, and replied with a frank account of himself. Various matters musical engaged his attention, including the Elgar part-songs and a recent performance of *Gerontius* under Wood, who continued the subject of Jaeger's suspicion. He was open about his anxieties over Elgar's ability to succeed in symphonic writing, and frank too over the terms in which he had written to hurry along the completion of the work. Jaeger knew that for him it was a race against time.

37 Curzon Road,
Muswell Hill, N.

13/4/8

My dear Loeb,

I *was* surprised at hearing from you. I haven't seen you, have I? since I dined at your House, years ago. I have been ill ever since & have had to leave Novello's, alas! & am now compelled to live on a small pension which they very Kindly granted me. I am quite unfit for work, & Heaven only Knows, whether I shall ever be about again: I doubt it, though my Dr promises me things at which I, who Knows the ways of Doctors, smile. Tomorrow I shall go for a much needed change to Exeter, where I shall stay with some Kind friends who, I Know, will look after me well. I can no longer afford Switzerland, much less a warm climate (Egypt, Riviera) Even the '*English* Riviera' is beyond my means now; So I am very glad of this chance of getting a change of air, surroundings, Diet &c. I haven't been to a London concert for years, it seems to me. The last one I attended was at *Munich*, last June, on my way back from Davos, when I heard the *Joachim* quartet for the last time (it must have been one of the grand old man's last appearances in public. He played frightfully out of tune, poor old thing).

What you write about Gerontius under Wood interests me greatly [.] I *did* so want to be there, but couldn't! Did you see Baughan's fierce onslaught on Senius & Culp (especially the Roosian Tenor) in this mng's Daily News? He is quite right: if these Foreigners can't pronounce English, they should not be engaged. It's an insult to Newman's memory, and to *Elgar*![8] But the way of Conductors who are also singing Teachers at £2.2.0. a lesson is passing strange – no! – wonderfully opportunist & commercial! (Entre nous! I MAY be wrong!) But what reason can there be, unless it is a question of £.s.d? I should like to read Wood's explanation. *Do* get the D.N.!

Yes! Gerontius wears well & it will want some beating yet! I saw Professor J. Buths in Düsseldorf shortly after he had heard the Yorkshire Chorus perform the oratorio at Cologne under Coward. He (Buths) said to me: 'Ja, Herr J, Gerontius mit doch ein *einzig* schönen Werk'. That's it, *uniquely beautiful*! Elgar has just composed five very striking partsongs (I have the proofs by me). One, an 8 part setting of Tennyson's 'There is sweet music here' is a perfect *gem*, a little masterpiece, an inspiration. It has the peculiarity that it's written in two keys. The 4 female sections sing in *Ab*, & the 4 male sections in G. The effect is lovely. The whole piece is pp & ppp, light as gossamer & ravishing to the ear when performed *well* (it's difficult), I am sure. *Do* get these things if you are interested. There is a weird, quite uncanny piece amongst them called 'Owls', an Epitaph; *most* original & strange. A setting of Byron's 'Deep in my soul the tender secret dwells' is quite beautiful, & most expressive.

I am always worrying E. to do more. He wont reply, but Lady E. wrote to me some 2 months ago, that the long-delayed Symphony, which I worried him about once more, & which I said I wanted to hear ere I died, would be heard by me many times yet, she hoped. So *perhaps* he is really at work on it. It is about time. But I fancy he must be sketching or getting ideas for the *third* 'Apostles' oratorio, to complete the Trilogy. He cant get out of that. And as it means *Cash* (from the B'ham Festival Committee) I fancy *that* work will tempt him more than the Symphony. But there is no guessing what E. may be doing. He is in *Rome*. That place ought to in[spire] him.

I must close, for I must pack my trunk. My address for the next few weeks will be

A J.J.
at Southcroft,
Heavitree Road,
Exeter.

I send my Kindest regards & am

Yours very sincerely,

A.J. Jaeger.[9]

P.S. Both W.H. Bell & H Walford Davies have written to me within a week, that they mean to write a Symphony each, as a sort of protest against the everlasting 'Symphonic Poem'. I hope they will do something good & big. It *would* be funny if Elgar's work came out about the same time & I fear the interest taken in *his* work rather [*sic*] Kill the others – at least for a time. Somehow I *fear* lest E is *not* at his best in the Symphonic Form.

A.J.J.

A week later, comfortably established with his old friends the Boundys at Exeter, Jaeger wrote again to thank Parry, whose financial generosity had not ceased. As a result of his own recent breakdown, Parry had again been sent abroad in order to create a break from his routine of overwork. After a spell cruising round the Mediterranean, he had returned to England at the beginning of April and, against medical advice, was preparing to resume his duties at the College in May. Aghast at the news, Jaeger wrote outspokenly and persuasively to dissuade him, putting his finger on the conflict between the private and the public Parry which had bedevilled his health – and the quality of his output as a composer – for many years. The letter concluded with a calm and realistic assessment of Jaeger's own future; now, in addition to the coughing, weight loss and fever associated with tuberculosis, the strain was beginning to tell on his heart.

'Southcroft'
Heavitree Road,
Exeter.
(Miss Kate Boundy's Home!)

20/4/8.

My dear Sir Hubert,

It is a long time since I felt such a thrill of happiness & Expectation as when I saw your handwriting on the Envelope the maid handed to me last night. I have so many times been tempted to write to you & enquire how you were. Mr Graves & Mr Brewer Kept me informed to a certain extent and I understood that You must not write or receive letters. So I kept 'mum', hoping greatly that I might hear good news about your Health. But nothing has filtered through my channels lately. Hence my delight on recognizing your handwriting. Now I had wished & hoped your news about yourself might be better than it seems. I am so sorry your stay at Taormina has not resulted in greater benefits to your precious health, & I am quite concerned when I read that at the End of this month you will go back to the College & 'face it out if you can'. I am sure all your multitudinous friends & admirers do wish you would let the College *go to the D* – & that you would look after yourself & the prolongation of your life, a life splendidly spent & filled with sufficient first-rate & unequalled work to 'adorn' half a dozen ordinary men's existences. You have done *enough* work, dear Sir Hubert, – enough of the College Drudgery, the 'presiding' at innumerable Dinners & meetings, the speechmaking & advice & encouragement-giving, the bracing up & cheering of *other* people. Do rest on your laurels, and devote yourself to composition only, within such bounds as your Doctors prescribe. What the College & your 1001 Societies & Associations may lose by your partial retirement, the great, general music-loving public & England, & the world of music will gain. It is the everlasting 'rush', the working against time, the sweat & anxiety of getting your compositions ready 'in time' for this & that fixed date, that plays such havoc with your health. *Do* halt; do be *content* with less work & honour & – I do not know of course whether that counts with you? – with less income, for your own your Family's & your many friends' sake, who love you if ever a man was truly *loved* by his fellows. Why *risk* another relapse? Do not give your heart a *chance* of playing pranks again. But there, is it quite useless imploring you?

From all I have heard, the R.C.M. is, thanks to your administration, in such a position, that your retirement cannot affect it – except, of course, that the loss of your commanding personality & your matchless Brains & all that makes for artistic nobility of thought & life cannot be made good. But when you have retired to lovely Highnam Court & feel content in the production of new, serene, & lofty big works, the memory of your influence will be sweet & evergreen at the College. A good, great man's shining example does not cease to work for good because he is compelled, by ill health, to leave the scene of his labour.

I Know how *fearfully* difficult it is, for a man used to a busy life, to retire & lie fallow. I am but a nobody, a mere fly on the wheel of musical life; but I felt I must go mad when I first came to Davos, & was made to lie down for days *without being allowed to do a* THING. My dear Sir Hubert, by forcing my nerves into a quiet 'mood', because I *wanted* to get better, I gradually got used to the *awfully* lazy life & now, though I still protest occasionally, I can be content without the bustle & excitement & the happy *and* anxious Hours at Novellos. And, believe me, you, though your life has a thousand interests where I have one, you will get used to the quiet & calm of the retirement which your Health *Demands.* Life does not cease to be sweet & full of interest because worry & sweat & fifty thousand anxieties have gone out of it. You of all persons, will enjoy it to the utmost, if in a different way from that of the last 20 years; your wonderful Brain, your matchless animal spirits will keep you going, never fear. I am sure you won't mind my preaching at you like this. You won't think it impertinent, I hope, for I feel most deeply what I write & that thought of you going back to the R.C.M. WORRIES me.

Your letter, dear Sir Hubert, affected me greatly. Illness may have made me 'soft', I don't know; But I do Know that concern about your Health *and* the proof of your exceeding Kindness to me, & your enquiry about my state & your generous gift brought tears into my eyes. I don't know how to thank you sufficiently & I ask myself again, as I have done before when you have helped me, 'Why?' & 'What have I done to deserve it?' I thank you from the bottom of my Heart, dear Sir Hubert, & can only assure you that your Cheque will *help us* splendidly & is most welcome & opportune. When I discovered at the end of last quarter that we had spent more than we had 'earned' – and in spite of strictest economy at Home, – my Heart sank into my Boots. Your gift will make up the deficit & much more, and with my wife's brave & so far fairly successful attempt to earn money by teaching (Vn. & Singing) & playing in Brewer's orchestra we may Keep things going in a way. I Know we ought to move into a smaller, cheaper House, but in the winter I felt so wretched that the *thought* of a 'move' upset me. Dr Brewer & Mrs Brewer have been & are MOST Kind to my wife & help all they can. Br. like yourself, has been a true friend 'in need', because he helped her to *work.*

You ask how I am. Well, since I have been down here, I feel rather better. The change, offered (& gratefully accepted by me) by Kind friends, has done me good & I shall return to Muswell Hill on Friday next in better spirits than I have 'enjoyed' for months. But I still cough a good deal, have fever nearly every day, am generally weak & unable to take more than a *little* exercise and, worst of all, my heart has of late played the fool with me. I get *bad* palpitations occasionally, which leave me quite limp afterwards. As my Heart has never troubled me before, I don't appreciate this change for the worse. Since I have been here I have worked a little (writing for the 'Musical Times') & *that* has put more 'Heart' (of the *right* sort) into me than all Dr's medicines & stuff. Talking of medicines & stuff, it is *they*, which make my expenses run up so. My Dr made me buy patent food-preparations (to keep up my weight) which cost me, plus the medicines, about 10/- a *week*! I simply could *not* afford that, so let the patent foods go hang, except one.

I have no idea what the near future may bring, good or bad. But I live in no fool's paradise & Know well enough what is before me as regards my *Health.* My disease goes steadily on, & soon there will be no more to cough up. I have days when I feel fairly well & then I enjoy life, & friends come to see me & we talk & make music & if I am as 'well' as I've felt here *occasionally*, I may venture into London one day soon & re-visit my old Haunts & Perhaps I may be able to travel to the R.C.M. to try & see you! That would rejoice my Heart! My devotion & gratitude I send to you, dear Sir Hubert & all good wishes for your Health.

Ever sincerely yours,

A.J. Jaeger.[10]

Jaeger had also been keeping in touch with one of Elgar's American admirers, Professor Sanford's friend, Julia Worthington. The Elgars first met her during the

American visit of 1905, and subsequently she had attended various Three Choirs rehearsals and concerts where she would have encountered Jaeger. He seemed to know her well enough by this time to confide his anxiety about Elgar's apparent lack of progress on the Symphony, an anxiety which Mrs Worthington passed on to the composer himself. Jaeger had written Elgar a lengthy letter about the part-songs – which had gone unanswered – in preparation for a major critical review which he would offer to the *Musical Times*. He sent a reminder, and was rewarded with a long, intimate letter in the old style, dealing fully with various points over the songs and including reasons for the Symphony's non-appearance which might appear special pleading. It was the first written communication to Jaeger since a note enclosed with a letter of Alice's the previous December, and was the longest letter he had written to Jaeger for some years.

Rome

Ap 26 1908

My dearest Nimrod: Your very welcome p.c. has just arrived & I hasten to send the reply you ask for. I was delighted to receive your last jolly long letter & should have written in answer to that but – my hand *jumps* when I write as you will see from this letter & I avoid writing as much as I can – sort of cramp & rheumatism mixed. I am *so* glad you are writing some notes & reviews & that you take pleasure in it.

... Now I have made a sort of name by writing some big things & can only get *commissions* to write rot – ah! & a! I must *talk* to you some day about my avoiding work on great things – I have too many people *now* alas! (& the clog gets heavier every day) to allow me to think of anything I would wish to do: it is painful but it is the only reward I get: I say this because I saw a portion of the letter you sent to Mrs W. – More of this when we meet.

... You are an old gooooose to think (Mrs W's letter) that I was annoyed: I am only somewhat heartbroken; I cannot afford to get a *quiet* studio where I might have worked & my whole winter has been wasted for the want of a few more pounds: it seems odd that any rapscallion of a painter can find a place for his 'genius' to work in when a poor devil like me who after all *has* done something shd. find himself in a hell of a noise & no possible escape! I resent it bitterly but can do nothing. It is just the same now at Hereford, noise has developed in the neighbourhood – I dodged it doing the Kingdom at great expense by going to Wales but I can't do it again: my lovely works do not pay the rent of a studio!

Much love to you & great rejoicing that you are having a change.

Yours ever

E.E.[11]

A few days earlier, Elgar had written to Ivor Atkins in much the same vein. Rome had indeed proved noisy, with unwelcome sounds of pianos near the flat that had been taken in the Via Gregoriana, and he had neglected the Symphony for the part-songs, together, after much persuasion, with a *Marching Song* commissioned by the Worshipful Company of Musicians and shortly to be given its first performance at an Albert Hall Empire Day Concert.

Jaeger, realistically facing sterner difficulties than these, stoically began to put his affairs in order.

> THIS IS THE LAST WILL AND TESTAMENT of me AUGUST JOHANN JAEGER of 37 Curzon Road Muswell Hill. I hereby revoke all wills and testamentary instruments heretofore by me made. I appoint John Blackwood McEwen of The Doon, Pinner, and William Henry Bell of 'Senwick', Radlett Park, Radlett, Hertfordshire, to be the EXECUTORS of this my will. I direct my executors to pay my just debts and funeral and testamentary expenses. I give and bequeath to my wife Isabella Jaeger Everything of which I may be possessed at the time of my decease.
>
> WITNESS my hand this twenty-first day of May one thousand nine hundred and eight (1908)
>
> AUGUST JOHANN JAEGER
>
> Signed by the above named testator as his last will in the presence of us both being present at the same time who in his presence and the presence of each other have hereunto subscribed our names as witnesses
>
> GEO L BOUNDY Merchant Exeter
>
> W.G. BOUNDY 'Southcroft' Heavitree Rd Exeter

Elgar, too, was making preparations. A few weeks later, on 3 June, the day after his birthday, he sketched a song *In Memoriam – In memory of a Seer.*[12] The words were left as fragmentary as the music in the sketch, and it has not so far proved possible to identify the poem from which they were taken; it seems to begin 'Silence and sorrow'. But Elgar's inability to confront the now inevitable annihilation of his intimate friend and mentor, together perhaps with a degree of the kind of guilt which he would know in the wake of his wife's death, affected even such musical promptings and the song was never completed. It would be some years before he could contemplate a direct musical reference to Jaeger, and that through the *Nimrod* persona. But that very day he wrote to Jaeger, repeating creative and financial frustration with bitter harshness; it might be an echo of the complex of strong feelings behind the earlier 'enigma'. The concluding Oratorio would be abandoned, and there was no mention of the Symphony.

> ... here it is very lovely but too suffocatingly *stuffy*. I can't write – there are too many other composers singing their own or traditional compositions loudly on every bush ...
> I can only write sadly about myself – I have done some good work in my life & now I can only get orders (which will keep my people in necessaries) for rot of kinds & I *must* do it. I have no intention of completing my oratorio cycle or whatever it is – I am not allowed to beg a dispensation of a benevolent providence who objects to the world being saved or purified or improved by a mere musician. Of course I have the thing – the biggest of all sketched – but I cannot afford for the sake of others to waste any time on it. Alas!
>
> Well: I am well & strong except my eyes & must be thankful to be allowed to breathe somebody else's air I suppose & walk on somebody else's roads – but I am not thankful at all.
>
> What an object lesson is poor dear Madam Albani: one of the best of women: she has sung to these delightful English their own *oratorios* & sacred things for years. – her husband loses all their money – she has to advertise for pupils! Now look at a battered old w-e like

Melba & Co: – !!! My beloved countrymen and women wd. & will subscribe anything to keep her if necessary – it makes ones blood boil – where is providence? NOTHING[13]

It was a letter that caused Jaeger, in his own words, to 'explode.'

Fired up over Elgar's music as he had not been for a long time, Jaeger had been investing his formidable perceptiveness and commitment in producing a review of the new part-songs for the *Musical Times*, but, ominously, its publication had been delayed. Elgar commiserated, and Jaeger sent a copy. Its full title was 'Sir Edward Elgar's New Part Songs, with some remarks on his vocal writing in general', and it was the sub-title that enabled Jaeger to come to Elgar's defence. Beginning with an expression of disappointment over Elgar's recent lack of production, Jaeger went on to extol the achievement of the part-songs in the highest terms, with a warning over the unconventional nature of the vocal writing.

He discussed each song in eulogistic terms, concentrating on expression and interpretation. *There Is Sweet Music* he thought 'one of the loveliest and most remarkable things that modern art can show. *Deep In My Soul* Jaeger described as a 'deeply affecting musical setting'. He gave encouragement to choirs to tackle the difficulties of *O Wild West Wind*, and offered direct exhortation over the unusual *Owls, An Epitaph*: 'Look at the printed pages … study them, and the musician's art … will both delight and impress you.' Finally, he gave the separate number, *The Reveille*, a full and vivid treatment. The whole article, despite its predictable enthusiasm, was a considered and detailed piece of writing, produced free from the constraints of Berners Street deadlines. Considering, too, that Jaeger had not heard a note of the songs in performance, it was a masterpiece of imaginative projection as well as Elgar propaganda.[14] It was Alice who responded, paying tribute to Jaeger's insight and defining his rôle as intermediary between her husband and the public. She hinted too that Elgar was deeply occupied in composition.

I must be allowed to send you a few lines to tell you how immensely I appreciate your beautiful & valuable article on Edward's pt. Songs.

You have shown such true insight into their depth of meaning & so truly recognize all their wonderful, poetic atmosphere like a *true* interpreter. Such an interpreter is a necessity between the genius & the outer world; the thoughts of a genius are always in advance of the ordinary world's understanding, & intense gratitude is due to the one who can see the new & beautiful thing offered to the people & reveal it to their more slowly perceiving eyes.

Everything that you have said is so absoloutely true & it is a record of the capability & mind of the Composer – Any curtailing would be a very great disappointment.

Edward is so absorbed in some work (I trust you will hear some day) that I know you will understand the delay in his reply to your letter …[15]

Jaeger replied by return of post; the lengthy letter and the attendance at a London concert which it mentions, taken together with the production of the part-songs article, seems to show that he had regained some of his old emotional and physical energy, even if only temporarily. Such an upsurge of vitality could be characteristic of the later stages of tubercular illness, and it enabled Jaeger to make his last great effort of many on behalf of Elgar and his music. He certainly had not lost his blazing faith in 'heart-music' and with the Symphony no doubt consistently on his mind, the letter is perhaps one of the greatest of his inspirational efforts. Jaeger revealed too his anxieties over Elgar's reaction to the now lost letter which contained the 'explosion', and his anger with F.G. Edwards; even now, the *Musical Times* editor was insisting that the part-songs article be cut for publication.

37 Curzon Road,
Muswell Hill
N

13/6/8

Dear Lady Elgar,

I am greatly obliged for your kind words respecting my article & very glad that you like it. You are of course quite right in saying that an 'interpreter' is generally needed between genius & the public, & it is because I feel the truth of this so much, & fear that there will be comparatively few conductors or singers who will appreciate those partsongs at their *real* worth, that I wrote what you have read. For I fancy I *can* get right at the heart of E's works & realize from the printed note what the effect of a PERFECT performance (none other must be taken into account) must be. These pieces are so much more than stereotyped partsongs. They are wonders, pieces of E's very being, of his heart & soul.

I thought my 'interpretations' would be welcomed by amateurs & conductors, & especially by the *M.T.* But I'm told I 'must not give a chance to scoffers'! Did 'scoffers' undo me (or E. for that matter) over my 'Gerontius' analysis in 1900? If there were scoffers, they must feel supremely silly now, because they failed to appreciate E's wonderful work & tried to make me look a fool. I didn't mind & I laugh at them now.

What annoys me is this,: that after being a writer for the M.T. for some 16 years & having done some of the best critical & analytical work for the paper; after all my successes in hailing new composers, conductors, &c with Enthusiasm, I am still treated like a novice who wants careful Editing. And I'm truly surprised that dear, kind Mr A.H.L lets that old fogey of an Editor persuade him into agreeing with him. I feel more & more that it's futile offering now good work to the M.T.

However, the 'stuff' must be boiled down, as I have marked it, and you see from enclosed (which please destroy) that Mr E[dwards] wants my 'copy' at once!

I hope E. is not cross with me – I wrote my letter in quite a fever & you know I would not 'explode' as I did if I were not such a 'ridiculous' admirer of & believer in E's gifts, & wanted not to see him *the* composer of the day, *the* deliverer of messages such as no other composer has the genius (& the *heart & soul*) to conceive. E. MUST be great in his works, & great in his contempt of the world which may not repay him his due.

I went to a Philharmonic (Beecham) concert this afternoon – the first concert I have been to for years. I heard Delius's 'Appalachia' a typical example, I take it, of the crazy 'colour' school. Well, D. is a genius in his way, & I heard sounds from the orchestra such [as] I have never heard before. Some of the Scoring is perfectly marvellous, I fancy; but – apart from the length of the thing (*70* minutes) which is impressive, or oppressive, there is nothing to remember, nothing to dwell over, nothing to take to your heart & hug. Colour, Colour, colour, awful Harmonies, a vulgar nigger tune varied in a number of impertinently long sections. no melodic ideas, only colour & Harmony. And 70 minutes of it! I met some friends afterwards & ventured the opinion that the first great *melodist* coming along will sweep the Whole colour-school into the Sea of forgotten failures. The Human race wont alter its hearing apparatus within a few years, nor its primitive love of *rhythmical tune.* That the great melodist must be a colourist also seems true, for the charm of colour such as E & Delius have on their palettes is great & undeniable.

I fancy E will develop more & more as a strong, original melodist, & see his special mission in that direction. Colour & Harmony can never move us & lift us out of ourselves (Delius would have done that with his stuff this afternoon if it were possible). But finely presented noble tune will go to the Hearts of all, now & always.

To me E. has only begun his career as a *great* man, as a genius. Excepting, say, the prologue to 'King Olaf' (one of the finest things I know), his early works (before Gerontius) do not sound the note of *Genius*. Gerontius & the 2 oratorios are full of it. So I look forward to E's future with high hopes. He will grow stronger & stronger, more original & beautiful, more melodious, & more inventive in Colour, Harmony & Form with every passing year. He will be *the* great melodist, & hence *the* great composer for the world's *need* of *Heart*-music. I have heard Delius; I am more than ever an upholder of the Banner of Edward Elgar as *the man of the times*.

Sincerely yours,

A.J.J.[16]

The Elgars had a copy of Jaeger's article made, in Alice's words, 'for its joy & its great value … it is not lost'. She thanked Jaeger for his 'beautiful' letter and went on to suggest that he find another journal which would publish the article in full. She felt sure that Julia Worthington – who was intending to visit Jaeger – would have it published in the New York Review. But most heartening of all must have been the long-awaited news that Elgar had now resumed work on the Symphony, for Alice concluded, 'E. sends his love, you have heard from him by now, & he wants to say to you the Sym is A1 [:] it is *gorgeous*, steeped in beauty, he is quite absorbed in it.' Elgar had recently sent Jaeger a cheque in respect of the analyses royalties; apologizing again for not writing at length, he wrote 'I can't answer your letter at this moment. I can't say I have anything more *important* to do, but it must be done & done now. Oh! such a tune[.]' The composition and scoring of the work now occupied Elgar intensively until the end of September. He reluctantly spent a few days in London at the beginning of July for a meeting of the Musical League, and played work in progress to Frank Schuster. He wrote to Walford Davies, 'I hoped to have seen Jaeger but it was not possible when I was in town: I feel he is better.' Davies was intending to visit and offered to send news, but Elgar made amends in mid-August. While he was staying at the Langham Hotel after conducting his music at Ostend, he made the journey to Muswell Hill in a hired car. Alice recorded the visit in her diary; it may well have been the last meeting between the two men. Certainly there seems to be no documentary evidence that Elgar visited Jaeger at Curzon Road on any later occasion.

Jaeger was continuing with the 'air-bath' regime, but he was becoming physically weaker, and sheer exhaustion made him abandon a planned visit to Parry. Instead he wrote his gratitude for past help together with concern over the older man's own precarious health; and he repeated his intense feelings over the inevitable detachment from musical life which he was continuing to experience. But if F.G. Edwards had made matters worse by his inflexibility, a greater man showed understanding, when Hans Richter gave him a rehearsal pass.

37, Curzon Road,
Muswell Hill,
London,
N.

29/8/8.

My dear Sir Hubert,

I have been on the road to H–ll for a long time, & if I haven't got there yet it is not due to any particular virtue developed, nor to any good deeds done in the meantime. My 'good intentions' were to go to the R.C.M. one day while you were in town, just to say 'Good Day' & see for myself How you were, and to thank you once more for all your Kindness to me.

But I had to combine in my infrequent visits to London all the 'calls' I could think of, such as at the Bank, Novellos, the Tailor's, the Doctor's &c, and when I was about half through my list of 'appointments', by which time the afternoon had been reached, I was always so done-up, that I had to make for Home & my chaise-longue, on which I take the open-air cure that is supposed to help me. And so, Prince Consort Road being so far away, it came about that I could not carry out my intention.

Last week I was at Novellos & heard from Mr May that you had returned from your 'yachting trip'. I hope sincerely that it has done you good, as usual, & that you feel really well. I read some months ago of the Prince of Wales's speech at a meeting of the R.C.M. Council (or whatever it was) when he congratulated you on your being 'restored to Health'. I hoped then, & hope now that the remark stated the truth & that you are *fully* restored to man's prime possession, to lose which reduces us all to pessimists, not to say misanthropes.

I have *three* times tried to procure a copy of your Worcester work, but in vain; it was 'not yet ready'. I had hoped they would ask me to write an (advance) review of the piece, as I did so often in years gone by. But no such luck; and as I had lately been quarrelling with the Editor about another thing I wrote, I did not want to *ask* for the little job.

Perhaps Mr May will send me a copy to-day, so that I may play through it before I go to the Rehearsal, as I want to do if I feel well enough (I have been far from well the last fortnight).

I am glad to see that the London Symphony Orchestra will do your fine Variations. Good! May I be well enough to go at least to the Rehearsal. (Dr H. Richter has given me special leave to come whenever I like).

I do feel being 'out of' things musical most dreadfully. It is an appalling sensation this Knowledge that one is thrown on the scrap-heap. I often wish it were all over! But I must clutch at every straw for my dear ones' sake.

Now, dear Sir Hubert, do *not* waste any of your rest in writing to me. I *hope* to see you next week, if only for a few seconds, & may I find you quite well & jolly.

With my Kindest regards,

I am ever yours devotedly and gratefully,

A.J. Jaeger.[17]

Parry sent a copy of his Worcester Festival work, *Beyond These Voices There Is Peace,* and at the beginning of September Jaeger managed to take himself to the rehearsals at the Queen's Hall, where he would have heard parts of *Gerontius* and *The Kingdom* as well as the second *Wand of Youth* Suite. The experience, an emotional one for Jaeger, was greatly welcome, despite the depredations of an erratic singer. It called forth another deeply felt letter which repeated Jaeger's view of the ethical value of music, alongside a romantic view of the lonely artist. There was also a vision of Elgar's creative future.

37 Curzon Road,
Muswell Hill

3/9/8

My dear Edward,

I had a happy day to-day, for I heard once more, after many months' starving, some *music.* Your works struck me with *all the force* I felt years ago, when I studied them & I was as deeply moved (Tilly K. notwithstanding) as ever. I shed a few happy, silent tears over so much beauty & my whole being was thrilled, elevated & purified & braced up. I feel morally & physically better for having heard your music, & I thank you. It was a wonderful experience, after many months in the Desert, to drink those refreshing, strengthening draughts of divine water of Healing.

Do let us have that third oratorio directly you have completed your Symphony. You owe it to us who *do* appreciate your genius fully & to whom your music *is* an inspiration and a moving power & the 'most beautiful of God's revelations' (Goethe). If we are only a few hundred or thousand to-day, be sure that we shall number *all* genuine music lovers in days to come.

Your works are too new, too original, too great to be appreciated by the average amateur or musician straightaway. Be happy that you made so many converts in so few years. And fear no rival! Your music has a greatness of conception & ideality & an *ethical value* possessed by the work of *no* living composer I know of. You are unique, a single & perhaps sometimes rather lonely wanderer in Elysian fields & on Olympian heights, yet surrounded by the love & admiration of many, many genuine 'disciples'. Go on, & give us more. Never cease. Be sure that the Best that is in you is just good enough for us greedy, starving enthusiasts. Make *no pause* when the Symphony is finished. By that time you should just be in the *right mood & trim to go on* with Part III of your sacred Trilogy.

Gluck auf!! and may you be helped in your work by the love of your friends, including

Your old Nimrod.[18]

Ivor Atkins kindly invited the Jaegers to stay for the Festival, but it was out of the question for the sick man to accept. The Elgars' house party at the King's School House – suitably equipped with rattles and toy drums to make up for the lack of servants' bells – included their old friends the Kilburns, Frank Schuster, Pippa Worthington, Lady Maud Warrender and others, and the week was made particularly memorable by the popular 'hit' scored by the 'bear' movements from the *Wand of Youth.* After the week was over, Elgar responded to Jaeger's letter, beginning with 'we *did* want you at Worcester & were a learned party'; Jaeger, who had received messages from various of its members, noted sadly in the margin, 'this is no doubt wrote sarcastic as I know they were a very *jolly* party'. But Elgar went on to discuss the Symphony in terms of its harmonic procedures, again paying Jaeger the compliment of being, in Dora Penny's words, 'the only musician with whom Elgar discussed his work in technical detail' and writing out some chord progressions for the sick man to play at the piano.

Jaeger had been taking the opportunity – at some cost to himself – to collect proofs of Elgar's Symphony from Novello's during his London visits, but he was not yet prepared to offer comment on the work to Sydney Loeb, to whom he wrote a letter of thanks for some photographs of his father-in-law Hans Richter, together with a proposal for a visit.

37 Curzon Road
Muswell Hill N.

6/X/8

My dear Loeb,

I must apologise for procrastinating over my acknowledgement of the two Richter portraits you so Kindly sent me from Bayreuth & Home. I would have written to You in the Franconian Mecca if I hadnt feared that you would have left it before my screed could reach you. And the delay over saying 'thank you' for the Summer – undress – picture of the dear, great Hans (which I was delighted to get, believe me), is due to the fact that I have had another bout with illness & have only just got out of Bed, where I was Kept for over a week. My heart went wrong after I had ventured on a journey to London (chiefly to Novellos) & rather overtired myself. I dont want any more heart attacks of that sort; the pain was excruciating. I find I have to lead a *very* quiet life & must never exert myself. It's dreadful, but there's nothing for it but to bear it & say 'Kismet' (and D—!)

You lucky man, to have the Health, Enthusiasm & means to go to Bayreuth! I have the second still, but the other necessaries are sadly lacking. I fear I shant even be able to go Manchester, to hear the first performance of Elgar's Symphony. Naughty Dr R. not to 'produce' it (Nr – Süffühing) in London, as I had hoped.

I have studied the proof of the first three movements of the work & hope to see those of the finale soon, if I'm well enough to call at Novellos. I heard 'Gerontius' & 'The Kingdom' at the London Rehearsals & was as much & as deeply stirred as when I studied these works years ago. That Gerontius after 8 years' intimate acquaintance with its every note should still move an old stager like me, (who might well be blasé by this time) is a powerful proof of the greatness of the work. As for 'The Kingdom', there are *wonderful* things in it, but it lacks the continuity of 'story' of Gerontius. The Finale to Part 1 & the End are glorious.[19]

I had been invited with my wife to stay with the Atkins' for the Gloucester [*sic*] festival, but considerations of Health & 'wealth' made me decide against the Kind proposal. I received several Kind messages during the Festival saying 'we miss you very much'. Nice of my many friends to say say, [*sic*] but – !

Why don't you come & pay me a visit one day in our modest, humble Tusculum on the Muswell Hill. I could show you some interesting Elgariana. But let me Know beforehand, in case I should be too ill to receive anybody, in which case I would write to you. Sunday, Saturday & Tuesday are our best days, as my wife is in Gloucester Wednesday & Thursdays & in London on Mondays.

With Kindest regards,

Ever sincerely yours

A.J. Jaeger.[20]

Walford Davies was also encouraged to visit the increasingly house-bound Jaeger, now facing the prospect of winter. He was happy to engage in some gossip over the *In the South* Overture, repeating his criticism of the Coda as well as stating some doubts over the quality of the *Canto popolare* section. There was still no comment on the Symphony, but the serious-minded, sympathetic Davies continued to be the friend with whom Jaeger was most easily able to share his feelings about death. Anger and bitterness were giving way to a growing acceptance.

37 Curzon Road,
Muswell Hill
N.

[undated][21]

My dear Davies,

I was very happy to receive your letter of Sunday week. Dont for a moment imagine that I 'grin' sarcastically or in any other nasty way at your expressions of Sympathy. They are very dear to me, *very*.

Yes, I feel better as regards the heart; but the thing is daily threatened with fresh ruin by the fearful attacks of coughing I have to put up with several times a day, especially after Breakfast (in Bed) in the morning. Of course nothing could be worse than this daily & hourly strain – a *great* strain – put upon poor ticker.

I feel at present as if I could never again venture to go to London, and, frankly, I dread the winter. It may easily put coda & Finis to my life's symphony. I'm sometimes (this afternoon e.g.) for hours at a time all but choked with phlegm. It's a dreadful sensation.

Yes, 'In the South' is a *fine* piece, but, like you, I think it too long; there's too much of the idyllic section, the thematic invention of which is not strong enough (though nice in its way) to bear the spinning out. The thread becomes too thin. It's *not* a 'Siegfried Idyll' for Invention. And he has spoiled the fine rush of the coda by those few bars of foolery: ratattatattata-tta in the Brass & the final 'Jauchzer'. They dont fit in with the scheme of the Coda. I felt that from the first, when I wrote my analysis for the last Worcester Festival (1905) & think so now. However, on the whole, what an ADVANCE on Stanford & the old guard (incl *dear* C.H.H.P.) in *every* way. I have studied his symphony a little from the proofs, but can't give an opinion. Were you at Sheffield for 'Everyman', & were you satisfied? When are you coming to see me?

My love to you!

Ever yours sincerely and devotedly,

A.J. Jaeger.[22]

Parry had at last taken the advice of his doctors and reduced many of his official commitments, and he would undertake only one more Three Choirs Commission, the celebrated *Ode on the Nativity* of 1912. Jaeger now wrote belatedly to acknowledge receipt of a copy of *Beyond These Voices*, and to offer his generous judgement on the aims and intentions of Parry's ethical cantatas. He was at last able to report that the *Musical Times* was asking him for contributions, although he blamed his recent heart trouble, significantly enough perhaps, on annoyance caused by a visit to Novello's.

But in discussing his health, Jaeger painted a self-deprecating picture of himself in comparison to Parry.

37 Curzon Road,
Muswell Hill,
N.

12/10/8.

Dear Sir Hubert,

It is over a month since you sent me your last very Kind letter & a copy of your 'Beyond these voices' – and I have not yet replied to say 'thankyou'! I am ashamed of myself & would cry 'peccavi' if I had any voice worth speaking of. Yet I know that you will forgive me when I tell you that the greater part of the time I Have been very ill & even now I feel – in one expressive word – 'rotten'! My heart collapsed one day after I had been to Novellos & came back much annoyed over sundry matters. I was packed off to bed, suffered great pain & had to lie low & say & do 'nuffin', like Brer Rabbit. And though I get up now, I never feel a human being till the evening, i.e. I am not fit to do *anything* till then, and if a bad fit of coughing should shake me, even my evenings are spoiled, and I live in constant fear of my heart playing its tricks again – for the weakness of that organ is of course chiefly due to all the coughing I do. It's a common accompaniment to the other ailments that are ruining my life. I daresay that you with your refractory heart have suffered & – maybe, though I ardently hope you are *not* just now – are suffering much more than I do. And you never complain! I admire you in this as in so many other respects. But then you are a philosopher & a deep thinker, & I am made of *very* ordinary clay & Kick with all my futile strength against the Kind fate that chains me to the procrustean bed of an aimless useless life. Cui bono? You may say. I know it's useless, yet a D–! does occasionally relieve one's feelings.

Well, strange to say, since you so very kindly expressed a wish in your letter that the people of the 'Musical Times' might give me some work, I *was* asked to take up the 'foreign notes' again which I used to write years ago, before I broke down. And I might 'submit anything else'! So I spent whatever 'fair' evenings my Health vouchsafed me in scribbling, & the result is that I have over 6 columns in this month's paper.[23] *Nothing* of ANY importance (they always refuse anything I have put my heart & Enthusiasm into!), but I get *paid* for it, & that must be the main thing to me just now. I shall continue trying to earn a few £ as long as my strength suffices for the not very heavy work.

And now let me say how sincerely I hope that you have returned to work feeling refreshed after your rest. I learned at Novellos that you have written yet another choral work for some celebration at Eton College. Well, I don't Know how you manage it; and if it upset your health again, I can only say & all your friends will say: You shouldn't have undertaken this task. People will *not* leave you alone & yet they must Know that your precious Health is of more account than the supplying of a pièce d'occasion, even if H.M. *is* going to be there.

I have spent many evening hours over your 'voices', & fancy I have got right into it & Know how to appreciate it. You have once more selected superb passages from the Bible, though the first half of your 'Book' is terrible in its negation of happiness as we poor mortals understand it. That first 'energico' theme is a 'discovery' on your part. Certainly, nothing could better express the spirit of the opening Sentences. (By the way it's a beast to play correctly on the P.F. the *first time*; I stumbled over it more than once, which proves what a poor Pianist A.J.J. is!) The 'Peace' motive is a beautiful, soaring thought, worthy of you at your best. And then we are floating on the stream of yet another of those elevating, dignified & beautiful musical creations of which C.H.H.P. has already given us so goodly a number; – creations which in their appeal to the best that is in us mortals, in their power to take us out of ourselves & lift us up into purer regions of thought, to cleanse & console us, have not had their equal – looking at the long series of work *all of them bringing this great message of hope & comfort*, – since Bach's Church Cantatas. I Know of no composer since the Great J.S.B. who is the creator of such a long series of choral works of such uniformly deep moral, ethical import. That in this matter You are so splendidly served by the beautiful words you have either compiled or written for these works is fortunate & there you have the advantage over J.S.B.! And I think that England is fortunate to count amongst her musicians of the present day three leading men (there may be many more of whom I Know little or nothing as regards their outlook on life) who place their gifts at the service of the Highest, men pure, good & true, whose lives are shining examples to us of commoner mould, men whose art is but a reflex of their pure, good & true selves. I mean C.H.H.P., E. Elgar & H. Walford Davies. You may not think much of Elgar's choral works (I mean the oratorios), I do not know your opinion of them; but that they *are*, like yours, the outpouring of a deeply feeling, pure, & good man I know. As for H.W.D. I daresay you Know him better than I do.

I say England is fortunate in the possession of such men, for the art which we love is in these days dragged into the mud to serve 'ideals' that are anything but noble. She is to do 'duties' for which one would have thought *music* was absolutely unfit, & certainly should be exempt from.

But what a chatterbox I am! My great fault. Pardon me.

Yes, your finale is allright, bless your great Heart, & the last page beautiful, tender, soothing, tear-compelling.

I was greatly interested in your news re your J.S.B. Book. Yes, YOU had to write that & nobody else in the Kingdom. But how did you find the time for such a big task? I could not come to your Worcester Rehearsal at the R.C.M. The day was too boisterous for a weaklunged fellow like me. I have now had to give up all idea of getting as far as the College once more.

Yours v. sincerely,

A.J. Jaeger.[24]

'Autumn is a bad season for persons in consumption', states Hippocrates, and Jaeger certainly continued in a low condition, confined to bed, as preparations for the Symphony performance wore on. Elgar corrected proofs during October and early November, in readiness for a visit by Hans Richter, who would conduct the première. The first rehearsal was arranged for 23 November at the Queen's Hall, although Jaeger's presence on that occasion was not possible. He felt, too, that he could not attempt the preliminary notice of the Symphony for the *Musical Times* that Elgar had evidently asked him to write, and requested Walford Davies, who visited Jaeger on 11 November, to take on the task. Walford wrote to Elgar that he would gladly undertake to 'send a notion', while confessing that 'probably a friend will write it for me', and mentioned Jaeger's conviction that there was a programme 'at the back of it all'. He received the familiar response, '... There is no programme beyond a wide experience of human life with a great charity (love) and a *massive* hope in the future.' Elgar also wrote – as he had done to Jaeger himself – of his grief over Jaeger's illness, and of his hopes and prayers for improvement, '... but it is dreadfully heartbreaking & weary for him: bless him!'

Weary indeed. Jaeger was now in the grip of daily variations of temperature with evening fever and sweating, and so weak that he was obliged for a time to dictate his correspondence to Isabella. With characteristic kindness, Walford Davies had offered to provide an oxygen cylinder to relieve his breathing.

[In the hand of Isabella Jaeger]

37 Curzon Rd
Muswell Hill
N.

Nov 15th [1908]

My dear, good friend

Many thanks for your kind letter. I am still in bed, feeling much the same as when you saw me, though I have been considerably worse during the same period; for the same evening you called my temperature rose to 104, & it has mounted as high another evening[.] I have spoken to my doctor about your very kind offer of a Cylinder of Oxygen, but he does not think it would be of the slightest assisstance [*sic*] to me. He says it is difficult to manipulate, that I could not possibly do it myself, & that any careless overdosing might knock me down. So there is another hope gone[.]

I have found that letter which Elgar wrote to me about the symphony some time ago. I will enclose it, because I thought it might possibly throw light on a dark place.[25]

I also send you, for private perusal, a very interesting letter Elgar wrote to me exactly 10 years ago. It refers to the Gordon scheme, & how it 'possessed' him. Fancy poor E. having to score some fool's Comic Opera for a living, while he was carrying two such works as the Variations, & the symphony in his head.! It seems a tragedy. I must stop for I am very tired. With my devoted love, & many thanks for all your kindness[.]

I am your ever

A.J. Jaeger[26]

Kindly return the Elgar letters to me when next you write. I must explain with reference to some remark in the old letter, that we were married on Dec. 22nd. 1898.!

Jaeger had evidently discussed his earlier suggestion for a *Gordon* Symphony with Davies, and he went on to reveal the extent of his rôle in that plan in a dictated letter to Sidney Loeb a few days later. It was making his present weakness all the harder to bear, for he had begun to despair of being able to attend the forthcoming performances of the Symphony.

37, Curzon Road
Muswell Hill
N.

Nov. 17th 1908

My dear Loeb.

How awfully kind of you to send me these beautiful & most delicious grapes. I greeted them as I would Manna from heaven; for many days now I eat all food under protest, & because I must live. These grapes, however, are a genuine luxury, & I eat them with real appetite. Once more many thanks.

Isn't it cruel of fate to debar me from hearing Elgar's symphony, for which I have been waiting so long? For it is exactly ten years this month that Elgar wrote to me that a 'Gordon' symphony, for which I had sent him a synopsis was 'possessing' him, but that he could not yet write it down.

I know that the present symphony has nothing to do with Gordon, yet I have been waiting for *a* symphony from him for 10 years. I am still in bed with fever, & very weak, & have no idea when I may be able to get up.

With my kindest regards

Yours very Sincerely

A.J. Jaeger (per I. Jaeger)[27]

In another few days Jaeger wrote to Walford Davies, who had sent a proof of the Symphony article for the *Musical Times* over which he had worked in collaboration with the critic H.C. Colles (1879–1943), an ex-pupil. Jaeger gave some first reactions to the work, which revealed a degree of disappointment. He cited the quality of some of the thematic invention, the length of the first movement, the nature of the orchestration and the work's conclusion, and went on to hope for a work in which Davies could combine his fundamental seriousness of purpose with Elgar's skill at instrumentation.

37 Curzon Road,
20/XI/08

My dear Davies,

Here is your proof. I have nothing much to offer in the way of criticism for the article is excellent & I couldn't have written one half as good, from most points of view. My lack of the Knowledge of musical technique handicaps me terribly.

I think however you should have made more of the jolly, bouncing theme which E draws upon for the last pages of the peroration. See my remarks on proof.

The more I study the work (and I have P. F. proofs of the Finale now) the more I feel that fine though the work is in many parts, yet it is not the great, elevated, philosophic 'aloof' work which I had *hoped* E. *might* write. The thematic invention is too unimportant for that, & the way he belabours that

&c is really too much for me. The idea is impressive in slow time; in Allegro time it *worries* me. However all this may seem futile criticism when I hear a performance (if I

ever do hear one). By the way, I think E. has once more spoiled his close by springing surprises on us where no one having been put into an elevated frame of mind by *the* big (Heroic) theme *wants* surprizes. He has a weakness for this sort of thing which ruins his Cockayne, In the South, Variations (before revision) & now this Symphony. That *first* allegro chief theme I *can't* get used to. It is for all in the world the Kind of 'Overture' theme that Spohr & his contemporaries might have thought 'fine'. The first movement *is loquacious.* Your proposed cut (too late to be carried out) would have done something to improve matters. There is altogether too much playing with sounds in those 'lyric' parts. Just as 'in the South'.

However, let us be thankful for what we have got; for that is much. *The* great serene, philosophically aloof Symphony that shall link on to Brahms No 4 will have to be written by *You* now, my friend. Elgar's nerves are too bad to get into the right 'attitude' for writing the work I had hoped he would have written. And I fancy he is really now the slave of His mistress, the wonderful art of his orchestral command. I wish *you* possessed that in the same degree! What with your outlook on life & art, & humanity, friendship, code of morality &c &c (I express myself badly), you are the man for *my* Symphony. How E's art of instrumentation would help you in writing an *effective* work. For in these days everything you write MUST *sound well*!

My dear friend, I'm still in Bed, as weak as any mouse, and full of pain, fever &c. I can't yet think of going down. Not for weeks I fear. I shall love to see you any day, as you know, but as for playing to me, that alas! is a pleasure I can't enjoy *yet.*

I laughed at a remark in one of your last letters that you thought Colles thought I thought not much of him. As I had *never read a line* of his stuff (as far as I know) I had absolutely *no* 'views'. After reading this article (if it is largely his writing) I think he is a very good writer.

My love to you

Ever thine

A.J. Jaeger[28]

Shortly afterwards, Jaeger's condition improved sufficiently for him to be able to leave his bed. Coming downstairs for the first time, he told Sydney Loeb, he made for his piano and the score of *The Mastersingers of Nuremberg*, finding the point in Act III when the festive crowds, gaudy apprentices and dignified Masters have ceremonially assembled at dawn on the town meadow, amid fanfares and banners, in preparation for the trial of the Art of Song. They salute the wisdom of Hans Sachs, whose love and understanding of music goes beyond mere observance of rule, and break into the famous 'Wach auf ' chorus. The great moment was full of poignancy for Jaeger, something of a Hans Sachs himself.

37 Curzon Road
Muswell Hill N.

[26 November, 1908]

My dear Loeb,

You are very Kind, and I thank you sincerely. The grapes are lovely. I laughed at the Tradesman's blunder, but thought you should Know, in case he expected *double* payment. Yes, I believe I am getting on a little now. To-day, by the Dr's leave, I'm down in my Drawing room, for the first time for 4 weeks! I even had half an hour's music on my beloved old Piano. The first thing I went for was 'Wacht auf! es nahet gen dem Tag' from the last Scene in Die Meistersinger. It brought tears into my eyes, for apart from the glorious music, the sentiment of the words seemed somehow to suit my condition. Now I'm bothering my brain how I can manage to be at the first performance of E's Symphony on Dec 7! I do hope I may. I Know the work well by this time.

With my Kindest regards

Yours Sincerely,

A.J. Jaeger.[29]

Jaeger was also able to take the proofs of the piano transcription of the Elgar Symphony to the piano, and in a letter to the composer the next day he admitted how much difference an opportunity to hear the sounds had made. He focused on the slow movement, which seemed to match his need to see the greatest music as a moral force. His gratitude was touching.

37 Curzon Road,
Muswell Hill

26/xi/8

My dear, great Edward,

I was allowed to come down today for the first time for a month, and I spent some happy quarter Hours over your Adagio in the Symphony (P.F. arrangement.)

My dear friend that is not only one of the very greatest slow movements since Beethoven, but I consider it *worthy of that master.* How original!, how PURE, noble, elevating, soothing. &c &c. I can't find the words. How exquisitely beautiful in every detail. I cried happy tears of 'Wonne' over so much beauty. It's the greatest thing You have done. I almost admire most of all the PURITY of Sentiment & the absence of all sensationalism. The music was written by a good pure man, & only such a character can feel & invent such music. I detected one or two places, where the great adagio of the Choral Symphony was recalled to my memory. Nothing in the way of a reminiscence (the Satz is *quite* your own), but just the feeling of nobility of sentiment. At 104 we are brought near Heaven. That is a lofty and inspired thought.

Until today I had only *looked* at the printed pages, & though I thought the music very fine, I was not prepared for this revelation of Beauty. You see, poor old mosshead *must* have his old Broadwood to help him. He is such a rank amateur. Yet he's not a bad Critic when he can HEAR sounds.

I must go to bed, though I Know that haunting Adagio won't let me sleep soon.

I wish I were near you that I might press & kiss your hand & say: thank you, my friend, for this great piece of music.

My love to you

Always yours

A.J.J.[30]

To Walford Davies Jaeger now opened his heart more fully than ever before as the damage to his lungs continued to worsen and he rehearsed his farewells to the beauty that he had sought to cherish all his life. Despair drove him to condemn his elderly paralysed mother, who was part of the Muswell Hill household, and he revealed too the terrible extent to which tuberculosis had been prevalent in the family. But continued study of the Elgar Symphony had enabled him to step outside his misery, and he revised many former criticisms, becoming all the more determined to attend the first London performance on 7 December. And behind it all it is possible to glimpse Isabella – burdened as she must have been by years of commuting to Gloucester and elsewhere for violin teaching, and by the care of her sick husband and their two children – putting the bravest possible face on things.

37 Curzon Road,
Muswell Hill.

2/XII/8

My dear friend,

I was relieved to get your letter. Many thanks. Oh yes, I still take Sanatogen regularly twice a day, but nothing will help me. I'm today in the lowest depths of despair, for I Know I cannot last much longer. I feel that during these 4 weeks in bed I have coughed away a great chunk of Lung & I am continuing the process every day. My most intimate friends Know my fate as surely as I do, but my dear, good wife, bless her, *quite* expects & hopes & 'feels sure' that I shall be quite 'allright' soon. Yes, in one sense I shall be but not in the way *she* imagines, poor woman. It seems strange, dear friend, & I cannot help pondering much over the strangeness of it, that here we have our old mother aged 83, paralysed, leading an utterly useless life consisting of eating, drinking, sleeping & sitting in a chair staring into vacancy. She, poor old dear looks 'like eternal life' as the Germans say, all her chief organs being in perfect condition. She has been a burden to me & a '*drag*' in more ways than one for many, many years, though for my mother I have gladly put up with it all. As I say, she seems (apart from her brain) in perfect health & may easily live to be 100!

And here I am, who should provide for a wife & 2 dear children & who could still do some good work in various directions, doomed to an early & terrible death of this fearful 'white plague'. My wife has never seen consumptives die, in fact, somehow my doctor's tarradiddles have set it into her head that I am only suffering from 'Bronchial catarrh'. Poor woman! We have lost three brothers & sisters through the dread disease. I'm no 4, & I'm only waiting from day to day for the time when I get confined to Bed, never to rise again. When I think over it all, and realize how beautiful life is & what work I might & could do & what intellectual beauty (E's Symphony) there is still brought forth by men of genius – and how very soon I shall be dead to it all, dead to family & friends & Sunshine & green fields and Symphonies & quartets & poetry & pictures & all that makes life the great thing it is, then my heart feels heavy, – heavy as lead, and tears flow readily. When I came down for the first time last Thursday, I went to the piano & the first thing I played was that glorious chorale 'Wacht auf! es nahet gen dem Tag' in Act III of Die Meistersinger (my musical Bible) I sobbed & cried. Wach auf! Oh! if only my Health could 'Awaken' once more. Vain aspiration!

I *Know* some of my friends think I 'exaggerate' & am too pessimistic. Ah. They Know not how I FEEL, how utterly weak & worn out, how short of breath, how impotent in every way, except as regards my Brain which Keeps bright enough (my brother was fully conscious till a second or two before his last, feeble breath).

E's Symphony has been a perfect Godsend to me, for it has made me forget for some happy hours that I'm a doomed man. I have played the work till I Know it inside out, and now I *love* it, think it a tremendous effort of genius (Just think what it means in these days to write an absolutely individual work, individual from the first bar to the last!) That first Satz *will* be appreciated when it is Known. It is a tremendous thing[.] The Scherzo is one of the most astounding in all Symphonic literature, the Adagio is Heaven. (I have shed many happy tears over it) & the Finale a real 'invention' & a real 'rouser'. I really did not give E credit for such powers as he here displays. What a pity that 'circumstances' kept him from devoting himself to Symphonies years ago, instead of, say, 'Caractacus', 'Banner of St George' &c &c.

Ill as I am, I am determined to hear the performance next Monday[.] Two old (lady) friends of mine are going to 'stand' me a Taxi cab from my door to Q. Hall & back. I have ordered a ticket (I can't rely on Elgar sending me one & I won't beg for one). So I do hope & pray the weather may be 'passable', at least. I don't mind Rain, but a bad fog might undo me. Of course I shall leave directly after the Symphony. Wrapped in my old Fur coat & otherwise warmly clad, I should be allright on the long journey. Oh! if only my health keeps as 'good' (this is wrote sarcastic) as it is at the present moment, & if but the weather is respectable I shall hope to *enjoy* what I fear will be the *last* great musical event of my life. After that – Silentium!

I must close & rest. My love to you, dearest friend. Come & see me one day when you can *spare the* time.

Ever yours

A.J.J.[31]

This needs *no* reply

The day after this letter, the historic Symphony première took place at the Free Trade Hall, Manchester, under Hans Richter, to great acclaim. On 4 December, Jaeger wrote again to Elgar about the work, and dealt with his reactions to the whole piece. He gave some clues as to his programmatic understanding of the music, and evidently concluded the letter in much the same terms as he had to Walford Davies; Elgar tore the lines away.

… I want to say that I do not 'see' only the Adagio, but since I have been able to spend many happy hours over your Sym. at the P.F. I see it *all* & feel most intensely all it implies & expresses,: The tremendous strife, alternated with delicious moments of hope & faith, imploring, sighing, smiles & happiness. I love it all, but of course the dramatic fights against the unsympathetic world, the proud assertion of your manly self & your belief in yourself & your powers thrill me most. There is one passage over a Pedal F# … where the discords … bite like acid into my musical feelin [*sic*]. But 'I likes it'. And there are as many passages that affect me as powerfully as anything you have ever done, or as anything in modern music as far as I know it.

The Scherzo is a real joy & one of the biggest things of the Kind in all Symphonic literature. And then that mysterious Lento with its abysmal depths of tone colour & the astounding Finale, an overpowering outburst of optimism & joie de vivre that carries one away in spite of oneself until the superb peroration crowns the whole splendid structure. [illegible] It's a great & masterly work & will place you higher amongst the world's masters than anything you have done. Ill as I am (& I feel so ill to-night that I want to go to the nearest Ry Station & throw myself under a train to end my misery) I hope to go next Monday. I have bought a ticket & am looking forward to what I fear will be the last great …[32]

However weak and frail he was, nothing short of a complete collapse would have kept Jaeger away from the London première of the Symphony at the Queen's Hall on Monday 7 December. Despite the warmth of Schuster's fur coat and the ease of the taxi journey, he must nevertheless have been anxiously aware of the possibility of embarrassing, painful paroxysms of coughing during the performance. But the music and the occasion absorbed his attention completely – he broke down during the slow movement – and made the efforts and risks of attending worthwhile. His first chance to hear the sounds in their orchestral guise also enabled him to continue to develop his evaluation of the work itself. He wrote to Dora Penny, who was unable to attend.

> How I wish you had been there. I never in all my experience saw the like. The Hall was packed; any amount of musicians. I saw Parry, Stanford, E. German, J. Corder, E. Faning, P. Pitt, E. Kreuz, etc. The atmosphere was electric … After the first movement E.E. was called out; again, several times, after the third, and then came the great moment. After that superb Coda (Finale) the audience seemed to rise at E. when he appeared. I never heard such frantic applause after any novelty nor such shouting. Five times he had to appear before they were pacified. People stood up and even on their seats to get a view. As regards my impressions, I must say I was delighted. The lovely Heavenly Adagio reduced me to tears. The Scherzo both amused and charmed me. The Coda is superb and winds up the Symphony in a blaze of glory. That Coda is quite new in laying out and effect. On the whole a splendid & noble & highly individual work, full of the most lovely detail work & any amount of Brains & Heart …[33]

So with just five months of life left to him, Jaeger's hopes and plans of ten years for a symphony from Elgar were finally realized. The day after the performance, he received a collection of press reviews of the concert, and the day after that a letter from the ever-attentive Sydney Loeb. Jaeger replied at length, coming to life, discussing the Symphony again, this time in terms of intimacy as between two sophisticated music-lovers with something of a shared German background. He repeated some doubts concerning the outer two movements, but praised the inner two, especially again the slow movement, which had affected him so deeply at the Queen's Hall. Beethoven, Brahms, Mendelssohn, Schumann, Strauss, Tchaikovsky and Wagner provided various points of reference, and Jaeger argued for judgements based on repeated hearings of the Symphony; he himself had come almost full circle in revising some of his earlier views on the work, although he continued to repeat his criticisms of Elgar's codas. He reverted, too, to another old worry, the uncritical patriotism which he sensed behind the frenzied reception accorded the work by the Queen's Hall audience.

> 37 Curzon Road
> Muswell Hill
> N.
>
> 9/12/8
>
> My dear Loeb,
>
> Many thanks for your interesting letter & the equally 'interesting' grapes. You are good to me!

Yes, I got home quickly in the motor brougham which two dear old friends of mine had 'stood' me, to drive me from my door to Q. Hall & back. I could not possibly have gone to the concert under any less comfortable conditions, say by Bus & Rail, for I was too utterly weak & breathless. My friends' largesse enabled me to enjoy the concert in luxurious 'peace', & to get Home with the greatest comfort by *9.50*.

Well, & what do I think of E's work? I know it *thoroughly*; I might say every note of it, for I had to study it carefully with a view to writing an article for the 'Musical Times', which article I could not after all accomplish because of my serious illness. I fancy I told you this before. Excuse! I enjoyed the performance hugely & was greatly stirred by it. The wonderfully beautiful, pure, pensive, elevating Adagio reduced me to sobbing & copious tears (my nerves are very 'slack' just now). That movement I consider the most beautiful & perfect message of peace, chaste feeling, aloofness from all things mundane & common that has been given to the world since Brahms penned the marvellous adagio in the 'Clarinet Quintet', his last specimen of chamber music. Or I will say *I Know* nothing to match Elgar's Adagio since the Brahms work. I have frequented concerts so little during the last years, that I must speak cautiously. Strauss has done nothing so pure and ennobling. He, the sensualist & sensationalist can only give us 'passion' & [illegible]. Elgar's music is passionless – using the word 'passion' in the vulgar sense – but oh! so wonderful in its sheer, abstract beauty of idea & workmanship. It is a *gem of the purest water.* The Scherzo is perfect & a magnificent movement full of 'go', vigorous fun brilliancy & charm. The Trio is simply haunting in its tunefulness & most exquisitely treated by a master's supreme art. The orchestration throughout this Trio is one long Delight.

Now I come to the first movement. I must confess that I too felt that E. has *not yet* attained to that big symphonic Sweep of the *true Symphonist*, & the same remark applies to the Finale. No wonder! This is E's *first* essay in the Symphonic (Sonata) form, except his Organ Sonata.[34] Beethoven, Schumann, Mendelssohn, Brahms were prepared for their first Symphony by having written many chamber works in the form. But I & 'we' generally must not do E. the injustice of imagining that we can 'take in' & exhaust such an elaborate movement at one hearing. *No one* can. It requires as much loving 'Entgegenkommen' – approaching with a *desire* to Know & understand it, – as does the first movement of Beethoven's Choral Symphony or the first of Brahms's No. 1. Those 2 movements *cannot* be appreciated unless one *knows* them thoroughly. Then let us be just to Elgar & trust to time – i. e. repeated hearings – to reveal the very many beauties there are lying hidden behind the masses of black crotchets & quavers. I Know the beauties are there, but they are not 'stated' in Bill-poster fashion, with Tchaikovskian brutality in the way of doubling parts to get a thick, fat, 'palpable' tone for every theme. E.g. that long drawn second subject (*not* quoted by Webb in his rotten analysis – he quoted a little episodical phrase of 9 notes as the 'second subject') is 'stated' by the Violins *piano*, and its sweet & tender melancholy might easily go for nothing at a first hearing, especially if the fatheaded analyst does not draw attention to it. Yet it is a beautiful, even haunting idea. And the sighing & longing[,] the playing with lovely sounds (such passages as where you thought you recognized a Götterdämmerung bit) will all appeal to us more & more as we learn to Know the work.

The coda to the 1st. movement is tantalizingly, perversely 'affected', but *in*effective & the same remark might be applied to the last page of the Score, where after a really superb peroration, nobly crowning a splendid structure, he *must* be 'original' & out of the way & thus spoil the great effect produced by what's gone before in the said superb peroration. The ending is really as ineffective as was that of the Variations until I made him add 90 Bars & thus got a Coda that has *made* the work the success it is. NO classical master ever 'played the fool' in his codas. Elgar spoils *all* his codas (except in the Adagio in this Symphony) by trying to be 'unconventional'.

Well, taking the work as a whole it is a magnificent effort, full of beauty & suggestiveness, of power & tenderness, individuality and 'newness'. *Because* it is so individual, it will require much 'getting at', and many hearings will not exhaust the stock of beauties to be found in it. The first & last movements are not perfect, but in spite of that I feel inclined to say Thank God for such a work.

Now I can't help feeling that the tremendous enthusiasm of last Monday was *exaggerated.* NO foreign audience, American or European is likely ever to display a fifth part of that white-heat, frenzied rapture. You English are *now* proud of E. who is the chiefest 'asset' in English music, the *one* man who is recognized abroad. Hence a charming but somewhat uncritical patriotism enters largely into the display of appreciation of a work which on the whole is DIFFICULT to appreciate at a first hearing. I certainly did my share in applauding & I dont say that the work does not deserve all the applause it can get. But Monday's Frenzy was uncanny.

The critics too have gone slightly 'dotty' I think, when they go in for lengthy dissertations on the 'inner significance' of the work. To judge it as *music* is quite enough for me, for as such it will be judged by the world.

Some Kind friend sent me a whole bundle of papers yesterday. Was it you, perhaps? If so, many thanks. I do wish I could go to the performance on Dec 19 & take my wife (the Handsome, tall lady you saw me with was *not* my wife)[35] but unless I am much better than at present I must not think of it, and Motor Broughams 'is off'.

Kindest regards,

Sincerely yours,

A.J. Jaeger[36]

Tell your friend who complained of 'no ideas' that he couldnt see the forest for trees. He no doubt admires the climax of the 1812 overture.

Jaeger's love of letter-writing to a wide circle of friends continued. To his old friend C.L. Graves he wrote at this time in much the same vein,

It is only fair to extend to the composer that goodwill with which all amateurs *must* approach the greatest works of the classics (including our beloved Brahms) if they wish to enjoy their music. They take the quality of the classics for granted and *go to enjoy* them. A modern composer is *abgeschlachtet* [butchered] after one hearing ... Well, the work will have to go through the crucible of foreign opinion, where no patriotic enthusiasm affects the public verdict. I consider the enthusiasm of last week exaggerated, certainly greatly affected by a display of patriotic pride in the composer. No foreign audience, American or European, will display a quarter of that frenzy. In fact I shouldn't be surprised to hear of fiascos in Germany.[37]

Jaeger was able to attend the repeat performance of the Symphony with Isabella as he hoped, for Elgar sent two tickets, and Loeb offered to pay for the necessary taxi. Another hearing of the work would help Jaeger to practise what he preached as far as understanding the Symphony was concerned, and enable him to transcend his sufferings once more.

37 Curzon Road,
Muswell Hill,
N.

17/12/8.

My dear Loeb,

I have not written before to thank You for your letter & most kind offer of a Taxi, because I did not Know whether I could avail myself of your 'largesse', i.e. whether I should get any *tickets!* but now Elgar has sent me two, I mean & hope to go, and I have therefore ordered a Taxi. Once more, very heartfelt thanks!

My seats (I'm taking my *wife* this time) are *bad*: Stalls Row 11 nos. 5 & 6, regular 'dead heads" seats, where one can't hear properly. Still, I wont examine this 'gift Horse's' dental apparatus too closely.

I have been in the lowest Hell of Hopelessness & despair these last few days. I hope Elgar's splendid music may lift me, for a short space of time at least, onto a higher plane, say some gentle, stimulating 'purgatory'. I fear I shan't get any higher even with the aid of E.E.! I lead a joyless, dark, & absolutely *hopeless* life now, & my heart fails me when I think of the future.

Did you send me the cutting from the 'Observer' re Elgar's Work?[38] If so, thanks! I never read anything so preposterously asinine as the clown's attempts to charge E. with plagiarism.

We hope to arrive at Queen's hall in good time, say 2.45. Could you come and speak to us in our seats? or shall we perhaps see you *after* the Symphony? We mean to get out & Home after the Symphony.

I must close, for I have to do some work for the Musical Times.

Very sincerely & gratefully yours,

A.J. Jaeger[39]

The letter crossed in the post with another from Loeb, enclosing a single ticket for a better seat in the Queen's Hall. In declining it, Jaeger paid touching tribute to Isabella and to the relationship they shared, and perhaps as something of a peace offering, went on to mention his collection of Elgar letters from the period of the turn of the century. To re-read these letters, to live over again the heady days of the Variations and *Gerontius*, and to remember his own contributions towards these works, must have brought comfort, pride and satisfaction. He wrote of them in characteristically Romantic terms, of how they 'laid bare' an 'artist's soul', although presumably that artist would have been horrified to think that his letters were to be the subject of discussion with a third party, even so genuine a devotee as Sydney Loeb.[40]

[18/12/08]

My dear Loeb

You are awfully good to me. Why?

I'm VERY much obliged for the Ticket, just received (9.50) but really, dear friend, I *must* sit next to my wife, she has been looking forward to it so & *I* want to sit next to her too. She is my best musical chum (a professional Violinist & *much* more 'musical' than I am[)], & we always enjoy music better when we sit together. I must risk the Stairs down & upstairs & never mind the 'bad hearing' in Row 2.

Now I can think of nothing else but to return the ticket which no doubt, if you don't arrive at the Hall too late, the ticket office will be glad of & return you the money for.

I'm sure you will understand, or you *will* when you have married a wife who is a real *Chum* to you!

Once more a thousand thanks from yours very sincerely,

A.J. Jaeger[41]

I spent a few hours last night looking through scores and scores of letters of Elgar, dating from 1897 to 1902 (I have plenty of others)[.] They would, I fancy, vastly interest you. A crucial time of the man's life (Caractacus, Variations, Gerontius, Cockaigne), *deeply* interesting Real human documents laying bare an artists soul!

Jaeger was able to continue his letter to Dora Penny, 'I went on Saturday too & took my wife & we enjoyed the work immensely. The House was packed again, & Busby, the managing director of the Symph: Orch: Co. told me the day was a record for them in the way of selling tickets …'.[42] The Symphony was proving an unprecedented success, with further performances being urgently arranged. Novello's issued specially bound copies of the full score for Christmas presents. Jaeger again wrote his impressions of the work to Loeb – who had risen to the bait over the Elgar letters – and was able after this second performance to claim a better understanding of the first movement.

37 Curzon Road
Muswell Hill
N.

21/X11/8

My dear Loeb,

Many thanks for your letter. As you ax me, I'll tell you that the townward journey (I having ordered a Taxi from King's Cross – there are none here!) cost 8/8 – which is of course for journey from town *& back, to Q. Hall* –; and the journey (single) *Home*, all uphill, 4/8. I did not retain the first chauffeur, because the waiting for over an hour runs up the expense so. I enjoyed the performance *very* much & think more of the work after the second hearing than ever. That puzzling first movement is now as clear as daylight to me, & *very* striking & dramatically beautiful it is. It requires a real *elucidatory analysis* (such as A.J.J. *could* write) though[,] to make the musical & emotional value of such a big movement clear to the average amateur. I cant make out that so few people speak highly of the Scherzo. I, who Know it thoroughly, consider it a truly *splendid* achievement, & one of the greatest Scherzos outside Beethoven's Symphonies. It is full of espirit, 'go', boisterous joie de vivre, fun, humour, tune, wonderful Scoring, ingenious workmanship, brilliant individuality. That Scherzo will dawn upon English amateurs & critics gradually, but gloriously, I'm sure.

I like the Finale least until the peroration is reached. That is superb in 'laying out' & Effect *quite new* & original. I Know nothing like it. I fancy Nikisch or Elgar would give us a much more Emotional & truly Elgarish reading than dear old Hans, though *his* performance is superb in its sanity, health, dignity & force.

The work will stand hearing over & over again, my boy, & each time you will hear *new* points of interest, new beauties. My wife, who is no mean judge thought the work *splendid*, and the Adagio heavenly. I'm glad you liked it better too.

As regards your coming to-morrow, I'm VERY sorry to say I have an appointment with my Dentist to morrow afternoon & can't say when I shall return from his torture chamber. Certainly, I fear I shall be *quite unfit*, physically, to receive anybody; I am so utterly weak (my legs tremble under me even as I walk on the *flat*!) that a dose of dentist's attention will quite undo me. Yet I *must* go, for I'm suffering much pain & have sleepless nights through it. If I do not take steps to get relief, I shall feel weaker than ever, for to suffer pain wears out the body as you *may* Know (?) And Oh! isnt toothache a hellish infliction!

I'm disgusted with things because I'm forced by circumstances to deny myself the pleasure of your visit to morrow. It's too bad. But after Xmas I hope you will be able to come & have tea one day with us (4.30, or 5, or 5.30, whichever you prefer) & then I'll show you my Elgariana. As far as I can see ahead, *any* day will suit us (*incl Sundays*) & any day my dear Frau & I shall be most happy to see you. Oh! by the way, on Mondays my wife is teaching in London (through the Holidays too) so please, *not*, on a Monday. I must close. With my best regards, in which my wife joins, & renewed thanks for all your kindness to me, and Heartiest season's wishes, I am,

Very Sincerely Yours,

A.J. Jaeger[43]

Loeb replied suggesting a firm date for his visit to Muswell Hill, and Jaeger now wrote with careful directions for finding Curzon Road, as meticulous as had been his calculations of the Queen's Hall taxi fare. Characteristic too was his refusal of Loeb's thoughtful suggestion that he earn some extra income by helping to judge scores submitted to the Patron's Fund, a body set up some years earlier to organize performances of new works by promising young English composers. Such work might seem ideally suited to Jaeger, but he remained fully aware of his lack of formal technical training.

37 Curzon Road,
Muswell Hill
N.

23/X11/8

My dear Loeb,

Very many thanks for your two letters & P.O. & suggestion re examining Scores for the 'Patron's Fund'. As regards this matter I must reply *NO*, I could not undertake such work for the simple reason that, like yourself, I am an *amateur* who cannot read full Scores like a trained musician & certainly would consider himself a *fraud* if he were to offer his opinion on a score after looking at it! I never had a lesson in Harmony, composition, orchestration &c in my life. I have 'picked up' a 'little Knowledge' which I hope has *not* been a 'dangerous thing' to me, but I *dare not* & *must not* pose as a person capable of sitting in judgement on a M.S. score. So with very many thanks to you & Dr E. Faning I fancy I *must* say 'no'. By the way, Parry, dear man, Knows my limitations & would smile at the proposal or suggestion.

As regards next Tuesday, that day will suit us very well. We will have Tea when you turn up; So we will not fix an Hour. Come when you can, the earlier the better. You can take a ticket through to Muswell Hill by the *Tube* from Moorgate Street to Finsbury

Park. There you get out & change into a Great Northern Train (There are 'sign posts' on the Platforms showing the Words 'Alexandra Palace' or 'Muswell Hill'. [)] That train you take. (not *all* the the [*sic*] Trains go as far as the Palace)[.] Now when you reach M. Hill Station you will observe that some of the passengers leave it by one way and others by another. You follow those going out of the *front* way (i.e. in the direction of towards the *Engine*) up some wooden steps. When you get into the Street, you'll find exactly opposite the exit a Street called 'Elms Avenue'. Go through that until you come into Muswell Road, running at right angles to Elms avenue, then turn to the right down Muswell Road, and Curzon Road is the second on the *left*. No. 37 is on the left of Curzon Road about 2/3rds down the Road.

We shall be truly delighted to see you & hope nothing will intervene to upset these plans.

Supposing you catch a Palace train quickly at Finsbury Park, the journey from the City should take about 35–40 minutes, for it is only a 3–4 minute's walk from Muswell Hill Station to my House.

All else when we meet.

With our best wishes for a pleasant Holiday time & a happy & prosperous New Year

I am Yours Sincerely & gratefully,

A.J. Jaeger[44]

The rapid exchange of letters continued, with Loeb now invoking the support of Parry and Eaton Faning[45] in his campaign to involve Jaeger in the Patron's Fund. Jaeger replied again on Christmas Day.

37 Curzon Road
Muswell Hill
N.

Xmas Day, 8

My dear Loeb,

You & Dr Faning & Sir Hubert Parry are too Kind, but you are all wrong. I wish you were not, for I should dearly love some work at which I could earn an honest penny. It is an extraordinary thing that for many years I have to *defend myself* against the 'grave charge' (!) of being a musician. When I tell my musician friends that I am a raw amateur they protest that I am as good as a musician & all the time I Know my own limitations perfectly well, and because I Know them & have never undertaken work to which I Knew I was not equal, I have been fortunate enough *not* to make a d – ass of myself.

Give me something to *play* (in my amateurish way) on the Piano and I fancy I can get right inside a work as well, & successfully as any musician, and better than a great many of them. But I *cannot* read a full Score so that I can get a proper impression of a work. Because I *describe* orchestration in my analyses of Gerontius, Apostles, Hiawatha &c, i.e. say 'this passage is scored so & so & brilliantly or sombrely ['], it does not follow that I can get at the emotional, structural & general value of the piece from studying the Full Score. In all my analyses I have had a *vocal* Score to tell me the value of the work, See? Even Elgar's Symphony, where I may take the value of the Scoring for granted, & a great deal besides, would be a sealed book to me until I *heard* it, or had a Pianoforte arrangement to help me (as, as a matter of fact, I did, though it is not yet published.) Do you see now? What could I make of a youngster's perhaps faulty score? *No*, NO, **NO**! I can't be an adjudicator without laying myself open to the charge of being a fraud.

There are plenty of frauds in the Profession & they make fortunes at the game. I *wont* be one & So I must say most emphatically I WILL NOT, since I'm not fit for it, undertake the work. I'm GREATLY & *sincerely* obliged to you, believe me, but I'm firm on this point, while regretting that I cant earn a few shillings that way. I'm at Home this winter & shall have to remain there. No funds for visiting Invalid's climes. Till Tuesday!

Very sincerely Yours,

A.J. Jaeger[46]

Jaeger's continued refusal reflected not only his own integrity, but also perhaps the diffidence that had prevented him from seeking personal publicity or membership of an acknowledged musical 'establishment.' And however much he bemoaned his lack of formal musical training, many a more accomplished score-reader might have lacked his ability to seize on the weak point in a work and know intuitively how to strengthen it.

Jaeger's contribution had already been made, his illness had caused him to retire from Novello's, his day as a professional critic was done. But that year, score-reader or not, he had through a final upsurge of that need to feel, understand and explain which was his *raison d'être*, penetrated to the heart of great new music – the part-songs and the Symphony – by the composer he still revered above all, despite the vicissitudes of their relationship. The great Symphony, that he had wanted so much and asked for so many times, was a final vindication of Jaeger's life's work. As she wrote her New Year's Eve entry in her diary, Alice Elgar gratefully acknowledged 'Deo Gratias for much – Symphony – Part Songs – Dear friends still spared ...'.

14 1909: 'I can no more … '

> … for now it comes again,
> That sense of ruin which is worse than pain,
> That masterful negation and collapse,
> Of all that makes me man.

The year began with a performance of the Symphony at the Queen's Hall on New Year's Day, conducted by Elgar. Alice thought he 'conducted splendidly & looked Nobilmente as he were his music' but Jaeger was not able to attend, much as he had wanted to hear the composer's own interpretation of the work. Loeb briefly visited Curzon Road, and again offered to provide a taxi to another performance of the work a week later, but Jaeger lacked a ticket and feared for his cough. Once more, the correspondence devolved upon Isabella.

37, Curzon Road,
Muswell Hill,
N.

Jan. 2nd. [1909]

Dear Mr Loeb,

My husband wishes me to thank you very much for your kind offer of a taxi, but he does not think it likely that he will go to the Concert, as he has no ticket, & his cough is sometimes rather troublesome in the evening. We wonder if you were at the concert yesterday, & if so, whether you saw any new beauties in the work as interpreted by the composer personally.

It must be interesting to compare the two readings. Thank you very much for coming to see my dear invalid last Tuesday. We thought it very good & brave of you to come all this way, & in such weather,! unfortunately it was such a short visit, there was no time to discuss anything.

Did you catch your train? Wishing you a happy 1909, & with my husband's kindest regards

Yours Sincerely

Isabella Jaeger.[1]

In the depths of the winter, Jaeger did not dare leave the house, although he seemed to be continuing with work for the *Musical Times*. Loeb now added to his generosity with an offer of tickets for the Symphony performance.

37 Curzon Road,
Muswell Hill
N.

[Postmark 6th January, 1909]

My dear Loeb,

Very many thanks for your letter & the Kind offer of tickets. You are *very* good, but I think I had better *not* go to the Concert. I'm really not fit & it might exhaust me beyond my strength, in spite of a comfortable Taxi cab. I need hardly say I *want* to go & ardently wish I *could* go. But my Health must be my first consideration, Alas!!

With our Kindest regards & heartiest thanks,

Ever Yours,

A.J. Jaeger.[2]

I'll write again soon I'm pressed tonight.

The deprivation of having to miss another hearing of the Symphony suggests in eloquent measure the weakness of Jaeger's condition, and he was never again able to attend a concert. While he could, however, he continued his correspondence, virtually his only link now with the world of music, criticism and friends which had been his life. He wrote again to Loeb the next day.

37 Curzon Road,
Muswell Hill
N

7/1/9

My dear Loeb,

Many thanks for the paper. I saw it weeks ago, for I receive the Signale regularly in connection with my work for the 'Musical Times'. Yes, I Know Karlyle, a small fat-bellied, broadshouldered German with a typical German Walrus moustache. Surely you have seen him many times? He is at all the concerts a nice sort of chap. The article is *very good* I think.

I have no idea of the Elgars' whereabouts; if they in London after tonight, you are almost sure to find them at Frank Schuster's ('Frankie') (22 Old Queen Street, S.W. isnt it? I *forget*!) Else of course Plas Gwyn, Hereford.

No, my friend, I feel no better. I am in bodily pain; sometimes *acute*, so that I *groan* under it *incessantly* (take that *literally*) *day & night*, and, as I have just written to my Doctor, feel only fit for the crematorium. My patience is getting worn out, & I have had a lot of it. But this suffering would try the divine patience of an archangel.

It's a good thing I did not go to to-night's concert, *though* I wanted to so badly.

We send our Kindest regards

& I am very sincerely yours.

A.J. Jaeger.[3]

There is no record of any contact between the Elgars and Jaeger at the Queen's Hall performances of the Symphony that he was able to attend, and his professed ignorance of their whereabouts may have been somewhat pointed. But Dora Penny, who that day had arrived at Plas Gwyn to stay with the Elgars, suggests that Edward and Alice had at any rate seen Jaeger at some point, and the very sight of him was enough to verify their worst fears. The result was a confirmation of the self-protecting reticence which had characterized Elgar's reaction to Jaeger's illness from its earliest stages.

> That first evening at Plas Gwyn we had much to say about the Symphony: the splendid performances: three since the production at Manchester on 3 December! I told them how delighted dear Nimrod was with it and how he had written me a huge long letter all about it. I thought they both looked very grave and the Lady changed the subject very quickly. Afterwards I heard that they had both been so dreadfully shocked and grieved to see such a change in him that it had rather upset them. I don't wonder. It is really amazing that he managed to go to Queen's Hall, even by 'motor cab', and enjoy it. 'I am sure it was an immense pleasure to him to be there,' I said, 'and he can have so few pleasures now.'[4]

One such pleasure had been in annotating the proof sheets of the piano reduction of the Symphony. The later binding sometimes partly obscures the often faint pencillings of a very sick man, and time has also done its work; much of the writing is now too faded to be recoverable. Of what remains, some of the comments duplicate other documented remarks, but there is much that is unfamiliar and full of interest that has been overlooked.[5]

In his determination to submit the Symphony to the most demanding scrutiny, Jaeger grappled with all aspects of the work – scoring, melody, harmony, form, key-structure, style and expression. Evidently the proof sheets had accompanied him to the performances, for there was no diffidence about his opinions about the orchestration. 'Oh! what a golden stream of sound E can get out of the full orchestra', he wrote of the restatement of the motto theme at Cue 3 in the first movement, and he noted too the 'barbaric splendour of scoring' at Cue 61 of the Scherzo together with the 'charming flute duet' of Cue 66 at the Trio section. Jaeger would not let an instrumental cliché pass, however, and in an aside perhaps for Arabella Wright's benefit he asked, 'what would composers do without trumpet triplets in fighting music?', nine bars after Cue 26 in the first movement.

Jaeger repeated his dislike of the first movement's D minor theme after Cue 5, finding it 'impetuous but commonplace', and described its continuation as 'excited, panting'. He admitted to some doubt in distinguishing between 'episodical matter' and the beginning of the second subject, and suggested 'perhaps 2nd subject really a *string* of themes (sighs)'. He noted the 'second subject proper' as beginning at Cue 12, and found it a 'long drawn melody, full of feeling & tenderness (regret?)'. He thought there was a 'touch of Caractacus' nine bars later, and noted too the 'Wagnerian turn, the first I know of in Elgar's music', at the semiquavers seven bars after Cue 13. The only other suggestion of another composer's influence came at Cue 94 in the slow movement, which he found '*ornate*! Un poco Schumannesque'. But he was fully and characteristically aware of the programmatic implications of the contrasts of mood contained in the first movement, writing at Cue 14 'soon storm rages again[,] passion, strife impetuous' and noting of the later recapitulation of the material at Cue 45, 'once more in whirlpool of passion or fight – dramatic to a high degree.' The music at Cue 24 was 'mysterious passage foreboding [and] throbbing we expect strife (tragic) [...] & are not disappointed.' He was struck by the transitions to quieter moods, finding Cue 18 a '*sudden* change' and describing the music as a 'silent prayer in trouble[,] hushed', while he found that the continuing music at Cue 19 'engenders a sad spirit/feeling' and was a 'change to tender thoughts & reflections'. He emphasized the point again at Cue 48, 'always *sudden* change to *p*, after frantic outburst', and thought the movement's last few bars contained an 'awfully sudden change to Ab'. Many of these points may count towards Jaeger's earlier expressed doubts about the movement, doubts which never entirely left him. He seems in particular to have remained unhappy over its overall structure and form, and his doubts over the identification of the 'second subject' were echoed later in a comment querying the commencement of the recapitulation.

The other movements were less fully annotated. Jaeger noted the contrapuntal treatment at Cues 74 and 75 in the Scherzo, and the transformation of the movement's main theme in the slow movement. This was always the part of the work that he loved most, and he wrote at its beginning, 'A most exquisite movt. Chaste, deeply felt real heart music[,] "holy" purity of expression most rare in these days[,] no sensation[...]any where.' He found the opening lento of the Finale 'very impressive' and wrote of the 'boisterous *optimism*' of the allegro, and how it 'wants hearing'. He thought it 'an emphatic affirmation [of] life as a [fine?] noble thing', and thought it done in '*manly* fashion (work, energy, deeds of derring do ...&c &c [)]'.

The notes form the basis of a document that would have been an important addition to Jaeger's Elgarian writings, had not serious incapacity stood in the way. But even at this stage, some humour shows through. He found a fellow-Variation in the Scherzo, writing of the clarinet and bassoon demisemiquavers immediately before Cue 70, 'the bewitching Dorabella casts a merry glance', and noted 'this theme is a caution to rattlesnakes' of the music at Cue 119 in the Finale.

Sydney Loeb's thoughtful kindness continued, and he was keen to visit again. But Jaeger felt unable to cope with the demands of acting the host, preferring the quiet companionship of his favourite child, his eight-year-old daughter Mary, who was often allowed to sit at his bedside at this time.

37 Curzon Road,
Muswell Hill
N.

12/1/9

My dear Loeb,

I received a pot of Turtle (*real* Turtle!) soup the other evening, but no hint as to the Kind giver, nor has one reached me since. I can only suppose that I have to thank you for the 'Delientesse' (which I never in my life tasted before) and if I'm correct in my surmise I hope you'll accept my warmest thanks for the gift. I ate (or drank!) the soup with relish without waiting for the sender to declare himself. Just as well that I did, it might have turned bad & the lovely pieces of green fat rancid if I had procrastinated.

Are you going to Saturday's concert to hear *the* Symphony once again? Of course you are. I want to go too, but I ***must not.*** Verb. sap. sat.

I'm in a wretched state & too full of pain to receive anybody just now[.] I must write again, *if* I get rid of my torture, as to Your coming here, as you Kindly suggested.

My wife joins me in sending Kindest regards, and I am

Yours Sincerely & gratefully

A.J. Jaeger[6]

Later that day another time-honoured gift arrived from Loeb, requiring another letter of thanks. Jaeger included some musical gossip and concluded with a touch of gallows humour.

37 Curzon Road,
Muswell Hill
N.

12/1/8[7]

My dear Loeb,

Once more I have to thank you for a Kind gift. You are a brick, & I cant say more than I have so often done to express my gratitude. The grapes were lovely, rich in *sugar*!

Are you going to the opera? Of course! I wish I could hear the Meistersinger once more, that wonderfullest of all Wagners works to me. But I mustn't think of it. Have you read E. Newman's 'Richard Strauss', lately published? It's *excellent.* What a clear, lucid brain the man (N.) has & how fearlessly he expresses his views! I hope you are well. Wish I were. My Doctors speak now of sending me once more to a Sanatorium. I shall strike. I prefer dying at Home if I am so bad.

Ever yours

A.J. Jaeger[8]

The formidable Ernest Newman had been a fellow-contributor to the ill-fated *Musician* of 1897, and came to play his own rôle in Elgar's life and work. His book on the composer had been published some two years previously, perhaps in place of the one that Jaeger decided not to write. The two men seem never to have met, but in admiring Newman's fearlessness, Jaeger reminds us of his own, one of his cardinal qualities as a critic since the days of his clashes with Grove.

The fatally ill man struggled on through that January, sinking so low that once again he thought of suicide. Loeb continued to bolster his weakening constitution with gifts of nourishing food, and in writing to him towards the end of the month, Jaeger revealed a touch of his old self and enjoyed a chance to express trenchant views on English critics. Hans Richter was directing the Wagner performances – three *Ring* Cycles and three *Mastersingers* – during a season of Opera in English at Covent Garden, repeating a successful experiment of the year before. Wagner himself had sanctioned the idea of performances of his works in the vernacular, and Richter quoted Cosima as being fully in support, stating her opinion that 'a profound influence on the public was only possible through the *national language*.'[9] For Jaeger, the idea did not work in practice.

37 Curzon Road,
Muswell Hill
N.

26/1/9

My dear Loeb,

I received late last night a magnificent bunch of grapes – from You, no doubt, & I send you once more heartiest and sincerest thanks. You seem bent on 'sweetening' my wretched existence as far as my palate & tummy are concerned, at any rate, and I fully appreciate your great Kindness, as you Know.

To-day especially my life stands in need of some 'sweetening', for I am in a suicidal mood, I'm so full of pain & misery – I sometimes fancy I cannot stand the never-ending agony any longer. Yet I have days when I get some respite at least in the degree of *intensity* of the pain, and then, though still feeling a wreck & an utterly useless thing, I feel life is sweet after all. Yesterday was such a day; I wish they were not so rare. Enough of this!

I suppose you are patronizing the English 'Ring' & 'Meistersinger'. How do they Compare with Bayreuth performances? Some English friends came last week. They had heard 'Siegfried', & when I asked whether *now* they could follow the *Drama* (POEM) throughout, as we, who *Know* German, can generally do in German performances, they replied, 'oh dear me, no, I understood about a dozen words'!! Well, I said, that's not Wagnerian singing, & the performances are not Music *drama* performances, but old fashioned opera, where the words mattered not one bit. No wonder English singers can pay attention to nice phrasing & Italian 'bel canto' if they drop their consonants, & their vowels are not distinguishable one from the other. English critics dont Know what true Wagnerian singing implies. Clear enunciation of the text is a *first* & almost foremost consideration.

I see Nikisch will conduct E.E.'s Symphony at the Philharmonic in May. Good! That should prove interesting, as will also be Wood's reading on Feb 3.

Goodnight! I hope you are keeping well.

Very Sincerely Yours

A.J. Jaeger[10]

Performances of the Elgar Symphony continued to proliferate. Nikisch conducted the work at the Leipzig Gewandhaus early in February, by which time it would also have been heard in the United States and Vienna, with many further performances booked at home and abroad. Nikisch's Philharmonic performance in London would take place just five days before Jaeger died. His condition worsened towards the end of February, when he was forced to take to his bed once more with an attack of bronchitis and a recurrence of heart strain. He managed another short note to Sydney Loeb, who had again offered transport to a concert.

37 Curzon Road,
Muswell Hill
N.

10/3/9.

My dear Loeb,

Very many thanks for your Kind letter with offer re Taxi, and for the lovely grapes, which I eat with relish (I have just had some) – You ask; 'Wie gehts'? Why, my dear friend, it 'geht' badly. I am, & have been for a fortnight now, in Bed with a terrible Bronchitis which gives me Hades! Fever, heart collapsed once more, consequent extreme weakness, Blues, Hump, pip – I have *everything*, & feel fit for the crematorium. Can you imagine my wishing to go to any concert under the circs? Not yet! But I will bear your most Kind offer in mind & meanwhile: Vielen Dank! The German critics are going for E's Sym. in fine style. I thought they would. No chauvinism over E. over there. My wife who has a wretched cold too, sends Kindest regards.

So does your Nim.[11]

Jaeger seems never to have properly recovered from the bronchitic infection, and more than a fortnight elapsed before he had the strength to write to Loeb again. In the misery of his illness, and at some distance now from the sounds of the music heard in performance, he continued even at this point to fret over a final judgement on Elgar's Symphony, and began almost perversely to complain of that need for repeated hearings of the work which he had earlier advocated. He now felt an inability on the composer's part to produce themes that might impress an 'average audience,' and repeated, if with disapproval, the criticisms of the quality of Elgar's invention that he was finding in the German press. Jaeger continued also to worry about the 'chauvinistic over-appreciation' accorded to the Symphony by English audiences, and about the potential power of the press to boost such responses on the one hand, and destroy reputations on the other. It was a last opportunity for a dig at the critics and a last opportunity, too, to plead the cause of a little-known composer.

37 Curzon Road,
Muswell Hill
N.

28/3/9

My dear Loeb,

I came downstairs for the first time this afternoon after 5 weeks of Bed & misery. I haven't the strength for a long letter, and I want to thank you for the two lots of lovely grapes you so kindly sent me since I last wrote to you. They were highly appreciated, I need not say.

It seems to me you are hearing every performance of E E's Symphony that London offers to an evidently insatiable public. Are you not getting surfeited; & does E's music stand this re-iteration well? The more I think over the work the more I feel that E. must do much better yet, if he wishes to write the first English Symphony to be worthy of being added as a link to the chain of great, classic Symphonies. He has everything in his favour except that sine quâ non, the power of coining really striking themes that shall leave their impress upon your brain the first time you hear them, and do not require that repeated hearing & loving meeting-you-halfway, which we E enthusiasts are prepared to give to his music, but which the average audience cannot be expected to indulge in, pour les beaux yeux de M. Sir Elgar. *All* the German (Vienna & Leipzig) reviews I have seen complain of this lack of invention ('trocken in der Enfindung', 'der Componisten ist nichts eingefallen' &c). No! in these days of sensationalism critics won't extend to any new work the Kind treatment so many masterpieces in the past days have demanded & received. They hear once, fail to understand – and condemn. Meanwhile, as regards this native, chauvinistic over-appreciation, I can't understand it, & can only hope that its *genuine* after all & not merely press-made. What can't the press cause the public to wax enthusiastic over? And what can it not utterly undo & Kill? Vide Maclean's Annunciation, *unjustly* slaughtered the other day, though a work worth any few dozen average Festival novelties for which the critics find words of praise.

I must stop & rest. I hope you are well, & jolly.

My wife joins me in sending Kindest regards & I am, as ever

Yours, very sincerely,

A.J. Jaeger[12]

Alexander Morvaren Maclean (1872–1936) had already enjoyed success as a conductor and composer, mainly of Opera. He won the Moody-Manners prize for a one-act opera by a British subject in 1895, and had another, full-length, work produced at Mainz some ten years later. The tone and content of the review of *The Annunciation* which appeared in the *Musical Times* for March 1909 vindicates Jaeger's anger and demonstrates the gap left by his absence from the world of music criticism. The values of the English Church style persisted still.

> Whether Mr Maclean has at once succeeded in finding an appropriate idiom for oratorio or sacred drama is somewhat doubtful. It would seem rather that his operatic training has too strongly dominated his style. The subject of the 'Annunciation' demands lofty treatment and artistic restraint. It is easy to give Mr Maclean credit for much originality and power to vivify by strong colours and sudden contrasts, but there are probably many who will find the colours too glaring for such a solemn subject. He is able to work up orchestral and choral forces to powerful climaxes which, however are sometimes not obviously congruous. Some of the choral passages . . . were highly dramatic and exciting as music, and there were often charming touches of varied orchestration the left one wistful [*sic*] for more. Mr Maclean's use of the *leit motif* is ingenious, and throughout the work considerable technical skill is displayed.[13]

Browsing through the musical press, in fact, must have been another of the pleasures left to Jaeger in these last weeks of his life. The columns of the *Musical Times* would have been a major link with the world of music ever since his retirement, despite the irritation which they caused. The continued staple diet of leading articles was on the great cathedrals and churches and their organs, varied occasionally by features on such subjects as Chinese music and folk-song, and the continued recyling of Grove's Analyses of familiar repertoire classics. But there were always the reports of the familiar Festivals to provide interest, with news from Sheffield, Leeds, Bristol,

Norwich, the Three Choirs and the Proms. Henry Wood continued to direct the Queen's Hall concerts – although he probably still played too much Russian music for Jaeger's taste – and Hans Richter carried on, solid and reliable as ever. Some notable links with the past had died, including Richard Mühlfield, Joachim, Sarasate, Grieg and Rimsky-Korsakov, but new names began to appear in their stead – Beecham, Percy Grainger, Beatrice Harrison, Landon Ronald, Marie Hall, Mischa Elman, Nikisch, Kreisler. Among composers, works by Jaeger's protégés – Coleridge-Taylor, Walford Davies, Bell, Holbrooke, Scott, McEwen – continued to gain attention, but now another new generation was beginning to emerge, including Vaughan Williams, Delius, Ireland, Bax, Frank Bridge and Havergal Brian. Jaeger had already expressed his dislike of the music of Delius and it is difficult to think of him viewing many of the new trends with approval, had he been able to maintain his concert-going.

He would have read of Debussy's visits to London to conduct his music and of the première of Strauss's *Elektra*, although he could not have known that the first performance of *Le Sacre du Printemps* was just four years away. Nor that the supremacy of German musical tradition and technique would pass, even as her political and military strength collapsed in a conflict that might have seen Jaeger treated with short shrift, deported or interned as an enemy alien. It is impossible, too, to see him accepting the procedures that Arnold Schoenberg devised in the attempt to ensure the position of German music 'for the next hundred years'. Within a short period of time, Jaeger's whole world would have collapsed; tragic and early as his death was, perhaps August Jaeger died at the right time, as Benjamin Britten believed people did.

Certain reports would have given particular satisfaction, such as those concerning the activities of the new Musical League, formed to further the cause of music in England, and of the series of concerts organized by Thomas Dunhill to present chamber works by young English composers. And there were occasional major features on now established figures such as Granville Bantock, Walford Davies and Coleridge-Taylor, whose output as catalogued by the *Musical Times* now ran to some 72 opus numbers.

A month to the day after his last letter to Sydney Loeb, Jaeger found the strength to write briefly to Walford Davies, who had asked him to preview his new Three Choirs work, another song-cycle with orchestra, *Noble Numbers*. Jaeger, now at the weakest point that he had known, responded diffidently, admitting that he was low in mind and that the thought of undertaking the task frightened him; and he knew full well that he was unlikely to live long enough to complete the work. This is Jaeger's last preserved letter, and Davies later told Elgar that he thought it 'had a touch of quietude and resignation in it which I do not remember ever before.'

37 Curzon Road,
Muswell Hill
N.

28/4/9

My dear Davies,

Very many thanks for your Kind letter. I appreciate your writing it in the midst of all your work. And how I envy you; to *have* so much work to do, & to be strong enough to stand the strain!

I hardly like dragging you out of the hurly burly of Your work to come & see this old, damaged (moltissimo!) piece of crockery, vastly as I would appreciate your visit. I am in Bed once more & in a state of such weakness as I have never in my life experienced. Fever, due to Tuberculosis *plus* this ghastly Bronchitis has Kept me down, down down (the temperature is up up up!) for months now. For four months now (literally) I reach 100° & rise above it up to 102 occasionally every afternoon & continue in that purgatory through the night. How *can* a man fight against that sort of thing? Well, I'm a weakling to write like this.

I feel honoured at your request to say something re your Hereford work in the M.T. But, my dear good friend, I can make *no* promise in my present state of collapse. I may be dead in August, when I suppose the stuff should be ready for the press. And I may in any case be unfit to undertake a task which will require a great deal of study to enable me to get 'right inside' your music. Forget not I'm a raw amateur. At present the task *frightens* me & I'd rather say 'no'. I'm too feeble in body *AND* mind. Better ask Colles who is a better musician critic & journalist than old Nim.

I must stop for I'm exhausted with this exertion of writing. Please thank Mrs Matheson very heartily for her Kind letter which I was happy to receive. My dutiful respects to her, & my love to you, dear D.

Ever Deine,

A.J.J.[14]

Tuberculosis is one of the oldest diseases known to man, going back to Classical times and beyond. The appearance of an advanced case was described in vivid terms by the Greek physician Aretaeus during the second century A.D.

> Voice hoarse; neck slightly bent ... fingers slender, but joints thick; of the bones alone the figure remains, for the fleshy parts are wasted; the nails of the fingers crooked, their pulps are shrivelled and flat ... Nose sharp, slender; cheeks prominent and red; eyes hollow, brilliant and glittering; swollen, pale or livid in the countenance; the slender parts of the jaw rest on the teeth, as if smiling; otherwise of a cadaverous aspect. So also in all other respects, slender, without flesh; the muscles of the arms imperceptible ... one may not only count the ribs themselves, but also easily trace them to their terminations ... the spine of the vertebrae formerly being hollow, now protrudes, the muscles on either side being wasted; the whole shoulder-blades apparent like the wings of birds.[15]

The eighteenth-century Shropshire specialist Thomas Beddoes also contributed a classic picture of the later stages of tuberculosis, emphasizing the symptoms and the final spreading of tubercle to the stomach, making the retention of any nourishment impossible.

> … the … hard rending cough, attended sometimes by retching and vomiting, sometimes by stitches which necessitate the most violent struggle against the continued solicitation to cough, and severely punish a moment of inattention; the expectoration sometimes nauseous, always offensive to the eye and harassing when it is not free; the languour with which the patient finds himself over-powered, when his attention is not occupied by some among his various fixed or flying pains; the extremes of cold or heat through which he is carried by the daily returns of hectic; the sweats in which his repose by night drenches him; the breathlessness on motion or without motion, arising by degrees to a sense of drowning, and terminating in actual drowning, when there is no longer strength to bring up the fluids, secreted in the chest; the disorder in the bowels, towards the last always threatening, and finally unrestrainable, while it cuts off those indulgences which the very thirst it creates or aggravates impatiently demands; – these are but a part of the torments under which the physician … sees the consumptive labouring.[16]

Stendhal thought that part of every man's biography should be written by his doctor. Yes, Jaeger may understandably have asked, but which doctor? And given the many variations and developments in the treatment of the illness which was such an important background to his life and work, it might seem appropriate to ask for not one, but a variety of second opinions.

It is easy, and not perhaps entirely inappropriate, to see in August Jaeger many of the romantic myths about pulmonary tuberculosis which grew up during the nineteenth century and which had gained currency among doctors and laymen alike. Some of these myths were centred on the attempted definition of a tubercular 'type,' characterized not only by complexion and eye-colour, and the other outward signs of cough and flush alternating with pallor, but also by an intense capacity for passionate feeling and an unusual flow of spirits. In such people, a mysterious kind of 'inner burning', as of creative drives wrecked by thwarted hopes and blighted desires, led to bursts of euphoria and hyperactivity in a reckless expenditure of energy, followed ultimately by the 'consumption' of the individual. Tuberculosis came to be seen as the disease of artists and creative people – Jaeger was certainly in historic company in this respect – and certain writers sought to invest it with a kind of glamour, creating pale languishing heroines and beautiful, intelligent children whose early passing was described in deathbed scenes which were meant to be somehow peaceful and ennobling.

More scientific counsels remind us that in fact a great many people of all types and classes fell victim to the disease. In the first decade of the twentieth century tuberculosis was responsible for the deaths of one third of men of Jaeger's age, and for one death out of every eight in overall terms. For the vast mass of the population, the disease had become inextricably linked with the unhygienic post-industrial conditions of large cities, characterized by poverty, malnutrition, overcrowding, poor ventilation and an atmosphere polluted by dust and fumes. Here too there may be some clues to Jaeger's illness, as there may be also in his largely office-bound lifestyle and even in his proximity to printers, among whom the rate of tubercular infection was twice that of the general male population. Some doctors, also, would have pointed to Jaeger's early connection with the cattle trade, and the possibility of infection through milk or meat, while others might have emphasized an evident family susceptibility.

A huge proportion of the population fell victim almost routinely to a primary infection by the tubercle bacillus, which might then remain dormant for months or years. A significant factor in the development of a secondary infection would be the weakening of an individual's immune system, at the mercy of persistent overwork and associated stress. Modern medicine might emphasize the obsessive-compulsive aspects of Jaeger's fascination with detail, his perfectionism and apparent need to work long hours and deny himself rest. Such factors often go together with a high sense of duty and high ambition, blocked despite all efforts. And if we question the underlying reasons for such behaviour, a standard answer seems to be that the overwork may be part of a search for love and affection, presumably rooted in childhood experiences. Certainly it seems accepted that some kind of deep emotional upset, related to work or private life, may precede or precipitate the onset of tuberculosis. Professionally, Jaeger was often frustrated and unhappy at Novello's, but such feelings seem unlikely to have produced a severe enough inner conflict. On a more personal level, some authorities have identified a bereavement, or break in a significant relationship, as being a factor that may be associated with lowered resistances to tuberculosis. It may sound unscientific, but then August Jaeger was the most unscientific of men, and he spoke his own truth when he told Dora Penny, of his efforts on Elgar's behalf, 'I have worked terribly hard for E.E. and ruined my health over it very likely ...'. The gradual distancing in his relationship with Elgar must indeed have been hard to bear.

Sadly the developments in bacteriology and radiology which had taken place in Jaeger's lifetime seem to have had little or no place in the treatments he received. An historic breakthrough had taken place in 1882, when the German researcher Robert Koch achieved the first scientific identification of the tubercle bacillus, thus identifying tuberculosis as a contagious disease and aiding diagnostic precision. England was slow in responding to the discovery, and Jaeger's condition, like that of so many others, was only fully confirmed when it was too late. Koch's development of tuberculin, a supposed inoculation-cure, in 1890, and Röntgen's discovery of X-rays in 1895, also attracted little early interest among the medical profession in England. But public concern was high and in 1898 the National Association for the Prevention of Consumption and Other Forms of Tuberculosis was formed under the patronage of the Prime Minister and the Prince of Wales. Within twenty years it had resulted in a comprehensive state-controlled scheme for the eradication of the disease. Surgical approaches were developed, collapsing the lung in order to rest and heal it, and finally came the arrival of drug treatment and the feeling – illusory it now seems – that tuberculosis, Bunyan's 'Captain of all these men of death', had been conquered once and for all.

There was little therefore that Isabella and the doctors could do to alleviate Jaeger's sufferings as, with his sister Joanna's help, they nursed him through his final dreadful weeks, complicated by the constant need to guard against the possibility of family infection. Doses of opium may have brought the patient himself some ease but Isabella's load was a heavy one indeed, for there was her weekly burden of teaching to be maintained, in addition to her share of the care of her elderly mother-in-law, as well as her own two children. Finally, in May, two months to the day after his forty-ninth birthday, Jaeger's sufferings came to an end.

37, Curzon Rd.
Muswell Hill, N.

May 18th [1909]

My dear Sir Hubert,

My dear Husband wished me to write to you, & give you his love, & bid you goodbye. He had the greatest love & admiration for you, & he would have loved to see you again. He died very peacefully early this morning.

Yours very Sincerely,

Isabella Jaeger.[17]

The two women busied themselves in the necessary tasks. Joanna registered the death – 'Pthisis Pulmonalis 5 years, Exhaustion' – and Isabella continued to write the brave valedictory letters, to Dora Penny, Elgar, Walford Davies and many others, that her husband had asked for. The gift of warm and generous friendship had been one of the secrets of his influence and achievements, and his friends were in his last thoughts. For many of them, the message must almost have seemed to come from beyond the grave. Walford Davies preserved the letter that he received.

37 Curzon Rd.
Muswell Hill
N.

May 18th [1909]

My dear Dr Davies,

My dear husband's last wishes were that I should write to his friends, & bid them goodbye for him. He sent his dear love to you. I know how I can rely on your sympathy when I tell you he died early this morning. Peacefully, serenely, as such a good man should.

He wished me to tell you he was not afraid of death[.]

Yours very sincerely,

I. Jaeger[18]

Hubert Parry received Isabella's letter on the day of Jaeger's death, and replied, characteristically and immediately, with warm appreciation of her husband and another cheque. She replied at once.

37, Curzon Road,
Muswell Hill, N.

May 19th [1909]

My dear Sir Hubert,

Your very kind letter of sympathy has warmed my heart, & I thank you most gratefully for thinking of me. Your praise of him makes me very proud. What his loss is to me I do not think anyone can quite realize, & I fear my courage is not great, but I have my children & they will help me.

How I wish he could have read the letters I have, telling of the warm appreciation, & admiration everyone has for him. But maybe he knows now.

It is good of you to send me the cheque. It will help me greatly. Thanking you again from my heart for your kind sympathy. Believe me,

Yours ever Sincerely,

Isabella Jaeger.[19]

Elgar was staying with Pippa Worthington in Italy, and did not receive Jaeger's message for some days.

Careggi

May 21: 1909

Dear Mrs Jaeger:

Thank you most sincerely for your great kindness in writing: you know our deepest sympathies & prayers are with you & yours. The news came as a great shock & I cannot realize that the end is come & I am overwhelmed with sorrow for the loss of my dearest & truest friend.

May God bless you

Yrs ever sncly

Edward Elgar[20]

And in the course of a letter to Ivor Atkins the next day he wrote, 'My heart is heavy. I have just heard of poor dear Nimrod's death. I say no more now.' He seems to have said little further to anyone about Jaeger, except to Dora Penny, who recorded that during a visit she made to Plas Gwyn that August,

... a batch of proofs came from Novello's and I unpacked them. It seemed so dreadful to have no exuberant letter from dear Nimrod and I spoke of it.

'Don't talk about it. It's too sad. I can't bear it.'

But that evening, sitting in the study, – the Lady having said 'Good-night' early and departed to bed – we talked much about him. I told E.E. how I had spent the whole afternoon at Muswell Hill the previous winter; how I had tried my utmost to cheer him, and how I had cried most of the way home in the train afterwards.[21]

15 In Memory of a Seer

Jaeger was cremated at Golders Green, in a simple ceremony with music provided by the choristers of the Temple Church accompanied at the organ by Walford Davies. His ashes were scattered in Coldfall Woods, alongside Creighton Avenue in Muswell Hill, a favourite walk. Probate was granted to Jaeger's executors, John McEwen and William Bell, early in June, with the gross value of his estate assessed at two hundred and forty-two pounds, seven shillings, and twopence. With every prospect of a precarious financial future for Isabella and her children, to say nothing of the other Jaeger dependants, the idea of a benefit concert was soon mooted, with evident support from Novello's. Hans Richter accepted an invitation from Elgar to act as conductor-in-chief, along with appearances by others of Jaeger's composer friends. Originally planned for the autumn, the concert was put off until the new year, possibly due to concerns over its success. Elgar himself seems to have had his doubts, and expressed them in a letter to Walford Davies at the beginning of October.

> The whole thing depends on the attendance – this I have said depends upon the people in London who are arranging the concert, getting the thing known *and* people (audience) to come – in this matter I was a nonentity. The expenses must I imagine be very large. I cannot feel that much will be made although, for the sentiment, I should love the concert to take place. I cannot *decide* whether it is rash or not.
>
> I have written about the guarantee – but – [1]

He kept the extent of his own contribution to the guarantee fund confidential but the overall amount, bolstered by generous contributions from Parry and Walford Davies, seemed to be sufficient for Elgar to happily accept a smaller contribution from the wealthy Frank Schuster. 'Thanks for your letter about the Jaeger concert: I have put you on the list for five pounds – Novellos name 50, Parry & Walford Davies 21 each &c. &c I think financially it shd. be all right. Your five is quite enough.' He was depressed and in poor health for much of the time, and seemed able only to complete smaller works, while working fitfully at sketches for the Second Symphony and Violin Concerto. Both the *Elegy* for string orchestra, written for the Musician's Company in memory of their Warden, and the anthem, *They are at Rest*, for the anniversary of Queen Victoria's death, were necessarily imbued with the spirit of mourning; that year saw not only Jaeger's death but that of another Variation, Basil Nevinson, and of Henry Wood's wife Olga. But he conducted the Symphony at the

Hereford Three Choirs in the autumn, and later embarked on a conducting tour of northern cities.

Another distraction was a meeting in Liverpool of the Musical League, of which Elgar was President. The League's purpose was to promote the music of unfamiliar composers, a cause of which Jaeger would surely have approved, and Elgar would follow his example and maintain interest in young composers and use his influence on their behalf even into the 1920s when musical tastes and styles had undergone a revolution. One early result of that Liverpool meeting was a performance of a work by the young Arnold Bax at the following season's Promenade Concerts on Elgar's recommendation. Towards the end of the year, his creative interest was kindled by some poems by Gilbert Parker which might provide a cycle of songs of frustrated love, and then by a series of passionate songs to words of his own; his intense friendship with Lady Alice Stuart Wortley seems to lie behind them all, as it would lie behind the Violin Concerto that would emerge during the first half of the following year.

Mention was made of the Memorial Concert, now arranged for 24 January 1910, at the beginning of an article about Jaeger which appeared in the Christmas number of *The Spectator*, written by his old friend of the Novello Choir days, C. L. Graves. It was the fullest and most informative public statement about Jaeger's life and career, and a final kindness from the man who had smoothed his entry to Novello's. The writer paid tribute to Jaeger's 'simple, generous nature' and stressed how the anonymity of his writings, and his modest nature, meant that he was little known to the public. He gave a brief account of Jaeger's life since his emigration from Düsseldorf, covering his 'uncongenial labours' with the map-making firm, his career at Novello's and subsequent retirement, and the courage with which he faced his end. Graves justly considered that Jaeger's letters were 'like the man, – sincere, outspoken, impulsive', and ranked his unflagging enthusiasm with that of Grove himself, 'another really great amateur'. There was appreciation of the services that Jaeger had rendered British composers, for his praise and his criticism, for his enthusiasm, sincerity and indefatigable propagandizing, all characterized by his unashamed enjoyment of the emotional in music. Graves pointed to the essential duality of Jaeger's life, how the great Romantic had earned a disciplined living. 'Men so charged with emotion are not often practical, but, by a happy anomaly, Jaeger did not allow his romance to interfere with routine. Musicians are often terrible egoists, but Jaeger was an eminently unselfish enthusiast.' Perhaps in one sense it was the secret of his success and all that he had achieved. And the writer finished with the tragic sacrifice of himself that Jaeger had been compelled to make. 'Despondent about himself, he was full of hope for others, and spent himself in smoothing their path to fame.'[2]

As the date of the Memorial Concert drew nearer, Elgar arranged to orchestrate three of the projected cycle of six Parker songs – the others were never completed – so that their première would enhance the occasion. He wrote to Hans Richter to tell him of his firm intention to attend the concert – 'I wish to shew my love & respect to my departed friend' – and to ask him to conduct the Variations, 'as at present settled'. But Richter wanted Elgar himself to conduct the Variations, self-evidently the core of the programme. The veteran conductor pressed the case with an eloquent tribute to Jaeger and his feelings for Elgar.

> I am very happy that you come to the Jaeger-Concert, it would be incomplete without you. I hope and everybody expects that you will conduct the 'Variations'. You must *not* disappoint the Public who are anxious to show you their respectful sympathy towards the composer of so many masterpieces. Please *do it*, not only for the sake of the audience but – chiefly – in memoriam of your dead friend who loved and adored you with all his noble heart.[3]

In the event Elgar avoided the kind of direct confrontation with Jaeger's 'good honest soul' that conducting the Variations would have made unavoidable. Some years earlier he had written to Jaeger after conducting the work at Liverpool, 'my procession of friends dear to me was nice to see – I mean hear – but the sounds I have connected with them are very vivid (to me) & I feel the corporeal presence of each one as the music goes by'. He was content to conduct his three Gilbert Parker songs, while Parry conducted his *Overture to an Unwritten Tragedy* – an entirely appropriate choice – Coleridge-Taylor his *Ballade*, and Walford Davies four songs from his cycle, *The Long Journey*. Richter, in addition to presiding over the Variations, conducted the *Alto Rhapsody* of Brahms, Hans Sachs's Monologue from Act Three of *Mastersingers*, and brought the concert to a close with the triumphant affirmation of the Prelude, music from a work which Jaeger dubbed his 'musical Bible'. Perhaps the concert's greatest tribute lay in its combination of English and German music on equal terms; that so much native work was fit to measure up to the standard of the greatest German composers was partly Jaeger's achievement. Other distinguished performers contributed to the concert's success including Muriel Foster, who emerged from retirement to take part, and Plunket Greene. All concerned, together with Harold Brooke, Augustus Littleton, Charles Graves and Alfred Kalisch, signed a copy of the Programme[4] to be presented to a proud Isabella, who was present with the children. The feelings of the audience – drawn from all sides of musical life, English and European, and a large one despite foul weather – must have been with them as the Ninth Variation, the heart of the whole concert, majestically unfolded under Richter's outspread arms. Alice Elgar noted in her Diary, 'Wonderful Concert, very large audience. Richter conducted *splendid* performance of Vars. He turned to the Orch. spreading out his arms as if to draw every sound & made the Nimrod gorgeous ... Saw Mrs Jaeger & children, very touching.' Many years later Ivor Atkins recalled the deeply emotional nature of the concert, and for all those who had known Jaeger, and particularly for fellow-Variants, it must have been a deeply moving performance. Winifred Norbury noted in her diary with characteristic stoicism that she thought the Variations performance 'magnificent', and Dora Penny would later write with English euphemism, 'I found it rather a trying experience, particularly the *Variations*. I noticed, however, that others found it "trying" besides myself.' Richter was recalled three times at the conclusion of the work.

The programme contained a short appreciation of Jaeger by Alfred Kalisch, and a reprint of Graves's *Spectator* article was also available separately. Isabella carefully preserved, mounted and bound them, together with some thirty articles and reviews taken from London and provincial newspapers and journals.[5] While many of them focused on the occasion of an Elgar première, and on the galaxy of famous names involved in the concert itself, others were written by critics who had known Jaeger and who had taken the measure of his life and achievements. *The Times* wrote of his earnestness, ardour and infectious enthusiasm, and described the transformation he had worked at Novello's, 'which, when he entered upon his work there, stood for all that was most academic and even reactionary in music, but which at the time of Jaeger's death had learnt to give proper attention to the movement and progress of the art.'[6] The *Daily Telegraph* combined a warm salute to the man and his qualities with an awareness of the elusiveness of his achievement:

> Time was, and that not so very long ago, when among musicians not to know A.J. Jaeger was, indeed, to argue oneself unknown. Now he is gathered to his fathers, and the turf rests lightly on him, and many musicians who knew him and loved him – synonymous terms in his case – paid a tribute to his memory at the concert which took place in Queen's Hall last night. What Jaeger achieved in the furthering of the cause of British music no man knows. We, all of us, know this or that fragment, but only the future will comprehend the real value of him who had a genius for enthusiasm and 'rightness', and was entirely devoid of cant, hypocrisy, and supercilious superiority. A man without an enemy, but with countless friends, such was A.J. Jaeger, and never in Queen's Hall has been paid a more justifiable tribute to the memory of one gone ...[7]

E.A. Baughan wrote in *The Daily News*[8] of his earliest memories of meeting Jaeger the clerk in the gallery at the Richter concerts, and subsequently in the Novello's years, meeting him 'almost every day at lunch, and the long and heated arguments we had remain as a vivid remembrance'. 'Crescendo' of *The Star* thought

> ... it is not often that anyone renders such peculiar service as he did, or inspires such genuine affection as it was given him to do. All British composers were his kin, and it would have been possible to make up a programme of the works of only his intimate friends which would have lasted into the small hours.[9]

The World emphasized one of Jaeger's strengths, his independence of position. 'Just because he worked unofficially, impelled thereto by overmastering zeal, he was able to attract more attention than if he had been speaking in virtue of some place in a hierarchy.' At the same time, the writer thought Jaeger's work 'a very necessary one, and anywhere else it would have been undertaken and done by someone marked out for it by official or other position. Here it would have remained undone but for a lovable enthusiast who occupied a humdrum position in a great publishing firm.'[10]

The critic of the *Sunday Times* dwelt on Jaeger's obscurity, and concluded with a worthy poetic flourish.

> To the general public the late Mr August Jaeger was known not at all; even in musical circles he was not a celebrity, and 'Grove' makes no mention of him. He was neither a composer nor a public performer, nor a newspaper critic; he was simply 'Jaeger of

> Novello's', yet in that comparatively obscure position he found the opportunity by his enthusiastic love of art to exercise a far-reaching influence, and to champion the cause of English music and English musicians with singular effectiveness. He was one of those exceptional men who 'in narrow circles live radiant lives', asking nothing of fame or fortune for their recompense, content that they may add in their measure to the growing good of the world.[11]

But perhaps the review that went deepest, 'In Memory of an Idealist', was published anonymously in the journal *Truth*, although it bears every sign of being written by someone who had known its subject a long time and understood him well, possibly Graves. Once more there were memories of Jaeger's early days in London, with a reminder of the sacrifices he would make in the cause of music.

> A quarter of a century ago Jaeger formed one of a group of young and enthusiastic music-lovers generally to be found in a particular gallery at all the best concerts in the old St James's Hall; and the love of music which induced him then to spend every shilling he could afford, and sometimes more, on concert-going, remained with him to the end of his all too brief existence the consuming passion of his life.[12]

The writer continued by touching on the moral basis of Jaeger's approach to music:

> There never was a more whole-souled devotee of the art than Jaeger, or one who in his unpretending way laboured more strenuously in its cause. It is, indeed, just such men as Jaeger who are most sorely needed in these cynical hypercritical days when no one feels very strongly about anything, and enthusiasm is regarded as bad form. This was not Jaeger's way at all. Music to him was something more than a mode of entertainment, or even an art. It was a religion, and evoked sentiments to correspond. Hence he was never indifferent or lukewarm in regard to the developments of the art, which he judged almost as much in relation to their moral as to their purely musical aspects.[13]

In support of this, the writer invoked Jaeger's gradual disillusion with the music of Richard Strauss, which despite its technical achievements, was to his mind spiritually inferior to that of the greatest of Elgar, 'leaving all the finer feelings untouched and unexpressed'. Jaeger's admiration for the high seriousness of purpose of the music of Max Reger was cited, as was his devotion to the greatest German Classic-Romantic figure.

> ... Jaeger found much to admire in the serious brooding art of Reger, which if often enough difficult and obscure could certainly not be reckoned meretricious or unworthy. Brahms was another of Jaeger's major divinities among composers for much the same reason. Not that he was foolish enough to suppose that any amount of spiritual fervour or good intentions could compensate for musical weakness, but it was one of his strongest convictions that the highest art could never find expression in ignoble subjects or spring from unworthy natures or fail to exercise a bracing and uplifting influence, and so the depth and earnestness and consistent loftiness of aim of Brahms found in him a ready response.[14]

And so too, the writer might have added, did the *nobilmente* of Elgar, and for the same reasons. If Jaeger's philosophical seriousness might be a Germanic trait, the article concluded by emphasizing the importance of a quality highly valued in English life, amateurism.

> Sometimes, no doubt, Jaeger's enthusiasm ran away with him, but this is a fault which leans so much to virtuous side that it is to be accounted only another reason for honouring his memory today. 'Why is it,' asked the late Sir George Grove once, 'that in music the greatest enthusiasm is so often displayed by those who have the least technical knowledge?' and the question comes back to mind in considering the case of Mr Jaeger. While he was certainly not lacking in very considerable technical knowledge, as his many excellent analyses attest – analyses as admirable in their way as any ever written, considered either technically or otherwise – Jaeger never pretended to be anything but an amateur, and herein lay, perhaps, the secret of the influence which he exercised. For while his knowledge of the art on its technical side was wide and deep, he at the same time never lost the enthusiasm of the amateur and the idealist.[15]

Perhaps most succinctly and appropriately of all, the *Glasgow Herald*[16] wrote simply of Jaeger's 'single-minded enthusiasm and his genius for discovering genius'.

If August Jaeger was given more recognition in death than he had ever sought in life, the story of his widow and children as they continued their lives without him has been largely undocumented. Isabella of necessity continued to develop her teaching connections in Gloucester and elsewhere, with her ever-helpful sister-in-law Joanna on hand to look after the children, Mary and Edward.[17] Mary in particular seemed to possess her father's sense of fun.

> Memories of her childhood in Curzon Road include tying a length of string to the lamp-post on the pavement & over the hedge so that gentlemen walking down the road in their top hats would be de-hatted. Also of throwing a coin into the street & being delighted & full of mirth as the unfortunate passerby hunted for 'his' dropped money. Mummy also loved tree-climbing in the fields where now is the Wood Green area.[18]

In the immediate aftermath of her husband's death, Isabella is recorded in Alice Elgar's diary as having visited twice during April 1910, accompanying Carice to a matinée on one occasion. In November she was re-admitted a British subject, having taken German nationality by virtue of her marriage, and that month also she was present at the première of Elgar's Violin Concerto at the Queen's Hall, where her husband had been such a frequent and familiar presence. Elgar offered to send tickets for another performance of the work at the end of the month, but continuing family responsibilities meant that she had to refuse. 'My husband's old Mother passed away late on Thursday last, & I do not think I could leave Miss Jaeger so soon,' she wrote. As for the Concerto itself, the first major work of Elgar that Jaeger never heard, Isabella's responses were in terms of her dead husband.

> I heard the first performance of the concerto, & was deeply impressed, & touched with it. Will you let me say how wonderfully the entrance of the solo violin appeals to me? The unpretending greatness & nobility of it is beautiful. I cried from the shere [*sic*] feeling of it. The second subject of the first movement haunts me too. My greatest wish is that my dear husband might have heard it too – maybe he did – ! How enthusiastic & full of joy he would have been.'[19]

Elgar, now arrived at the creative peak of his career, continued to devote himself to orchestral music with the Second Symphony, given its première in May 1911. The following month Isabella wrote to congratulate him on the award of the O.M., 'I am so delighted it has been given to you. It is so fitting.' But no message from her has been preserved over the work in which Elgar was finally able to exorcise his repressed grief for Jaeger, a setting of Arthur O'Shaughnessy's ode, *The Music Makers*, with its overwhelming reworking of the *Nimrod* Variation at the passage

> But on one man's soul it hath broken,
> A light that doth not depart;
> And his look, or a word he hath spoken,
> Wrought flame in another man's heart.

In his broken English – and none the less eloquently for all that – Julius Buths wrote to Elgar about the work, with memories stirred of Jaeger's involvement in the Düsseldorf *Gerontius* performances of ten years before.

> I got your dear letter last week and was heartily pleased by, but the copy of your 'Music Makers' is not yet arrived. I long really for to know it, so more I can tell you, that I have read in the September Musical Times an article about it. You are quite right to say, that I will like the poem. The strophes I read, made a deep impression on myself. That is a fine poetry and how actual for yourself! 'But on one man's soul it hath broken', really, 'dear Jaeger' and I feel happy, that it was myself, to whom 'he hath spoken a word'. Please, please, send me the copy![20]

The *Musical Times* preview of the Ode had been written by Ernest Newman, who had taken over something of Jaeger's position as Elgarian analyst. In writing to Newman about the work's creative background, Elgar chose to explain the *Nimrod* reference in terms which emphasized Jaeger's achievement as a journalist and as a man.

> ... I do not mean to convey that his was the only soul on which light had broken or that his was the only word, or look that wrought 'flame in another man's heart'; but I do convey that amongst all the inept writing and wrangling about music his voice was clear, ennobling, sober and sane, and for his help and inspiration I make this acknowledgement.[21]

When, on the 4 August 1914 and very much as Jaeger had predicted, 'Der Tag' finally arrived, Isabella anglicized the family name in the face of violent anti-German feeling, as did so many, including the royal family. Thus the Jaegers became the Hunters. Even such a close friend as Dora Penny seems to have destroyed her letters from Jaeger at this period, although she later made amends by dedicating her book of Elgarian memories 'To the Memory of A.J.J.'. Had he lived, Jaeger would have seen his adopted country's admiration for things German transformed into the sudden discovery that German militarism had all along been a menace to civilization. He presumably would have agreed, but that may not have stopped him from being attacked, as German-born citizens were in Deptford, Poplar, Crewe, Keighley and

Liverpool. Jaeger, who had retained his German citizenship, would have been further at risk after the sinking of the *Lusitania*, when Government policy came to favour the internment of 'enemy aliens' – and, as if to add insult to injury, there was an internment camp at the Alexandra Palace itself. An old German colleague from Novello's, the master-craftsman who had worked closely with Jaeger and Elgar, was threatened with repatriation. 'Mr B[rause], Novello's head engraver, called to see me in great distress about being repatriated which he didn't want at all,' noted Parry in May 1915. 'I tried to comfort him.'[22]

As the years passed, there seems to have been little enough continuing contact between Jaeger's widow and his old friends, although Marguerite Swale appears to have remained close to the family. At Christmas 1914, Sydney Loeb sent Isabella a copy of a book containing reprinted articles from *The Musician*, including the Wagner letters that her husband had translated and for which he had not been paid.[23] Her continuing sympathy for the cause of Coleridge-Taylor, who had died in 1912, was shown in the assistance she gave his biographer Berwick Sayers, whose book on the composer appeared in 1915; later she would help Basil Maine with his biography of Elgar. Alice Elgar's diary records an occasion at Severn House just after Christmas 1916, when 'Mrs Hunter & 2 children came – (formerly Jaeger) Gave them little presents. They seemed to enjoy visit & the Gramophone.' Elgar was unwell at the time, and Mary, born during the composition of *Gerontius* and now sixteen, later remembered him lying on a sofa while Lalla Vandervelde, another visitor that day, was looking on 'adoring him'. Four years later, on hearing of Alice Elgar's death, Isabella wrote a letter of condolence. Even though it was eleven years after her husband's passing, she wrote as if he were a continuing presence: 'Will you accept my deepest sympathy? I know what this terrible loss means to you & Miss Elgar, & my heart aches for you both. My husband understands too, & if it is possible he is sending you a message of hope & comfort'.[24] In return, Elgar sent her an inscribed copy of his Violin Sonata, with the message that it had been Alice's wish.

Teaching work, if available in sufficient quantity, would no doubt have ensured Isabella a modestly comfortable existence, although it became expedient in 1919 to sell the copyright in Cyril Scott's *English Waltz* to Messrs Elkin & Co, and in later years there would be a sad procession of documentary material sold at auction. The family continued to live in the north London area for some time, although the Curzon Road house had to be given up in favour of a flat above shops along Muswell Hill Broadway. Here ill luck continued to dog them with the occurrence of a serious fire in the premises below, which destroyed virtually all their possessions, including a grand piano which had been purchased with part of the proceeds of the Memorial Concert; Isabella managed to rescue her treasured Guadanigni, and the family was accommodated by friends nearby for some considerable time.

The young Felix Aprahamian met both Isabella, as an afternoon tea guest of his mother's at their home in Methuen Park, Muswell Hill, and Mary, who became private secretary to the headmaster of nearby Tollington Boys' School, which he attended. Mary's role on one occasion included ushering the youngster into the

Head's study for an episode of physical retribution; more happily, Isabella readily offered an Elgar letter from her husband's collection[25] on learning of the miscreant's possession of a signed photograph of the composer. Both Jaeger's children – Maimie and Ted to the family – displayed musical talents, Mary took enthusiastic part in Gilbert and Sullivan productions with the Muswell Hill Choral Society, and Edward developed his childhood interest in the piano, playing by ear but '... better than his cousin Brian, who was a trained musician.'[26] Professionally Ted demonstrated more of a technical bent than his father, adopting a career with the Cable and Wireless Telegraph Company which involved several periods in Rio de Janeiro.

Mary left her post at Tollington School in 1929 to marry Alec Fraser, a colleague of her brother, now married himself, and the foursome enjoyed a final posting to Rio, where they began their families, until most expatriates were withdrawn in the early 1930s. There would be seven Jaeger grandchildren altogether. Having lost an eye in an accident in Rio, Ted became head tutor at the company's training department in London, and as a member of the Home Guard during the war, was restricted to light duties such as fire-watching, although he commanded an ancient anti-aircraft gun for a time during the Blitz. He developed a heart condition and died in 1960. Something of his father's qualities of enthusiasm and meticulousness were demonstrated in the beautifully detailed maps he contributed to a magazine devoted to steam trains which he produced jointly with his Yorkshire cousin Brian Tunstall, a multi-talented artist, writer, musician, naturalist and linguist, who provided the illustrations. Brian continued living at Ivy Cottage until shortly before his death in 1981, welcoming many of the grandchildren on holiday visits and sharing with them favourite hobbies such as fell-walking and climbing. Relations with the Yorkshire side of the family had remained close, and earlier the indefatigable Donnie had gone to keep house at Ivy Cottage on the death of Isabella's sister Lucy.

In her later years Isabella made loyal efforts to keep the flame burning, lending her late husband's collection of Elgar letters to Basil Maine, the composer's first biographer and the first writer to offer a public account of Jaeger's role in Elgar's life. In 1933 and approaching 70, she wrote to Henry Colles, the critic and friend of Walford Davies whom Jaeger had admired so much, to suggest that her husband's work merited mention in Grove's Dictionary of Music. The reply was sympathetic.

> I think a memorial of your husband's work in 'Grove' would have been very suitable and I am sorry it was not done in my edition of five years ago. Whether another opportunity will occur I do not know at all. No further edition is in contemplation at present so far as I know, and when it is undertaken it may not be in my hands. However, I keep an interleaved copy in which I write all sorts of corrections and addditions, & if you would care to send me a note of the essential facts I wd put them in for possible use.[27]

The brief article duly appeared in the fourth edition, some seven years later.[28] Isabella did not live to read it, dying in 1938; in accordance with the terms of John Rutson's benefaction, the precious Guadanigni was returned to the Royal College of Music, where, after some 45 years, its condition was duly noted as 'excellent'.

The correspondence with Colles had been taken over by Mary, who wrote also to Walford Davies, just over a year before his death, with a musical anecdote of her son which Jaeger himself might have enjoyed. Davies replied warmly from wartime Bristol where he was working for the BBC.

The British Broadcasting Corporation
Broadcasting House,
21-25 Whiteladies Road,
Bristol 8

29th February, 1940

Dear Mrs Fraser,

Thank you so much for your letter which I value greatly, not only for its own sake, but for the way it links me to your dear father and your little son, a true grandson. Give Neville my love. I hope some day we may meet somehow.

The remark 'I don't like that voice, it spoils the tune' shall be duly passed on to many a singer. They are not too willing to learn out of the mouth of babes.

With warmest greetings,

Yours sincerely,

Walford Davies[29]

Isabella was affectionately remembered by those grandchildren who knew her as a good-humoured, gracious presence, taking a particular interest in their music lessons and exercising a grandmotherly influence on occasion: 'Mummy on landing & me in hall had a rather noisy altercation & granny's hand rested on my back & she spoke very gently and the anger was totally diffused.'[30]

There were memories too of Jaeger's sisters, the 'German Aunts', Donnie and Mollie, who both lived on until the early 1950s and in their different ways shared much of his rich humanity. Both unmarried, they made a strikingly contrasted pair; Donnie, kindly, selfless, independent, somewhat gaunt and austere-looking, spent her life helping others in the family. Mollie, buxom and humorous but rather demanding and autocratic, lived in Bayswater and was one of the principal language teachers at the London School of Languages, where she made a speciality of coaching members of the diplomatic service. Stories of their various eccentricities survive in the family, of how Donnie would tie a handkerchief under her beaky, dripping nose and in a bow over her head when plagued by sinusitis, and of how she would arrive for a regular Sunday lunch with the Frasers during the war bearing her week's meat ration, a chump chop. 'She would be glimpsed arriving slowly up the alleyway at the side of the house – red cherries in her black straw hat bobbing about as she walked, & just visible above the top of the fence.'[31] Mollie by contrast cultivated a certain 'style', sporting high ruched collars and pince-nez and making regular use of henna to maintain her auburn hair, with a bun and curls above the forehead; something of a continuing burden, she confessed, advising her niece not to imitate her example because 'once you start, you can never stop!' She thrived on attention from others, so much so that Mary Fraser was advised by her doctor not to have her to live with the family on retirement. Her visits could be memorable nevertheless.

> She was plump and jolly with a somewhat wicked sense of humour. She was, however, quite happy to sit back and be waited on. Her visits, though welcome, were not quite as welcome as Donnie's. Mollie would sit plumply in our lounge gazing round and would eventually call to my mother working in the kitchen, 'Maimie, I'm bored, come and talk to me.' On one occasion when I was … 3 or 4 years old, there was some programme on the radio. I was sitting on the arm of great-aunt Mollie's chair and must have been shuffling my feet in time to the music. Mollie called out, 'Maimie, look, the child is quite musical.' She gave me a great hug, knocked her glasses askew, and laughed and laughed![32]

Eventually Mary Fraser and her husband left London in 1954 to retire to Bexhill on the Sussex coast, where for a short time they ran 'Jane's Treasure Chest', a toy shop and dolls' hospital. She continued to do whatever came to hand to further the cause, helping Jerrold Northrop Moore, contributing to the fund for the Elgar statue at Worcester, and attending a special ceremony at St Sepulchre's, Holborn Viaduct in 1975 to commemorate the centenary of Coleridge-Taylor's birth. She was always affected on hearing *Nimrod* performed, feeling that it brought her very close to her father, and with the passing of the years she came more and more to idealize his memory. At the age of 81 she wrote to a niece, of the father who had died when she was a child of nine, 'One woman wrote of Daddy – "He was a small man," etc. He was tall, slim, fair and very elegant, *very* particular about his clothing, shirts, ties, etc.' Her reverence for her father and her understandable – and entirely justified – concern that he should be properly and more widely recognized extended also to a modern classic of Elgar popularization.

> 23, Ladbroke Sq
> London
> W11
>
> Sunday
>
> Dear Miss (?) Fraser,
>
> I have just come across a letter you wrote me last year when I was away on location – forgive the late reply.
>
> Believe me I was fully aware of Jaeger's role in Elgar's life – but in the time allotted to me – 50 minutes it was only possible to give the briefest outline of Elgar's life, though on reflection, I think we did your father a great injustice by not even mentioning him. I have often thought of making a sequel to the film concentrating on the more intimate relationships in Elgar's life. If I ever do it, Jaeger will of course have pride of place.
>
> All honour to your father for championing the work of such a great man.
>
> Yours Sincerely,
>
> Ken Russell[33]

After her husband's death Mary lived on in Bexhill until 1991, remembered as a bright old lady with a distinct presence, who maintained her active love of music and her pride in her father's name until the end. She is remembered thus by a fellow-passenger on a concert outing.

> ... in the winter of 1989–90, going over to Hastings for a concert, I found myself sitting beside a lady who was clearly knowledgeable about music. Then, suddenly, she turned to me and said 'You know the music of Elgar?', and, when I replied that I did, she went on 'Do you know the Enigma Variations?', and when I said that indeed I did, she continued 'You know the one called "Nimrod"?' and, when I agreed again, more firmly, to my absolute astonishment, she added 'He was my Father'. I was so amazed that I immediately countered, in disbelief, with 'A.J. Jaeger was your Father?', at which point I don't know which of us was the more amazed – I that I was sitting beside the daughter of the 'legend' Nimrod, or she that I actually knew his name![34]

If wider public recognition has never come,[35] August Jaeger, the most modest of men, may not have minded. The best tribute to his life and work is after all to be found in the large and varied body of musical works that he encouraged, urged and sometimes goaded into existence. Many of them remain ripe for rediscovery but others are enduring repertoire classics, masterpieces by a great composer for whose sake Jaeger made willing sacrifice of himself.

Elgar's own story can still appeal to us on the most basic level, almost as one of 'rags to riches', piano-tuner's son to Master of the Musick. His encounter with an obscure music-loving clerk, the son of a cattle-dealer, who came close at times to holding the future of English music in his hands, is, in its way, another such story, and one of the happiest accidents of the English musical renaissance.

August Jaeger came to England as something of a refugee, in search of simple freedoms and decent values – civilization, in a word. His own total commitment and unique enthusiasm, his heartfelt love of music which never abated and which sustained to the last a determined mind in a frail body, has enhanced that civilization for us now and for all the future. And if Jaeger's 'riches' were mainly of the mind and heart, then, after all, ...

'What will survive of us is love'.

Notes

Abbreviations

AJJ	C.L.G., 'August J. Jaeger', *The Spectator*, 25 December 1909, pp. 1100–1101.
EAF	E. Wulstan Atkins, *The Elgar-Atkins Friendship*, David & Charles, 1984.
DNB	L.G. Wickham and E.T. Williams (eds), *Dictionary of National Biography 1941–1950*, OUP, 1959.
EHP	J.N. Moore (ed.), *Elgar and his Publishers, Letters of a Creative Life*, Clarendon Press, 1987.
ESJ	*Elgar Society Journal.*
LN	Percy M. Young (ed.), *Letters to Nimrod: Edward Elgar to August Jaeger*, Dennis Dobson, 1965.
LoL	J.N. Moore (ed.), *Edward Elgar Letters of a Lifetime*, Clarendon Press, 1990.
MoM	P.A. Scholes (ed.), *The Mirror of Music 1844–1944*, Novello & OUP, 1947.
MT	*Musical Times.*
MV	Mrs Richard Powell, *Edward Elgar: Memories of a Variation*, 4th edn, Scolar Press, 1994.
RF	R. Burley and F.C. Carruthers, *Edward Elgar: the Record of a Friendship*, Barrie & Jenkins, 1972.
WRO	Worcester Record Office, Fish Street, Worcester.
YUML	Yale University Music Library.

Chapter 1 1860–95

1. MT June 1909, p. 381.
2. AJJ.
3. B. Maine, *Elgar, His Life And Works,* New Portway Edition, 1973, p. 176.
4. Undated biographical memorandum of August Jaeger by Isabella Hunter, in the possession of Neville Fraser.
5. EHP, p. 48, n. 10.
6. For a time the Düsseldorf Academy was thought to be one of the leading art schools in Germany, making a speciality of narrative-historical, sentimental painting with links to the theatre. Its Director in the 1820s was Peter Cornelius, uncle of the composer. See Geraldine Norman, *Biedermeier Painting*, Thames and Hudson, 1987. Jaeger seems to have possessed a degree of interest in painting and both the *Gerontius* and *Apostles* Analyses make reference to the Pre-Raphaelites. For further discussion see P. Young, *Elgar O.M.*, 2nd edn, White Lion Press, 1973, pp. 307–8, and ESJ, Vol. 10, No. 6, November 1998, *Elgar's Favourite Picture*, by Geoffrey Hodgkins.
7. MT October 1908, p. 644.
8. Ibid.

9. 'Honley Link with Elgar's "Nimrod"', *Huddersfield Daily Examiner*, 18 August 1966. Jaeger's daughter was quite clear that the family came to England 'to escape the rigours of imperial Germany under Bismarck', EHP, Vol. 1, p. 48, n. 9.
10. The firm had connections with another *Enigma* character, for in 1898 Bacon published reproductions of the Toposcope Indicator on the Worcestershire Beacon, designed by Arthur Troyte Griffith for the Diamond Jubilee of Queen Victoria.
11. *Reminiscences of a Middle-Aged Amateur*, RCM Magazine, Vol. 9, No. 3, 1913.
12. MT July 1897, p. 463.
13. MT June 1882, p. 320.
14. H.C. Colles, Jaeger entry in *Grove's Dictionary of Music and Musicians*, 4th Edition, ed. H.C. Colles, 1940.
15. Undated biographical memorandum of August Jaeger by Isabella Hunter, in the possession of Neville Fraser.
16. I have drawn gratefully in what follows from Michael Hurd's *Vincent Novello – And Company*, Granada Publishing, 1981.
17. C.L. Graves, *The Life And Letters of George Grove, C.B.*, London, 1903, p. 356.
18. Quoted in P. Young, *Elgar O. M.*, White Lion Edition, 1973, p. 26.
19. *The World*, 3 August, 1892. Quoted in *Shaw's Music*, ed. D.H. Laurence, Vol. 2, pp. 686–7. Bodley Head, 1981.
20. H.O. Anderton, *Granville Bantock*, John Lane, 1915, pp. 38–9.
21. Revd H.R. Haweis, *Music and Morals*, Longmans, Green & Co., 1898, p. 528.
22. Coleridge-Taylor entry in *Grove's Dictionary of Music And Musicians*, 4th Edition, ed. H.C. Colles, 1940.
23. In a letter to Alice Elgar of 13 June, 1908, Jaeger said that he had been a writer for the *Musical Times* 'for some 16 years'. EHP p. 698.
24. MT August 1894, p. 535.
25. MT March 1895, p. 166.
26. MT April 1895, p. 236.
27. MT August 1895, p. 528.
28. G. Self, *The Hiawatha Man*, Scolar Press, 1995, p. 61. Jaeger and Isabella Donkersley were not in fact married at this point, as Self states.
29. P.M. Young, *George Grove*, Macmillan, 1980, p. 197.
30. RCM Library, transcribed by Celia Clarke.
31. MoM p. 474.
32. MT May 1896, p. 333.
33. David Rattray, *Masterpieces of Italian Violin Making 1620–1850*, Royal Academy of Music, London, 1991, p. 9.
34. '… my impression is that a fine Guadanigni would have fetched about £200–250 in 1896.' Letter from Charles Beare to the writer, 8/4/97. This would equate roughly to £11,200–£14,000 at 1998 values.
35. *Royal Collegians*, in *The World*, 25 March, 1891. Quoted in *Shaw's Music*, ed. D.H. Laurence, Vol. 2, pp. 296–301, Bodley Head, 1981.
36. MT December 1896, p. 811.
37. MT October 1896, p. 663.
38. *A Few Words on the Successive Editions of Beethoven's Ninth Symphony.* Proceedings of the Musical Association, Vol. XXI, 1894–95, p. 65.

Chapter 2 1896–97

1. MT July 1896, pp. 480–82.
2. Ibid.
3. G. Grove, *Beethoven And His Nine Symphonies*, 2nd Edition, Novello, 1896, p. 357.
4. Quoted in E. Newman, *Musical Studies*, 2nd Edition, John Lane The Bodley Head, 1910, p. 249.
5. MT July 1896, p. 481.
6. Ibid.
7. MT July 1896, pp. 484–5.
8. Kate Emma Boundy, 1865–1913. Pianist, teacher and composer. She was one of the first intake at the RCM in 1883, with composition as principal study, and was said to be the first student to have a work performed in public, an 8-part Psalm sung at Westminster Abbey. She also produced songs for voice and piano, and various unison songs (with 'ad. lib. actions') and operettas for schools which were published by Novello's in response to a rising demand for such material. She would have been a part-contemporary of Isabella Donkersley at the RCM, and became a family friend and supporter of the Jaegers.
9. He was not, presumably, responsible for summoning Elgar to London to ask him to delete a note from the orchestral score on the grounds that it was below the compass of the organ. See B. Maine, *Elgar, His Life And Works*, New Portway Edition, 1973, p. 138.
10. Parry's *Pied Piper of Hamlyn* had been abandoned in an advanced stage of composition when one of his pupils made a setting of the poem. It was later completed and first performed at the 1905 Norwich Festival. An analysis by Jaeger appeared in the *Musical Times* for November that year, pp. 726–8.
11. Shulbrede Priory.
12. MT May 1897, pp. 313–14. Jaeger's presence at this concert is further attested in his letter of 15/9/1897 to Elgar, EHP p. 50.
13. MT May 1897, p. 318.
14. Ibid., p. 339.
15. R. Nettel, *Ordeal by Music*, OUP, 1945, p. 26.
16. MT June 1897, pp. 376–7.
17. Among the Walford Davies papers in the RCM Library is an empty envelope marked 'Brahms – a photograph (amateur) taken after death given to me by Miss Jaeger Nov 16 1901'.
18. See R. Nettel, *Ordeal by Music*, OUP, 1945, p. 21; R. Burley and F.C. Carruthers, *Edward Elgar: The Record of a Friendship*, Barrie & Jenkins, 1972, p. 96; J.N. Moore, *Edward Elgar, A Creative Life*, OUP, 1984, p. 212, and Elgar's letter to Novello's of 8/4/1896, EHP p. 32. R. Anderson, *Elgar*, Dent, 1993, p. 32, is sceptical about the excision of orchestral interludes, and discusses the nature of the cuts in *Elgar in Manuscript*, British Library 1990, pp. 29–32.
19. Elgar to Jaeger, 6/8/1897. EHP pp. 49–50.
20. Jaeger to Elgar, 15/9/1897. EHP pp. 50–52.
21. Ibid.
22. RCM Library.
23. MT January 1898, p. 25.
24. Ibid.
25. Ibid.
26. Ibid.
27. Jaeger to Elgar, 10/12/1897. EHP pp. 59–60.
28. *Wagner in London in 1855*, by A.J. Jaeger. *The Musician*, 13, 20 and 27 October 1897.
29. Jaeger to Elgar, 10/12/1897. EHP pp. 59–60.
30. Jaeger to Elgar, 31/12/1897. EHP pp. 61–2.

Chapter 3 1898

1. MT October 1893, pp. 586–7.
2. For a discussion of the relationship between the two composers, see W. Kearns, *Horatio Parker, Edward Elgar, and Choral Music at the Turn of the Twentieth Century*, ESJ Vol. 10, No. 1, March 1997.
3. MT March 1989, pp. 171–2.
4. Edgar Frederick Jacques (1850–1906), music critic, writer of programme notes, and lecturer; he had a special interest in Indian music. Obituary MT February 1907, p. 94.
5. MT March 1898, pp. 171–2.
6. A. Jacobs, *Henry J. Wood, Maker of the Proms*, Methuen Paperback Edition, 1995, pp. 56–7.
7. Ibid., p. 55.
8. H. Wood, *My Life of Music*, Gollancz, 1938, Chapter 7.
9. Jaeger to Elgar, 28/2/1898. EHP pp. 66–7.
10. Jaeger to Elgar, 8/3/1898. EHP pp. 67–8.
11. RCM Library.
12. MT August 1897, p. 533.
13. MT December 1897, p. 818.
14. RCM Library.
15. Quoted in A. Boden, *Three Choirs, A History Of The Festival*, Alan Sutton, 1992, p. 133.
16. *August Johannes Jaeger. An Appreciation.* Jaeger Memorial Concert Programme. Westwood-Brookes Collection.
17. MT March 1909, pp. 153–8.
18. *Huddersfield Daily Examiner*, 18 August 1966.
19. Perhaps the 'Then said they' Chorus reflects the advice Jaeger gave to Elgar in his letter of 10/12/1897 (EHP p. 60), pointing out the absence of 'a developed broadly melodious lyrical movement with the "fat" given to the *chorus* where the ear can *rest* & just drink in *quietly* moving strains of a broadly melodious type' in *King Olaf*.
20. W.C. Berwick Sayers, *Samuel Coleridge-Taylor, Musician.* Augener, 1927, pp. 63–4. The Jaegers were not in fact married until some three weeks after the première of *Hiawatha's Wedding Feast*.
21. MT June 1898, pp. 388–9.
22. 'Cautery might well have been used to control severe or recurrent nose bleeds: I cannot think of any other reason for using it.' Undated letter to the writer from Dr E.F. Laidlaw.
23. RCM Library.
24. EHP p. 88.
25. MV pp. 131–2.
26. EHP p. 89, n. 26.
27. MV p. 131.
28. The suggestion has been made that the *Enigma* theme was itself a variation on the melody of the slow movement of Beethoven's *Pathétique* Sonata. See J.A. Westrup, 'Elgar's Enigma', *Proceedings of the Royal Musical Association*, 1960, reprinted in C. Redwood, (ed.) *An Elgar Companion*, Sequoia Publishing, 1982.
29. M. Hurd, *Vincent Novello – and Company*, Granada Publishing, 1981, p. 98.
30. O. Newman and A. Foster, *The Value of a Pound: Prices and Incomes in Britain 1900–1993.* Gale Research International, 1995.
31. As at August 1998 values, Jaeger's salary would equate roughly to £250.00 weekly. *Equivalent Contemporary Values of the Pound*, Bank of England.
32. MT October 1898, pp. 661–2.
33. RF p. 115.
34. Vide infra Jaeger's letter of 17/11/1908 to Sydney Loeb.

35. EAF p. 43.
36. Elgar to Jaeger, 20/10/1898. EHP p. 93.
37. R. Anderson, *Elgar in Manuscript*, British Library, 1990, p. 190.
38. MV pp. 23–4.
39. Elgar to Jaeger, 11/11/1898. EHP pp. 95–6.
40. W.C. Berwick Sayers, op. cit., p. 63.
41. Jessie Coleridge-Taylor, *Coleridge-Taylor, Genius and Musician*. John Crowther Ltd, 1942–43.
42. MT October 1898, pp. 673–4.
43. MT November 1898, p. 728.
44. AJJ.
45. Ibid.
46. W.C. Berwick Sayers, op. cit., p. 63.
47. MT December 1898, p. 808.
48. Elgar to Jaeger, 17/12/1898. EHP p. 100. Jaeger had earlier expressed particular admiration for the *Valse Gracieuse* from German's Symphonic Suite of 1895, composed for the Leeds Festival. 'I fancy it is the most beautiful piece of yours I know. You have done more stirring and impressive things, especially in "Romeo", but nothing so full of the very spirit and soul of music', he wrote to the composer. W.H. Scott, *Edward German: An Intimate Biography*, Chappell & Co., 1932.
49. Elgar to Jaeger, 21/12/1898. EHP p. 101.
50. Letter to the writer from Jane Nagy, 9/3/1996.
51. MT December 1898, p. 803.
52. C. Scott, *My Years of Indiscretion*, Mills & Boon, 1924, p. 104.
53. MT December 1898, p. 803.
54. MT December 1898, p. 804.

Chapter 4 1899

1. W.C. Berwick Sayers, *Samuel Coleridge-Taylor, Musician*, Augener, 1927, p. 82.
2. There was a belief at Novello's that Julius Buths was invited to the 1900 Birmingham Festival first and foremost to hear *Hiawatha*, Coleridge-Taylor being rated above Elgar by the Littletons. See D. McVeagh, *Edward Elgar, His Life And Music*, Dent, 1955, pp. 32–3.
3. W.C. Berwick Sayers, op. cit., p. 83.
4. H. Plunket Greene, *Charles Villiers Stanford*, Arnold, 1935, pp. 157–8.
5. LoL p. 74 n. 4. Parry's diary for this period has no mention of this incident.
6. All quotations from the diary of Alice Elgar have been taken from the transcription by Dr J.N. Moore, Elgar Birthplace.
7. Jaeger occasionally acted as Sub-Editor for the *Musical Times*, but never became Editor.
8. '... [Elgar] is, in fact, a most eclectic composer, his most obvious influences being Wagner, Tchaikovsky, and Franck.' Benjamin Britten, 'England and the Folk-Art Problem', *Modern Music* 8, January/February 1941, quoted in *Letters From A Life*, ed. D. Mitchell and P. Reed, Faber and Faber 1991, p. 924.
9. RF pp. 96–8.
10. MV p. 131.
11. MT January 1899, pp. 15–16.
12. Coleridge-Taylor to Elgar, undated. WRO 705: 445: 8018.
13. MT February 1899, p. 90.
14. Ibid.
15. MT June 1893, p. 356.

16. MT October 1893, pp. 586–7. Jaeger was diffident about his ability to read a score, *vide infra* his letter of 25/12/1908 to Sydney Loeb.
17. MT February 1899, p. 91. Lorenzo Perosi (1872–1956), Italian priest and composer, was Maestro di Capella at St Mark's, Venice, and subsequently at the Sistine Chapel. He was a prolific composer of religious choral works, and a trilogy of oratorios gained great success in Italy. All three were given at the London Music Festival in May 1899. Perosi's success was spectacular but short-lived: his mixing of earlier church styles with modern orchestral effects had novelty value only.
18. MT March 1899, p. 175.
19. MT April 1899, p. 247.
20. Novello's had published a Violin Sonata in E minor, Op. 5, in 1894, and one in D minor, Op. 7, in 1896. H.C. Colles, in his *Walford Davies, A Biography*, OUP, 1942, refers to two earlier works, in E flat and A, which are unpublished. Jaeger appears to be referring to the D minor work here.
21. RCM Library.
22. Barry to Elgar, 10/4/1899. WRO 705: 445: 3034.
23. Alice Elgar Archive, Elgar Birthplace. There is every likelihood that this Essay was written before marriage, like most of her major writings.
24. J.N. Moore, *Edward Elgar, A Creative Life*, OUP, 1984, p. 259.
25. MT May 1899, p. 320.
26. Ibid.
27. EAF pp. 39–40.
28. MT July 1899, p. 464.
29. Ibid., p. 471.
30. Approximately £57. 00 as at August 1998.
31. Elgar to Jaeger, 28/5/1899. EHP p. 124. The word also appears in Jaeger's letters to Elgar of 7/11/1899, EHP p. 148, and 27/6/1900, EHP p. 204.
32. MT November 1899, pp. 742–4, and December 1899, pp. 813–15.
33. MT December 1899, p. 821.
34. Jaeger to Elgar, 14/11/99. EHP pp. 149–50.
35. Jaeger to Elgar, 17/11/99. EHP pp. 52–3.
36. MT December 1899, p. 819.

Chapter 5 1900

1. Elgar to Jaeger, 10/1/1900. EHP pp. 157–8.
2. MT January 1900, p. 34.
3. Jaeger to Elgar, 4/2/1900. EHP p. 161.
4. MT March 1900, p. 165.
5. Ibid.
6. Ibid., pp. 184–5.
7. Jaeger to Elgar, 13/4/1900. EHP pp. 173–4.
8. Ibid.
9. MT April 1900, p. 246.
10. Ibid.
11. W.C. Berwick Sayers, *Samuel Coleridge-Taylor, Musician*, Augener, 1927, p. 93.
12. MT April 1900, pp. 256–7.
13. Ibid.
14. Jaeger to Elgar, 27/4/1900. EHP pp. 176–7.

15. Elgar to Jaeger, 29/4/1900. EHP p. 177.
16. MV p. 36.
17. Claud Powell suggests that the destruction of the letters may have been due to feelings of shock and betrayal at the idea that 'Jaeger's homeland, and the home of so much that was good in the realm of music, had become "the enemy"'. MV p. 5.
18. Ibid., pp. 38–9.
19. Ibid., p. 39.
20. Jaeger to Alice Elgar, 8/5/1900. EHP pp. 179–80.
21. MV p. 39.
22. Jaeger to Elgar, 29/5/1900. EHP pp. 183–4.
23. MT June 1900, p. 408.
24. Ibid.
25. Ibid.
26. Ibid.
27. Ibid., p. 409.
28. MV p. 40.
29. Ibid.
30. Jaeger to Elgar, 16/6/1900. EHP pp. 190–91.
31. Alfred Bruneau (1857–1934). French composer, mainly of opera. His *L'Attaque du Moulin* was successfully produced at Covent Garden in 1894. *Grove's Dictionary* (4th edn) described it as ranking 'with the masterpieces of the modern stage', adding 'his most striking gift was his power of building up a scene to a climax'.
32. Jaeger to Elgar, 16/6/1900. EHP pp. 199–200.
33. The relevant correspondence is most effectively presented as a 'dramatic dialogue' in M. Kennedy, *Portrait of Elgar*, 3rd edn, OUP, 1987, pp. 108–12.
34. Jaeger to Elgar, 30/6/1900. EHP p. 208.
35. In other words, 'as far as you are concerned'.
36. YUML.
37. MT September 1900, pp. 598–602.
38. Jaeger to Elgar, 12/8/1900. EHP pp. 221–3.
39. YUML.
40. C. Grogan, 'My Dear Analyst', *Music & Letters*, Vol. 72, No. 1 (February, LXXII, 1991), pp. 48–60 considers Elgar's reference to his wife's opinion to be a diplomatic ploy. I most gratefully acknowledge my general debt to this article.
41. Quoted in L. Foreman (ed.) *From Parry to Britten, British Music in Letters 1900–1945*, Batsford, 1987, p. 14.
42. YUML.
43. Jaeger to Alice Elgar, 18/9/1900. EHP pp. 233–4.
44. MV p. 40.
45. Otto Lessmann (1844–1918), celebrated music critic, at one time editor of the *Allgemeine Musikzeitung*.
46. MV pp. 44–5.
47. Diary of Hans Richter, 3 October 1900, quoted in C. Fifield, *True Artist and True Friend, a Biography of Hans Richter*, Clarendon Press, 1993, p. 345.
48. EAF p. 52.
49. Elgar Birthplace.
50. Jaeger to Alice Elgar, 7/11/1900. EHP pp. 254–5.
51. Ibid.
52. Pianist, composer and conductor. In 1907 he would form a Symphonic Orchestra Society consisting of professional players, 'which composers could on payment of a small fee conduct their own compositions … and invite Agents and Publishers'. MoM p. 404.

53. Jaeger to Elgar, 2/12/1900. EHP pp. 258–9.
54. Charles Macpherson (1870–1927) had been sub-organist of St Paul's Cathedral since 1895. His setting of *By the Waters of Babylon* for choir and orchestra was programmed by the Worcestershire Philharmonic in 1902.
55. Jaeger to Elgar, 2/12/1900. EHP pp. 258–9.
56. MV p. 45.
57. MT November 1900, pp. 734–5.
58. Diary of Sir Hubert Parry, 30 May 1890, quoted in J. Dibble, *C. Hubert H. Parry, His Life And Music*, Clarendon Press, 1992, p. 283.
59. MT December 1900, p. 818.
60. Elgar to Jaeger, 31/12/1900. EHP pp. 265–6.

Chapter 6 1901

1. MV p. 45.
2. EHP p. 191.
3. Jaeger to Elgar, 28/1/1901. EHP p. 273.
4. Ibid.
5. MV p. 45.
6. D. Tovey, *Essays in Musical Analysis*, Vol. 4, OUP, 1936, p. 151.
7. Jaeger to Elgar, 7/2/1901. EHP p. 276.
8. Jaeger to Elgar, 11/2/1901. EHP p. 278.
9. MV pp. 45–6.
10. Brotherton Collection, Leeds University, MS 361/154/2.
11. Diary of Dora Penny, 5/3/1901.
12. MV p. 46.
13. Ibid.
14. I am indebted to Dr John Harcup of Malvern for this information.
15. Rodewald to Elgar, 25/5/1901. WRO 705: 445: 7880.
16. '... the idea of an operation which could or would delay or prevent the development of TB is, I think, utterly remote from modern ideas. ' Letter to the writer from Dr E.F. Laidlaw.
17. Elgar to Jaeger, 26/6/1901. EHP p. 292.
18. Jaeger to Alice Elgar, 18/7/1901. WRO 705: 445: 8808.
19. Jaeger to Alice Elgar, 19/7/1901. WRO 705: 445: 8800.
20. Jaeger to Alice Elgar, 24/7/1901. WRO 705: 445: 8799.
21. Isabella Jaeger to Alice Elgar, 24/7/1901. WRO 705: 445: 8811.
22. Jaeger to Elgar, 11/8/1901. EHP pp. 297–8.
23. Jaeger to Elgar, 16/10/1901. EHP pp. 304–5.
24. Jaeger to Elgar, 26/10/1901. EHP p. 309.
25. MT December 1901, p. 805.
26. Jaeger to Elgar, 13/12/1901. EHP pp. 319–20.
27. Kalisch to Elgar, 19/11/; undated as to year. WRO 705: 445: 1815.
28. Buths to Elgar, December 1901. WRO 705: 445: 7968.
29. 20/12/1901. Quoted in L. Foreman, *Elgar and Gerontius, The Early Performances*, ESJ Vol. 10, No. 5, July 1998, p. 227.
30. *The Times*, 20/12/1901.
31. *Manchester Guardian*, 20/12/1901.
32. 19/12/1901. Quoted in L. Foreman, loc. cit., p. 227.

33. 27/12/1901. Quoted in L. Foreman, loc. cit., pp. 229–30.
34. RCM Library.
35. Among the Powell papers in the Royal College of Music is a letter from Isabella Hunter to Dora Powell in explanation of this usage. 'I think my husband meant the English word "filed." I read it that Buths curbed & "filed" the tone of the orchestra until it was down to the beautiful softness beloved of Elgar's soul. My sister-in-law says it is *not* a German word. It is a word often used by Conductors & those careful musicians who practise ensemble music.'
36. MV pp. 60–64.

Chapter 7 1902

1. Elgar to Jaeger, 13/01/1902. EHP pp. 325–6.
2. Elgar to Jaeger, 22/02/1902. EHP pp. 335.
3. John Blackwood McEwen (1868–1948). He became Principal of the RAM in 1924. 'His craftsmanship and musical invention in writing for string quartet is impressive, and he can in truth be called a pioneer of the renascence of British chamber music composition which took place during the first quarter of the century.' L.G. Wickham and E.T. Williams (eds), *Dictionary of National Biography 1941–1950*, OUP, 1959.
4. Jaeger to Elgar, 28/2/1902. EHP pp. 339–40.
5. Jaeger to Alice Elgar, 9/3/1902. EHP p. 341.
6. 'A little man with a big head' is a description of Jaeger that has survived in family circles. I am grateful to Mrs Patricia Pamment for this information.
7. WRO 705: 445: 8398. Not published in EHP.
8. MT April 1902, p. 255.
9. Ibid., pp. 255–6.
10. Ibid., p. 256.
11. Ibid., p. 256.
12. Ibid., pp. 249–50.
13. MT June 1902, pp. 402–3.
14. *The Times*, 23/5/1902.
15. MT June 1902, p. 402.
16. Ettling had written to Elgar on 3 July 1901, 'Novello ought to send Variation scores to Germany – Emil Steinbach, Mainz, Gustav Kogel, Frankfurt am Main.' Later that year Elgar presented Ettling with the MS Full Score of the *Cockaigne* Overture.
17. MT July 1902, p. 481.
18. Ibid., p. 473.
19. Elgar to Jaeger, 18/8/1902. EHP p. 370.
20. MT October 1902, p. 676.
21. Ibid., p. 675.
22. H.C. Colles, *Walford Davies*, OUP, 1942, p. 74.
23. RCM Library.
24. H.C. Colles, op. cit., p. 75.
25. Ibid., pp. 76–7.
26. MT September 1902, p. 603.
27. Ibid.
28. Ibid., p. 604.
29. Ibid.
30. L. Foreman (ed.) *From Parry to Britten, British Music in Letters 1900–1945*. Batsford, 1987, p. 16.

31. MT November 1902, pp. 729–30.
32. Jaeger to Elgar, 7/10/1902. EHP p. 374. 'Difficult to offer an explanation of all these symptoms. Pain around the heart is often due to acid regurgitation from the stomach into the gullet … a dagger-like pain which catches on inspiration is very suggestive of pleurisy. And this might well occur in the course of TB, & would lead to significant shortness of breath …'. Letter from Dr E.F. Laidlaw.
33. Arthur Jacobs considers that Newman's bankruptcy at Queen's Hall may have been partly responsible for Wood's illness. *Henry J. Wood, Maker of the Proms*, Methuen Paperback Edition, 1995, p. 84.
34. Jaeger to Elgar, 16/10/1902. EHP p. 376.
35. YUML.
36. Jaeger's love of horseplay led to accident on one occasion, when a pole he was trying to balance on his head to entertain his children slipped and seriously hurt his nose. Letter from Mrs Patricia Pamment, 23/8/98.
37. Arthur Reynolds collection.
38. 'Elgar, Master of Music', *Music and Letters*, Vol. XVI, No. 1, January 1935, reprinted in *Essays and Lectures on Music*, OUP, 1945.
39. YUML.
40. Jaeger to Elgar, 22/12/1902. EHP p. 391.
41. Ibid.

Chapter 8 1903

1. £1 in 1903 was worth £51.16 as at August 1998 (Bank of England).
2. Jaeger to Elgar, 4/11/1903. EHP p. 402.
3. Jaeger to Elgar, 8/2/1903. EHP pp. 404–5.
4. Scott, *Bone of Contention*, The Aquarium Press, 1969, p. 73.
5. Ibid., pp. 147–8.
6. RCM Library.
7. Shulbrede Priory.
8. Ibid.
9. Ibid.
10. MT July 1903, p. 478.
11. Jaeger to Elgar, 8/7/1903. EHP pp. 456–7.
12. Jaeger to Elgar, 29/7/1903. EHP pp. 464–5.
13. RCM Library.
14. Jaeger to Elgar, 10/8/1903. EHP p. 471.
15. Jaeger to Elgar, 18/8/1903. EHP pp. 478–9.
16. D. McVeagh, *Edward Elgar, His Life and Music*, Dent, 1955, p. 39.
17. Including *The Epic of Sounds, An Elementary Interpretation of Wagner's Nibelungen Ring*, by Freda Winworth, 1898, and *The Master-Singers of Nuremberg, A Musical Explanation With Numerous Musical Examples*, by Albert Heintz, translated by Constance Bache, 1892.
18. *The Apostles, Book of Words, with Analytical and Descriptive Notes by A.J. Jaeger*, Novello, 1903, p. 6.
19. Jaeger to Elgar, undated, August 1903. EHP pp. 480–81.
20. Jaeger to Elgar, 28/8/1903. EHP pp. 484–5.
21. Elgar to Jaeger, 14/9/1903. EHP p. 489.
22. As early as 1906 Ernest Newman, in his book on Elgar, based his *Gerontius* comments on Jaeger's Analysis, done 'with full knowledge of the composer's intentions'. His discussion of *The Apostles* likewise followed Jaeger's Analysis, 'which may be taken to have the composer's sanction'.

23. E. Newman, *Elgar*, John Lane, 1906.
24. Ibid.
25. Coleridge-Taylor to Nicholas Kilburn, 18/2/1904. Quoted in G. Self, *The Hiawatha Man*, Scolar Press, 1995, p. 141.
26. Jaeger to Elgar, 16/9/1903. EHP pp. 490–91.
27. MV pp. 75–6.
28. Jaeger to Elgar, 28/9/1903. EHP pp. 503–4.
29. Elgar to Jaeger, 29/9/1903. EHP p. 504.
30. Jaeger Memorial Concert Programme, p. 4. In possession of Richard Westwood-Brookes.
31. Arthur Reynolds collection.
32. Jaeger to Elgar, 22/10/1903. EHP pp. 509–10.
33. Writer of programme-notes. Percy Scholes thought him 'superficial and sometimes inaccurate'. MoM p. 217.
34. Jaeger to Elgar, 22/10/1903. EHP pp. 509–10.
35. MT November 1903, p. 726.
36. *Manchester Guardian*, 21/10/1903. Elgar Birthplace.
37. Undated press cutting, Elgar Birthplace.
38. Ibid.
39. Actually 92.
40. *The Times*, 14/10/1903. Elgar Birthplace.
41. Gorton to Elgar, *c.* 12/10/1903. WRO 705: 445: 2451.
42. Rodewald to Elgar, 3/11/1903. WRO 705: 445: 2745.
43. Jaeger to Elgar, 10/11/1903. EHP pp. 523–4.
44. Shulbrede Priory.
45. MT December 1903, p. 809.
46. Quoted in J.N. Moore, *Edward Elgar A Creative Life*, OUP, 1984, p. 401.
47. ESJ, Vol. 10 No. 6, November, 1998, pp. 278–80.
48. Elgar to Jaeger, 13/12/1903. EHP p. 527.
49. Ibid.

Chapter 9 1904

1. Jaeger to Elgar, 5/2/1904. EHP pp. 533–4.
2. MT February 1904, p. 119.
3. RCM Library.
4. Jaeger to Elgar, 16/2/1904. EHP pp. 535–6. Novello's had issued a reprint, the third, of Jaeger's Analysis for the performance. The second reprint had been for the Westminster Cathedral performance the previous year.
5. Jaeger to Elgar, 24/2/1904. EHP pp. 538–9. Robert Anderson considers that the timpani solo in the bar before Figure 61 was 'probably' the result of Jaeger's complaints. *Elgar*, Master Musicians Series, Dent, 1993, p. 310.
6. Jaeger to Elgar, EHP p. 543.
7. Elgar to Jaeger, 9/3/1904. EHP pp. 546–7.
8. Jaeger to Elgar, 26/3/1904. EHP pp. 552–3. Novello's published both McEwen's String Quartet in A minor and his Piano Sonata in E minor in the early part of 1904.
9. MV pp. 79–80.
10. MT April 1904, pp. 241–3.
11. Ibid.
12. Kalisch to Elgar, 19/4/1904. WRO 705: 445: 1834.

13. MT April 1904, p. 243.
14. Isabella Jaeger to Alice Elgar, 10/4/1904. WRO 705: 445: 8812.
15. MT June 1904, p. 391.
16. MV p. 80.
17. EAF p. 114.
18. MT June 1904, pp. 391–2.
19. Gorton to Alice Elgar, 15/6/1904. WRO 705: 445: 2444.
20. A composer of music for the London theatre. See MoM p. 267.
21. Shulbrede Priory.
22. WRO 705: 445: 4360.
23. WRO 705: 445: 5361.
24. Jaeger to Alice Elgar, 28/6/1904. EHP pp. 567–8.
25. MT July 1904, pp. 462–3.
26. Ibid.
27. Jaeger's review of *Don Juan* at the Lower Rhine Festival. MT July 1896, p. 480.
28. The notorious *Symphonia Domestica* had been premièred in New York on 21 March and repeated in Frankfurt in June. It would be played for the first time in England on 6 November. Grove, Vol. V, p. 162.
29. Taylor Institution, Oxford.
30. MT November 1904, p. 723.
31. Shulbrede Priory.
32. This and other extracts from the diaries of Sydney Loeb are by kind permission of Sylvia Loeb.
33. Diary 11/10/1914.
34. Westwood-Brookes Collection.
35. Jaeger to Elgar, 24/9/1904. EHP p. 582.
36. Ibid.
37. RCM Library.
38. Ibid.
39. Possibly *Lift Up Your Hearts*, a Sacred Symphony for Bass Solo, Chorus and Orchestra, premièred at the Hereford Festival of 1906, although Davies also produced a purely instrumental work in 1911. Havergal Brian remembered, 'Jaeger thought highly of Walford Davies, placing him a peer with Elgar, and was frankly enthusiastic about his Choral Symphony. Davies was at the time away in Switzerland working on this symphony; and I recall Jaeger turning to me and saying, "Can't you see, my boy, what sort of symphony it will be? Davies in the Alps: thousands of feet up in the air: writing away at his score".' *Musical Opinion*, May 1934, reprinted in *Havergal Brian on Music*, ed. M. MacDonald, Toccata Press, 1986, p. 253.
40. RCM Library.
41. Jaeger to Elgar, 17/10/1904. EHP p. 589.
42. Jaeger to Elgar, 28/10/1904. EHP p. 595.
43. Westwood-Brookes Collection.
44. Holbrooke to Elgar, 13/12/1904. WRO 705: 445: 2366.
45. Shulbrede Priory.
46. Ibid.
47. Ibid.

Chapter 10 1905

1. RCM Library.
2. Jaeger to Elgar, 8/1/1905. EHP p. 605.

3. RCM Library.
4. *Davos-Platz, A New Alpine Resort for Sick and Sound in Summer and Winter, By One Who Knows it Well*, Stanford, 1878.
5. *Piotr Ilyich Tchaikovsky, Letters to His Family, An Autobiography*, trans. Galina von Meck, Stein and Day, Scarborough Books Edition 1982, p. 317.
6. Elgar to Jaeger, 16/2/1905. EHP pp. 610–11.
7. Published in England by Constable in 1902.
8. Parry's incidental music to Aristophanes' *The Clouds*, parodying the styles of Tchaikovsky, Wagner, Richard Strauss, Mendelssohn and Bach among others, had first been heard at the Oxford University Dramatic Society production on 1 March that year.
9. Buths had conducted a performance of Stanford's Requiem on 24 February, with the composer being recalled many times at the conclusion.
10. Parry had conducted the work there on 3 March. Of the rehearsal he wrote, '... Choir really tremendous. Their volume and decision of tone was stunning.' Of the performance itself he thought it was 'the best it has ever had. Chorus magnificent'.
11. Shulbrede Priory.
12. MT May 1905, pp. 326–7. The article appeared over Jaeger's initials. It was reprinted in the July 1997 number (Vol. 138, No. 1853) as part of a 'From the Archive' series, without attribution.
13. Many of Elgar's points in his Birmingham Lectures echo ideas of Jaeger.
14. WRO 705: 445: 8860.
15. It is not entirely clear what may be cause and effect here, but the seriousness of Jaeger's condition is indicated by the existence of a lung cavity, which would inevitably lead to the coughing up of infected tissue and its spread through the bronchial tree. '... the operation [Jaeger] describes is ... for the drainage of the maxillary antrum, one of the paranasal sinuses – spaces in the facial bones which are lined by mucous membrane and which drain into the nasal cavity: if they become inflamed or infected, they may become obstructed, leading to pain and intermittent nasal discharge, – the "disgusting symptoms" of which he complains. The operation employed to deal with this (Caldwell-Luc operation) involves drilling a hole into the sinus from below: I think it can be and is (or was) done with local anaesthetic ("Cocainisation") though it must have been fairly uncomfortable.' Letter from Dr E.F. Laidlaw.
16. Shulbrede Priory.
17. MT September 1905, p. 624.
18. Jaeger to Elgar, 23/8/1905. EHP pp. 621–3.
19. *Sic.* I suggest 'gamin', '(street) urchin; impudent child' (Concise OED).
20. Jaeger to Elgar, 25/8/1905. EHP pp. 621–3.
21. H. Brian, *Josef Holbrooke, English Composer*, in *Tomorrow*, 4/11/1939. Quoted in *Havergal Brian on Music*, ed. M. MacDonald, Toccata Press, 1986, p. 280 et seq.
22. '... your nice friend ... came (& Wendt) on Saturday – lunch & a walk found us deadly dull I know & pitied himself for having expended two marks on railway fares.' Elgar to Jaeger, 26/11/1899. EHP p. 155.
23. J. Foulds, *Music To-Day*, Nicholson & Watson, 1934, p. 232.
24. RF p. 183.
25. Arabella Wells to Dora Powell, 25/6/1938. Powell Papers, RCM Library.
26. Jaeger to Alice Elgar, 20/9/1905. EHP pp. 627–8.
27. Ibid.
28. Elgar to Schuster, 29/10/1905. LoL p. 166.
29. His uncle was the painter Peter Cornelius, Director of the Düsseldorf Academy from 1821 to 1824.
30. *Manchester Guardian*, 21/5/1909, 'Memorial Notice. Mr A.J. Jaeger'.

31. Gorton to Alice Elgar, 2/11/1905. WRO 705: 445: 2483. I am grateful to Geoffrey Hodgkins for drawing my attention to this letter.
32. Alice Elgar to Jaeger, 17/11/1905. EHP p. 631.
33. Alice Elgar to Jaeger, 14/12/1905. EHP p. 633–4.

Chapter 11 1906

1. *Davos Courier*, 27/10/1905, p. 2.
2. Elgar to Jaeger, 26/1/1906. EHP, p. 636.
3. Shulbrede Priory.
4. Alice Elgar to Jaeger, 17/3/1906. EHP pp. 639–40.
5. Shulbrede Priory.
6. Shulbrede Priory.
7. MT March 1906, p. 188.
8. Ibid., p. 178.
9. MT April 1906, p. 261.
10. In an article for the *Musical Opinion* of September 1934, 'The Elgar Manuscripts', reprinted in *Havergal Brian on Music*, Vol. 1, ed. M. MacDonald, Toccata Press, 1986, pp. 88–92, Brian wrote 'The first glimpse I had of an Elgar manuscript was in Jaeger's office at Novello's. The American mail was in, and with it had come the first instalment of the full score of *The Kingdom*, on which Elgar was working during his visit to the States. We both pored over those first pages with the deepest interest, admiring the unerring rapidity of the work and the extraordinary skill shown in scoring and the bold handwriting.' MacDonald footnotes this as having taken place in April (loc. cit., p. 92, n. 18) although Jaeger was still at Davos at this time and I can find no evidence that Elgar sent any portions of *Kingdom* full score to Novello's from the States. MacDonald's footnote includes also another account of the incident, contained in a letter Brian wrote to Granville Bantock on 23/12/1916. 'Do you know I was once at Novello's with Jaeger when Elgar had sent the first instalment of his "Kingdom" from America. Jaeger had been talking about Elgar and swelled head. As Jaeger turned the pages he said – "he's got it bad this time, growing pains all over." Elgar had written – " I am the chosen of the Lord." Jaeger cut it out.' These words do not appear in the *Kingdom* libretto, and in any case it is out of the question for Jaeger to have cut passages of text from an Elgar MS full score; nor can I find any extant correspondence or evidence of any discussion between Elgar and Jaeger over the matter. MacDonald considers that the account might refer to the arrival of parts of the (vocal) score at Novello's during January, but again, Jaeger would have been abroad. Given these difficulties it is hard to know what weight to give to Brian's description of Jaeger's words about Elgar. MacDonald points out that the nearest approach to the offending phrase is found in the words 'The Lord hath chosen you to stand before Him to serve Him; you shall be named the Priest of the Lord' and says 'it is known that Jaeger criticized this passage to Elgar'. In fact it was the ensuing chorus, 'O ye priests!' that Jaeger appears to have criticized.
11. Grogan (*My Dear Analyst*) considers that Jaeger began the analysis on his own initiative, but a letter from Elgar to Littleton of 7 June 1906 (EHP p. 645) might appear to suggest that the work was undertaken at Littleton's suggestion. See also Jaeger's letter of 27/9/1906 to Parry, in which he says that he was made to undertake the analysis against his will.
12. Jaeger to Elgar, 3/9/1906. EHP p. 659.
13. WRO 705: 445: 8845.

14. Elgar to Jaeger, 5/9/1906. EHP p. 659.
15. *The Soul's Ransom: A Psalm of the Poor,* Sinfonia Sacra, for soprano, bass, chorus and orchestra, given its first and only performance during Parry's lifetime at the Hereford Three Choirs Festival on 12 September.
16. Shulbrede Priory.
17. RCM Library.
18. EHP p. 661.
19. Shulbrede Priory.
20. MT September 1906, p. 609.

Chapter 12 1907

1. Doctor Faust.
2. From *The Complete Poems of Heinrich Heine*, trans. H. Draper, Suhrkamp/Insel, Boston, 1982.
3. Presumably of Koch's much vaunted but unsuccessful tuberculin.
4. Elgar?
5. Edward Hunter became a proficient amateur pianist, playing jazz and various classical pieces, including Grieg's *Butterflies*, by ear.
6. Shulbrede Priory. Novello's published two sets of Parry's *English Lyrics* in 1907, with the Violin Suites and the *English* Symphony appearing later in the year. The *Cambridge* Symphony had been published in 1906.
7. MV p. 148.
8. RCM Library.
9. RCM Library.
10. MV p. 96. I have placed this item here as Jaeger may have misdated it; he did not leave Davos for Lippspringe until about the first week in May.
11. Alice Elgar to Jaeger, 7/6/1907. EHP pp. 672–3.
12. Shulbrede Priory.
13. EHP pp. 677–8.
14. 'Jaeger was one of the really quickening forces in the music of his day, and his generous enthusiasm was a stimulus and inspiration not only to Elgar but to many other musicians of the time, notably Hubert Parry.' I. Atkins, 'Elgar's *Enigma* Variations', MT May 1934, pp. 411–14.
15. Published in EHP pp. 192–7.
16. Shulbrede Priory.
17. MV p. 98.

Chapter 13 1908

1. Parry's letter of resignation from the Oxford post was not in fact written until 22 February. His successor was Sir Walter Parratt.
2. Writing to Dora Powell, Arabella Wright remembered, 'You, I met once! – I wonder if you will remember? At Muswell Hill station on a very wet afternoon & I offered you a lift in my cab … & when I asked you where you wanted to go & you said 37 Curzon Road – I said "Dorabella"! I often used to go there …'. Letter of 25/6/1938. Powell Papers, RCM Library.
3. RCM Library.
4. Recte *Tap o' The Hill.*

5. Recte *Infant Joy*.
6. RCM Library.
7. MV pp. 98–9.
8. Baughan had written, '… "Mr" Senius cannot pronounce English properly … "To the God of earth and heaven" became "To ve Gott of eart' an' t'eaven"; "A maze of things" was pronounced as "a maze of thinks"; "I ever had believed" as "I efer hat belieft," and so on. This foreign accent entirely spoilt the religious atmosphere of the oratorio.' 'Foreign Soloists in "The Dream of Gerontius"', *Daily News*, 13 April 1908.
9. Westwood-Brookes Collection.
10. Shulbrede Priory.
11. Elgar to Jaeger, 26/4/1908. EHP pp. 693–5.
12. Elgar Sketchbook 8, B.L. Add. MS 63160, ff. 52–3. I am grateful to Professor Brian Trowell for sight of his edition of this song-fragment for the Elgar Complete Edition.
13. Elgar to Jaeger, 3/6/1908. EHP pp. 696–7.
14. Jaeger's article was published in full for the first time in an edition by Ron Taylor, of a copy of the original made by Elgar's niece May Grafton, in ESJ, Vol. 6, No. 3, September 1989, pp. 19–23.
15. Alice Elgar to Jaeger, 12/6/1908. EHP pp. 697–8.
16. Jaeger to Alice Elgar, 13/6/1908. EHP pp. 698–9.
17. Shulbrede Priory.
18. Jaeger to Elgar, 3/9/1908. EHP p. 709.
19. Jaeger possibly changed his mind over 'O Ye Priests!' but it may be more likely that he was referring to the conclusion of the Pentecost scene, which was Elgar's suggested point for an interval in performance.
20. Westwood-Brookes Collection.
21. The Sheffield Festival performance of *Everyman* referred to in the last paragraph took place on 7 October 1908.
22. RCM Library.
23. These included Jaeger's memories of Brahms and Schumann in Düsseldorf, and a short article headed, 'Is the Symphony Doomed?'
24. Shulbrede Priory.
25. Presumably Elgar's letter of 19/9/1908, EHP pp. 710–11.
26. RCM Library.
27. Westwood-Brookes Collection.
28. RCM Library.
29. Westwood-Brookes Collection.
30. Jaeger to Elgar, 26/11/1908. EHP p. 715.
31. RCM Library.
32. Jaeger to Elgar, 4/12/1908. EHP p. 716.
33. MV pp. 99–100.
34. Jaeger presumably discounted Elgar's three Concert Overtures because of their programmatic nature.
35. 'I went with him to hear E.E.'s first performance by Richter at the Queen's Hall of his first Symphony (but I was not one of the friends who sent him in a taxi there!) We met at the Hall, & he gave me the proof sheets of it all with his marginal notes – a great possession which I value highly.' Letter from Arabella Wright to Dora Powell, 25/6/1938. Powell Papers, RCM.
36. Westwood-Brookes Collection.
37. AJJ.
38. 'A writer in The Observer is among those who detect certain plagiarisms from "Parsifal"; more than that, he ventures the opinion that the composer may have gone a-rummaging

among the sketchbooks of his salad days and used some of the material he found there in serving up a "Wand of Youth" Symphony.' Unidentified press cutting, Elgar Birthplace.

39. Westwood-Brookes Collection.
40. 'He also let me sort out & put in chronological order (as best I could) all E.E.'s letters to him – a somewhat difficult (but most enthralling) task as many of them were undated ...'. Letter from Arabella Wright to Dora Powell, 25/6/1938. Powell Papers, RCM.
41. Westwood-Brookes Collection.
42. MV p. 100.
43. Westwood-Brookes Collection.
44. Westwood-Brookes Collection.
45. Eaton Faning (1850–1927), teacher, conductor and composer. In addition to professorships at various of the London colleges, he was Director of Music at Harrow School, which Loeb had attended.
46. Westwood-Brookes Collection.

Chapter 14 1909

1. Westwood-Brookes Collection.
2. Westwood-Brookes Collection.
3. Westwood-Brookes Collection.
4. MV p. 101.
5. Elgar Birthplace Document 1407.
6. Westwood-Brookes Collection.
7. *Sic.* I have placed this letter here as January 1908 seems too early, bearing in mind the beginning of Jaeger's letter to Loeb of 14 April that year. Jaeger was apt to misdate letters after the turn of the year, and the Newman book he refers to was not reviewed in the *Musical Times* until November 1908. Loeb's diary makes no mention of attending a *Meistersinger* performance in January 1908, although he did so on 25 January 1909.
8. Westwood-Brookes Collection.
9. C. Fifield, *True Artist and True Friend, A Biography of Hans Richter*, OUP, 1993, p. 400.
10. Westwood-Brookes Collection.
11. Westwood-Brookes Collection.
12. Westwood-Brookes Collection.
13. MT March 1909, p. 177.
14. RCM Library.
15. Quoted in R.Y. Keers, *Pulmonary Tuberculosis, a Journey Down the Centuries*, Baillère Tindall, London, 1978.
16. Ibid.
17. Shulbrede Priory.
18. RCM Library.
19. Shulbrede Priory.
20. Elgar to Jaeger, 21/5/1909. EHP pp. 722–3.
21. MV p. 106.

Chapter 15 In Memory of a Seer

1. Elgar to Walford Davies, 1/10/1909. WRO 705: 445: 2195.
2. AJJ.

3. Richter to Elgar, 16/1/1910. LoL p. 216.
4. In possession of Richard Westwood-Brookes.
5. In possession of Arthur Reynolds.
6. 25/1/1910.
7. 25/1/1910.
8. 25/1/1910.
9. 25/1/1910.
10. 2/2/1910.
11. 30/1/1910.
12. 26/1/1910.
13. 26/1/1910.
14. 26/1/1910.
15. 26/1/1910.
16. 25/1/1910.
17. 'They were naughty & were always dissolving into giggles when Donnie wagged her large, knobbly index finger at them ...'. Letter from Mrs Gillian Scully, 12/1/1998.
18. Ibid.
19. Isabella Jaeger to Elgar, 27/11/1910. WRO 705: 445: 3627.
20. Buths to Elgar, 5/11/1912. WRO 705: 445: 7643.
21. Elgar to Newman, 14/8/1912. LoL pp. 248–50.
22. Diary of Sir Hubert Parry, 20/5/1915.
23. Robin Grey (ed.), *Studies in Music by Various Authors*, Simkin, Marshall, Hamilton Kent & Co., 1901.
24. Isabella Hunter to Elgar, 10/4/1920. WRO 705: 445: 0385.
25. Reprinted in EHP p. 630.
26. Letter from Richard Hunter, 31/8/1998.
27. H.C. Colles to Isabella Hunter, 1/7/1933.
28. The entry was revised for inclusion in *The New Grove.*
29. In possession of Neville Fraser.
30. Letter from Mrs Gillian Scully, 12/11/1998.
31. Ibid.
32. Letter from Neville Fraser, 10/9/1998.
33. In possession of Arthur Reynolds.
34. Letter from Joyce Kemp, 7/7/1998. Miss Kemp continues, 'After that meeting Mrs Fraser invited me to tea ... and I particularly remember her telling me how, as quite a small child, Elgar would sometimes call to her to go and sit beside him when he was playing the piano – I imagine when he was trying out parts of a composition. She said that he liked her to sit beside him, rather than her brother, as her brother could never sit as still as she did!'
35. English Heritage turned down a request for a commemorative blue plaque at 37 Curzon Road, as they did not consider Jaeger to be 'of sufficient historical interest'. The Elgar Society erected its own plaque on 19 June 1999, the centenary to the day of the first performance of the *Enigma* Variations. The unveiling was performed by Wulstan Atkins, MBE, son of Ivor Atkins.

Index